THE PSYCHOLOGY OF POLICE DEADLY FORCE ENCOUNTERS

ABOUT THE AUTHOR

Laurence Miller, PhD is a clinical, forensic, police, and neuropsychologist based in Boca Raton, Florida. Dr. Miller provides clinical and training services for the Palm Beach County Sheriff's Office, West Palm Beach Police Department, Florida Highway Patrol, and other regional and national law enforcement agencies. Dr. Miller is a forensic psychological examiner for the Palm Beach County Court and serves as an independent expert witness in civil and criminal cases across North America. He is an adjunct professor at Florida Atlantic University and is the author of over 400 print and online publications and books, including two previous volumes with Charles C Thomas: *Practical Police Psychology: Stress Management and Crisis Intervention for Law Enforcement,* and *Criminal Psychology: Nature, Nurture, Culture.* Dr. Miller has consulted and/or testified in a number of high-profile police shooting cases in the United States and Canada. In February 2015, he was selected to be a panel member testifying before the *President's Task Force on 21st Century Policing* in Washington, DC. Dr. Miller can be contacted at (561) 392-8881 or at docmilphd@aol.com.

THE PSYCHOLOGY OF POLICE DEADLY FORCE ENCOUNTERS

Science, Practice, and Policy

By

LAURENCE MILLER, PhD

With a Foreword by

Alexis Artwohl, PhD

CHARLES C THOMAS • PUBLISHER • LTD.
Springfield • Illinois • U.S.A.

Published and Distributed Throughout the World by

CHARLES C THOMAS • PUBLISHER, LTD.
2600 South First Street
Springfield, Illinois 62704

ISBN 978-0-398-09326-6 (paper)
ISBN 978-0-398-09327-3 (ebook)

Library of Congress Catalog Card Number: 2019057519 (print)
2019057520 (ebook)

With THOMAS BOOKS *careful attention is given to all details of manufacturing and design. It is the Publisher's desire to present books that are satisfactory as to their physical qualities and artistic possibilities and appropriate for their particular use.* THOMAS BOOKS *will be true to those laws of quality that assure a good name and good will.*

Printed in the United States of America
MM-C-1

Library of Congress Cataloging-in-Publication Data

Names: Miller, Laurence, 1951-author.
Title: The psychology of police deadly force encounters science, practice, and policy / by Laurence Miller, PhD.
Description: Springfield : Charles C Thomas, Publisher, Ltd., 2020. | Includes bibliographical references and index.
Identifiers: LCCN 2019057519 (print) | LCCN 2019057520 (ebook) | ISBN 9780398093266 (paperback) I ISBN 9780398093273 (ebook)
Subjects: LCSH: Police shootings--United States. | Police psychology--United States. | Firearms--United States--Use in crime prevention. | Police training--United States.
Classification: LCC HV8141 .M475 2020 (print) | LCC HV8141 (ebook) | DDC 363.201/9--dc23
LC record available at https://lccn.loc.gov/2019057519
LC ebook record available at https://lccn.loc.gov/2019057520

This book is dedicated to the men and women in law enforcement, medicine, mental health, criminal justice, military service, and education who work to reduce the risk and lessen the suffering of their fellow citizens.

FOREWORD

There are a handful of behavioral scientists who combine scholarship with real-world experience working with law enforcement. Dr. Laurence Miller is one of those rare individuals. His areas of practice include working with officers in a clinical setting, providing training and consultation services to police agencies, and entering the battleground of the courtroom to provide expert testimony in high profile officer-involved shootings and other cases.

Miller is neither a cheerleader for cops nor a critic. When examining police operations, he recognizes that the vital questions are: "what do the facts and the research show?" This scientific inclination gives him an evidence-based approach that can be sorely lacking with the media, politicians, anti-police activists, and others who want to exploit officer-involved shootings to score political points or for personal gain.

Miller and I agree that law enforcement, like all professions, has a small number of bad apples, but the rest are honorable people trying hard to perform one of America's most demanding occupations. Each officer and every incident deserve what all other Americans desire and are entitled to: objective, forensically reliable investigations without rushes to judgment before the facts are known.

Miller's latest book is an important contribution to the practice of psychology and the legal system. All critiques of critical incidents involving cops or citizens must take into account the science of human performance. Miller delves deep into the research and applies it to police use of force, but the same body of knowledge is essential to understanding a wide variety of high-stress events.

This outstanding volume makes a unique and much-needed contribution to law enforcement training, police operational assistance, investigation procedures, the courtroom, the clinician's office, police officers and their families, and anyone who wants to understand how human beings operate under extreme stress.

Alexis Artwohl, Ph.D., Police Psychologist
and co-author with Loren Christensen:
Deadly Force Encounters, Second Edition (2019)

PREFACE

This was supposed to be a shorter book. I had originally intended to provide a concise, coherent guide to the psychology of deadly force that would summarize and integrate the existing literature on the subject and offer a few pithy recommendations of my own. What I discovered is that this field is neither concise nor coherent, but that there are multiple nuggets of data and insight scattered among disciplines as diverse as neuroscience, cognitive psychology, sociology, and politics. I also came to realize that when you are trying to understand and explicate the scientific and social foundations of life-and-death encounters, you inevitably run up against conflicting opinions and swirling passions that require some measure of time, patience, and perspicacity to unravel and comprehend.

Meanwhile, I'm hopefully able to draw on my 30 years' experience as a clinical, forensic, police, and neuropsychologist to flesh out and humanize some of the empirical data and theoretical models reported in this volume. Make no mistake: the science is paramount if we are ever going to come to a rational understanding of human nature and use it to devise practical measures for improving society. That's why this book may seem a bit top-heavy with empirical research from neuroscience, cognitive psychology, and social theory, but facts are facts, and understanding them and what they mean is vital to our system of justice.

But I want this volume to be a practical one, too, because for attorneys and expert witnesses who work on contested deadly force and other police misconduct cases, the lives, careers, and sanity of the involved officers may depend on our ability to explain to a factfinder (judge or jury) why that officer acted as he or she did, and why what may appear to be a case of excessive force may have, in fact, seemed reasonable from the perspective of that officer's brain at the scene. Thus, some of the recommendations offered herein stem from my experience in consulting and testifying in contested deadly force cases, as well as other types of cases in the civil and criminal justice systems.

Throughout, I try to portray a balanced, realistic view of police officers in general; neither a defeatist, cynical "they're all crooked cops" trope, nor a Pollyannish, overromanticized "noble guardians of civilization" homage.

Mostly, these are just ordinary men and women trying to do their jobs, carrying the full range of virtues, faults, and foibles that characterize the warp and woof of humanity in any society. Except that they are authorized to kill you if they have to, and then face the consequences of their actions–and that's where the not-so-ordinary complications lie.

This book contains nine chapters, arranged in three sections. Chapter 1 discusses the nature of police use of force, including deadly force, and some of the legal standards that apply. In Chapter 2, I describe the various circumstances that may cause a police-citizen interaction to evolve or explode into a deadly force encounter. Chapter 3 deals with features of officer attitude, personality, training, and job experience that may make some officers more likely than others to consider and deploy force as a preferred option, as well as to misuse their police authority more generally.

Chapters 4, 5, and 6 dive into the cognitive neuroscience of emergency responding in describing how officers perceive, react to, and remember deadly force encounters. An accurate understanding of these matters is essential to the fair adjudication of police deadly force cases, and one of the goals of this volume is to bridge the gulf between the dense productions of wonky researchers and the need for practical tools for police managers, law enforcement investigators, legal personnel, mental health consultants, and expert witnesses in dealing fairly with use of force cases.

Nowhere is this more important than in the area of race and policing, and Chapter 7 endeavors to focus the cold light of scientific scrutiny on the hot zone of police-community conflict and perceived bias in law enforcement. One of the encouraging experiences in researching this chapter has been the discovery that brain and behavioral scientists are taking these matters seriously in empirically studying the cognitive psychology of alleged race-based deadly force actions, but this important information has largely remained buried in professional journals. Hopefully, this chapter will spur more general interest in, and support for, vital research in this area.

But it's not just all about confrontations and court cases. The overwhelming majority of police deadly force actions are ruled justifiable, but the act of taking a human life can nevertheless reverberate in the lives of many officers. Chapter 8 describes the types of psychological reactions officers may display to any type of deadly force encounter and offers a suite of suggestions for practical management and psychological counseling of such personnel, including special considerations for those officers who are enduring the additional seismic pressure of surviving day-to-day under investigation or indictment for their alleged actions.

Chapter 9 jumps into the legal arena itself, describing the range of potential outcomes in a contested deadly force case. It then describes the structure and process of a law enforcement forensic psychological evaluation, and offers a set of recommendations for officers on how to cope with the stresses of living under the microscope and how to deal with the challenges of investigation, litigation, and court testimony.

This book will thus be a useful guide and reference volume for police managers and supervisors, investigators and attorneys, mental health clinicians and psychologist expert witnesses, law enforcement educators and trainers, and rank and file police officers who may find themselves involved in a deadly force incident and need an authoritative roadmap for the complex journey ahead.

A note on terminology: to avoid the linguistic clumsiness of repetitive he/she, his/her, and him-/herself bumplets, I've elected, with a few exceptions where appropriate, to use the male pronoun for most descriptions in this book, rationalizing that, since most cops are still male, my readers will let me get away with it for the sake of readability. If I offend anyone, I'm sorry, and please feel free to do it your way in your next book.

In addition to poring over oceans of print, much of the content of this volume is informed by my own experience in working on police deadly force and other cases, and in this, I have been aided by the advice, counsel, and expertise of a short list of respected colleagues. A special shout-out goes to Dr. Alexis Artwohl, who, in addition to being one of the premiere researchers, authors, and teachers the field of police deadly force encounters and police psychology generally, has been extraordinarily gracious and supportive of my own work in this area, and it was a pleasure to meet her during one of my court trips to Arizona. One of the motivations for writing the present volume stems from the example of Dr. Artwohl's special ability to mold the ore of cognitive and social science into practical tools for helping cops on the job.

Within the broader field of police psychology, I've gained valuable experience in providing clinical, consultative, and training services to several local police agencies, particularly the dedicated personnel of the West Palm Beach Police Department, Boca Raton Police Department, Palm Beach County Sheriff's Office, Troop L of the Florida Highway Patrol, and also many other local, regional, and national law enforcement organizations. Captain Patrick Kenny of PBSO and Dr. Bradley Feuer, Chief Surgeon at FHP deserve special mention as the kind of law enforcement supervisors, trainers, and mentors who inspire their troops with the constructive amalgam of confidence, commitment, and authority that defines true leaders.

The rank and file officers whom I've evaluated, advised, and counseled over the years have highlighted the importance of mutual trust and respect in encouraging tough, resilient service members (that also goes for military personnel) to open up and share their thoughts, perceptions, and feelings. This kind of work reinforces the responsibility of mental health clinicians and law enforcement leaders to promote a practice model that allows these tough guys and gals to see our counseling interactions with them, not as a threat, but as a resource, as a way of building them up, not breaking them down.

Contributing to this effort has been the work of several law enforcement personnel, clinicians, and scholars–some embodying all three descriptors. Dr. Richard Levenson of the New York State Highway Patrol presented many of this book's formative ideas in the pages of the *International Journal of Emergency Mental Health,* and then provided valuable guidance when I later inherited that editorial mantle from him for the next several years. Going decades back is the literary support of author, editor, and Agent James D. Sewell of the Florida Department of Law Enforcement, in who's learned and practical anthologies I still have the privilege of sharing my observations and ideas. Same goes for forensic-police psychologist and prolific author Dr. Jack Kitaeff, with whom I still enjoy a productive collaboration and friendship, and who possesses a unique and singular insight into Elvis (yes, that one).

In the field of forensic psychology you meet a lot of lawyers, and we've all heard what they say about lawyers, and some of that is more true than you want to know. But I've also worked with a few skilled and honorable attorneys who have represented their police officer (and other) clients with vigor, integrity, and compassion, and law enforcement is lucky to have these dedicated professionals on their side. The same goes for the hard-working State Attorneys and Public Defenders I've worked with at the Palm Beach County Courthouse, who understand that justice is never a part-time job.

To sharpen your ideas and consolidate your knowledge base, there's nothing like having to field questions from inquisitive and sometimes skeptical interlocutors. Over the years my students at Florida Atlantic University, Palm Beach State College, and the Police Academy-Criminal Justice Institute of Palm Beach County, as well as the law enforcement, criminal justice, and mental health professionals who have attended my continuing education and training seminars, have managed to keep me on my toes and remind me how much there still is to learn in any domain of study and practice.

And sometimes even the professors can help a little. My research and clinical work in psychology in general has been bolstered by the intellectual stimulation, collegial support, and friendship of a number of university faculty members, most significantly, Drs. David Bjorklund and Paul Peluso at FAU, Dr. Vincent Van Hasselt at Nova Southeastern University, and Dr. Paul Friedman at the Palm Beach County Criminal Justice Institute. These scholars embody the principle that teaching is not just an activity, but an organic state of being, and that those who teach most effectively are those who never stop learning.

Other professionals in law enforcement, mental health, and criminal justice who have contributed directly, philosophically, or inspirationally to this volume include Nancy Bohl, James P. Cummings, Gerald W. Garner, John Violanti, and Howard Webb. I'm sure there are others I'll think of right after this manuscript goes to press, and to those I can only offer my assurance that such oversight is mnemonic, not motivational, and in recompense, I offer to send them a copy of this book or buy them lunch, whichever is cheaper.

As with several of my previous books, editor-in-chief Michael Thomas and the editorial and production staff at Charles C Thomas Publishers are a writer's dream to work with: helpful, courteous, efficient, and always dedicated to bringing out an author's message in the most authentic and expressive way. I look forward to a continuing productive relationship.

Of course, once again, gratitude to my wife, Joan, for her enduring support, and who, by now, has become used to my periodic sequestrations as I complete yet another project of this type. And thank you, Dr. Halle, for your substantive input and discussion into many of the clinical concepts that underlie this volume. It has been a pride and a pleasure to watch you mature from daughter to colleague.

Laurence Miller
November, 2019

BOOKS BY LAURENCE MILLER, PhD

Inner Natures: Brain, Self, and Personality.
Freud's Brain: Neuropsychodynamic Foundations of Psychoanalysis.
Psychotherapy of the Brain-Injured Patient: Reclaiming the Shattered Self.
Shocks to the System: Psychotherapy of Traumatic Disability Syndromes.
Practical Police Psychology: Stress Management and Crisis Intervention for Law Enforcement (Charles C Thomas).
METTLE: Mental Toughness Training for Law Enforcement.
Counseling Crime Victims: Practical Strategies for Mental Health Professionals.
From Difficult to Disturbed: Understanding and Managing Dysfunctional Employees.
Criminal Psychology: Nature, Nurture, Culture (Charles C Thomas).
Posttraumatic Stress Disorder and Forensic Psychology: Applications to Civil and Criminal Law.
Clevenger, S.M.F., Miller, L., Moore, B.A & Freeman, A. (Eds.). *Behind the Badge: A Psychological Treatment Handbook for Law Enforcement Officers.*
The Psychology of Police Deadly Force Encounters: Science, Practice, and Policy (Charles C Thomas).

CONTENTS

THE PSYCHOLOGY OF POLICE DEADLY FORCE ENCOUNTERS

Part I

DEADLY FORCE: FACTS AND FACTORS

Chapter 1

OFFICER-INVOLVED SHOOTINGS AND DEADLY FORCE

Law is order in liberty, and without order liberty is social chaos.
Archbishop Ireland

Death is always and under all circumstances a tragedy, for if it is not, then it means that life itself has become one.
President Theodore Roosevelt

The gun. Any account of police use of force must begin and end with the gun—as both weapon and symbol. Among all public safety and emergency personnel, no other civilian service group is mandated to carry a lethal firearm as part of their daily equipment, and no other service member is charged with the responsibility of instantly fusing strict rules of engagement with their own discretion and judgment in making the split-second decision to take a life. Watching any typical TV cop show or movie might convince viewers that most officers pop off multiple rounds every day. But in reality, the discharging of one's weapon in the line of duty is typically a rare and profound event, one that can leave a lasting trace on the officer involved (Henry, 2004; Loughlin & Flora, 2017; Miller, 2006e, 2019b).

Commentators have noted that the power invested in the police to use coercive physical force against citizens, up to and including killing, may often put them at odds with a civil society which, ideally, does not countenance violence as a regular means of maintaining domestic tranquility (Bittner, 1970; Fyfe, 2000; Klinger & Brunson, 2009; Klockars, 1985). Accordingly, nothing places the police under more scrutiny than when officers exercise their ultimate power to take the lives of citizens through the use of their firearm in an **officer-involved shooting/deadly force encounter (OIS/DFE)**. Of course, deadly force is itself a rare and extreme example of other

use of force (UOF) actions that may become necessary in the course of police work.

PATROL POLICING

When most people think of police officers, they think of the traditional cop on the beat, and indeed, the police patrol function, on foot or in vehicles, continues to be the backbone of community law enforcement (Nhan, 2019, Peak, 2003). This seemingly simple police role is really composed of a variety of complex daily decisions and activities, which include the discretionary use of authority and the prevention of criminal activity by an assertive police presence. It also involves maintaining good relations with citizens in the community, because police may at times have to depend on the cooperation of those citizens to help them do their jobs effectively. Examples include obtaining useful information in trying to solve a crime, or helping to cool down contentious family members' or neighbors' anger to forestall a potential violent escalation. Officers know they will encounter the same people—"repeat customers"—on a regular basis, and so maintaining good relations works in everybody's favor (Miller, 2006i).

While the actual effect of patrol officers on crime statistics continues to be studied, surveys show that, overall, citizens feel safer and more confident in their local police department when the officers are a living, breathing presence in their daily lives. However, this is only true if there exists a baseline level of trust between community members and the police that serve them (Kim, 2018; Morin et al., 2017, Nhan, 2019). Another irony is that, in lean fiscal times, foot or vehicle patrols are often the first to undergo budget cuts in favor of more flashy special tactics and investigative units (Thibault et al., 2004).

Survey research has identified a number of tasks and responsibilities that officers must carry out in order to successfully perform their patrol duties (Peak, 2003). Although TV cop shows often portray police work as nonstop action, in real life the patrol officer's job is more like that of a firefighter, paramedic, or air traffic controller: long periods of monotony punctuated by brief episodes of intense activity. Officers have to be able to react quickly and go from "zero to sixty" at a moment's notice. They have to be able to respond courageously and aggressively in critical situations, yet possess sufficient tact and presence of mind not to overreact and risk inflaming the situation further. In between, they must deal with various and sundry crises, ranging from traffic violations, to citizen disputes, to gang activities.

For patrol officers to do their jobs effectively, they must adopt a constructive territoriality about their patrol areas, sometimes known as "owning the beat" (Peak, 2003). By becoming increasingly familiar with the geography, economy, personality, and sociology of their patrol areas, officers come to know intuitively what's normal or what's out of place for their respective neighborhoods, thus making them able to spot and respond to problems before they spiral out of control (Johnson & Morgan, 2013; Sacks, 1972; Stroshine et al., 2008). This practical expertise further enables officers to quickly size up situations and make prompt, effective decisions with regard to what specific actions to take, such as a crime in progress, family crisis, or citizen dispute–a type of experiential wisdom known as **recognition-primed decision making**, or **RPDM** (Hardy & Kroenig, 2016; Klein, 1989, 1993, 1996, 1998; Miller, 2008i; Orasanu & Backer, 1996; Orasanu & Connelly, 1993; Ross et al., 2004), which we will discuss further in Chapter 4.

By adopting an optimal blend of professional objectivity and emotional investment in their neighborhoods, patrol officers develop what the business world calls "buy-in," a personal stake in the welfare of their patrol community, a situation in which it is important to them to keep the peace and provide the highest quality of service: "This is *my* neighborhood, and I'm going to do everything I can to make sure that it stays safe." Importantly, officers who feel they are an integral part of their patrol communities are less likely to resort to physical force to resolve crisis situations that they might verbally de-escalate. In return, citizens come to trust and respect those officers whom they perceive as earnestly trying to keep order, but without excessive harshness, and who truly try to understand the community's concerns (Toch & Grant, 2005; Wadman & Ziman, 1993).

While not all officers can be Olympic athletes, they are expected to maintain basic standards of physical conditioning and psychomotor skill with respect to strength and endurance, manual dexterity, proficiency with firearms and equipment, driving skill, and other fundamental police functions. In the same way, while not all officers can be paragons of mental health and moral virtue, they are expected to possess the basic cognitive skills of mature judgment, problem-solving, independent thinking, and effective communication. Indeed, even more so than other emergency responders, police officers are given wide latitude in how to handle many types of routine and complex policing scenarios, ranging from the decision to write a traffic citation to whether to use their Taser or firearm in a dangerous criminal confrontation. In this regard, police officers need to be able to work under varying levels of supervision, from tight micromanagement of their every move to the most meager oversight that leaves crucial decisions to the officer's discretion.

Important psychological skills extend to the interpersonal domain as well. Patrol officers, especially in larger metropolitan areas, will have to deal with a wide range of citizen ages, ethnicities, cultures, economic strata, personalities, and psychopathologies. Officers must sometimes endure impolite or verbally abusive behavior, while at all times maintaining vigilance and a professional presence of dignified strength and resolve. Effective officers must be able to utilize appropriate conflict-resolution skills to prevent situations from escalating, while maintaining objectivity, balance, and the perception of fairness. They must be able to cope with different kinds and varying levels of stress, and yet at all times maintain a high level of personal integrity and ethical conduct. This is not just a nice-sounding, politically correct idea; it is essential to the officer's maintaining and reinforcing his or her authority and credibility on patrol.

POLICE USE OF FORCE

As noted above, police **deadly force encounters (DFE)** are a small subset of a broader range **use of force (UOF)** scenarios, which have been defined as "acts that threaten or inflict physical harm on subjects" (Terrill, 2003, p. 56). Law enforcement officers are the only civilian branch of service providers that are authorized to utilize coercive physical force with citizens (Bittner, 1970; Reiss, 1971; Scharf & Binder, 1983; Sherman, 1980; Walker & Fridell, 1993). Police use of any kind of force is a statistically rare event in any community, but a small percentage of officers are disproportionately involved in such incidents, as well as the recipients of citizen complaints, at a factor of up to 7 to 1 (Albert & Dunham, 2000; Brandl & Stroshine, 2012; Brandl et al., 2001; Dugan & Breda, 1991; Garner et al., 1995, 1996; Klinger, 1995; Lersch & Mieczowski, 1996; Reiss, 1971).

As we'll discuss further in Chapter 3, a common response of officers to use of force complaints is some version of "you have to crack eggs to make an omelet," that is, if an officer has a productive arrest record, he or she will probably be using more than a little force (albeit justified in the officer's mind) to rack up the collar stats. Research (Brandl & Stroshine, 2012) seems to partially support this: officers with high use of force rates do make over twice as many arrests as low-force-rate officers. However, force alone cannot be the only factor because the same research shows that other officers with equivalent high arrest rates do not have greater than average use of force complaints. Why?

Perhaps it has to do with another finding from this research. Officers who are authorized to carry a Taser have higher use of force rates than non-Taser qualified officers, but their force is no more likely to involve the Taser itself than any other kind of force. One explanation is that officers who are attracted to the forceful aspects of policing are more likely than others to apply for Taser certification because they regard it as yet one more tool for the intimidation and control of citizens.

Police Attitudes Toward Use of Force

Not that overly forceful officers will regard their own use of force as abusive, per se. An early analysis (Reiss, 1971) found that 78 percent of documented excessive force instances occurred in police-controlled settings, such as the precinct station, patrol car, or public streets. Almost all victims of force were young, lower-class males from a variety of ethnic groups, who were regarded by police as chronic offenders. Among this group, 39 percent of suspects openly defied police authority, 9 percent physically resisted arrest, and 32 percent were persons in what were at the time considered traditionally "deviant" offender roles, such as drug addicts. However, the study also found that, even in the face of clearly antagonistic behavior, many officers opted to restrain their own use of force.

Subsequent surveys have shown that police officers rarely regard the level of force used by themselves or their colleagues as excessive (Grant & Grant, 1996); however, over a fifth of officers in one anonymous survey (Carter, 1976) believed that extra force is sometimes necessary to establish an officer's authority, while almost two-thirds felt that officers have the right to use force in retaliation for physical attacks by suspects. Force does not necessarily have to be physical: about half the officers in this sample felt that "rough talk" was sometimes the only way to get some citizens to obey police commands. Less than one in six officers felt that their use of force reflected primarily ethnic or racial discrimination per se. However, endorsement or tolerance of verbal and physical aggression toward unruly citizens was associated with those officers' overall dissatisfaction with their own jobs, suggesting that some officers may be taking out their frustrations on citizens, albeit often on the citizens who may themselves be the source of many of those very aggravations.

Some police officers regard excessive force as a less serious offense than sleeping, drinking, or having sex on duty, taking bribes, accepting free services, or lying under oath (see Chapter 3). In anonymous surveys, police officers who strongly identify with their "cop's cop" role are more likely to admit that they would participate in the street execution of a suspect known to have killed a police officer, although an event like this is, thankfully, rare (Lester & TenBrink, 1985; TenBrink & Lester, 1984). Yet, as will be discussed subsequently, even when deadly force is justified to apprehend a fleeing felon, many officers report that they would refrain from using such force in these situations due to possible departmental sanctions and/or legal repercussions (Brown, 1983; Cloherty, 2004; Hughes, 2001; Kappeler, 1997; Kappeler et al., 1993; Miller, 2004, 2006i, 2008a, 2008c, 2011b; Nhan, 2019; Vaughn et al., 2001).

OFFICER-INVOLVED SHOOTING

Since most law enforcement DFE cases involve use of a firearm, it is important to understand how police officers become involved in shooting incidents. This will be expanded upon in subsequent chapters.

Rates of Officer-Involved Shooting and other Use of Force

Physical force of any kind is used in less than 1.5 percent of police-citizen contacts, and officer-involved shootings are rarer still. According to the FBI's annual *Law Enforcement Officers Killed and Assaulted* (LEOKA) report (FBI, 1994, 1998, 2006, 2015), U.S. police are assaulted about 60,000 times each year, with approximately 11,000 of these attacks involving a lethal weapon, of which 3,000 are firearms. Up to 80 percent of officers are assaulted in the line of duty, and these officers are assaulted an average of seven times over their careers. If you are a police officer, you are most likely to be slain in the line of duty in the following circumstances, in descending order of probability: making an arrest (29%); responding to a disturbance call (26%); conducting a traffic stop (18%); being ambushed (14%); investigating a suspicious person call (11%); transporting a felon (1%); and interacting with a mentally ill person (1%). In one study, 82 percent of the officers slain were killed within six feet of their assailants (Aveni, 2003). Following a peak in the early 1970s, assaults on, and homicides of, U.S. police officers have been declining steadily.

Data from the U.S. Department of Justice (Durose et al., 2007; Eith & Durose, 2011; Langan et al., 2001) indicate that police use or threaten any kind of force in approximately 1.3 percent of total citizen contacts, and male citizens are three times as likely as females to be involved. The average annual rate of justifiable deadly force by U.S. law enforcement is about 360-390 cases per year. Police deadly force incidents declined from a peak rate in the early 1970s, but then began rising again in the early 2000s (Blair et al., 2011; Bohrer et al., 2008; FBI, 2015; Geller & Scott, 1992; Hickman et al., 2008; Loftin et al., 2003; McElvain & Kposowa, 2008; Petrowski, 2002a; Schouten & Brennan, 2016). Collating data from several sources, Ross and Brave (2018) calculate the overall probability of a U.S. citizen being killed by a police officer to be approximately 0.0003 percent. Put another way, the average New York City police officer would have to work 694 years to shoot and kill a citizen (think of the overtime!), and in most municipalities, the rate is even lower.

Officers Ambushed and Killed

The LEOKA reports characterize **ambush incidents** as attacks that involve entrapment and premeditation. These are situations in which an unsuspecting officer is targeted or lured into danger as the result of conscious consideration and planning by the offender, as opposed to spontaneous aggression against police officers that often erupts from an episode of police questioning or attempts to arrest a citizen. Ambush incidents account for 22 percent of officers killed during the period between 2004 and 2013, close to the rate (24%) of officers feloniously killed during arrest actions.

In fact, although the actual number of officer deaths has declined, there has been a steady increase in police ambush deaths since the 1980s, including some very recent cases involving officers attacked in their cars or shot at by snipers (Blake & Miller, 2015; Schouten & Brennan, 2016; Sheets & Sprouse, 2019), perhaps due to a more brazen attitude on the part of recent offenders. Of note, in almost 60 percent of police ambush killings, the officer was on assignment alone.

Not Shooting: Officer Hesitates or Refrains

Given the volume of contentious and often potentially dangerous interactions with citizens in the work life of an average patrol officer, it is noteworthy how often police officers restrain themselves from utilizing force, even in the face of an imminent threat where such force would be legally justified (Fitzgerald & Bromley, 1998; Kesic et al., 2012; Klinger, 2005; Loughlin & Flora, 2017).

In fact, in the majority of potential deadly force situations, the officers fire no rounds because the very act of displaying a firearm is sufficient to discourage the suspect from further dangerous action. Sometimes, however, this does not suffice, and the officer is forced to shoot (Bohrer et al., 2008). In such cases, officers typically conceptualize the situation not as their actually *deciding* to use deadly force, but as reacting naturally to the suspect's threatening actions that *require* it: "He made the choice to die when he aimed that gun at me."

Even in the military, where a soldier's mandate is precisely to kill the enemy, a large number of individual soldiers in combat hesitate or decline to kill an identified adversary even when they know that this hesitation might endanger their own lives. This no doubt reflects a natural human reluctance to kill another person that most people (fortunately) have (Grossman & Christensen, 2007; Miller, 2008b, 2013a).

FBI data reveal that approximately 85 percent of officers killed in the line of duty never discharged their service weapon (FBI, 1992; Hickman et al., 2008; McElvain & Kposowa, 2008; Petrowski, 2002a). Review of individual case studies has revealed that the slain officers often hesitated, even in the face of an immediate, credible threat. In a number of cases, officers repeatedly ordered suspects to drop their weapons and were killed when the suspect ignored the commands and fired at the officer. Some of these incidents were recorded on the slain officers' dash cameras (Bohrer et al., 2008; Petrowski, 2002a).

Research on officer-involved shootings (Bohrer et al., 2008; Pinizzotto et al., 1997, 2000; U.S. Department of Justice, 1992) has identified several potential reasons why officers may be reluctant to fire their weapons in a deadly force encounter:

General Unwillingness to Kill People. Many law enforcement officers believe that their primary mandate is to help people and to keep the peace, i.e., "to protect and serve." Many of these officers who survived deadly force encounters state that they were trying to wait until the last possible moment before using their firearm; obviously, they miscalculated. In these surveys, officers chose to withhold deadly force in three out of four incidents where they would have been justified in using it.

Misperceived Threats. Many officers may not recognize the full range of threats that can affect them, leading them to underestimate the dangerousness of certain citizens, weapons, or situations. In simunitions training, officers shoot at targets, and even when the figures are designed to look as lifelike as possible, they almost always depict adult males as the assailants, who are wielding firearms or other obvious weapons. But officers have been injured and killed by schoolchildren and little old ladies, using kitchen utensils or office supplies, which argues for a wider range of more realistic training scenarios. Disturbingly, a number of cop killers have stated in interviews that they "knew" or "sensed" that the officer would not fire at them, and this emboldened them to attack.

Departmental Policies. Many officers can readily recall their departmental policy on when not to shoot, but have more trouble remembering when they can. Although every conceivable circumstance cannot be anticipated, this apparent ambiguity suggest that police agency policies and training programs should make the protocols for deadly force utilization as clear and objective as possible and should ascertain that each officer understands these policies thoroughly.

Detriment to Career. In some departments, the organizational culture, intentionally or not, seems to promote the idea that if officers have to shoot someone, they are doing something wrong. Not infrequently, the brass send a mixed message to their troops to "maintain officer safety," but at the same time will admonish them to avoid doing anything that will embarrass the department or create liability. This will be discussed further is Chapter 9.

FORCE AND DEADLY FORCE

Largely based on fictional accounts and media reports, many citizens have an unrealistic view of how deadly force encounters develop and what the appropriate responses to them should be (Jeffries et al., 2016; Henry, 2004; Kowalyk & Tasse, 2019; Miller, 2006a, 2008a, 2015a, 2017, 2019b; Loughlin & Flora, 2017; Remsberg, 2008; Ryan, 2013). This is one area where law enforcement educators have a vital role to play, inasmuch as such potentially misinformed citizens are the ones who may eventually serve on citizen review boards, on juries, and as voters.

What Is An "Armed" Suspect and What Is "Deadly" Force?

We all know the joke about the dumb schmuck who brings a knife to a gunfight. But keep laughing while the schmuck jumps you from behind and shivs you in the neck while you're unsnapping your holster. Police officers know that subjects who threaten lethal violence may be "armed" in any number of ways. Yet, commentators seem to assume that unless a citizen closely matches the police in physical power or weaponry, he or she cannot possibly be much of a menace, or that a potential attacker is entitled to the equivalent of a "free shot" before the officer is allowed to respond (Blair et al., 2011). Use of deadly force by police in such circumstances may be viewed by citizens as violating some street-chivalrous notion of a fair fight. But every cop understands just how unpredictably dangerous a police-citizen encounter can be when dealing with a subject who may be enraged, intoxicated, or delusional. A look, a word, a gesture, and–boom–a compliant citizen can turn into an adrenalized assailant.

Don't believe me? Stop reading and try this: ask a buddy lie on the floor, face down, spread-eagle, head facing away from you. Stand 10-12 feet away with your back turned to your prostrate partner. Now tell him, whenever he's ready, to get up, rush at you as fast as he can, and tap you on the shoulder (this exercise comes from Massad Ayoob, a firearms trainer and police safety advocate, going back to the early1970s). When I do this in my classes (usually with me playing the victim), it takes about three seconds for the volunteer to go from prone on the floor to hand on my shoulder–which could just as easily be on my neck, utility belt, or pistol if I were wearing a police uniform and gear. That's why every officer knows that an unsecured suspect, even with no weapons, can pose a deadly threat in less time than it may take that officer to notice and react to the danger.

Care to try the same exercise, but this time have your partner hold a hammer, a pair of scissors, a belt, or a frying pan? Didn't think so, because another thing police know is that, in a life-and-death confrontation, virtually any nearby object can become a lethal weapon at any time; a firearm or blade is not required. I've interviewed officers who have been choked with a bathrobe sash, brained with a flowerpot, had shop tools or industrial chemicals hurled at them, been clawed, bitten, spit on, peed on, and worse. One officer suffered permanent knee damage after being kicked by an intoxicated amputee who was literally unarmed (actually, he had one arm). A fist to the face or a pair of strong mitts around the throat can quickly render an officer unconscious. Even full use of one's own body is not required; in one case, a suspect on the ground in full hogtie restraint was able to twist around and chomp on an officer's ankle.

Another point of confusion attends the very concept of what "deadly force" means. Following an officer-involved shooting, citizens and media pundits often issue expressions of outraged puzzlement that go something like this: "All right, I get it that if an officer's life is truly threatened, he has to defend himself, but did they need to use all those bullets? Was it really necessary for five cops to fire forty rounds to bring down this one guy?" The answer lies in the starkly fundamental rule for a deadly force encounter: Do not use deadly force unless there is absolutely no other choice. But once that decision has been made, *deadly means deadly,* and the responding officers must assure that the force used is as lethal as possible, as quickly as possible.

Why? Because in a real emergency, to prevent a dangerous assailant from killing or injuring someone else, the primary goal is not to wound the suspect or even to kill him, but to *stop* him. If an officer shoots a charging suspect multiple times, it won't make much difference if the attacker dies of his wounds several seconds after he's had a chance to slash the officer's throat or crush his skull with a brick. Once an assailant has presented a clear and credible threat, the goal is to neutralize that threat immediately, and while four bullets may not swiftly drop an aggressive juggernaut, 40 bullets might—assuming that at least some of them hit their intended target, which will be discussed later.

Reasonable Force: A Reasonable Standard?

In life-and-death situations, we expect our guardians to protect us, yet we also expect them to somehow always use just the right amount of force necessary to mitigate the danger. But how much is that? In most law enforcement conceptualizations, **necessary** or **reasonable force** is the amount of force needed to control a given situation, so as to preserve the life and maintain the safety of police officers and/or vulnerable civilians at the scene. **Excessive force** is any use of force beyond that required for such safety and control. The severity and intensity of the force used—from verbal commands, to handcuffing, to baton, pepper spray, Taser, or firearm—must be proportional to the dangerousness of the suspect's present actions and should not be based on the suspect's attitude or the presumed moral blameworthiness of the crime in question.

That is, whether the suspect is being detained for shoplifting a candy bar or battering a disabled neighbor, the purpose of any police action is to secure the suspect for further processing, not to judge or punish him, which is the province of the courts (Blau, 1994; *Graham v. Connor,* 1989; Mastrofski et al., 2002; Miller, 2006i, 2015a; Nhan, 2019; Petrowski, 2002a, 2002b; Scrivner, 1999; *Tennessee v. Garner,* 1985).

Thus, a gratuitous finger-flick upside the head of a suspect who is already safely restrained constitutes excessive force, while multiple gunshots fired at a suspect who is aggressively assaulting an officer or civilian may not be. In law, the term **justifiable homicide** is used to describe any confrontation in which one person kills an attacker as a last resort to prevent imminent death or injury to themselves or a third party (see also Chapter 9). In a police deadly force encounter, this would describe a situation in which an officer kills a suspect who presents a clear threat to the life of that officer or others (Flowers, 2002; Miller, 2012; Palermo & Kocsis, 2005). This sounds straightforward enough, but in most real-life situations encountered by police, the line between excessive and reasonable force is hardly clear-cut. The amount of force necessary to secure the situation is almost always in some part a judgment call. And this means that occasional *mis*judgments may be made (Scrivner, 1999).

Court Decisions on Reasonable Force

All regulated professions have standards of practice. For example, when we're injured or ill, we want our doctor to do everything possible, go the extra medical mile, to ensure that we recover quickly and safely. But the law knows it cannot stipulate the highest possible levels of excellence, it can only enforce the minimal baseline standards of acceptable practice for a given profession, because who could decide in each case what the absolute highest level of care is? That's why your doctor can only be cited for malpractice if he or she failed to observe the established baseline criteria for competent medical practice. In other words, you're not statutorily entitled to the "best" medical care, only to that which follows the mandated basic requirements for that profession.

In a like manner, the law does not require police officers to invariably utilize the absolute minimum level of force necessary in a given situation, because how could one instantaneously judge what "minimum" means in every conceivable circumstance? Rather, the law requires only that the level of force used be **objectively reasonable** to control a deadly threat, and courts typically afford officers a degree of latitude in using their own judgment as to what is reasonable in a given confrontation (Bohrer et al., 2008; de Carmen, 1994; Gross, 2016; Meadows & Trostle, 1988; Petrowski, 2002a). This has been codified in a number of important legal decisions, two of which are well-known (for a comprehensive review of deadly force legal standards, see Ross, 2018).

In the case of *Sherrod v. Berry* (1988), Berry, a police officer, shot and killed Sherrod, whom he thought had a gun. When no gun was found, Sherrod's family sued for wrongful death, and the jury found for Sherrod's family. However, the Illinois Appellate Court reversed the decision, noting that a jury must base their assessment of reasonableness on what was known to, or believed by, the officer at the time of the event (thinking the suspect has a gun), not upon information acquired post hoc (subsequent investigation finds there was no gun).

In the case of *Graham v. Connor* (1989), Graham, a diabetic, asked a friend to drive him to a store to get some juice to counteract an insulin reaction. The line at the store was too long, so Graham hurriedly left and hopped back into the car, hoping to find his juice more quickly elsewhere. Officer Connor observed Graham "fleeing" the store, became suspicious, and followed the friend's car for a block, then made a traffic stop. Graham and his friend tried to explain the medical nature of the emergency, but Connor detained the pair and called for backup.

Meanwhile, Graham got out of the car and, probably due to the effects of hypoglycemia, began behaving erratically, leading arriving officers to handcuff him, believing he was drunk. Graham sustained cuts, bruises, joint injuries, and a foot fracture. The store owner later confirmed that no illegal or suspicious activity had occurred, and Graham subsequently sued the police. However, the case was dismissed on the basis of insufficient evidence that the police acted maliciously or illegally in light of the knowledge they were assumed to have possessed at the time.

In reviewing the case, the U.S. Supreme Court acknowledged that an officer's lawful action in making an arrest or investigatory stop necessarily carries with it the right to use some degree of physical force or coercion to effect it. The Court went on to rule that judgments about the constitutionality of all physically coercive police actions must be based on the Constitutional Fourth Amendment's **objective reasonableness standard**, which is to be applied on a case-by-case basis, from the perspective of a reasonable officer at the scene, possessing knowledge that is available at the time, and not from a perspective of 20/20 hindsight informed by data gathered subsequently (Klinger & Brunson, 2009; Ross, 2012, 2018).

The Court, in *Graham,* acknowledged that it still left undetermined what precise standard officers should use in assessing the reasonableness of their use of force in any given police-citizen interaction, and that reasonableness under the Fourth Amendment is "not capable of precise definition or mechanical application" in each and every split-second, life-and-death confrontation. The Court did, however, attempt provide some guidance about the kinds of criteria to be taken in to consideration–subsequently known as the **Graham factors**–in judging the constitutional objective reasonableness of an officer's actions (Klinger & Brunson, 2009; Petrowski, 2002a):

1. The officer's use of force must be assessed by examining the facts and circumstances of the incident as it unfolded.
2. The actions of the suspect must be considered, including the severity of the crime committed or believed to have been committed; whether the suspect possessed a weapon or otherwise posed an immediate threat to the safety of the officers or others; and whether the suspect was actively resisting arrest or attempting to flee and evade arrest.
3. The human factors affecting the officer's decision-making and responses need to be carefully evaluated, including the perception and cognition of a reasonable officer, and the need to make split-second decisions under rapidly evolving circumstances. These must be viewed from the perspective of the officer at the scene, not based upon facts and perspectives acquired post-hoc. It is just these perceptual and cognitive factors that often form the basis for an officer's defense in a contested abuse of force or deadly force case (see Chapters 4, 5 and 9).
4. The totality of the environment of the incident must be considered, including the quick-changing and unpredictable circumstances of the unfolding confrontation and the various actions of others at the scene.

Thus, the overall question in each deadly force case before a court is whether the officer's actions were objectively reasonable in light of the facts and circumstances confronting that officer, without regard to the underlying intent or motivation.

Since the *Graham* decision, other agencies have sought to refine and extend the definitional parameters of objectively reasonable force (see Ross, 2018 for a comprehensive review). One example is the *Model Use of Force Policy* of the International Association of Chiefs of Police (IACP), which states:

> Force that is likely to cause death or serious injury is properly judged through the eyes of a reasonably prudent and well-trained police officer under the same or similar circumstances. This "reasonable man" or, more accurately, reasonable officer, standard is an objective test. That is, it is not based on the intent or motivation of the officer or other subjective factors at the time of the incident. It is based solely on the objective circumstances of the event and the conclusion that would be drawn by any "reasonable officer at the scene." (IACP, 2005, cited in Klinger & Brunson, 2009)

Criteria for the Use of Deadly Force

However, this still leaves unexplained exactly what circumstances and what levels of danger and threat actually warrant the use of force, no matter how "reasonable" it may later be judged to be. In other words, just what does a suspect actually have to do to be perceived as dangerous enough to justify being killed by the police? As noted earlier, many citizens seem to feel that an assailant should be entitled to draw first blood before police respond with deadly force, and that anything less is unreasonable. Therefore, in attempting to address this issue, the Federal Bureau of Investigation (FBI) cites four categories of deadly threat (Klockars, 1996; Petrowski, 2002b):

The suspect possesses a weapon or is attempting to gain access to a weapon. This is the most obvious and common precipitator of a deadly force encounter.

A suspect with the capability of inflicting death or serious injury, with or without a weapon, is demonstrating an intention to do so. The law empowers police officers to use deadly force to prevent an imminent and credible threat to a victim's life; it obviously makes no sense to wait until *after* the suspect has taken lives to then attempt to prevent it; i.e., there is no "free shot."

The suspect is armed and running to gain the tactical advantage of cover. Police (and military) tactical training teaches that an armed assailant is far more dangerous once he has achieved the defensive advantage of cover, which may serve to embolden him in his efforts to attack police and civilians. This is a key problem, for example, in hostage-barricade scenarios (Call, 2003; Greenstone, 2005; Miller, 2005c; McMains & Mullins, 1996).

This tactical principle may also account for those "shot in the back" accusations against police when it appears that an officer fired at a suspect when all he was doing was trying to get away. But get away for what? Most people unconsciously conflate fleeing from an assailant who is trying to harm them with fleeing from a police officer who has just issued a lawful command to halt. In the first case, stopping in your tracks will almost certainly end badly because the attacker already intends to hurt you and your stopping will just make it easier for him. In the second case, stopping and surrendering might well *save* your life because in all probability, the officer's first choice is not to kill you; he just wants to control the scene and minimize danger.

The suspect is attempting to escape the vicinity of a violent confrontation in which he or she inflicted or attempted to inflict death or serious injury. This is related to the above description, but here, the suspect has already demonstrated his lethal intent by killing or trying to kill an officer or citizen, and it is thus assumed that he will show little compunction about subsequently harming others to effect his escape. This issue often arises when a suspect in a vehicle attempts to barrel through a cordon of cops, knocking them aside or causing them to scatter, at which point the officers fire at the fleeing car, evoking another round of criticism for "shooting an unarmed motorist," as if a recklessly driven, two-ton vehicle that just almost squashed a police officer equates to "unarmed."

Statistics vary from study to study but, overall, law enforcement deadly force actions which result in the deaths of citizens are most likely to occur in the following circumstances: (1) domestic or other residential disturbance call; (2) robbery in progress; (3) burglary in progress; (4) traffic stop or traffic offense' (5) personal dispute and/or accident; and (6) stake-outs and drug busts. Note that these circumstances are all characterized by high potential danger to police and civilians.

CONTINUUM OF FORCE

Even acknowledging that use of force, up to and including deadly force, may be reasonable in a given police-citizen encounter, this still does not seem to address the commonplace observation that most such encounters are rarely static: the level of threat posed by a given suspect can cascade up and down the threat-meter, it can move slowly or abruptly, and it can escalate or de-escalate reciprocally, based on the evolving interactions among citizen, officers, and others at the scene.

In what some commentators regard as a case of misapplied good intentions, police agencies have traditionally tried to address this issue by teaching and reinforcing the **continuum of force** principle (Table 1.1). That is, at any given moment in the encounter, the level of force used should be proportional to the level of threat posed by the suspect. Training programs and

Table 1.1.
CONTINUUM OF FORCE

Officer Presence: Calm show of force, uniform, vehicle, several officers respond.

Dialogue: Verbalization, warnings, orders, statement of consequences.

Empty Hand-Soft: Physical guidance, control, and passive restraint.

Empty Hand-Hard: Physical strikes, forceful restraint, chemical agent.

Impact Weapon: Baton, conducted energy device (Taser).

Lethal Force: Firearm or lethal use of other weapon.

manuals are often replete with charts and graphs, illustrating what levels or categories of subject threat (e.g., vocally resistant vs. physically combative) warrant the commensurate level of force by the officer (e.g., verbal command vs. Taser).

It sounds good on paper, but a number of authorities have criticized the use-of-force continuum concept as being impractical, legally unnecessary, or both. As noted earlier, from the legal side, the process of utilizing the absolute least forceful intervention is not constitutionally required, only that the level of force be reasonable, that is, not excessive, based on the exigent circumstances (Harper, 2000; Lewinski, 2000, 2009; Lewinski & Redmond, 2009; Petrowski, 2002a, 2002b).

From a practical standpoint, the continuum of force principle is almost impossible to apply consistently because most use of force encounters do not predictably march up a neatly unfolding staircase of severity; instead, many such encounters can go from calm to explosive in an instant. In some opinions, training in force continua only perpetuates hesitation and exacerbates the natural reluctance of officers to apply significant force, thereby increasing their vulnerability and compromising their safety (Petrowski, 2002a, 2002b). Additionally, what are the potential liability issues if a department trains their personnel in continuum of force, and an officer fails to follow the prescribed sequence appropriately? In the real world of police-citizen confrontations, there will be some situations that lend themselves to a continuum of force approach and some that don't, and this illustrates just one of the complexities of policing that require adequate knowledge, judgment, and skill.

HOW MUCH FORCE?

The force continuum concept concerns itself mainly with how officers can avoid the unnecessary escalation to deadly force with a firearm, but once circumstances have compelled a decision to shoot, corollary considerations involve how much to shoot and when to stop—the "why all those bullets?" question noted earlier. In this regard, various training protocols have been developed for appropriate use of deadly force—from "tap and look" to "pop to drop."

For example, a number of law enforcement agencies train their officers to fire one or more rounds ("single tap," "double tap," "triple tap," etc.), then assess the outcome, and decide whether to shoot again. Another, increasingly common, approach has been to train officers to shoot and assess simultaneously (Harper, 2000; Lewinski & Redmond, 2009)—despite the fact that such a level of perceptual and cognitive precision may be beyond the average officer's brain to handle in a rapidly unfolding deadly force encounter (see Chapters 4 and 5).

From an officer safety perspective, all this shooting, stopping, and assessing on the part of police officers may well confer a tremendous tactical advantage to the armed bad guy who has no hesitation about indiscriminately blasting away at anything that moves (see Chapter 5). Hence, the surest way for an officer to effectively and definitively neutralize the threat in a firefight is to continue to direct accurate fire on target until the threat stops ("pop to drop"). Problematic from a public perception standpoint is when several officers simultaneously utilize the same tactic on a single subject, resulting in that notorious "hail of bullets." This is compounded by the fact that different officers are likely to perceive the threat in different ways, and therefore some will begin firing or cease firing at different times, or fire differing numbers of rounds, depending on their individual perspectives of danger, leading to the assumption that those officers who fired more rounds than others were using "excessive" force (Lewinski, 2000; Lewinski & Redmond, 2009).

Accuracy of Shooting

Another practical reason for firing multiple rounds is that, as noted earlier, in a typical shooting scenario, only a limited number of those rounds will actually hit the target. Most civilians–and many police officers, until they have been in the situation themselves–are likely to give far more credit to officers' ballistic accuracy in critical life-and-death circumstances than exists in the real world. In the movie, *Die Hard III,* fictional New York City police officer John McClane uses a .38 caliber revolver, with just two rounds left, to snip off an electrical wire several hundred feet away, at night, in order to bring down the escaping villain's helicopter. Never mind that such a feat of marksmanship would be the envy of any trained military sniper or law enforcement sharpshooter equipped with a high-powered rifle and telescopic sight, but many civilians who grew up on police movies and TV shows also wonder why an officer can't just unerringly wing a threatening suspect and thereby nonlethally disable him like the Hollywood cops do. (Actually, this goes back even further, to the old cowboy movies, where the white-hatted lawman shoots the varmint's pistol right out of his hand.)

The reality is that, even with extensive firearms training in simunitions or live-fire scenarios, the average police officer (or soldier) misses his intended target at least as often as he hits it (Aveni, 2003; Donahue & Horvath, 1991; Geller & Scott, 1992; Grossman & Christensen, 2007; Pinizzotto et al., 2012; Schader & Bruns, 1989; White, 2006). Studies of police departments in New York, Los Angeles, Memphis, Miami-Dade, and Michigan find shooting accuracy to be between 25-56 percent; notable exceptions include San Antonio and San Francisco with shooting accuracy rates reported to approach 100 percent (what do they know?).

Suspects are more likely to be struck by police bullets if they are armed and have assaulted the officer, and if they have serious past criminal histories, which probably accounts for why they are more likely to attack an officer in the first place. Distance plays an important role, in that there seems to be a relational "Goldilocks zone" that determines the likelihood of a subject being killed or injured by police gunfire. Too far–greater than 20 feet–and shooting accuracy drops precipitously. Too close–especially where officer and subject are within grappling reach of each other–and firing again goes askew. Unsurprisingly, shooting accuracy deteriorates when both officer and suspect are running, and when a stationary officer fires at a fleeing subject, probably in large part accounted for by the distance factor. Shooting accuracy is also diminished when officers have to respond to a scene quickly and have less time to prepare. Whereas some studies (Aveni, 2003) cite environmental factors, such as ambient light, as important influences on shooting accuracy, others (White, 2006) find this to be negligible. Also apparently unrelated to shooting accuracy in some studies are whether or not an officer uses cover or has his gun drawn before confronting the suspect.

As noted above, if the fundamental rule for a deadly force encounter is to neutralize the threat as quickly and as effectively as possible, then firing additional rounds to compensate for decrements in accuracy makes tactical sense. Even with this rationale, the number of shots being fired per incident and per officer has shown gradual escalation over the past decades, which some have attributed to the increasing use of high capacity, semiautomatic pistols. However, it probably also has at least as much to do with the way police are being trained to use these weapons, that is, moving away from the continuum of force model in favor of the "fire till your foe falls" or "pop to drop" protocol.

Yet, as described earlier, despite the high priority placed on ending a potential threat to life, it is impressive how often police officers restrain themselves from utilizing deadly force even in circumstances where it would be justified. Thus, the deadly force conundrum: react a second too fast, and you may be vilified as a trigger-happy rogue cop, with career-ending and possibly criminal and civil liability consequences. Hesitate a second too long, and you may spend the rest of your life in bitter self-reproach and peer condemnation for letting an innocent civilian or fellow officer die.

SUMMARY AND CONCLUSIONS

Most cops don't want to kill people, but every officer knows that he or she may someday have to make that choice. Police have the state-sanctioned authority to order citizens to do things against their will. Citizens have the obligation to comply with lawful orders by police. Police have the power to use physically coercive force against citizens, up to and including deadly force, guided by a set of legal standards combined with their own judgment and discretion. Herein lies the potential for misunderstanding and abuse because, while most citizens would like to believe that their adherence to the values of civil society, and the laws that express those values, ensure their immunity from adverse police action, some citizens feel they cannot afford to allow themselves such entitled reassurances (see also Chapter 7).

Successful patrol policing relies on some degree of mutual trust and respect between police and most members of a given community. Like other professionals, police must meet minimal standards of practice as set by their law enforcement agencies, statutory requirements, and legal precedents. In daily police work, any use of force is exceedingly uncommon, and deadly force is a fraction of that. In fact, police are attacked by citizens many times more often than police act forcefully on civilians, and many officers hold their fire even when deadly force would have been statutorily justified–but these are typically not the stories the public hears and reads about.

Court decisions have stated that deadly force is reasonable to prevent or stop a citizen from taking an officer's or another citizen's life. Suspects have killed and injured police officers with all manner of common objects, from ashtrays to automobiles, or just with their rage-, panic-, or intoxicant-fueled hands and feet. Large numbers of rounds may be fired at a threatening suspect because it can never be known how many of those rounds will be sufficient to neutralize an extant deadly threat. Public education about the realities of police work represents time and effort well spent in fostering safety and understanding between police and their served communities.

Chapter 2

FACTORS MOST LIKELY TO LEAD TO A DEADLY FORCE ENCOUNTER

True heroism is remarkably sober, very undramatic. It is not the urge to surpass all others, but the urge to serve others at whatever cost.

Arthur Ashe

As noted in Chapter 1, given the volume of contentious and potentially dangerous interactions with citizens in the work life of an average patrol officer, it is noteworthy how often officers *don't* use force, even in circumstances where it would be legally justified to do so (Fitzgerald & Bromley, 1998; Kesic et al., 2012; Klinger, 2005).

But what about those cases where the force used is legitimately assessed to have been excessive? Based on analyses from internal investigations, criminal prosecutions, civil litigation, court decisions, and case law, a considerable literature has developed around the factors that characterize those deadly force encounters that could potentially have been avoided, or at least nonlethally contained. Some of these characteristics are inherent in the situation itself, while others stem from insufficient training, human factor variables, improper procedure, or abuse of authority on the part of one or more involved officers (Table 2.1). For more detailed information, the reader is encouraged to consult the following primary sources, from which this chapter's discussion is distilled and adapted (Alpert & Dunham, 2004; Alpert & Smith, 1994; Alpert et al., 2005; Askey et al., 2018; Aveni, 2003; Beeson, 2017; Campbell, 1999; Crawford, 1973; del Carmen, 1994; Dorriety, 2005; Dunham et al., 2005; Engel & Silver, 2001; FBI, 2005; Fishel et al., 2007; Friedrich, 1980; Fyfe, 1980, 1986; Garner, 2016; Garner & Maxwell, 1999; Garner et al., 1995, 2002; Geller, 1982; Geller & Karales, 1981; Greenfield et al., 1999; Griffin & Bernard, 2003; Hails & Borum, 2003; Hicks, 2003; Hill & Logan, 2001; Holmes, 2000; Johnson, 2011, 2017; Kaminski, 2004;

Table 2.1.
FACTORS CONTRIBUTING TO USE OF FORCE AND DEADLY FORCE

Situational Factors.

Low officer information about the incident.
Officer initiates contact.
Confrontation follows chase or pursuit.
Split-second decision making.
Contagious shooting.
Presence of bystanders or other officers.
Citizen is found with a weapon.
Police nonavailability of less-lethal weapons.
Arrest in progress.
Suspect already surrendering.
Use of extraneous equipment during arrest.

Citizen Factors.

Nonwhite ethnicity.
Male sex.
Younger age.
Lower socioeconomic status.
Citizen shows initial hostility.
Citizen resists police commands.
Citizen makes verbal threats.
Citizen wields weapon or dangerous object.
Citizen is intoxicated and/or mentally ill.
Citizen-citizen conflict.
Suicide by cop scenario.

Klahm & Tilyer, 2010; Langan et al., 2001; Lawton, 2007; Lee & Vaughn, 2010; Lewinski & Redmond, 2009; Lord, 2000; Manning, 1978; Mastrofski et al., 1996, 2002; McElvain & Kposowa, 2008; Meadows & Trostle, 1988; Meyer, 1980; Miller, 2015a; Mollen, 1994; Montgomery, 2005; Nhan, 2019; Novak & Engel, 2005; Nowicki, 2002; Ostrom et al., 1978; Parks, 2000; Petrocelli, 2006; Petrowski, 2002a; Pogrebin & Poole, 1993; Rayburn, 2007; Reiss, 1980; Ross, 2000; Skolnick, 2002; Spector, 2002; Terrill, 2001; Terrill & Mastrofski, 2002; Terrill et al., 2003, 2008; Van Maanen, 1978; Vaughn & Coomes, 1995; Weitzer, 1999; Westmarland, 2005; White, 2000, 2006; Williams, 2002; Wilson & Rashbaum, 2006; Worden, 1995; Worden & Catlin, 2002).

ENCOUNTER (SITUATIONAL) CHARACTERISTICS

Although every police-citizen interaction is unique, some commonalities and categories of deadly force scenarios arise out of the nature of the encounter itself.

Low Information

"Be prepared" is not just a motto for the Boy Scouts, but can have life-and-death implications for police officers responding to a potentially dangerous call for service. Officers who barrel into a perilous scenario with little or no background information, or have a mortal struggle suddenly burst upon them, are at a severe disadvantage, both tactically and psychologically. Who are the suspects and who are the bystanders? How many suspects? Where? Weapons? What kind? Armed robber or confused mental patient? Other officers responding? EMT or fire-rescue? What's happened so far? The question list is, of course, potentially endless and will be unique for each scenario. Sometimes, officers have to deal immediately with the world as they find it, but the more information they can glean from dispatch, other officers, and ancillary sources before rushing into a call, the safer they're likely to be (Askey et al., 2018).

High-Speed Foot Chase or Automobile Pursuit

If you've ever watched your dog chase a squirrel, you know that among hunting species, the predatory "heat of the chase" often accelerates and intensifies the lethality of the encounter once the prey is cornered. It can be pretty much the same when cops chase bad guys. In addition to the natural dopamine and adrenalin rush (see Chapter 4), officers naturally resent any behavior on the part of a citizen that makes their job more difficult or dangerous, which is why "don't make me chase you" is a common refrain heard from both TV cops and real ones. So, when the officers finally catch up with a fleeing suspect, there is likely to be an added aggravation factor that makes the situation even more volatile.

From a tactical perspective, a criminal suspect who has actively attempted to evade capture–called **fleeing and eluding**–is more likely to be combative to police and dangerous to innocent bystanders when finally surrounded. Erring on the side of caution, officers will be more inclined to "take no chances" and may pile onto the suspect once he's down, neutralizing the threat but posing a risk for accidental asphyxiation or other unintentional injury (Hall et al., 2014; Holman & Vilke, 2108; Savaser & Chan, 2018). If the suspect draws a weapon, there is apt to be minimal hesitation on the officers' part to return fire. And, under these high-arousal conditions, even a neutral movement by the suspect has a higher chance of being misinterpreted as threatening (see Chapter 4).

Split-Second Syndrome, Mistake-of-Fact Shootings, and Bunch Shootings

Many potential deadly force encounters require officers to make instantaneous decisions, often with incomplete or ambiguous information, which may ultimately have immediate life-or-death consequences. Low lighting, bad weather, vision obscured by obstacles, or the suspect's own aggressive or evasive actions may cause officers to misperceive a harmless object as a weapon, misidentify an innocent citizen as a dangerous suspect, or even mistake a fellow officer for an assailant, a phenomenon that has been referred to as **threat magnification** (see Chapter 4).

In the heat of the moment, officers have stumbled and fell or dropped their weapons, radios, or flashlights. Fellow officers may misinterpret their teetering comrade as being under attack; if the officer's fumble also results in an unintentional discharge of his firearm, the perceived threat will skyrocket, leading officers to erroneously retaliate at the perceived source of the danger (Aveni, 2003; Lewinski & Redmond, 2009). In other circumstances, an officer may underestimate the danger and fail to take cover or may prematurely emerge from a safe, barricaded position, which then leaves his colleagues no choice but to protect him from the heightened danger by directing cover fire at the suspect (Aveni, 2003; Garner, 2016).

In such perilous scenarios, further misinterpretation of the suspect's behavior may occur (Chapter 4). If a fired-upon suspect collapses to the ground, one officer may see this as the threat being neutralized, and appropriately cease fire. From a different visual vantage point, another officer may perceive that same suspect not as falling, but as crouching down or diving for cover, thereby posing an even greater threat, and that officer may commence firing or continue to fire. Other officers, hearing the exchange, may conclude that the threat is continuing or has even escalated, and they, too, may start to fire, continue firing, or begin firing again after ceasing.

Meanwhile, still other officers, hearing their companions' fire, can't know if their peers are shooting at an illusory danger or a real one, and, to protect themselves, may join in the exchange. In yet other cases, officers may perceive the shots of their comrades as coming from the suspect: again, firing commences, continues, or resumes. All of these factors, in various combinations, may collectively contribute to what Lewinski and Redmond (2009) call the **associative firing impulse**, and what others have referred to as **mistake-of-fact shootings** or **bunch shootings** (Aveni, 2003), frequently eventuating in the "hail of bullets" scenario.

For example, between 1990 and 2001, the Metro-Dade Police Department reported 33 shootings in which officers claimed they saw a gun, but no gun was later found. Similarly, in Los Angeles County, during the period of 1998-2002, 27 of 148 shootings (18%) were identified as likely mistake-of-fact shootings. Of that total, 20 (75%) occurred under reduced lighting conditions. Research in Portland, Oregon showed that mistake-of-fact shootings contributed to higher suspect fatality rates which were due to an overall greater number of rounds being fired in these circumstances, in one study amounting to an average of 9.3 hits per slain suspect (Aveni, 2003)–that's just hits, not the actual number of shots fired.

Analysis of the causes of such mistake-of-fact shootings (Aveni, 2003) has attributed them to three main factors: (1) the threat level is misidentified due to impaired visual contrast sensitivity in low ambient light; (2) the suspect's behavior is incorrectly perceived as threatening (threat magnification); and/or (3) context-based expectations associated with the nature of the call ("robbery in progress," "suspicious behavior," etc.) heighten officers' vigilance to danger (Aveni, 2003). In one well-publicized New York case in 1999, African immigrant Amadou Diallo was shot while withdrawing a wallet from his pants pocket, an incident widely ascribed to police racism (see Chapter 7). But would this DFE have occurred if not for the context of the event? That is, Diallo reportedly fit the description of a serial rapist being sought by police at the time of the incident. When approached by the NYPD's Street Crimes Unit, he acted "suspiciously" (probably confused), and when initially confronted by police, he fled, leading to a chase that eventuated in the fatal shooting (Lewinski & Redmond, 2009).

Are such scenarios inevitable? Do police officers simply fire en masse based on a misperceived triggering event? Be it a flock of birds, a school of fish, a herd of cattle, or a pack of wolves, we know from evolutionary psychology that most social organisms placed abruptly in perilous circumstances tend to mirror one another's behavior. Thus, in a deadly force encounter, it is not unreasonable to assume that if one officer perceives danger and opens fire, then other officers at the scene may reflexively do the same. For some time, this has been the accepted explanation for the "hail of bullets" scenario, where police are accused of overkill in reacting to the threat of a perceived perpetrator: essentially, "policeman see, policeman do."

More recently, researchers have begun to examine this assumption empirically by analyzing the decision-making processes of officers actually involved in shooting episodes (White & Klinger, 2012). The findings suggest that purely imitative behavior is in fact quite rare and that officers generally each make their own determination whether or not to shoot a suspect during a deadly force encounter, well- or ill-advised as those split-second decisions might be. Part of this may relate to the phenomenon of perceptual narrowing, or **tunnel perception** (Chapter 4), where a given officer may actually be tuning out the sights and sounds of surrounding officers, making it even less likely that he will be influenced by the actions of others.

There does appear to be evidence of a paradoxical relationship between the number of officers present, number of rounds fired, and the number of rounds that hit the suspect. Early data (reviewed by Aveni, 2003) collectively suggested that, in a given confrontation, an officer firing alone discharges an average of 2.7 rounds at a suspect, whereas officers firing in "bunches" discharge an average of 5.9 rounds per officer, amounting to a 118 percent increase in the number of shots fired when officers fire in groups. Yet, data from Aveni's (2003) more recent study of Los Angeles County police officers showed a significant decline from an average 51 percent hit ratio when single officers are involved in a shooting to as low as 9 percent when more than two officers fire, which amounts to an astonishing 82 percent decline in hit ratio from single officer fire to multiple officer fire.

Officers in groups, then, each appear to fire more rounds, but each also seems to be far less accurate than officers who fire alone. The reason is not clear, but could it be that a given officer, firing along with a supporting barrage from his companions, may feel less need to focus and aim carefully, and may just blast away, assuming that, with so many bullets flying, there must be a sufficient number of rounds to ultimately bring down the suspect? More research is needed.

Deadly Force Used Against a Suspect Who Is Already Surrendering

Firing at a suspect who seems to pose no threat might represent a blatant abuse of police power, or it could occur as the result of an officer's misperception of the suspect's actions. Most real-life critical police-citizen confrontations are characterized by uncertainty and ambiguity, and many citizens who decide to surrender to police authority don't necessarily wave a white flag or reach for the sky with both arms. What if a suspect wants to hand over his gun to an officer, but the officer thinks he's pulling it out to shoot? What if it's not a gun at all, but a wallet or cell phone? What if the suspect starts to comply or surrender and then abruptly changes his mind? Remember that consistency and predictability are not prime traits of criminal suspects, especially those who may be mentally ill or intoxicated. The subject may have felt overwhelmed by the police presence a moment ago and decided to give up. But wait–now he sees an opening and figures, what the hell, let me take a chance and flee or fight my way out of here. Often, it is just not clear what a suspect's intentions are and officers are then left to rely on their own perception and judgment in taking whatever they think is the safest action in that moment.

Officer Draws or Reholsters a Gun While Handcuffing a Suspect

This type of error is more tactical than psychological. An officer has just two hands and can focus his attention on just so many tasks at once. If he's trying to cuff a suspect and unholster or reholster his firearm (or Taser or baton or radio) simultaneously, there's a good chance that the officer will lose control of either the suspect or the object–or, worse, both at the same time–thereby endangering himself, his fellow officers, and anyone else in the vicinity. If this occurs, the officer and his peers may have no choice but to compensate for the breach in safety by applying overwhelming force to the suspect in order to protect their fumbling comrade and regain safe control of the situation.

Use of Deadly Force to Prevent Subject's Own Suicide

It seems obvious: you can't kill someone just to prevent them from killing themselves. Of course, it's rarely that simple. Unlike swallowing a bottle of pills or jumping from a roof, when a suspect threatens suicide with a firearm or other deadly weapon, the police are already dealing with a mentally unstable individual who can suddenly point that weapon anywhere he chooses. In fact, realistic simulation studies show that a suspect can go from pointing a gun at his own head to firing at an officer before that officer can return fire (Blair et al., 2011). That's why, even without making an overt threat to anyone else but himself, a suspect who resists police commands to drop the weapon will place officers on high alert, and any twitch of the suspect's gun hand in the wrong direction may earn him his own hail of bullets.

Contact is Officer-Initiated, Not Citizen-Initiated

In many cases, when citizens reach out to the police for help, whether through a 911 call or by physically flagging down an officer on patrol, the peak of the crisis is over by the time the police arrive, as in a burglary or domestic assault scenario. Even if the melee is ongoing, as officers rush to the scene they may at least have some lead time to prepare themselves for the forthcoming encounter, both informationally through dispatch input or citizen calls, and mentally by reviewing and anticipating appropriate tactics. But when patrol officers abruptly come upon a crime in progress, or attempt to investigate a suspicious circumstance, or question an edgy citizen who seems high on drugs, there is far less predictability and cognitive preparation, and that makes it much easier for the adrenalin index to ratchet sharply upward.

Research has found that, in general, when police proactively intrude themselves into an encounter with a community member, this is more likely to eventuate in the use of force than when the encounter is initiated by the citizen him- or herself (Klahm & Tillyer, 2010; McCluskey & Terrill, 2005; McCluskey et al., 2005; Paoline & Terrill, 2007; Terrill & Mastrofski, 2002). Once again, however, nuances of the interactional dynamics may influence any particular outcome. For example, where the citizen is generally compliant with police actions, whichever party initiates the contact appears to have little influence on whether force is used or how much is applied. But where the citizen resists the officers or acts belligerently from the outset, police-initiated contact is more likely to be forceful (Garner et al., 2002; Paoline & Terrill, 2004; Terrill, 2005; Terrill et al., 2003), no doubt because the police are unwanted in that situation in the first place. Still other research, however, has found no relation between proactivity and use of force in either direction (Engel et al., 2000), so additional complex variables are probably involved in different situations.

Presence of Bystanders, Including Citizens and/or Other Officers

Police are naturally wary of crowd scenes because of the characteristic contagion effect that occurs when groups of citizens, especially young males, reinforce one another's confrontational posturing. In these cases, a simple traffic stop or curbside conversation can flash over into a violent struggle. It is here that police de-escalation strategies can be vital (Miller, 2006i). In addition, the number of officers that respond to a scene, and how they respond, can influence the likelihood that a force scenario will erupt. Too few officers may constitute a weak deterrent to the aggressive proclivities of an agitated group of citizens. On the other hand, too many officers barreling into a scene may be perceived by citizens as an invading phalanx and heighten tensions further. Ideally, what is termed a **calm show of force** with multiple officers peacefully but assertively surrounding the scene may serve to quell a potentially aggressive citizen response that might have escalated further if just one or two officers were on hand.

Where this has been studied empirically, the evidence has been mixed (Engel et al., 2000; Garner et al., 2002; Klahm & Tillyer, 2010; Paoline & Terrill, 2007; Phillips & Smith, 2000; Terrill, 2005; Terrill & Mastrofsku, 2002; McCluskey et al., 2005), once again, probably because of the effect of a myriad of situational factors that affect how such scenarios unfold. For example, the location of the encounter–public area vs. private residence–can influence whether more responding officers lead to greater or lesser likelihood of force (Terrill et al., 2003). One obvious factor is that most people don't like it when they feel their homes are being invaded. Also, number of officers present may have different effects on whether those officers utilize physical presence, verbal commands, physical force, or other tactics (Paoline & Terrill, 2004).

Somewhat counterintuitively, no consistent relationship emerges between the number of citizens present at a given scene and the probability of the police using force (Klahm & Tillyer, 2010; McCluskey et al., 2005; Paoline & Terill, 2004, 2007; Riksheim & Chermak, 1993; Schuck, 2004; Terrill, 2005; Terrill & Mastrofski, 2002; Terrill et al., 2003; Terrill et al., 2008), although this finding no doubt occurs for the same reason noted above, namely, the situational and demographic heterogeneity that characterizes studies of complex social phenomena. Some research does support the anecdotal observation that an increasing number of bystanders increases the likelihood of police use of force (Engel et al., 2000), but it would be useful to know what kind of interaction dynamics characterize these incidents. For example, it would be surprising if force were used at the same level and frequency with a crowd of obnoxious but peaceful gawkers preoccupied mainly with recording the event on their cell phones, as opposed to a hostile mob cursing and throwing objects at the cops.

Indeed, the presence of a growing crowd of bystanders, even if initially quiet, may impel officers to take no chances and begin issuing commands and/or using physical restraint and coercion to control the citizens (Crawford & Burns, 1998), but the same line of research also finds that number of bystanders in and of itself actually appears to have no effect on the likelihood of police using chemical agents, less-lethal weapons, or firearms (Garner et al., 2002; Phillips & Smith, 2000). Again, it would be useful to have some idea of the characteristics of such crowds (e.g., political protesters vs. Saturday night partiers) that make it more or less likely that force will escalate, although, given the powerful role of perception and cognition in these cases (Chapters 4 and 5) it probably also has a lot to do with how unsafe the police feel in any given situation.

Suspect Possesses A Weapon Or Object That Can Be Used As A Weapon

This would seem obvious: if a subject is wielding a weapon or weaponizable object, responding officers are likely to feel threatened and may respond accordingly, especially if the subject ignores or refuses commands to relinquish the item: "I was just coming off a job and this cop tells me to drop my socket wrench and face the wall. Who the hell is he to tell me what to do with my tools? It's not like I had gun or something." In such circumstances, there may be a fatal misconception on the part of the average citizen as to what constitutes a "weapon" in the minds of police officers who are responding to a potentially dangerous call. As noted in Chapter 1, virtually any object can and has been used to attack officers, and simple work tools can quickly become bludgeons or missiles in the hands of a hostile assailant.

Surprisingly, however, despite police officers' understandabley heightened wariness in the presence of a suspect with a real or improvised weapon, research has not identified any consistent correlation between possession of such weapons and actual increased likelihood of police using force (Crawford & Burns, 1998; Kaminski et al., 2004; Klahm & Tillyer, 2010; McCluskey & Terrill, 2005; McCluskey et al., 2005; Morabito & Doerner, 1997; Paoline & Terrill, 2007; Sun & Payne, 2004; Terrill & Mastrofski, 2002; Terrill et al., 2003). Perhaps, in some situations involving a weapon-wielding suspect, police respond with extra caution, first attempting to use verbal suasion to talk the suspect down, whereas in other situations, the suspect more immediately and directly threatens police or other civilians, or the responding officers lack the requisite verbal skills to defuse the incident, leaving physical force as the only option.

Availability/Unavailability of Less-Lethal Weapons

In a number of deadly force cases I've worked on, the involved officers have lamented that budgetary or policy restraints limited the range of **less-lethal (LL)** weapons available to them, leaving them no option than to resort to their firearm. In a potential deadly force encounter, when police have beanbag munitions, chemical sprays, or conducted energy munitions (e.g., Tasers), it makes sense that they would first try to use these devices to contain a subject if this is in fact a safe option (Kroll & Brave, 2018; Sloane & Vilke, 2018), especially for officers who are trained in the continuum of force model. However, these devices don't always work as intended (Loughlin & Flora, 2017). In one study of 148 officer-involved shootings (Klahm & Tillyer, 2010), 12 percent of those incidents took place after officers failed to contain the suspect through the use of LLs, in some cases involving the deployment of more than one LL device.

Unfortunately, there is no universal requirement for police officers in the United States and elsewhere to carry and utilize LLs, and standards vary from agency to agency. For example, in some North American jurisdictions, police are not allowed to routinely carry LLs for fear that ready access to these devices would tempt responding officers to overuse them. Instead, LLs must specifically be requested in each given situation, in which case a sergeant or other authorized person assesses the need and brings the items to the scene. Whatever the underlying rationale for this rule, it is hard to make tactical sense of it in light of the fact that most potentially dangerous police-citizen encounters evolve over a matter of seconds to minutes. One recent study showed that, in 77 percent of non-firearm police-citizen confrontations, the "less lethal" option most readily available turns out to be the officer's own hands (Askey et al., 2018).

Another tactical problem with these devices is that most LLs are effective only at close range, usually a maximum of 12-20 feet, and officers who get closer than this distance usually must then have covering officers prepared to immediately employ deadly force by firearm if LL options fail to contain, or further inflame, the suspect. Finally, there are situations in which LLs are simply not an option, for example, a suspect aiming a firearm or who lunges at officers with a bladed weapon at close range.

Arrest

Unsurprisingly, police officers are more likely to employ force when making an arrest (Klahm & Tillyer, 2010; McCluskey & Terrill, 2005; McCluskey et al., 2005; Paoline & Terrill, 2004, 2007; Terrill & Mastrofski, 2002; Terrill et al., 2003), although the cause-and-effect relationship is not clear. That is, are suspects who are told they are under arrest more likely to show active resistance than nonarrested suspects, thereby eliciting a commensurately forceful response by police? Or are suspects who behave more belligerently at the outset of the encounter more likely to commit an arrestable offense, such as battery on a LEO, or to incur intrusive behaviors by police, such as interrogations and pat-downs, that prompt the citizen's physical resistance, leading to police use of force? Consistent with the principles of vicious cycles and tipping points, in many such encounters, it is likely to be some combination of both.

CITIZEN DEMOGRAPHIC CHARACTERISTICS

We know that citizens who habitually find themselves in hostile confrontations with police officers are not a random sample of the population. Most people do not violate the law with any frequency or severity, and most community members cooperate with, or at least tolerate, interactions with police officers when these occasionally occur, most commonly at traffic stops. Only a small proportion of individuals in any community are sufficiently impulsive, angry, desperate, dishonest, addicted, and/or mentally unstable to regularly find or place themselves in situations where confrontations with police are likely. In such circumstances, the potential for violence is always present. The police know this, and are apt to act warily and take safety precautions around certain citizens–behaviors that those citizens may then regard as intrusive or demeaning, leading to a potential vicious cycle of police-citizen confrontation (see also Chapter 7).

We also know that certain static personological factors are associated with a higher risk for police-citizen confrontation. For example, being young, male, and non-white is a ubiquitous demographic variable that arises consistently in both media descriptions and in reported research on police use of force, going back to the early 1900s. Why this should be so will be discussed more thoroughly in Chapter 7. Yet, some research has begun to challenge the factual basis for some of these assumptions.

Race–Ethnicity

It is often taken as axiomatic that nonwhite citizens are subject to a greater degree of police use of force, including deadly force, than white citizens, and some studies have indeed identified such a relationship (Terrill & Mastrofski, 2002; Terrill et al., 2003). The empirical evidence is mixed on this issue, however, because researchers have as yet failed to document a direct association between suspect race as a stand-alone factor and an increased likelihood of police using force (Engel et al., 2000; Klahm & Tillyer, 2010; Lawton, 2007; McCluskey & Terrill, 2005; McCluskey et al., 2005; Morabito & Doerner, 1997; Phillips & Smith, 2000; Sun & Payne, 2004). That is, in communities where black citizens seem to have force used against them disproportionately, this might be explained by such neighborhood contextual factors as economic instability, increased overall crime rate, and less citizen access to social services that might otherwise serve to diffuse and deflect criminal behavior (Kaminski et al., 2004; Paoline & Terrill, 2004, 2007; Schuck, 2004; Terrill & Reisig, 2003; Terrill et al., 2008).

Race does appear to interact with suspect behavior to affect the likelihood of police use of force. According to one study (Garner, 2002), when a suspect is actively resisting the police, race seems to have no bearing on whether or not force is used. That is, in a situation containing high potential danger to life, the officer really doesn't care if the person he's grappling with is black or white—that officer is intent on reducing the threat and stabilizing the situation, no matter who is provoking it. However, black citizens may be more likely to have force used against them in situations where they are already complying. That is, police may be more likely to attribute hostile or aggressive actions to a black suspect than to a white one, and then react accordingly. The possible reasons for this will be discussed further in Chapter 7.

Social Class

Starting with problems in even defining what is meant by "social class" (income? education? occupation? values?), research has been mixed in examining this factor as well, with some studies finding a greater likelihood of use of force in poorer neighborhoods (Klahm & Tillyer, 2010; McCloskey

& Terrill, 2005; Paoline & Terrill, 2007; Terrill & Mastrofski, 2002; Terill et al., 2003;Terrill & Reisig, 2003), and others finding no such correlation (McCluskey et al., 2005; Sun & Payne, 2004). A major complication, noted above, is that economic status and social class are typically cross-correlated with other factors, such as race, educational level, access to social services, and crime rate (Friedrich, 1980), so if police use force against a poor, unemployed, minority citizen with an undertreated addiction or mental health issue, to which factors are the police reacting?

Sex

In a sea of empirical ambiguities, one seemingly universal finding is that male citizens are more likely to have force used against them during police-citizen encounters than females (Garner et al., 2002; Klahm & Tillyer, 2010; McCluskey et al., 2005; McCluskey & Terrill, 2005;Phillips & Smith, 2000; Sun & Payne, 2004; Terrill & Mastrofski, 2002; Terrill & Reisig, 2003; Terrill et al., 2003). Yet, even here, some studies have produced uneven results (Crawford & Burns, 1998; Klahm & Tillyer, 2010; Paoline & Terrill, 2004, 2007; Schuck, 2004; Terrill, 2005).

For example, in one report (Kaminski et al., 2004), officers were equally likely to use a firm restraining grip on a female suspect as on a male; however, officers were more likely to use a higher level of force overall on male suspects compared to females. One reason might simply be that males are generally bigger and stronger than females, and thereby require greater effort to subdue. Other studies have found no difference in police use of force on males vs. females (Engel et al., 2000; Lawton, 2000; Morabito & Doerner, 1997). Again, wide disparities among levels of force used (wrist-grip vs. take-to-ground, vs. weapon use) and types of interactional dynamics (slow buildup of tension vs. abrupt violent assault), among other factors, likely account for the varying results.

Age

Where suspect age is found to be related to use of force, most evidence suggests that police are more likely to use force on younger than on older suspects (Klahm & Tillyer, 2010; McCluskey & Terrill, 2005; McCluskey et al., 2005; Paoline & Terrill, 2007; Phillips & Smith, 2000; Terrill & Mastrofsky, 2002; Terrill & Reisig, 2003; Terrill et al., 2003). This no doubt reflects the common finding that younger citizens are more likely to resist police than older ones and to use more aggressive kinds of resistance.

Interesting demographic cross-correlations emerge from this research. For example, in one study, male officers were less likely to use verbal or physical force against older citizens, whereas female officers were less likely to use physical force, but apparently just as likely to yell at the old-timers (Paoline & Terrill, 2004). Other research has found that suspect age does not influence whether an officer issues a verbal command, uses chemical spray, or deploys a firearm (Crawford & Burns, 1998), or how much force is used in responding to domestic disputes (Sun & Payne, 2004). A methodological issue in this research is that, whereas studies of sex ratios only yield two possible classifications, male or female, what do different studies mean when they say older vs. younger? A 20-year-old citizen compared to a 40-year-old– or a 70-year-old?

CITIZEN BEHAVIORAL CHARACTERISTICS

Consistent with the "tipping point" principle, all police-citizen encounters are dynamic in nature (Garner, 2002; Klahm & Tillyer, 2010; Terrill & Mastrofski, 2002), and citizen behavior influences officer behavior, which can turn an otherwise routine encounter into a deadly force confrontation. Such factors include the following.

Suspect Resists Command Given by Police Officer

Many citizens are not aware that they are legally required to obey a lawful command by a police officer. Noncompliant subjects–whether such resistance is verbal or physical, passive or active, defensive or aggressive–are more likely to have force used against them than compliant citizens (Klahm & Tillyer, 2010; McCluskey & Terrill, 2005; McCluskey et al., 2005; Paoline & Terrill, 2004, 2007; Schuck, 2004; Terrill et al., 2003, 2008), although, as noted above, black citizens are more likely to have force used against them even when cooperating (Garner, 2002). Furthermore, at least one study (Lawton, 2007) found no effect of subject resistance on police use of force.

Suspect Shows Hostile Demeanor or Overly Aggressive Behavior Toward Officers

Hostile and aggressive suspects are most likely to resist officers. While it is ultimately the officers' responsibility to behave professionally in any police-citizen encounter, citizens who derive satisfaction from goading or needling cops, or whose anger and resentment, real or imagined, at past police mistreatment boils over into the present encounter, may find themselves on the receiving end of more force than might initially have been necessary. One reason is that officers cannot automatically tell whether a citizen showing **contempt of cop** is just trying to impress his buddies by messing with the po-po, or if his truculent demeanor is a prelude to an imminent violent eruption that will seriously endanger the officers and others. However, individuals who purposefully provoke police can't be surprised when those officers take special precautionary measures in the form of physically restraining or subduing the obstreperous citizens.

Some research (Engel et al., 2000; Garner et al., 2002; Klahm & Tillyer, 2010; Sun & Payne, 2004) supports the common-sense notion that disrespectful citizens are more likely to be subjected to police use of force than more congenial citizens, yet other studies (McCluskey et al., 2005; McCluskey & Terrill, 2005; Paoline & Terrill, 2004, 2007; Phillips & Smith, 2000; Terrill & Mastrofski, 2002; Terrill et al., 2003) are not so clear. Again, the sheer diversity of individual police-citizen encounter dynamics, involving a range of both citizen and officer personality types and reaction styles, makes blanket generalizations problematic.

Suspect Displays Suspicious or Threatening Behavior

Survey research (Johnson, 2015, 2017, 2019, Johnson & Aaron, 2013; Worrall et al., 2018) has shown that police officers reliably rate certain nonverbal and interpersonal cues as portending a dangerous encounter, and that even nonpolice citizens recognize the same danger signs. These indicators fall into several categories.

Muscle tension cues. The suspect clenches his hands or jaw muscles, stretches his arms, neck, or shoulders, or tenses up his whole body in a rigid posture.

Facial cues. The suspect's face flushes red. He avoids eye contact, shifts his gaze rapidly, glares intently, or blinks his eyes repeatedly.

Vocal cues. The suspect cries, yells, or makes overt verbal threats.

Physiological cues. The suspect shows signs of high arousal, such as rapid breathing and/or profuse sweating.

Behavioral cues. The suspect paces back and forth, looks around the area, removes excess clothing, places his hands on his hips, conceals his hands, and/or makes exaggerated gestures. The following cues are considered especially dangerous: (1) placing or keeping his hands in his pockets; (2) assuming a fighting stance, especially a bladed stance, i.e., turning sideways to present a diminished target; and (3) deliberately invading the officer's personal space.

Citizen-Citizen Conflict

Many police calls for service involve a dispute, conflict, or outright attack by one citizen on another. On such calls, officers are likely to be in an already heightened state of vigilance when they roll up on the scene, and the citizens themselves are probably quite agitated, magnifying the risk of a forceful confrontation. Some research indicates that police are more likely to use force against a suspect if he or she is embroiled in a conflict with another citizen at the time of the encounter (McCluskey & Terrill, 2005; McCluskey et al., 2005; Paoline & Terrill, 2007; Terrill & Mastrofski, (2002), while other data show mixed results (Engel et al., 2000; Klahm & Tillyer, 2010; Paoline & Terrill, 2004; Terrill et al., 2003). Once again, the myriad dynamics of both citizen-citizen and police-citizen encounters no doubt account for the diversity of findings. For example, it is likely that arriving officers will respond differently to two citizens shouting at each other than they would to two citizens wrestling on the sidewalk or one citizen chasing another with a stick.

Suspect is Intoxicated

Substance intoxication is a well-recognized risk factor for violent behavior in general, for two reasons. First and most obviously, being drunk or stoned impairs judgment and may disinhibit aggressive behavior that might otherwise be restrained in a more sober state. But additionally, chronic substance abuse is a **proxy factor**, or demographic marker, for aggression and antisocial behavior in general. That is, characteristically reckless, thrill-seeking subjects whose preferred state at any given moment is being buzzed or blitzed are by nature apt to be less reflective and to have poorer overall impulse control and ability to tolerate frustration and other unpleasant emotional states without reacting (Douglas & Skeem, 2005; Miller, 1985, 1987, 2012). Even cold sober, such individuals may be especially volatile and dangerous in a police-citizen encounter.

In fact, when queried, more than half of suspects forcefully subdued by police report having been intoxicated at the time of their arrest and of resisting police by arguing, disobeying, or becoming combative (Langan et al., 2001; Parker, 1998; Parker & Auerbaum, 1998; Parker & Cartmill, 1998). These findings should be viewed with caution, however, since many suspects may consider it to be in their own interest to claim mental impairment by substances at the time of their arrest, thinking this will exculpate or mitigate their guilt, not realizing that, under the law, voluntary intoxication is typically not an affirmative defense (Flowers, 2002; Miller, 2012).

But while a relationship between suspect intoxication and police use of force seems intuitively obvious, empirical research on this subject, again, yields uneven results (Crawford & Burns, 1998; Engel et al., 2000; Garner et al., 2002; Klahm & Tillyer, 2010; Lawton, 2007; McCluskey & Terrill, 2005; McCluskey et al., 2005; Morabito & Doerner, 1997; Paoline & Terrill, 2004,

2007; Phillips & Smith, 2000; Schuck, 2004; Terrill, 2005; Terrill & Mastrofski 2002; Terrill et al., 2003, 2008). For example, whether officers perceive the suspect to be intoxicated with alcohol vs. narcotics may influence the type of force used. Drunk suspects are more likely to receive verbal commands, while those perceived to be high on other drugs are more likely to be subject to less-lethal weapon deployment and other physically forceful responses. Perhaps this is due to the fact that alcohol inebriation is a much more familiar state to many officers, via observation as well as personal experience, and therefore the besotted subject is regarded as more predictable and less dangerous than someone high on an unknown substance where a presumed greater degree of volatility is seen as warranting a more proactively forceful response.

Still other studies find no difference in police use of force between sober or intoxicated suspects. Since different people's behavior varies radically under the influence of even the same substance (e.g., marijuana makes one person placid, a second person belligerent, and a third person delusional), most likely it is the specific dynamics of each encounter that determine the decision to use force or not, with intoxication being one factor among many.

Suspect is Mentally Ill

Mental illness has a small association with risk for violence overall, and most mentally ill citizens are no more aggressive than members of the general population. In fact, mentally ill citizens are many times more likely to be the victims of crime than other citizens because of their cognitive disorganization, lack of access to resources, and high exposure to street criminals due to homelessness and bizarre behavior. Only a small proportion of police encounters involve mentally ill citizens, and violent exchanges or use of force in these cases is relatively rare, with mental illness calls comprise only one percent of situations in which police are killed (Deane et al., 1999; FBI, 2015; Hickman et al., 2008; Kesic et al., 2013). Nevertheless, many calls for service involve disturbed and potentially threatening speech or behavior on the part of a mentally ill citizen, and such a scenario may engender misunderstanding and overreaction on the part of the responders (Miller, 2007a, 2008h, 2010a, 2011a, 2015e).

Evidence suggests that a citizen's mental illness has a paradoxical relationship to the probability of use of force by police (Engel & Silver, 2002; Johnson, 2011; Novak & Engel, 2005). On the one hand, when officers perceive a citizen as genuinely lacking control over his own behavior, and especially if the citizen is known from previous encounters to be irrational but not necessarily malicious or confrontational, officers may be disposed to treat him more leniently. That is, they will take the necessary steps to prevent the mentally impaired citizen from hurting himself or others, but are more likely to release him to his family if he calms down, or to transport him to a hospital rather than jail if he remains agitated–assuming such a local facility is available.

Even if the mentally ill citizen acts abusively toward the officers, but does no real harm (e.g., just curses, threatens, pokes a finger, pushes the officer, or tries to wriggle out of the officer's grasp), he is less likely to be arrested for assault or for resisting arrest, because the police will probably take into account the citizen's deranged mental state. In fact, surveys suggest that mentally ill citizens themselves typically, at least in retrospect, regard officers as acting fairly with them (Livingston et al., 2014).

On the other hand, precisely because of his heightened agitation, disturbed perception, impaired judgment, imperviousness to reason, lack of self-control, and/or disregard for consequences, the mentally ill citizen, should he become combative, may require far more physically forceful restraint than the average citizen. Experienced mental health clinicians and law enforcement officers both know that the one thing that distinguishes a mentally ill subject from an ordinary citizen is sheer unpredictability: the subject with an active mental illness is far more likely than the average citizen, or even the typical criminal suspect, to go from subdued surrender to agitated fury in the blink of an eye. Officers who are caught off-guard by this eruption of violence may react with commensurate force to get the subject under control. And if the mentally ill citizen's reaction is misinterpreted as more dangerous than it really is, the result may be a deadly force encounter.

A fairly extensive data base (Arsenault et al., 2000; Engel & Silver, 2001; Johnson, 2011; Link & Stueve, 1994; Link et al., 1992, 1998; McCluskey et al., 1999; McNiel & Binder, 2005: Morabito et al., 2017; Novak & Engel, 2005; Rojek et al., 2010; Silver & Teasdale, 2005; Silver et al., 2008; Swanson et al., 1996, 1997, 1999, 2006; Swartz et al., 1998a, 199b; Taylor et al., 1998; Watson et al., 2008) has shown that the risk of a mentally ill citizen becoming aggressive and requiring police use of force to contain him is increased by the following factors. Note that, while some of these risk factors involve symptoms of mental illness per se, others relate more to behaviors that would make any citizen more dangerous to police, with or without a diagnosis.

Suspect displays psychotic symptoms, especially persecutory delusions with command hallucinations. This is found most often in patients with paranoid schizophrenia, but may be seen in other psychotic disorders, such as bipolar mania and some organic brain syndromes and drug intoxication states (Miller, 1985, 1986, 1987, 1994b, 1998a, 2012, 2013d). The combination of persecutory ideation ("someone is out to get me"), delusions of thought control ("they're making me think and do things against my will"), and command hallucinations ("voices are telling me that the only way to stop the intrusion is to destroy the persecutor") has been found to greatly heighten the risk of violence in actively psychotic subjects (Link et al., 1998; Swanson et al., 1996).

Suspect has co-existing substance abuse history and/or is presently intoxicated. For reasons noted above, intoxication can further impair judgment and self-control in an already cognitively compromised citizen. In addition, citizens most prone to an addictive lifestyle generally possess traits of impulsivity and unconcern for consequences that make them more likely to react with aggression to any real or perceived provocation. Combined with a comorbid mental disorder, this may render the subject's behavior especially volatile and unpredictable.

Subject has a clinically significant personality disorder. Police officers at a hot scene can't be expected to engage in formal psychiatric diagnosis, but many first responders have an intuitive grasp of personality-related behavioral patterns that signal extra caution. In addition, within a given patrol community, many citizens with mental disorders are likely to be well-known "repeat customers," that is, citizens with whom the officers have had previous encounters, in some cases multiple times. Some especially high-risk personality disorders include the following (Miller, 2007a, 2012, 2013c, 2015c; Millon & Davis, 2000; Sperry, 1995).

Paranoid personality disorder is a pattern of pervasive distrust and suspiciousness, so that others' actions and motives are almost invariably interpreted as deceptive, persecutory, or malevolent. For such a citizen, even an innocuous inquiry or encounter ("Sir, you have a broken tail light." "Ma'am, you seem lost; can I help you find something?") may evoke suspicion and anger, thus setting the stage for a hostile confrontation. Of course, citizens who have actually had unpleasant past experiences with police may simply be expressing their resultant wariness and resentment.

Borderline personality disorder describes a pattern of emotional instability, self-damaging impulsivity, erratic and intense love-hate relationships, and a tendency toward episodes of seemingly irrational, intense anger. In a police-citizen encounter, these individuals may seem calm and controlled at one moment, only to lash out at another. When in a rageful state, they may be almost impossible to calm down. This personality disorder is commonly encountered in the context of a domestic disturbance, and, although more commonly diagnosed in women, it may characterize either partner.

Antisocial personality disorder refers to a pattern of flagrant disregard for, and violation of, the rights of others, associated with an exploitive and predatory lifestyle, unconstrained by any sense of conscience or empathy. Essentially, these individuals regard other people simply as objects for their own gratification. They often employ guile and seduction to get what they want, but if that fails, intimidation and violence become the tactics of choice.

In a police-citizen encounter, this individual may first try to charm and cajole his way out of the jam, but if that doesn't work, he may have no compunction about trying to fight his way out, even if that means threatening or attacking officers and using nearby citizens as bait or hostages.

Suspect has a history of treatment noncompliance and/or is currently not taking prescribed psychotropic medication. Many citizens with even severe mental illnesses usually manage to stay out of trouble if they consistently take their prescribed medication. An inability or unwillingness to do so may be a further indication of a general rule-violating and consequence-disregarding mindset, an impairment in organization or memory, or paranoid fear of being "poisoned." Combined with the symptoms of the mental illness itself (e.g., angry manic state or delusional psychosis), this can render these subjects especially dangerous. Paradoxically, many patients who refuse prescribed medication are perfectly happy to self-medicate with alcohol or street drugs.

Suspect has recently been experiencing stressful life events. For any of us, work, family or other stressors, especially if persistent, can impair our coping skills and degrade the quality of our daily functioning. Mentally disordered individuals may be particularly susceptible to these disruptions because many of them already lack access to the kinds of material and social resources–job, home, family, friends–that most ordinary citizens can call upon in time of need. Thus, mentally disordered subjects are especially likely to experience more frequent and serious psychosocial stressors, such as family conflicts and homelessness. Under these adverse conditions, the mentally disordered citizen's mindset may turn to desperation, triggering depression, psychosis, and anger, which in turn may be projected onto any convenient symbols of societal authority, including the police.

Mentally ill citizen resists officers, becomes combative, or wields a weapon. These risk factors are the same for citizens with or without a mental illness, but in the case of the former, officers may be more primed for trouble, either from prior experience with this individual or others like him, or from their own preconceptions about how a "crazy person" might behave. In general, however, if police use a greater degree of force against a mentally disordered citizen in a community, it is usually not for illness-related reasons per se, but because that citizen either has presented a greater-than-normal threat to responding officers in the past or is acting in a dangerously unpredictable manner in the present encounter.

As noted earlier, even in these potentially threatening circumstances, whether dealing with mentally disordered or ordinary citizens, police officers often err on the side of less vs. more force, and will usually try to contain a subject, first verbally and then manually, before resorting to weapons. If the subject is posing a clear danger, but has not yet escalated to imminently life-threatening behavior, officers will commonly first deploy less-lethal control technologies, such as baton, pepper spray, or Taser (in one case, police used a ladder and a fire hose to control a psychotic suspect wielding a machete) before using their firearms (Garner & Maxwell, 1999; Henriquez, 1999; McElvain & Kposowa, 2008). Again, research shows that officers restrain their use of deadly force in the majority of circumstances where such use of force would be objectively justifiable and, in many cases, even when this puts the officers' own safety in jeopardy (Pinizzotto et al., 2012).

SUICIDE BY COP

Police departments take deadly force incidents seriously, so most disturbing to an officer involved in a shooting incident may be the feeling that he or she was forced or manipulated by the suspect into killing him. The idea that a citizen would deliberately expose himself to police gunfire in order to effect his own death has probably long been familiar to law enforcement officers, but the phenomenon was first formally articulated by Wolfgang in 1959 and the actual term **suicide by cop** was coined by police psychologist and sworn police officer Karl Harris in 1983.

Other terms for this phenomenon have been proposed, such as **officer-assisted suicide** (Homant et al., 2000), **law enforcement-assisted suicide** (Lord, 2000), and **suicide by victim-precipitated homicide** (Hillbrand, 2001), but it's easy to see why none of these alternative terms ever caught on. The first two wordings situate the officer in a Dr. Kevorkian-like role of willingly abetting the suspect's wish to die, while the latter designation is all but calling the cop a murderer. Though still not the most elegant terminology, **suicide by cop (SBC)** is the moniker that appears to have stuck, and is the term used by most law enforcement personnel, police psychologists, and media commentators when they talk about this phenomenon.

Suicide by Cop: Facts and Circumstances

It is estimated that approximately ten percent of the approximately 600 police shootings a year in the United States are intentionally provoked incidents. Most involve uniformed officers who are on duty at the time of the shooting, probably because such officers are easily identifiable by subjects seeking to exploit them as unwilling executioners. The greatest number of SBC incidents occur in the context of a police response to an armed robbery, the next most common being a domestic disturbance call. While some SBC incidents arise spontaneously out of the anger and panic of these situations, a good number of them appear to have been planned, as shown by the fact that, in nearly a third of SBC cases, investigators find a suicide note, some of which have even contained apologies to the police for deliberately drawing their fire.

Other SBC attempts begin as self-suicidal crises, but when police arrive on the scene, many of these subjects choose to make a virtue of necessity by delegating the lethal action to the responding officers. Officers involved in SBC incidents often feel a sense of powerlessness and manipulation, and this is typically reported to be an especially stressful and demoralizing form of shooting trauma for police. In general, SBC cases garner more departmental, community, media, and legal scrutiny than more common officer-involved shooting cases (Allen, 2004; Cloherty, 2004; Feuer, 1998; Hillbrand, 2001; Homant & Kennedy, 2000; Homant, et al., 2000; Hutson et al., 1998; Kennedy, et al., 1998; Kesic et al., 2012; Miller, 2006c, 2017; Parent, 1998; Pinizzotto et al., 2005; Praet, 2002; Van Zandt, 1993; Wilson et al., 1998).

Suicide by Cop: Patterns and Motives

The typical SBC subject is a white male in his mid-20s to mid-30s with a history of mental illness and/or substance abuse, although he may not actually be intoxicated at the time of the suicide. He has had prior contact with the law, but usually for minor offenses, although this may have given him some familiarity with how police operate and their responses to critical incidents. There is often a history of prior suicide attempts associated with a mental health treatment record; diagnoses typically include schizophrenia, bipolar disorder, depression, and/or substance abuse, although there is at least one report of attempted SBC in the context of a postconcussion syndrome following a brain injury (Bresler et al., 2003).

The critical episode is commonly precipitated by the rupture of some important relationship in connection with the subject's self-esteem or social support, such as a family or job crisis, which leads to feelings of hopelessness, anger, and despair. Up to two-thirds of SBC subjects take hostages, and up to 40 percent of subjects are intoxicated with alcohol, but other drug use at the scene is rare. The average duration of the incident itself from initial police arrival to death of the subject is under half an hour, but many of these episodes are over within a few minutes (De Leo et al., 2002; Fazel & Danesh, 2002; Feuer, 1998; Gill & Pasquale-Styles, 2009; Hutson et al., 1998; Kennedy et al., 1998; Kesic et al., 2012; Klinger, 2001; Lord, 2000; Lord & Sloop, 2010; McKenzie, 2005; Mohandie et al., 2009; Mumola, 2007; Parent, 1998, 1999; Perrou & Farrell, 2004; Wilson et al., 1998).

From studies of those who have survived SBC attempts, motives for the actions have been found to include: (1) not wanting to appear weak by committing self-suicide, i.e., aiming to go out in a "blaze of glory"; (2) wanting to "send a message" to family members or others who have hurt or betrayed the subject; (3) fear of incompletion of self-suicide: one self-inflicted bullet to the head might leave me a vegetable, but a hail of police bullets will surely finish the job; (4) religious proscriptions against self-suicide: if the police kill me, I'm technically not violating God's law against killing myself; (5) financial considerations: life insurance policy or family member's will excludes payment for suicide; (6) delusional motives, e.g., dying for the sins of the world; and (7) rare cases of a suicidal police officer or ex-officer who understands that drawing a weapon on fellow officers will leave them no choice but to return deadly fire (Hafenback & Nasiripour, 2005; Homant et al., 2000; Lord, 2000; Lord & Sloop, 2010; Mohandie & Meloy, 2000).

In still other cases, the dividing line between SBC and more direct aggression toward officers may not be clear-cut. Subjects who are apt to find themselves in armed confrontations with police have likely lived in a violent subculture where impulsive, manipulative, and aggressive behaviors have been characteristic problem-solving strategies. In such a life-and-death confrontation, such individuals may not be suicidal in the usual clinical sense of connoting despair and self-deprecation, but may be relatively unconcerned about dying as compared with the immediate impulse to take a desperate last stand (McLeod et al., 2014; Mohandie & Meloy, 2010; Van Zandt, 1993). In these cases, it may not be so much "I want to die so I'll let the cops do it," as "I'll show these cops they can't mess with me again, and if they kill me, well, then fuck it." In many such cases, mixed motives are likely to be more common than clear agendas.

Suicide by Cop: Police Response and Officer Reactions

In SBC cases, all of the issues pertaining to split-second judgment calls that attend ordinary officer-involved shootings are greatly magnified. In scenarios where the suicidal motive is clear, police may regard the citizen, not as a typical armed assailant engaging them in mortal combat, but rather as a pathetically disturbed person who may not really deserve to die, except for the fact of stupidly creating a lethal threat to officers or other civilians. As with similar situations involving a clearly distraught mentally ill subject, the suicidal citizen's presumed lesser blameworthiness may make responding officers more hesitant to take him down, but at the same time, the very instability of such an individual may render him unpredictably dangerous even when the situation appears calm, fostering a heightened hair-trigger reactivity on the part of the police. Unfortunately, as noted above, it is often not clear whether the subject is trying to get only himself killed or has more malevolently resolved to take as many officers and others as possible to the grave with him.

Officer reactions to having killed a subject in a SBC incident range from anger at having been baited into "doing this guy's dirty work for him," to sadness at the perceived senselessness of many SBC scenarios, especially when they have involved very young, very old, or very ill subjects. Where the SBC incident has followed a failed effort at negotiating a peaceful outcome, officers may experience a demoralizing sense of disappointment and self-criticism (Clagett, 2004; Van Zandt, 1993). Because of the increased administrative and media attention in suspected SBC cases, involved officers may walk around feeling like they're under a microscope, as suspicions of excessive force used against a "poor psycho" or a "dumb kid" may be fanned by the media and the general public. Such officers may well need extra support as they negotiate the aftermath of a SBC episode (Cloherty, 2004; Miller, 2000, 2006e, 2007g, 2013b, 2015d; see also Chapter 8).

SUMMARY AND CONCLUSIONS

It's all about vicious cycles and tipping points. What turns any given police-citizen encounter into an OIS/DFE scenario characteristically involves a melange of interacting factors ranging from the biological, to the psychological, to the sociodemographic, to the situational. It is rare for a firefight or grappling match with a suspect to begin immediately. Almost always, there is an emotional and behavioral buildup, an interactional dance that precedes the escalation into a forceful confrontation.

Both in media accounts of deadly force incidents and in administrative and forensic reviews of contested OIS/DFE cases, a strikingly similar pattern of these tips and cycles often emerges. At some critical juncture in the verbal exchange, one party says or does something that triggers a physical reaction from the other. For the suspect, it may be the cop imperiously barking an order or nudging the suspect to move onto the sidewalk. Especially in the presence of peers, a suspect who doesn't want to look like a chump may push the officer away, yell in his face, or dismissively saunter off. For the officer, the suspect is now guilty of "contempt of cop," ratcheting up the tension level.

Now, somewhere, somehow, somebody touches somebody, the officer tries to move or restrain the citizen and he jerks away. A hand goes here, an elbow there, and the officer feels something brushing his utility belt. Or the obnoxious citizen fails to obey a police command to step back, drop an object, and show his hands. Next thing you know, the situation has tipped over into a forceful confrontation, and the escalation proceeds from there. As we'll discuss in Chapter 4, all of the above may be complicated by misperceptions and misjudgments that are the consequence of the vagaries of human neurocognitive processing.

Not to be forgotten, however, is that *misuse* of force is the exception, not the rule, and in most confrontations, officers control the suspect and the scene, if not daintily, then at least lawfully and justifiably. However, the majority of law enforcement use of force training still focuses on strategies and tactics for safely and effectively subduing dangerous suspects once the battle has begun. Such training programs would do well to incorporate strategies for recognizing vicious cycles and de-escalating them in order to keep more points from tipping over into unnecessarily dangerous show-downs. Of course, the probability of this happening will depend in part on the policing attitudes and philosophies of the officers and their agencies in a particular jurisdiction, and a variety of individual and collective officer variables may actually make such use abuse of force more likely, as we'll discuss in Chapter 3.

Chapter 3

POLICE OFFICER FACTORS IN THE USE OF FORCE AND DEADLY FORCE

Nearly all men can stand adversity, but if you want to test a man's char acter, give him power.

President Abraham Lincoln

As noted in Chapter 1, police are unique among civilian public safety professionals in that the law and society give them the general right, and in many circumstances charge them with the obligation, to use coercive physical force to influence the behavior of citizens. Further, within the broad bounds of standard operating procedure (SOP), their decision to use such force is based largely on their own judgment as to what is appropriate in a given situation. No other class of service provider that citizens deal with on a daily basis has that power.

True, we give certain medical personnel, such as paramedics or emergency room physicians, special rights to do things to critically ill or injured citizens without their conscious consent, such as intubate them, stitch them up, and administer life-saving drugs, but even here, an otherwise mentally competent patient who assertively refuses treatment cannot be made to submit against his or her will. Certain provisions occur in clinical practice, for example involuntarily committing a patient who is imminently dangerous to self or others, or forcibly sedating an out-of-control patient in a medical or psychiatric facility. But these are exceptions. As noted in Chapter 1, only police officers have the statutory right to expect compliance by citizens with any lawful order they give, and only police officers are empowered to apply coercive physical force and control to enforce such compliance where necessary (Klockars, 1996). This confers great power, which engenders tremendous responsibility, and, when misapplied, creates commensurate opportunities for abuse.

Because our society imbues its police forces with such a mandate to protect us, we are willing to put up with occasional instances of intrusiveness if we feel this is necessary for our overall safety, much as we tolerate the sometimes brusque scrutiny of TSA agents at airport terminals because we know that, without them, it wouldn't be safe to fly. But when those charged with protecting life turn around and willfully abuse their authority to take or threaten life, they become **failed protectors**, akin to parents who starve, beat, or enslave their children, instead of nourishing, comforting, and empowering them. When the literal grownups in a family or the metaphorical grownups of society turn on us and betray our trust in them, we are filled with existential dread: if the safekeepers won't keep us safe, if the sheepdogs become the wolves, how will we survive? Who can we ever count on to help us in this treacherous world?

So to preserve some semblance of sanity and control, we sublimate our existential terror into vengeful anger: the perfidious betrayers deserve the worst of all possible fates. That's why "bad cop" stories almost always lead the daily headlines: we don't want to believe this could happen to us, and often grope for rationalizations for why the officer acted as he did ("he was provoked; he misperceived the danger; the suspect deserved what he got"). For citizens who believe that the police are rarely on their side to begin with (see Chapter 7), each personal or vicarious adverse encounter further fuels their cynicism and despair. Another group of professionals sometimes find themselves in the failed protector category because we depend on them, too, for our very lives: physicians. That's why "bad doc" stories are a close second to "bad cop" stories in the media.

But even those civilians who have no great love for cops may grudgingly admit that theirs is a difficult, dangerous, and often thankless job. Police officers have to deal with violent, impulsive, predatory, or just plain obnoxious members of society and sometimes must confront cruelties and horrors that the rest of us view from the sanitized distance of our newspapers and video screens. In addition to the daily grind, patrol officers frequently feel they are the targets of criticism and complaints by citizens, the media, the judicial system, adversarial attorneys, do-gooder mental health and social service personnel, and the sometimes pusillanimous law enforcement administrators who kowtow to political correctness and public opinion at their own officers' expense (Blau, 1994).

The nature of their job exposes officers to special kinds of traumatic events and daily pressures that require a certain adaptively defensive toughness of attitude, temperament, and training; without this resolve, they couldn't function effectively. Most police officers deal with both commonplace and exceptional stresses by employing a variety of situationally adaptive coping and defense mechanisms, such as suppression, displacement, isolation, and compartmentalization of feelings. Humor–often seemingly gross or crass humor–is another coping mechanism, one that may be mistaken for callous disregard in the aftermath of a deadly force encounter or other circumstance that results in the death or injury of a civilian (Blau, 1994; Miller, 2006i, 2009a).

Officers develop a closed society, an insular "cop culture," centering around what many refer to as **The Job**. For a few, The Job becomes their life, and crowds out other activities and relationships. For these reasons, officers have historically resisted formal outside review or criticism of their conduct on the grounds that civilians could not possibly understand what police work requires and are therefore in no position to judge or criticize their actions (Blau, 1994, Klockars, 1996).

As noted in Chapter 2, a number of situational factors may contribute to the likelihood of use of force and deadly force encounters between police and citizens. Equally important to consider is that certain characteristics of some officers themselves may make them more likely to utilize force in a police-citizen encounter. For many officers, this may seem intuitively obvious: most law enforcement supervisors can cite which of their personnel they would most and least trust to handle a sensitive call, and most patrol cops know which of their chucklehead peers they would least likely want to have with them on that call. In addition, for some officers, it may well be that misuse of force is just a subset of a more general pattern of officer misconduct. Recently, research has attempted to address the factors of officer attitude, temperament, and personality more directly (Table 3.1).

OFFICER DEMOGRAPHICS

Some influences on police officer conduct stem from innate personological characteristics, while other factors may be more malleable.

Officer Race/Ethnicity

Surveys seem to concur that "blue" is the color most officers identify with when interacting with citizens; that is, officer race/ethnicity appears to bear no systematic relationship to the likelihood or justifiability of police use of force, including verbal command, physical restraint, less-lethal weaponry, or firearm use (Crawford & Burns, 1998; Friedrich, 1980; Geller & Karales, 1981; Lawton, 2007; McElvain & Kposowa, 2004; McCluskey & Terrill, 2005; McCluskey et al., 2005; Morabito & Doerner, 1997; Paoline & Terrill, 2004, 2007; Terrill & Mastrofski, 2002).

It is always important to look closely at any correlational data, however, and further detailed analysis of the existing research yields some notable

Table 3.1
OFFICER VARIABLES ASSOCIATED WITH POLICE MISCONDUCT

Officer Race/Ethnicity: No consistent relationship to police misconduct.

Officer Sex: No consistent relationship to police misconduct.

Officer Age & Experience: In general, greater on-the-job experience correlates with less reported misconduct.

Officer Educational Level: Completion of a college degree correlates with less officer misconduct.

Officer Attitudes: Strict law-and-order approach to policing and/or distrust of, or contempt for, citizens in the officer's patrol area is associated with greater officer misconduct.

Officer Personalities: Too naïve-ingratiating or too cynical-aggressive officer personalities and behavior are associated with higher rate of force and other confrontations. Mature, proactive, assertive, and flexible approach to policing is associated with fewer force complaints and other officer misconduct.

Organizational Variables: Police agency endorses or overlooks police abuse of authority, actively or passively abets code of silence regarding officer misconduct, fails to adequately train personnel, and/or contributes to officer cynicism and burnout by lack of support: all factors associated with increased police misconduct.

findings (Klahm & Tillyer, 2010). For example, in one study, black officers were more likely than white officers to respond coercively when asked to resolve interpersonal conflicts between citizens (Sun & Payne, 2004). However, controlling for neighborhood characteristics reduced the significance of officer race as a factor; that is, black officers may act more forcefully because they are more likely to be assigned to communities with higher frequencies and intensities of citizen-citizen and police-citizen confrontations.

In these studies, it is also important to fully define what is meant by "use of force," that is, how often or how much? For example, one such study (Garner et al., 2002) found that Hispanic officers, but not black or other-race officers, showed a higher frequency of force utilization than white officers, but were not more likely to use higher levels of force than their white colleagues; i.e., their use of force was more frequent, but not more severe. Again, an interaction between any two parties is always a complex dance, and a description of officer behavior in such an interaction has to be interpreted in light of the actions of the citizens in question (see Chapter 7).

Officer Sex

Overall, the sex of the police officer, as a stand-alone factor, has not been found to be a consistent predictor of officer use of force (Crawford & Burns,

1998; Kaminski et al., 2004; Klahm & Tillyer, 2010; Lawton, 2007; McCluskey & Terril, 2005; McCluskey et al., 2005; Paoline & Terrill, 2007; Morabito & Doerner, 1997; Phillips & Smith, 2000; Sun & Payne, 2004; Terrill & Mastrofski, 2002; Terrill et al., 2008).

Male officers may be more likely to utilize higher levels of force against male subjects than against female suspects, while female officers appear to mete out force in equal proportion with regard to male and female suspects (Garner et al., 2002; Kop & Euwema, 2001; Paoline & Terrill, 2004). This probably relates to the fact that much of law enforcement authority in a police-citizen encounter comes not from the sheer size and strength of the officer, but from the symbolic authority inherent in the officer's societal status: the citizen knows that, if he resists or attacks the officer, he will ultimately be going up against the full weight of the local or regional law enforcement and criminal justice systems, either in the immediate encounter through officer backup, or subsequently in his arrest and prosecution.

This doesn't mean that a particular suspect might not make a swift calculation to try and elude the grasp of a small, rather than a large officer, but in doing so, he knows the pursuit will hardly end there, and the outcome is likely to be far more unpleasant when the cops finally catch up with him. Finally, some male suspects may actually consider it less of a threat to their machismo to surrender to a female in uniform—"I don't fight with women"—than to another male, who may be seen as more of a direct rival.

Officer Age and Experience

We might expect (or hope) that older, more seasoned, officers would know how to employ calmer, more measured tactics in dealing with citizens. However, officer chronological age, in and of itself, does not seem to bear any consistent relationship to the rate of use-of-force incidents (Klahm & Tillyer, 2010), although it might be related to lower severity of force per incident (Garner et al., 2002), and officers with more time and experience on the job may be more likely to utilize verbal de-escalation strategies or less-lethal weaponry than physical restraint or a firearm (Crawford & Burns, 1998).

Overall, although some studies have found no consistent association between experience and use of force (Klahm & Tillyer, 2010; Lawton, 2007; McCluskey et al., 2005; McCluskey & Terrill, 2005; Sun & Payne, 2004; Terrill et al., 2008), others report a relationship in the direction one might expect, that is, greater number of years on the job is associated with less favorable attitudes toward force as a first-resort tactic, along with lower propensity to resort to force in a police-citizen encounter, and, consequently, a lower number of force complaint investigations (Kop & Euwena, 2001;

McElvain & Kposowa, 2004; Paoline & Terrill, 2007; Terrill & Mastrofski, 2002). However, this last factor may also reflect the greater skill of more experienced officers in maneuvering within the investigatory process in their agencies. Added to this is the fact that different law enforcement agencies may have different criteria and thresholds for initiating and pursuing such investigations (investigate all claims vs. pick and choose the more "serious" ones).

Age is generally correlated with experience on the job, but not always: individuals may become police officers at different stages in their lives, some in their early twenties, others perhaps a decade or more later, often after working in other vocations. In these studies, therefore, officer chronological age might actually be a confounding variable, i.e., do older officers with more years of experience use less force because older age mellows one's personality in general or because more years on the job leads to greater tactical wisdom? Even if one could control for individual personality factors, would a 30-year-old cop who's been on the job since age 21 be expected to use less force than his 45-year-old partner who became an officer two years ago after working in sales or construction? These are questions for further research.

Officer Education Level

While absolute number of years of education may not correlate with propensity to use force (Sun & Payne, 2004), one consistent finding is that police officers who have completed a four-year college degree show a significantly lower likelihood of utilizing force than non-degree-attaining officers (Aamodt, 2004; Cascio, 1977; Hudzik, 1978; Kappeler et al., 1972; Klahm & Tillyer, 2010; Lynch, 1986, 1987; McElvain & Kposowa, 2008; Miller & Fry, 1976; Paoline & Terrill, 2007; Terrill & Mastrofski, 2002). But why? Is there something magical about filling one's head with science, philosophy, or humanities courses that somehow translates into more effective law enforcement tactics and better community relations?

It turns out that the actual course content of college study bears little relationship to later officer behavior; that is, officers who have earned their bachelor's degree in Criminal Justice or Psychology do not seem to have any advantage in constructive dealings with citizens than those who majored in Business or History. Second, sheer amount of knowledge-stuffing isn't the reason, either. Future officers who take multiple courses for five or more years, but never manage to complete their degrees are little different from those officers with no college at all when it comes to use of force rates.

The answer relates to cause and effect. It is not the specialized knowledge gained from any particular branch of college coursework that accounts for more restrained officer behavior. Rather, some officers-to-be already possess the innate traits of intelligence, perseverance, self-discipline, emotional stability, and communication skills that are necessary to maintain focus, overcome obstacles and frustrations, and stick to the task of completing four long consecutive years of a higher education curriculum. And it is these very traits that will also likely translate into a more reasoned and nuanced, less reactive and impulsive, approach to communication and interpersonal problem solving on patrol, and indeed, in one's life and career (Haier, 2017; Kashdan & Rottenberg, 2010; Mischel, 2014, Moffitt et al., 2010; Robson, 2019).

Finishing college, then, appears to be a marker (although hardly the only one) for the kind of reflective, mature approach to life challenges that also characterizes effective patrol policing. Those with this pattern of cognitive skills and temperamental traits will be better cops (or better at most human-oriented professions), whether or not they actually had the opportunity to attend college.

TYPES OF OFFICER MISCONDUCT

This book's focus is mainly on police use of force, excessive force, and deadly force, but psychological research and commonsense observation inform us that good or bad traits often cluster in the same individuals, and officers who show a propensity to abuse their authority and misuse force often commit other types of misconduct as well. Indeed, undeterred, one type often escalates to another. For example, a study of the New York City Police Department found that frequent rule-violating officers were more than five time more likely than other officers to have had five or more complaints filed against them for alleged use of unnecessary force (Miller, 2003b, 2004, 2006i, 2007d, 2007h, 2015b).

Corrupt Cops

Many of these activities are subsumed under the category of **police corruption**, which has been defined as "the use of one's status as a police officer for wrongful gain or benefit" (McCafferty & McCafferty, 1998). Studies (Beigel & Beigel, 1977; McCafferty & McCafferty, 1998) reveal the wide range of corrupt behaviors that officers may engage in, including: (1) receiving gratuities (free meals, discounted sports tickets), sometimes in return for preferential treatment or extra protection; (2) granting immunity from police action to certain citizens or peers, such as fixing parking or traffic violations, not enforcing regulations for certain businesses, or looking the other way during illegal activities by favored parties; (3) collecting bribes and kickbacks from lawyers for drunk driving arrests or auto accident investigations; (4)

explicit extortion of a cash payment in return for protection against police action; (5) stealing small items from unsecured places of business on one's beat; (6) taking property from recovered stolen vehicles; (7) stealing items from a crime scene and attributing their loss to criminal activity; (8) keeping weapons or drugs that are confiscated from suspects or crime scenes; (9) carrying out a planned burglary; (10) carrying or using unauthorized weapons; (11) having sex with informants in vice and narcotics investigations; (12) other sexual or physical assault, exploitation, coercion, or intimidation of suspects or citizens; (13) selling confidential information to lawyers and insurance companies; (14) using illegally deceptive or coercive means in interrogating suspects; (15) lying to protect fellow officers and/or oneself in a court of law (perjury) or during an Internal Affairs investigation; and (16) loafing or attending to personal business while on duty. Anyone who has worked for any length of time within a police agency can no doubt add their own items to this list.

Predicting Officer Misconduct

Every organizational manager learns, "If you don't want trouble, don't hire it." A recent study (Aita et al., 2018) factor-analyzed the pre-hire predictors of good vs. bad (i.e., excessively disciplined and/or terminated) officers from a sample of 1536 sworn law enforcement personnel. The strongest predictors of poor performance were a history of reprimands, suspensions, and referrals for fitness-for-duty evaluations in prior law enforcement positions. In other words, if someone was a bad cop in his or her previous agency, they'll probably be the same in yours. Other relevant predictors included failing to pay alimony or child support; frequent physical fights with people; and a history of arrest, mental health treatment, or substance abuse rehab.

Reinforcing the idea that bad things frequently come in the same package, what we seem to be looking at is a pattern of egocentricity, impulsivity, irresponsibility, and amorality that would probably characterize this person's activities in any vocation; it's just that the profession of policing affords such a bad apple greater opportunity to spoil the barrel for citizens and colleagues alike. Every officer can easily identify the high-drama members of their agency, so that when some bad stuff goes down, everybody rolls their eyes and says, "Oh, not *him* again!"

One surprising finding of this study was that some types of past behavior that might be assumed to spell disaster on the job turned out to have low rates of occurrence in both the good and bad cops. These included dishonorable military discharge, past felony conviction (how did he or she become a cop in the first place?), or prior citizen complaints of abuse of force, sexual harassment, or racial bias.

Police misconduct is rarely either-or, however. Even in challenging circumstances and on difficult patrol beats, becoming an active and enthusiastic participant in police corruption or abuse of force is hardly inevitable. Despite temptations and provocations, most officers are able to maintain their personal and professional integrity, while some become merely "passively" corrupt, e.g., racking up unearned overtime, accepting gifts of stolen items, or just turning a blind eye when their brothers or sisters in blue bend or break the rules.

Still other officers start out with small infractions, but become more aggressively corrupt and abusive as their ethical sensibilities erode and illicit opportunities expand. In a few extreme cases, they become the proverbial "rogue cops" of the department—those who actively seek out criminal activity in the pursuit of money, power, and prestige. For these officers, bribes, payoffs, theft, burglary, sexual misconduct, planting evidence, robbing drug dealers and citizens, vigilante street justice, and even murder, become a way of life (McCafferty et al., 1998).

OFFICER MISCONDUCT, USE OF FORCE, AND DEADLY FORCE

As discussed in Chapter 1, police use of force, even deadly force, does not automatically equate with excessive force, and the majority of police officers conduct themselves competently, legally, and ethically in both ordinary and extreme circumstances. In general, where mistakes occur due to tactical errors or cognitive-perceptual distortions (see Chapter 4), proper training may contribute to overall safer community policing. However, the following are situations in which some officers' intentions and actions may not be so benign, and which additional training will never overcome so long as those officers are unwilling to endorse and exemplify—and their agencies to inculcate and enforce—an ethical standard of law enforcement practice (Alpert & Dunham, 2004; Dunham et al., 2005; Engel et al., 2000; Klahm & Tilyer, 2010; Langan et al., 2001; Lawton, 2007; Terrill et al., 2008; White, 2002).

Abuse of Authority Escalates to Deadly Confrontation

Later in this chapter, I talk about authoritative vs. authoritarian approaches to law enforcement, but for now, let's just say that some officers apparently feel the need to project their police power in ways that grossly exceed the bounds of professionalism. These are officers that are likely to take affronts to their police authority as personal attacks and then forcefully defend their wounded pride under the guise of maintaining control and safety. If there is indeed anything like a contagion effect, it is more likely to play out in these scenarios, where other officers, who themselves might have responded more diplomatically, feel compelled to back up their brother in blue now that he has prematurely escalated to an aggressive approach and won't back down.

Police Retaliate Against a Suspect for Endangering Officers or for Showing Contempt of Cop

This is more serious because, in the previous example, the overreacting officers could at least rationalize that they were trying to forestall a dangerous confrontation. But in the present case, it's all about revenge. Even so, few police officers are going to risk their jobs by blatantly tuning up a citizen just for giving them a pissy attitude. More commonly, there may be some lawful cause for detaining or arresting the suspect, and the officers may sneak in a few extra thumps while taking otherwise justifiable action.

Improper Vehicle Operation

The relevance of this variable to abuse of force may seem less obvious, but recall Chapter 2's discussion of car chases. In their zeal to apprehend a suspect who is deemed dangerous, officers may be tempted cut corners (pun originally unintended but retained) on vehicle pursuit safety in order to nail their quarry. That's why many police agencies now have rules that specifically mandate no car chases of fleeing suspects because the risk of accidental injury or death by the suspect's or officer's vehicle is just too great. But another reason for the connection between cars and force may be correlational and demographic: those officers most prone to bend the safety rules for vehicle pursuits are probably also more likely to disregard the proper use of force standards when they catch up to their target, as well as incurring other violations and infractions. This is discussed in more detail below.

Inadequate Training and Supervision of Officers

As a general rule of organizational management, before you assume that any employee is deliberately misbehaving, first ascertain that he or she knows what the correct behavior or job description actually is (Grote, 1995; Miller, 2003a, 2008j, 2010b); that is, it is important to distinguish between *can't* and *won't*. Initial lessons learned at the Police Academy level quickly get stale if not reinforced by ongoing training and practice in diverse scenarios; this holds equally true for firearms use, vehicle tactics, communication skills, and ethical guidelines. Continuing education is considered important in any professional discipline, whether medicine, law, psychology, nursing, or any field whose practitioners impact human lives, and this is especially true for law enforcement (Miller, 2006h).

Maintaining a Code of Silence in Failing to Report Peers' Misconduct

This is a general factor that heightens the risk for any kind of officer misconduct. Cops who lack an internal ethical compass will pretty much do whatever they think they can get away with, as long as they can count on their peers, and sometimes their bosses, to look the other way.

Burnout and the Use of Force

A common assumption is that officers who experience a great deal of stress, disillusionment, and/or frustration on the job will, over time, grow less motivated, more jaded, and therefore more susceptible to taking out their frustrations and disappointments in interactions with citizens. But adverse experiences do not affect all officers equally, and stress effects are always filtered through the individual temperament and personality of each officer.

In support of this idea, at least one study (Kop & Euwema, 2001) has found that officers who score high on the depersonalization factor of burnout, which involves traits of cynicism and detachment, are more likely to endorse and use force as a default tactic. Not surprisingly, this typically sets up a vicious cycle wherein rough handling of citizens by the burned-out officer engenders resentment and hostility on the part of community members, which further fuels the officer's mistrust and contempt for those citizens, creating a vicious cycle which markedly increases the overall risk for violence in any given police-citizen encounter.

WHY DO POLICE OFFICERS MISBEHAVE?

Two main approaches have characterized the study of police misconduct (Worden,1996), which will serve as the framework for this section. One model is **psychological**–that is, it attempts to explain how the inner workings of an officer's personality influence his response to the demands of policing and thereby affect his behavior as a cop. This approach highlights individual variation among officers in their temperaments, personalities, and behavioral predispositions. Such individual differences are far less emphasized in the second, **organizational** model, which focuses on departmental, subcultural, and situational determinants of behavior. This latter approach is based on the premise that police behavior is influenced by departmental policies and the social dynamics of police-citizen encounters, and that these broad socialization factors can obscure or override individual differences in personality.

INDIVIDUAL/PSYCHOLOGICAL FACTORS

Individual factors are important for two reasons. First, certain types of people are more likely to be attracted to police work than others. Of course, this holds true for any profession: an individual's personality and cognitive style commonly play a significant role in what types of life work that person will find compatible (Miller, 1990, 2003a, 2008j). Second, the stresses and overall role demands of policing will likely shape and refine these existing cognitive and personality traits further in the direction toward which they're already inclined, leading to a continuing differentiation and concentration of individual work styles, as well as the development of certain stereotyped modes of perception, thought, and behavior, which is what some authorities may mean when they speak of a **police personality** (see below).

Individual factors in police misconduct can be described in several ways. The present discussion will follow the existing research in this area and break the discussion down to the relative roles of attitudes, personality traits, and psychological disorders.

ATTITUDES

Social scientists like to speak of **attitudes**, because the term connotes a perceptual and behavioral style that sounds less ingrained and immutable than **personality traits** (see below), and therefore potentially more amenable to change. Attitudes of police officers toward citizens, toward their own roles as law enforcement officers, and toward the profession of policing as a whole are likely to influence their propensities toward misconduct, including abuse of force.

Several attitude factors have been associated with officers' increased likelihood of using excessive force (Ostrom et al., 1978; Worden, 1996). The first involves officers who conceive of "real" police work in terms of action-oriented crime prevention and arrests, rather than handling interpersonal disputes or mental health crises, which many cops disparagingly regard as "nuisance calls" or "social work." A second attitude involves the belief that an easing of unnecessary restrictions on officers' discretionary use of force would allow them to "just do our job" and thereby make a meaningful dent in the serious crime problems that plague their patrol neighborhoods. A third attitude is that only fellow officers are qualified or entitled to pass judgment on what constitutes excessive vs. necessary force in a given situation. Finally, officers who believe that citizens on their beats generally disrespect and abuse law enforcement as a matter of course are more likely to use force on those citizens when tense situations arise.

A group of municipal and state police officers were surveyed with regard to their specific attitudes toward the Rodney King beating in Los Angeles at the time of the state trial in 1992 (Arcuri, 1994; Grant & Grant, 1996). Those officers supporting the police actions in the incident were more likely to believe that they themselves had been assaulted more often, to regard themselves as being in danger at their daily jobs, to say they would use physical force on suspects, and to report that they generally enjoyed the power and excitement of police work to a greater extent than those officers who did not endorse King's treatment. This use of self-perceived victimization or self-defense to justify an overly active and aggressive policing style appears to be an especially dangerous formula for community law enforcement efforts, perhaps having become even more acute in the modern policing era (Morin et al., 2017; Nhan, 2019; also see Chapter 7).

PERSONALITY: TRAITS, TYPES AND DISORDERS

As noted above, academic researchers, armchair theorists, and media commentators often make reference to the **police personality**, by which they typically mean a relatively uniform set of traits and behaviors that are supposed to characterize most working police officers (Adlam, 1982; Blau, 1994; Carpenter & Raza, 1987; Gallo, 2011; Gould, 2000; Hogan, 1971; Nhan, 2019; Peak, 2003; Russell & Biegel, 1990; Twersky-Glasner, 2005). This purportedly occurs either because of a selection factor that draws certain personality types to law enforcement, or because years on the job inevitably hammer an initially malleable mindset into a progressively hardened attitudinal alloy that, over time, becomes increasingly rigid and brittle. Members of few other professions are regarded as manifesting such cookie-cutter characteristics based on the type work they do: where are the expositions on the "doctor personality," the "firefighter personality," the "truck driver personality," the "CPA personality," and so on? The closest analogy might be the "military personality," which appears to share many features in common with its police counterpart (Grossman, 1996; Grossman & Christensen, 2007; Miller, 2008b, 2013a, 2019c).

Yet, even within the supposedly monolithic descriptor of the police personality, some observers and researchers have identified sufficient heterogeneity to generate a variety of subcategories, or typologies. If you work in or with law enforcement, some of these descriptions will seem familiar.

Police Personality Typologies: The Big Five Model

One such classification scheme (White, 1972; Worden, 1996) describes five types of officer personality.

The **tough cop** is the most likely to use force improperly because he thoroughly overidentifies with an extreme version of the Cop Culture and generally holds the cynical view that people basically can't be trusted because they're fundamentally motivated by selfish interests or evil intent (Graves, 1996; Johnson & Morgan, 2013). The tough cop believes that the citizenry is generally hostile toward law enforcement, and he conceives of the role of police officers as "keeping the lid on" or "drawing the line," that is, doing what it takes to control serious crime. He also believes that experience and common street sense are the best guides for dealing with the realities of daily law enforcement, and that "thumping" or other forms of curbstone justice are sometimes appropriate and effective.

The **clean-beat crime fighter** also emphasizes the law enforcement function of the police and justifies no-nonsense police action in terms of its deterrent effect on crime, but this officer is less adversarial in outlook and approach, seeing crime control as just part of his job as a good cop. While he is very proactive and energetic on patrol, he lacks the gritty street ethos and unyielding cynicism of the tough cop.

By contrast, the **problem-solver** holds a more "existential" perspective (Muir, 1977); that is, he understands people's actions to be influenced by complex sets of physical, economic, and social circumstances, not always malevolence or cold self-interest. He thus conceives of his police role primarily as providing assistance and solving problems, not just cracking heads, and his street instincts and judgments are likely to be in the direction of creative conflict resolution, rather than reflexive use of force. He may be skeptical of traditional police methods, as he is sometimes unable to reconcile the use of coercive measures with his personal moral code. This type of officer is probably the least likely to use force improperly, but may be at risk of underutilizing his legitimate police authority where it is truly needed, thereby making himself vulnerable to exploitation or attack by unscrupulous bad guys while he is trying to be too nice or too understanding.

Less high-minded philosophical or humanitarian motives drive the **avoider** who, unable or unwilling to cope with the daily demands of policing, is content simply to do the minimum amount of work he can get away with and still technically meet his supervisors' expectations. His basic approach is to lay low and not make waves.

A more healthy balance seems to be achieved by the **professional**, in whom an optimal blend of temperament, training, and experience allows the use of aggressive tactics when necessary, but flexibly moderated in proportion to the circumstances. This officer possesses a broader menu of interpersonal tactics, including verbal de-escalation. He believes that law enforcement is fundamentally about helping people, but he understands that this sometimes requires the judicious use of legitimate coercive control and that being fair and courteous doesn't mean taking crap. As a result, this officer is neither impulsively confrontational nor inertly passive, and he is less likely to resent the legitimate legal restrictions on his authority and actions, because he is confident in his ability to handle most situations successfully within the rules.

U.S. Department of Justice Psychological Model

Another police personality classification was derived from a study commissioned by the United States Department of Justice specifically to identify means of controlling police use of force (Scrivner, 1999). This study took the approach of directly asking a sample of police psychologists about the characteristics of officers who had been referred to them because of excessive force issues. From their responses, five distinct psychologically-based profiles of officer types emerged.

The first profile, smallest in number, identifies officers with overt **personality disorders**. These officers have pervasive, enduring personality traits (in contrast to job-acquired characteristics), largely in the antisocial, narcissistic, and paranoid categories (discussed further below). These extreme traits, which include egocentrism, cynicism, and a marked lack of empathy, predispose these officers to abusive behavior, especially when they perceive challenges to their authority.

These officers do not learn from their mistakes and are unlikely to change their behavior, so they tend to rack up a disproportionate number of repeated citizen complaints and internal disciplinary actions. In true squeaky-wheel fashion, the resulting departmental overfocus on this misbehaving minority may cause supervisors to overlook the more common everyday examples of rule-breaking activity by a wider range of officers, not to mention deflecting supervisors' recognition of the legitimate good works that the higher-functioning officers are doing because the brass is preoccupied with the troublemakers, further eroding departmental morale. Unfortunately, these personality disorder characteristics, disastrous as they become in daily police work, may not be apparent in their pre-employment psychological screening due to the superficial social adroitness and test-taking savvy of many of these individuals.

The second profile describes **traumatized officers** whose previous adverse job-related experiences place them at higher risk for using excessive force. Disturbing situations such as police shootings and other critical incidents, especially if severe, frequent, and cumulative, may contribute to the development of posttraumatic burnout and a sense of increasing isolation from their peers. Under pressure to maintain the typical tough guy cop image, this officer may conceal his distress for some time, until he loses control in a use of force incident. In contrast to the previously discussed intractable personality-disordered group, the functioning of these traumatized officers is more amenable to improvement with the use of appropriate administrative and/or psychological interventions (Blau, 1994; Miller, 1995, 1999b; 2007g, 2013b, 2019a; Russell & Biegel, 1990

A third group is composed of officers who have **problems at early stages of their police careers**. These are the "hotdogs" or "cowboys," i.e., young, inexperienced, immature, highly impressionable, and impulsive rookies with a high appetite for action and a low tolerance for frustration or boredom. They are not necessarily entrenched hard cases, however, and they may actually be quite effective in their police work if their gung-ho enthusiasm can be channeled productively. Unfortunately, without the proper early instruction and guidance by mature and experienced field training officers (FTOs) and first line supervisors, their initial law enforcement zeal may spiral into abusive behavior with citizens.

A fourth profile consists of officers who, in the course of their work, **develop inappropriate patrol styles**. Overly sensitive to challenge and provocation, officers in this category combine a dominant command presence with a heavy-handed "take-no-crap" policing style. They may once have been good cops, equipped with a flexible range of responses in dealing with citizens, but they have learned over time that it is often more expedient to just make the citizen do what they want, and this approach gradually congeals into a rigidly stereotyped approach to dealing with all citizen problems. In contrast to the chronic risk group, the behavior of officers in this category is more likely to be learned and reinforced on the job, which implies some potential for corrective change with appropriate retraining and supervision. The longer the patterns continue, however, the more entrenched they become, the more these officers become invested in coercive police power and control, and the more difficult these behaviors will be to modify.

This pattern is most commonly (but not exclusively) seen in the "old-timers" or "dinosaurs" in the department, and this group often includes those in upper administrative positions, with their attitudes filtering down to the rank and file. This group may be more responsive to peer programs or situation-based interventions in contrast to traditional counseling, which they tend to disparage. Finding ingenious and creative ways to make these officers part of the solution instead of the problem can foster a sense of "buy-in" and may be crucial for modifying their behavior and their influence on other officers.

The fifth and final risk profile in this typology is made up of officers with **personal problems**, who are going through serious life crises, such as divorce, parent-child issues, financial stresses, substance abuse, or intradepartmental conflicts that have destabilized their job functioning. These troubled souls often seem to have a tenuous sense of self-worth and high levels of anxiety and insecurity that they have been able to mask through intense, even obsessive, immersion in their work. They may not be innately aggressive and, before they resort to blatantly excessive force, these officers are often observed to exhibit more generalized erratic patrol behavior that signals the possibility of ultimately losing control in a confrontation.

This is the officer who may have been hobbling along with at least an adequate work record until one additional "last straw" event impacts his personal or professional life, critically undermining his confidence, and making it more difficult for him to squelch his fear and animosity in a tense patrol situation. In such incidents, he may lash out in an effort to restore some control both to the immediate situation and more broadly to his own fragile stability and identity. These officers may benefit from individual counseling, and the earlier the problems are identified and addressed, the less likely these officers are to erupt into an unnecessary confrontation (Blau, 1994).

Police Psychiatrist Typology

Still another typology, developed by police psychiatrists who worked extensively with law enforcement officers in Sausalito, California (Shev & Howard, 1977), utilizes only three categories. **Natural cops** constitute just five percent of all police officers studied. These are the men and women who seem to grasp instinctively how to handle the work and pressures of being a competent law enforcement officer. Their own basically healthy personalities form the basis for the discretion, confidence, and good judgment that daily patrol work requires, and they seem to absorb departmental training and on-the-job experiences in a naturalistic, intuitive way.

Treatable cops make up the second and largest category, comprising 60 percent of all police in this study. Most of the time these officers perform their duties reasonably well, but they have to work hard to master the complex skills of being a law enforcement professional. More importantly, each officer in this category has his or her breaking point, which, under sufficient stress, may jeopardize both police and citizens in a confrontation. Yet, in most circumstances, with proper leadership, supervision, and training, these basically healthy officers can perform as capably as the "naturals" if they are encouraged to recognize and work on their weaknesses and to overcome their tendency to overreact under the pressures that push their idiosyncratic buttons.

In this typology, the seriously dangerous officers are the surprisingly large 35 percent who make up the third category of **untreatable cops**. These bad boys in blue (and a few bad girls) are persistently inflexible, repressive, and psychologically unstable. They are unwilling to admit fault and will reject any form of coaching, counseling, or supervision that is aimed at encouraging them to function as better police officers. If these characterizations of one California police department actually generalize to the U.S. police population as a whole, then, alarmingly, fully one officer in three would be an untreatable bad cop, and the actions of this sizable minority may be responsible for the bad reputations of the police in many communities.

Police Personalities: Commonalities and Interactions

The various typologies outlined above were developed on the basis of studying diverse police agencies, in different places, at different periods in time. Nevertheless, if we boil down their essential characteristics, certain commonalities emerge, suggesting that all of these classifications are tracking a few fundamental and universal officer types (the following terminology is my own). Bear in mind, that each of these extreme types may be seen in more moderate gradations in individual officers.

At one end of the spectrum is the flinty **Officer Hard-Ass** who regards the majority of his patrol denizens as a collection of bugs, lugs, and thugs who must be intimidated, subjugated, or subdued for his and his fellow officers' safety. "You can't be nice to these people; they'll just take advantage of you," he tells himself, his colleagues, and his supervisors. He regards a fundamental aspect of his job as getting himself safely through his shift and going home, and he knows better than those clueless, politically correct desk jockeys and bureaucrats that, to keep order, you sometimes have to bust a few heads to show people they can't mess with you and get away with it.

Even this officer, however, is probably not going to go out of his way to sadistically abuse or otherwise mistreat a harmless citizen, and he typically does not regard himself as dishonest or corrupt–indeed, he prides himself on being an honorable cop's cop who won't hesitate to jump in to protect a deserving citizen or defend a fellow officer when necessary. Just don't ask him to feel any sympathy for the skells and freeloaders who devote all their time to making life miserable for everyone else.

Although these officers' attitudes and behaviors may be attributed to burnout from years of working tough, gritty beats, a fair number are young and only a few years into the job, and some may even be rookies. What Officer Hard Ass has done is brought his inherently and pervasively cynical attitude with him into the profession of policing, and he probably would have acted this way no matter what job he held. The difference is that law enforcement, unlike most other vocations, puts into this officer's hands the societally sanctioned power to force people do things they don't want to do–even, when called for, to take their lives.

At the other extreme is **Officer Friendly**, who exemplifies the service orientation model of police work, but whose desire to be liked and admired, and whose overly trusting and conciliatory approach to citizens, may backfire and lead to an erosion of the legitimate law enforcement authority that is essential for effective policing. As he often possesses good communication skills, Officer Friendly is more likely than other cops to try to negotiate a solution to a problem before intervening forcefully, but because of this, he is the officer who is most likely to be derided by his peers as a "social worker." Ironically, line-of-duty death statistics show that the two kinds of officers most likely to be shot and killed by citizens are Officer Hard Ass and Officer Friendly–the first, because his overly aggressive policing style angers citizens, some of whom may feel compelled to retaliate; the second, because a well-intentioned effort to be nice to people may induce a premature relaxation of vigilance and consequent exploitation and attack by some citizens who are mentally ill, intoxicated, or just opportunistic criminals.

In between these two extremes lies **Officer Tough-but-Fair**, the cop who genuinely tries to help people and treats citizens with basic courtesy and civility, but don't you try messing with him or he *will* take you down, and you know it. Precisely because his use of force is perceived as mostly justified and proportional to the situations he encounters, this officer may accrue a grudging respect from the citizens he patrols, and his ratio of words to actions in dealing with confrontations depends largely on the sophistication of his overall communication skills, the latter which can be enhanced by training if the officer is willing to learn.

Other common types encountered in the work of a police psychologist, and well known to the officer's colleagues and supervisors, include **Officer Slick Operator**, who may not necessarily be overly violent or abusive, but whose exploitive orientation may frequently lead him into areas of corruption and misconduct; **Officer Drama**, whose perennial personal problems, multiple service-related incidents, or untreated psychopathology impede his efforts to conduct himself effectively and professionally; and **Officer Bad News**, who may be an effective crime fighter, but whose continuously rule-breaking behavior on the job makes him a departmental liability. As noted earlier, there can be all kinds of gradations, permutations, combinations, and overlaps among the above basic officer types.

Authoritative vs. Authoritarian: Andy vs. Barney

In my training classes, I distinguish between two styles of patrol policing that have similar wording, but are worlds apart: **authoritative** vs. **authoritarian**. Although dated, I illustrate this concept by referencing the old *Andy Griffith Show* of classic TV, which features two main characters in the fictional Southern town of Mayberry (the show was actually filmed in the real-life town of Mount Airy, NC): Sheriff Andy Taylor and Deputy Barney Fyfe. If you haven't ever seen the show, it's worth Googling, YouTubing, Huluing, or Netflixing to get a sense of what these characters are like and why they have become immortal icons of TV policing.

Sheriff Taylor is physically imposing, but always has a smile. He walks slow, he talks slow, he wears his uniform open-collared, and most of the time he doesn't even carry a gun (probably not the best idea outside of Mayberry). Whatever sundry disputes and altercations the sheriff encounters in his quiet hamlet, he tries to resolve through diplomacy and mediation. There's a quiet confidence about the man, an understatedly strong presence that tells you he's prepared to handle any situation and face any challenge, and that you'd be well advised not to mistake his rustic affability for weakness. He's fair, he's strong, he believes in what he's doing, and that is what conveys his authority. You're apt to listen to him because he's the grown-up on the scene and can be trusted to make the right decisions and protect the citizens under his charge. He doesn't have to bluster or posture to pull rank because everything he does exemplifies his **authoritative** stance.

Along comes his foil, Deputy Fyfe, smaller both in stature and confidence, whose predominant reaction to challenges can be described as akin to a rooster who's just been sprayed with a garden hose. Deputy Fyfe always wears his complete service uniform–hat, tie, and gun belt. Equally well-intentioned in his efforts to serve the Mayberry citizenry, the deputy unfortunately can find no other way to do so than by affecting a cocky, supercilious attitude, asserting his police authority shrilly, frequently, and often unnecessarily, and as a result, he is alternately pitied and ridiculed by the townspeople, who recognize the weakness and insecurity underlying his buffoonish display. They may defer to him because he's the law, but they don't respect him. Any authority he manages to command lies in his badge, not his person. He is **authoritarian**, not authoritative.

Even if they haven't seen the show, the cops in my classes usually nod and chuckle knowingly at these descriptions (and occasional videos), because almost every department has a few Andys and Barneys in them. And then I ask the class what type of officer do they want to be, and the room gets a little quieter. After that, much of the training revolves around mastering the interpersonal skills needed to be an Andy, not a Barney.

Inevitably, however, a couple of hands go up: "In case you haven't noticed, Doc, we don't work in Mayberry. Where we patrol is more like Compton or Bed-Sty, South Central or South Bronx." Cops can be histrionic, but they've got a point. Many of them who may have started out with a well-meaning service orientation have, after many years on the job, had their good intentions stepped on and spat at way too many times to take seriously my little TV-Land homilies. As noted earlier, a persistently rough patrol setting may override the congenial and constructive personal qualities that, in more clement interpersonal environments, would have allowed this officer to function safely and productively throughout his career. But now he's just burned out from the bullshit, wants to coast through his remaining time, and pension out alive and healthy. On the way, however, his frayed patience may lead to hyperreactively forceful confrontations on patrol.

But it works the other way, too: "The fire that melts the butter hardens the egg." That is, different officers will react differently to different patrol environments precisely because their personalities are so different. Solving interpersonal problems through negotiation and diplomacy may be an onerous chore for the officer with poor communication skills and a rigid law-and-order orientation, but will be taken as an invigorating challenge by the more verbally adroit, service-oriented officer.

Officers who think they know it all when they leave the Academy and then have their eggs and butter singed in the frying pans of decidedly un-Mayberry patrol beats may find that their attitudes have curdled into a thick glob of cynicism and suspicion as they continue to deal with an ungrateful or hostile public. A more flexible-minded officer, on the other hand, may react to these sparks as the proverbial flame that is lit under his seat, impelling him to learn from experience and thus discoagulate his initially chilled and clunky patrol style into a range of more smooth and varied communication options with diverse citizens.

Having worked this breakfast metaphor to death (what, no donuts?), the salient point is that it is just this complex interplay between person and circumstance that makes the analysis and understanding of the "police personality" so challenging, but that must be addressed if we are to provide effectively targeted clinical and supervisory interventions to different kinds of officers. As we'll discuss in Chapters 4-6, this diversity also applies to the perceptual, cognitive, and behavioral responses to deadly force encounters.

PERSONALITY DISORDERS

Pre-hire psychological screening of police candidates usually manages to filter out gross forms of psychopathology like psychoses and severe mood disorders (Grant & Grant, 1996; Scrivner, 1999). Harder to catch, however, are the "normal abnormalities," the characterological idiosyncrasies and aberrations that may be masked by a superficially impressive interview style and good test-taking skills, but that may wreak professional havoc when unleashed on an unsuspecting public. More than mere traits, **personality disorders** denote a level of dysfunction that adversely and persistently affects major areas of life and work, and these disorders include many of the diagnosable syndromes that psychologists evaluate and treat.

We discussed personality disorders in Chapter 2 in connection with some of the citizens that police officers must confront. Here, we'll apply these clinical concepts to the officers themselves (APA, 2013; McCafferty & McCafferty, 1998; Millon & Davis, 2000; Miller, 2003b, 2006i, 2007h; Sperry, 1995; Tyre, 2001) to help better understand how these characteristics can influence policing styles and impact the communities the officers serve.

Note that prominent symptoms of a personality disorder–or any form of psychopathology–can lie dormant for some time until a severe stressor, or cumulative series of lower-level stresses, overwhelms an officer's coping capacity. Also note that different types and blends of personality disorders may intersect and overlap in a given officer. If you are a law enforcement manager or line supervisor, these descriptions will seem familiar, even if the terminology is new.

Borderline Personality Disorder

Borderline personality disorder is a pattern of erratic and intense relationships, alternating between over-idealization and devaluation of colleagues, departmental authorities, and citizens; self-damaging impulsiveness in the form of car chases, citizen harassment, and other abuse of authority; emotional instability, including inappropriately intense anger and/or depressive mood swings and possibly suicidality. These may be associated with persistent identity disturbance in self-image, professional goals and values, and interpersonal relationships. There is often a chronic feeling of emptiness that may lead to the quest for stimulation through provocation or escalation of law enforcement incidents or other inappropriate actions.

Narcissistic Personality Disorder

Narcissistic personality disorder is a pattern of grandiosity, sense of entitlement, arrogance, need for admiration, and lack of empathy for others' feelings or opinions. Officers with this pattern believe that rules are for other cops and that they are special and above the law because of their superior powers of perception, insight, and judgment. When afforded what they believe to be proper deference and respect from colleagues or citizens, they can actually be quite gracious, but they are often truly baffled as to why so many others don't recognize and acknowledge their uniqueness, and their reactions may range from mild irritation to explosive rage when asked to follow protocol like other, "ordinary" officers. Typically, they will rack up multiple complaints for insubordination or violation of standard operating procedures, all the while rationalizing that they are only trying to utilize their particular talents to "help" their colleagues and "improve the way things are done around here."

Antisocial Personality Disorder

Antisocial personality disorder is a pattern of persistent disregard for, and violation of, the rights of others, often associated with impulsivity, criminal behavior, sexual exploitation, substance abuse, and an exploitive parasitic, and/or predatory lifestyle. While possessed of similar characteristics of entitlement and self-importance as the narcissist, what distinguishes the antisocial officer is the complete lack of conscience that allows him to qualmlessly use and abuse other people for his own selfish ends. Antisocial individuals can be superficially charming and quite shrewd in a cunning-conning type of way, and the more intelligent of these officers may accumulate considerable illicit fiefdoms of wealth and power, or rise to positions of great authority within their agency before their complexly spun webs of deceit begin to unravel.

While the above discussion has focused on the more flagrant varieties of personality disorder that may affect police officers' job performance, in most police psychologists' clinical practices, the kinds of psychological traits and disorders that prompt referrals for evaluation and treatment are just as commonly found in what can be called the "less-explosive, more-corrosive" personalities that cause problems, not just for police departments, but in many kinds of employment settings (Miller, 2003a, 2003b, 2006i, 2007h, 2008j, 2010b).

Avoidant Personality Disorder

Avoidant personality disorder is a pattern of social inhibition, feelings of inadequacy, and hypersensitivity to negative evaluation or criticism, so that even relatively neutral interactions are approached with trepidation. Although it is unlikely that many individuals with this personality pattern would choose an interpersonally demanding career like law enforcement, some cops may have initially been attracted to the helping aspects of policing and may have been motivated (consciously or unconsciously) to assume the role of Officer Friendly as a vehicle for their own self-esteem enhancement by garnering good will and admiration from citizens and the camaraderie of fellow officers.

However, avoidant officers will be far less effective in a truly contentious interaction or physical confrontation with a citizen, and they may be particularly susceptible to burnout and depression when their kind and noble efforts earn only snickers from their more aggressive colleagues, while they're regarded as exploitable patsies by the manipulative and intimidating citizens on their beats.

Dependent Personality Disorder

Dependent personality disorder is a pattern of submissive and clinging behavior stemming from an excessive need for care and guidance. Whereas avoidants fear people and prefer to be away from them, dependents desperately need people and fear only their rejection or abandonment. Dependent personalities look to others to provide support and direction, and officers with this pattern may actually be good, dedicated workers, so long as any kind of independent decision-making is kept to a minimum. Interactions with colleagues, supervisors, or citizens are apt to be taken more personally than with other cops, as dependent personalities will always be looking for work-related validation, and will panic at any hint of rejection or disappointment on the part of peers or supervisors. To forestall this catastrophe, dependent officers may continue to pester coworkers and commanders with pleas for direction and guidance in matters that other officers will have long since independently mastered: "How many times do I have to spoon-feed everything to this guy—when is he going to learn to stand on his own two feet?"

Unfortunately, such critical blowback only heightens the insecurity of the dependent officer, leading to more strident pleas for guidance, and then more adverse feedback, resulting in a vicious cycle in which the dependent officer is chasing his peers and supervisors around, seeking greater and greater validation and support, while they are doing their best to avoid him or, worse, turning him into an object of departmental ridicule. In constant distress, he sinks into a demoralized state where his work performance further deteriorates, eventuating in the worst of all possible outcomes: a poor departmental evaluation, demotion, or reassignment.

This, then, becomes the very psychological death blow the dependent officer has always feared because, overly invested in the relatively secure position of the police role, the now-threatened loss of his job may seem literally like the end of the world. In severe cases, this may precipitate a suicidal crisis (Allen, 1986; Cummings, 1996; Hillbrand, 2001; Miller, 2005b, 2006j; Loo, 1999; Violanti, 1996; Violanti & Dryden, 2008; Violanti et al., 2011); more commonly, the officer may overcompensate by resorting to overly aggressive policing in an effort to "prove himself" to his peers and supervisors. To make matters worse, dependency also commonly characterizes his personal relationships, priming yet one more potent trigger of potential conflict and loss of support.

Historic Personality Disorder

Histrionic personality disorder is a pattern of excessive emotionality, attention-seeking, need for excitement, flamboyant theatricality in speech and behavior, an impressionistic and impulsive cognitive style, and the use of exaggeration to maintain largely superficial relationships for the purpose of getting emotional needs met by being cared for and admired by others. These are the "showboats" of the police department who love to be the focus of positive attention and who will do anything to get it from colleagues, supervisors, or the general public. They enjoy being in the news and will often work overtime and volunteer for extra assignments, as long as this keeps the spotlight on them. Fellow officers may tire of these officers' endless renditions of their own exploits.

Typically regarded as reasonably competent officers, the danger arises when their need for constant approval fails to be adequately met. Then, the histrionic officer may become depressed and angry, and is particularly prone to develop psychosomatic ailments and symptoms, leading to excessive use of leave and sick time. Worse, if attention can't be gained by doing good, he may resort to more aggressive policing, believing that this is what is required to gain further recognition. The intense drive to prove himself as a tough, effective cop, especially when unaccompanied by a commensurate level of judgment and common sense, may quickly flash over to an abuse of force incident. Then, when he receives criticism from his supervisors and complaints from citizens, he may react with shocked dismay at this flagrant lack of appreciation, precipitating a depressive tailspin and, in some cases, a request for a transfer or even resignation from his "ungrateful" agency.

Paranoid Personality Disorder

Paranoid personality disorder is a pattern of pervasive distrust and suspiciousness, so that others' actions and motives are invariably interpreted as deceptive, persecutory, or malevolent. Actually, because paranoid individuals spend a lot of time intently watching and studying other people, their perceptions may in fact be quite accurate–it's the interpretations and conclusions drawn from those perceptions that are problematic. Like psychologists and detectives who observe people for a living, paranoid individuals often show keen insight into human behavior patterns. The difference is that trained professionals know that there always exists a range of motivations for people's behavior, while the paranoid has only one all-fitting interpretation: people are basically mean and selfish, and they'll screw you every chance they get, unless you maintain self-protective vigilance at all times, and are prepared to counterattack or strike pre-emptively when threats are detected.

The job of law enforcement can in many ways reinforce paranoid tendencies, because a lot of police work involves getting information from people who have every reason to keep it from you. The paranoid cognitive style often includes a knack for technical details and many of these individuals are able to channel considerable energy in the direction of goal accomplishment (Miller, 1990; Shapiro, 1965). As such, paranoid individuals may actually achieve considerable success at work. In fact, they may often be found among the ranks of law enforcement investigators where their talent and enthusiasm for ferreting out "dirt" is actually encouraged and rewarded by the law enforcement culture.

Of course, healthy skepticism in investigators is not the same as clinical paranoia; indeed, an unchecked, overly cynical, us-against-them stance may result in overzealously pursued, ruinous investigations of honest citizens. In patrol policing, excessive vigilance and suspiciousness can lead an officer to misread interpersonal cues, resulting in hair-trigger reactivity with resultant street-level abuse of force confrontations. In many cases, it is not long before the hypercritical lens of the paranoid officer becomes trained on his own colleagues and supervisors, not to mention bringing his suspicious attitude and accusations home and alienating family members. Thus emerges a vicious cycle of mistrust and hostility as coworkers come to shun their obnoxiously mistrustful and standoffish associate, only confirming his suspicions of plots and intrigue, leading to more outright avoidance and hostility and perhaps even defensive moves on the part of others. Eventually, the old adage comes true: "Just because you're paranoid, it doesn't mean they're *not* out to get you."

Schizoid Personality Disorder

Schizoid personality disorder is a pattern of aloof detachment from social interaction, with a restricted range of emotional expression. These are people who don't need people, and are perfectly happy being left alone. Consequently, they are not typically drawn to intensely interactive professions like policing. However, some schizoid officers may function adequately in certain departmental settings, especially those that involve solitary, high-tech applications. They will be the "oddballs" of the department who keep to themselves, do their jobs, rarely cause trouble, but never seem to form any kind of solid bond or camaraderie with their fellow cops. In interactions with citizens, they are generally low-key, but in unfamiliar threatening situations, may have a tendency to impulsively erupt due to a dearth of social skills. Also, they may be more at risk of decompensating and becoming delusional under prolonged, intense stress, and they are more likely to be the source of citizen complaints about "that weirdo cop," rather than abusive force per se.

POSITIVE QUALITIES AND TRAITS

Implicit in the various typologies reviewed above, good policing should not be defined solely by the absence of bad policing. Indeed, research (McCafferty et al., 1998; Toch, 1996) has uncovered a range of qualities that appear to augur well for fair and productive law enforcement work. Even in rough, high-crime areas, there are often at least some officers in who patrol their beats, enforce the law, interact with citizens, make arrests when necessary, but do not accumulate excessive use of force or other complaints. These **high-quality officers** (McCafferty et al., 1998) are described as individuals of integrity and good character who are self-disciplined, honorable, honest, and basically incorruptible. Unfortunately, these model officers–the uber-Andys–are estimated to comprise only about three percent of police forces, a microminority even smaller than the natural cops category of Shev and Howard (1977), described earlier. The important question is, to what extent can these traits, skills, and behaviors be more broadly trained, instilled, and enculturated within a given law enforcement agency.

ORGANIZATION FACTORS: LAW ENFORCEMENT CULTURE

The above discussion implies that analyzing officers' individual attitudes, traits, and personality types may be a necessary but not sufficient, condition for understanding police misconduct, because all behavioral traits are expressed in a social context. In any hierarchical organization, members quickly learn which of the overt malfeasances or subtle rule-tweakings are officially condemned and which are tacitly condoned, which can be snuck under the radar or are even surreptitiously encouraged. Thus, in any law enforcement agency, understanding officers' behavior at the street level must be supplemented by examining the cultures and philosophies of the upper floors of that organization, cultures and philosophies that may have accreted over generations and are exemplified and reinforced by that agency's entrenched command staff. Such a top-down approach may have great practical potential in effectively guiding police reform, as organizational factors are sometimes more readily altered than are the attitudes and personalities of individual officers or the citizens they confront (Johnson, 2018; Miller, 2004, 2006f, 2006h, Worden, 1996).

Law enforcement enculturation begins at the recruiting stage. Like the rest of us, many officers-to-be get their first impressions of the world of policing from TV and movie portrayals, which almost always emphasize the excitement and action aspects of being a cop. Law enforcement recruitment videos commonly feature testosterone-fueled sounds and images of flashing police cars racing down the street, foot patrol officers chasing and tackling bad guys, heavily armored drug or gang unit team members busting down doors, siccing snarling K-9s on perps, or deploying high-powered weapons (Balko, 2014). In highlighting the thrill-seeking, adrenaline-pumping, butt-kicking aspects of law enforcement, what kind of recruits are these promos enticing to the profession of policing? Will these officers be able to adjust to a community policing patrol model that emphasizes conversation over confrontation, talk-downs versus take-downs?

Throughout my training classes and seminars, I typically have the cops go through a variety of role plays involving verbal de-escalation and communication strategies that we've discussed in the course. A few students get right into it; others initially squirm uncomfortably but ultimately manage to demonstrate that they've picked up a few useful interpersonal skills. However, there are always at least one or two students who, frustrated by their difficulty in learning and utilizing this verbal judo, blurt out with great consternation some version of: "Hey, I'm a cop, not a social worker. I don't get paid to talk to people, I get paid to catch crooks."

At which point, I slap my forehead (sometimes metaphorically, sometimes literally) and patiently reiterate that, no, talking to people is *exactly* what you get paid for, since that happens to be what most patrol officers do for 90 percent of their shifts. Crime interdiction and offender apprehension are essential components of police work, but proper mastery of de-escalation and other communication strategies is just as essential for preventing or mitigating potential crises and thereby contributing not just to better police-community relations, but to overall officer safety (Miller, 2005c, 2006i, 2013c, 2015e).

Administrative and Departmental Factors

In achieving such an integrated perspective, it is important to resist conflating the generic "**cop culture**" with the idiosyncratic cultures of different regional police departments and administrations (Worden, 1996). As noted earlier, the cop culture consists of general perspectives and behavioral norms that are shared by most officers as part of The Job. The cop culture has always emphasized the danger and unpredictability of police work, the collegial loyalty and reliance of officers on one another, a certain degree of discretionary autonomy in handling diverse situations, and the need to assert and maintain law enforcement's authority and credibility (Bittner, 1970; Lundman, 1974; Nhan, 2019). The cop culture thus endows officers with a great deal of latitude in exercising their individual judgments and styles of policing, but then may come down hard on them if certain, often unclear, protocols are breached (Miller, 2011b).

Chain of command and standard operating procedures (SOPs) are vital to any complex service organization. It has long been observed that larger police agencies tend to emphasize more coercive and restrictive policing tactics than smaller ones (Alprin & Wilson, 1974; Cancino, 2001; Etzioni, 1975; Morin et al., 2017). One reason may be that larger agencies are unable to provide the close, individualized supervision of officers that smaller ones can, or different supervisory approaches tailored to individual officers may raise concerns of fairness or equal treatment. Therefore, to err on the side of administrative caution, many of these agencies attempt to address use of force policies and other supervisory issues by setting up standardized, top-down, bureaucratic systems of oversight and discipline which, paradoxically, sometimes only seem to make the problems worse.

One study (Worden, 1996) found that officers in less bureaucratized departments were less likely to use force or, at the outset of the encounter, to engage in overly confrontational actions that could later spiral into a force incident. Instead, these officers were more likely to deflect and de-escalate tense situations, using force as a last resort. In this study, the differences in departmental culture far overshadowed any observed individual differences in officer attitudes or personality. Of course, one could argue the causality the other way: more flexible and resourceful personnel in a given agency may reduce the need for overly rigid and punitive bureaucracies.

As noted above, it is likely that administrators and supervisors in smaller, less bureaucratic departments can more effectively get to know and monitor the performance of their officers as individuals, and can have more of a personal influence on their subordinates' judgments and actions. Relatedly, less bureaucratized departments may be characterized by an overall increased attitude of trust and confidence in their officers and this may have positive feedback effects on confidence and morale. In such cases, individual officer personalities and department style may interact, with officers less suited to the department's culture of policing eventually leaving or being weeded out. Moreover, less bureaucratic departments may define good policing not predominantly in quantifiable terms such as arrest rates, but also by statistically fuzzier but interpersonally more meaningful criteria, such as positive community relations. Finally, it may partly boil down to location: larger police agencies are typically situated in more heavily populated urban areas with proportionately more crime.

Police researchers (e.g., Klockars, 1996) have identified certain features of departmental culture that may impede administrators from adequately controlling police excessive force. For one, the unspoken but ubiquitous code of loyalty that demands brother officers to go to extreme lengths to protect one another from censure and punishment may be found among the upper brass as well. In this philosophy, the "good" supervisor is the one who will back up his or her officers when they make a mistake, even to the point of covering up questionable behavior if performed in the line of duty. When this abrogation of accountability is combined with a departmental attitude that favors arrest statistics over community relations, the result is a recipe for corruption and abuse.

In such cases, a department's hard-nosed, "law and order" orientation may further encourage already violence- and corruption-prone officers to abuse their authority under the tacit imprimatur of the command staff. The pro forma legal and ethical training mandates—such as "observe due process and earn community acceptance"—may be conveniently tossed aside by officers favoring a "get 'em at any cost" approach to collaring offenders and racking up stats. Within such a department, aggressive crime-fighters are praised, rewarded, and promoted, while officers who hold back or engage in "social work" are denigrated or ignored, thereby further deflecting efforts away from community relations and more towards busting heads, keeping the lid on, and hauling in the trash (Toch, 1996).

One early study of officer-involved shootings among several Los Angeles County police departments (Uelmen, 1973) found that the major determinant of shooting rates was not their communities' level of crime and violence, but the personal philosophies and policies, official or implicit, of their chiefs and command staff. Similarly, the number of police shootings in Philadelphia was found to be relatively unrelated to the actual threats to police officers' lives or safety, but had more to do with whether the municipality was governed by a "law and order" mayor (Fyfe, 1988), highlighting the role played by a municipality's overarching political climate in influencing the attitudes and actions of its regional police managers, ultimately filtering down to officers on the street and affecting their proclivity to use discretionary force (Geller & Toch, 1996).

In still other cases, departmental control may be conspicuous by its absence. Police brass may tolerate officer abuses because the supervisors themselves simply lack the interest or ability to detect, prevent, or constrain them. The natural independence and autonomy of daily patrol policing and out-of-office special unit assignments means that, on a day-to-day basis, most supervision occurs at a distance, especially for officers who work alone and in low-visibility settings, essentially allowing them to operate much of the time as free agents (Fyfe, 1996; Miller, 2006b, 2015c). In this regard, appropriate management training may be essential to helping these departmental supervisors maintain better oversight and control of their personnel—assuming they want to.

Training and Supervision Issues

Problems with departmental philosophy and personal conduct often begin at the Police Academy level. Despite curricular lip-service about law enforcement ethics, community relations, and citizens' legal rights, instructors in many training programs still love to regale recruits with harrowing war stories that feature the use of justifiable violence against execrable evildoers (Grant & Grant, 1996; Waegel, 1984), "Hot calls"–harrowing chases, dangerous arrests, first-in-the-door scenarios–are, for many young officer-candidates, what "real" police work is supposed to be about, the heroic narratives that encourage the crystallization of a cop's identity as an aggressive crime-fighter (Toch, 1996).

During the probationary phases of training, the greatest influence on a recruit is from his **field training officer (FTO)**, who's attitude and behavior can powerfully shape the freshly minted rookie's conduct for years to come (Toch, 1996). A few of these FTOs might believe it is their obligation to disabuse their trainees of the stultified, by-the-book Academy lessons filling their precious little heads, and to supplant those with cynical doubts about the relevance of their just-completed education to the hard-bitten realities of policing on the street: "This ain't no classroom, probie, and that piece of metal on your belt ain't no pencil."

The attitude of these FTOs seems to be that effective police work would be impossible if officers had to follow all the pesky rules and procedures to the letter (Cancino, 2001; Hunt, 1985; Neiderhoffer, 1967; Sykes, 1986). In some cases, the FTOs may actually have a valid point, but that point may be too raw, jagged, premature, and unburnished by the requisite lathe of judgment, common sense, experience, and safety to serve as a practical guide to discretion and flexibility for the average new recruit. In these "real-world" narratives, officers may acknowledge that mistakes are sometimes made, but they reason that the risk of being killed by lowering their guard occasionally outweighs the consequences of being accused or even found guilty of an unjustifiable shooting or other use of force, i.e., the famous **6/12 argument:** "I'd rather be judged by twelve than carried out by six."

A reasonably intelligent, mature, psychologically stable new officer might actually learn to productively contextualize the strict protocols he's been taught in cop school with their flexible and sensible application on the beat. But garish war story narratives and derogations of "textbook policing" are exactly the wrong messages at the wrong time for officers who already harbor some self-doubt or feelings of inadequacy about their ability to handle their police role. The urge to demonstrate one's "cop chops" may impel such novice officers (and some disgruntled old-timers, too) to disregard normal precautions, such as calling for backup or adequately securing a scene, before charging into a situation (Cancino, 2001), which then greatly magnifies the likelihood of a forceful, and possibly deadly, encounter, with heightened danger to officers and citizens alike.

At the same time, those officers who are already overly aggressive, abuse-prone, or adrenaline-addicted will most likely take the slightest wink at minor rule-bending as an unrestricted license to kick ass at will. Further, as a result of the "ethic of masculinity" (Toch, 1996), some women rookies may feel particular pressure to prove themselves by acting even tougher than the guys.

Effective Policing: Proactive, Aggressive, or Abusive?

So, is this an argument for officers all becoming "social workers"? Of course not. Most citizens want the police to do their jobs, by which we generally mean we want them to protect us. At the same time, we don't want them to hurt us. As we've seen, the cop who naps in his car while the little old lady is mugged across the street is probably little better than the one who body-slams a young man for merely flashing a disrespectful look. But can we have it both ways?

Citizens who feel that the police have abused their authority might voice their displeasure in a formal complaint to the department. And we know that, within any given police agency, certain cops seem to garner a disproportionate number of complaints (Hudson, 1970; Lersch & Mieczkowski, 1996; Miller, 2003b, 2004). As we've discussed, these officers typically justify their actions by asserting that they're just zealously fulfilling their sworn crime-fighting duties and that, naturally, many of the people they encounter are not going to appreciate their efforts. "You can't make an omelette without cracking a few eggs," these cops will say. But is there any truth to this self-serving kitchen metaphor? (Don't worry, no more food analogies after this.)

Some research (Terrill & McCluskey, 2002) actually does support the idea that assertive, proactive policing is associated with higher rates of both prosecutable arrests and citizen complaints, but that arrest productivity does not necessarily have to equate with abuse. Indeed, the same research finds that some officers are able to maintain a kind of optimum balance between relatively high crime interdiction and relatively low citizen dissatisfaction, and it appears that they do this by embodying the type of Andy-policing described earlier. That is, they take no nonsense, call out the bad guys as they see them, but are all the while able to project an attitude of respect and confidence. They use as much force as necessary, but no more. They don't try to act like pals with suspects, but neither do they gratuitously insult or demean them. By factually explaining what they're doing ("I stopped you because your license plate came back as a stolen vehicle;" "You're under arrest for possession of a controlled substance"), their actions are less likely to be interpreted as arbitrary or authoritarian (remember Barney?). And if a suspect resists or becomes violent, they unflinchingly take the appropriate action necessary to neutralize the threat as they are trained and mandated to do.

Because there will always be citizens who resent any police intrusion, interference, or questioning about their various and sundry activities, these proactive officers will still garner more citizen complaints than less proactive officers, but still not as many as the cops swaggering around with their "egg-cracking" ideology. Most citizens understand that police officers sometimes need to use coercive force in fighting crime, but they also know that crime can be fought in their communities without abusing and alienating the very people the police are purporting to protect, and whose cooperation is often vital for officers to carry out their responsibilities. This issue will be further explored in Chapter 7.

SUMMARY AND CONCLUSIONS

It might seem intuitively obvious that officers who are prone to other types of misconduct would be more likely to use excessive force with citizens, but at this stage of the research, we just don't know. Extrapolating from data on workplace misbehavior more broadly, we do know that some malfeasors are specialists, that is, they stick to one or a few types of offenses, such as equipment theft or record falsification. Other workplace wrongdoers are generalists, their offenses running the gamut from electronic financial crimes to aggressive threats, intimidation, and bullying of coemployees and customers–and in the case of cops, the customers are all the citizens in a patrol community.

As with most forms of behavior–good and bad–people gravitate toward the types of activities that best match their skills and temperaments. So it is feasible that some police officers might feel that a badge validates their natural prerogative to do what they want and get away with it. Unlike most occupations, however, the role of a police officer puts such an ill-intended individual in daily contact with a large number and myriad variety of community dwellers as potential unwilling victims of exploitation and abuse. Probably, inherently nonviolent officers will display less aggressive misbehaviors, while inherently more impulsive or bellicose officers may be the ones who are especially force-prone, including acts of deadly force. Remember, however, that in all this, we're still talking about the exceptions: most police use-of-force scenarios, including deadly force, are justified and carried out by officers as a last resort to preserve life.

Can we screen out bad cops? Yes and no. Pre-employment background checks and psychological evaluations constitute a coarse net that can snag major historical red flags (prior arrests, drug use) and gross psychopathology (severe psychotic, mood, or personality disorders), but many officers' more subtle mental wobbles, and the resultant bad behaviors, only emerge later in their careers, as the combined result of innate psychology, patrol environment, and the policies and practices of their law enforcement agency. From an administrative perspective, it is the last of these variables that we can exert the most control over. Police leaders can't rewire their officers' brains or change the demographics of their patrol communities, but they can commit themselves to the goal of competent, ethical policing, and reinforce those goals through their own daily statements and actions.

Part II

DEADLY FORCE: BRAIN AND BEHAVIOR

Chapter 4

DEADLY FORCE COGNITION I: PERCEPTION

If the human brain were so simple that we could understand it, we would be so simple that we couldn't.

Emerson M. Pugh

So now it happens: an officer is suddenly faced with a deadly threat and has to act immediately. What actually goes through the minds of police officers during an officer-involved shooting or other deadly force encounter? What would go through your mind?

Typically, from the moment the 911 call is received or the officer rolls up on a potentially dangerous scene, that officer's internal threat radar snaps into high gear. Some use of force encounters escalate gradually, while others erupt explosively, but most officers can clearly recall the instant–that "oh-shit moment"–when they realized this is life or death, and they must make the decision whether or not to draw their weapon and fire at another human being.

Under emergency conditions, the brain does extraordinary things to allow its owner to escape danger and survive. But officers in a deadly force encounter must do more than survive and, under most circumstances, their job descriptions don't give them the luxury of fleeing. We admire firefighters who rush into a burning building while everyone else is racing away, because we know that these responders risk their lives to do the dangerous but necessary job of containing the blaze and protecting people and their property. In the same way, when faced with a deadly force scenario, a police officer's responsibility is to face the danger, move in, control the scene, and preserve life.

But the firefighter's unambiguous enemy is the blaze itself and no one takes sides with the fire. Firefighters are not likely to undergo questioning about whether they gave the flame a chance to surrender before turning on the hose. They will probably not be asked whether a less forceful approach could have been used, say, deploying just foam instead of a high-speed water jet. And they will rarely be accused of singling out a particular fire for extra-aggressive quenching because of the color of its glow or the neighborhood of the burning house. You will be hard-pressed to find any "conflagration abuse" civil lawsuits on the legal books. Firefighters may have to risk their own lives in battling a fire, but they don't have to hurt or kill other people—on the contrary, because many firefighters are also trained as paramedics, theirs is an explicitly life-*saving* orientation. That's why, in many of the same communities where police are reviled, firefighter-paramedics are almost always welcomed, or at least tolerated.

Thus, while both police and fire-rescue personnel must act skillfully within the standards of their professions, a police officer has the added burden of making sure he acts lawfully, ethically, and defensively, because to save a human life, that officer may well have to take a life, and be able to explain why later. Now imagine having all this swirling around in your head as somebody points a weapon in your direction, and you instantaneously have to decide what to do. It is for this reason that OIS/DFE scenarios are among the most stressful and dangerous circumstances in civilian public safety work.

This chapter and the next one describe how the human brain perceives and responds to critical emergencies, while chapter 6 discusses how memory works in processing, storing, and recalling details of the traumatic event. Naturally, in the response to any emergency scenario, perception, cognition, action, and memory all interact and mutually influence one another in a reciprocal, moment-to-moment relationship, but for the sake of chapter readability and intellectual digestibility, Chapters 4, 5, and 6 will discuss these topics individually. Keep in mind, however, that because the brain operates as an integrated whole, some overlap in chapter subject matter is inevitable.

THE BRAIN'S EMERGENCY RESPONSE SYSTEM

Neuropsychological research has taught us that, during an acute emergency of any type, a number of systems in the brain and body mobilize to deal with the threat to life (Anderson et al., 2003; Armony & LeDoux, 2000; Bremner, 2006; Charney et al., 1993; Frewin & Lanius, 2006; Gazzaniga et al., 2018; Kandel, 2012; Kolb, 1987; Lambert & Kinsley, 2011; LeDoux, 1996, 2000; Lobo et al., 2011; Ohman, 2005; Ohman & Mineka, 2001; Ross & Murphy, 2018; Ross et al., 2012; Sapolsky, 1996; Sharps, 2010; Weyandt, 2019; Yehuda, 1998, 2002). These will be summarized here and expanded in the sections and chapters to follow (Table 4.1; Figures 4.1, and 4.2).

Initially, the threat is perceived by the senses (vision, hearing, etc.) and

Table 4.1
THE BRAIN'S EMERGENCY RESPONSE SYSTEMS

Perception: Visual, auditory, and other sensory pathways from the sense organs, through the brainstem and thalamus to perceptual processing areas in the cerebral cortex. Reticular formation–selects, attends, and guides perceptual information.

Thinking: Temporal lobes–access to memory stores of skills, knowledge, and accumulated practical wisdom. Frontal lobes–evaluation, integration, conceptualization, planning, goal-directed activity and behavioral flexibility.

Emotion: Limbic system, includes the following: Amygdala–assesses survival value of experiences and situations, "how important." Hippocampus–formats experiences for memory consolidation, based on their significance for survival.

Alarm System 1: Locus coeruleus-norepinephrine system–fast alarm system for jolting the organism into action ("adrenalin dump").

Alarm System 2: Hypothalamic-pituitary-adrenal (HPA) axis–stimulates the secretion of the hormone cortisol which has energy-enhancing and anti-inflammatory effects.

Action: Frontal cortex–planning and decision making. Motor cortex–programming actions. Spinal motoneurons–communicating with muscles to execute movements. Cerebellum–coordination and fine-tuning of rapid, complex actions and course corrections. Basal ganglia–stabilizing and postural movements, motivation for action.

this sensory information is routed to a brain structure called the **amygdala**, which instantaneously assesses the threat to survival posed by the event. If there is time to make a complex assessment, the **frontal** and **temporal lobes** of the cerebral cortex access the person's stored neural data bank of memories, experiences, and cumulative expertise. The brain then surveys the current situation and attempts to integrate the present perceptual input with the stored knowledge to formulate an effective plan of action. But many acute threats do not allow this luxury of time; the responder has to act immediately, so in these cases, the amygdala's message temporarily bypasses higher cortical processing and communicates directly with the behavioral programs of the **basal ganglia**, **cerebellum**, and **motor cortex** ("motor memory") that rely on both innate instinct and well-practiced training to generate an immediate response that will enhance the probability of survival.

To maximize the brain's efficiency of responding, a neural network called the **reticular formation** selectively channels sensory and perceptual attention to only those aspects of the rapidly unfolding scenario that require moment-to-moment action, and restricts focus on extraneous environmental stimuli that are of no immediate survival value. The brain structure that normally processes incoming sensory data for later memory storage, the **hippocampus**, may temporarily be placed on emergency standby mode, so

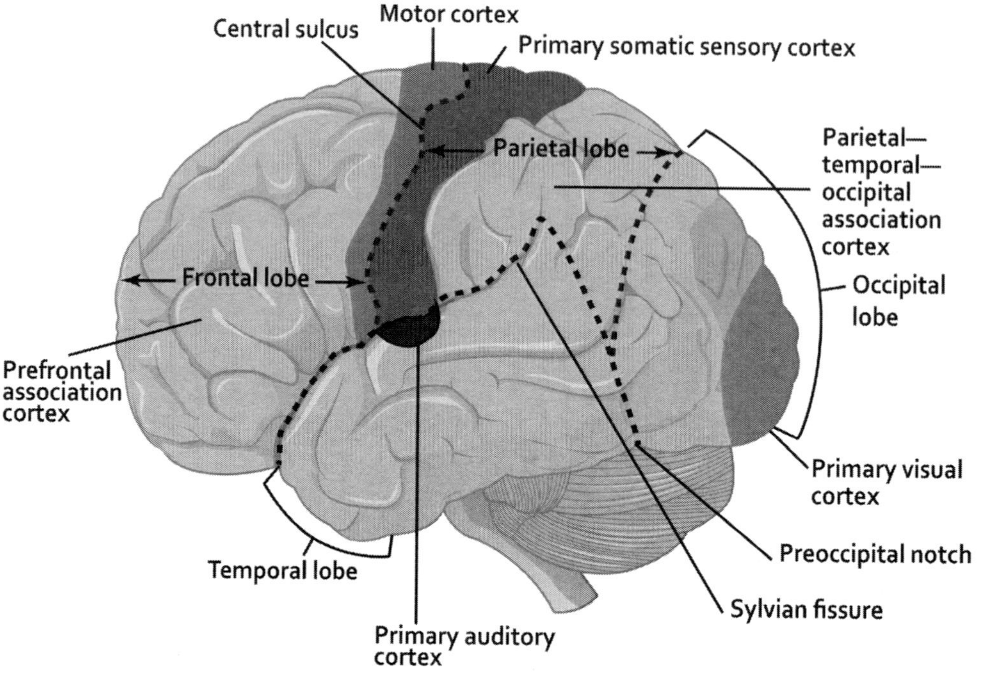

Figure 4.1. Perceptual and Response Systems of the Brain.

that encoding and remembering the ongoing events take a back seat to focusing all mental energies on surviving the encounter; that is, if the person does not live through the experience, there is little point in forming a memory of it.

At the same time, the person's reaction is not just perceptual and cognitive, but highly emotional as well, as the amygdala alerts another deep brain structure, the **locus coeruleus**, to secrete **norepinephrine**, a chemical cousin of **adrenalin**. This puts the entire brain and body into a physiologically hyper-aroused emergency state, aided by the release of large amounts of actual adrenalin from the adrenal medulla above the kidneys. Meanwhile, the **hypothalamic-pituitary axis (HPA)** energizes the hormonal system to stimulate the secretion of **cortisol** from the **adrenal cortex**, which has anti-inflammatory and energy-enhancing effects throughout the body and also acts on the hippocampus to suppress memory formation (Figure 6.2 in Chapter 6).

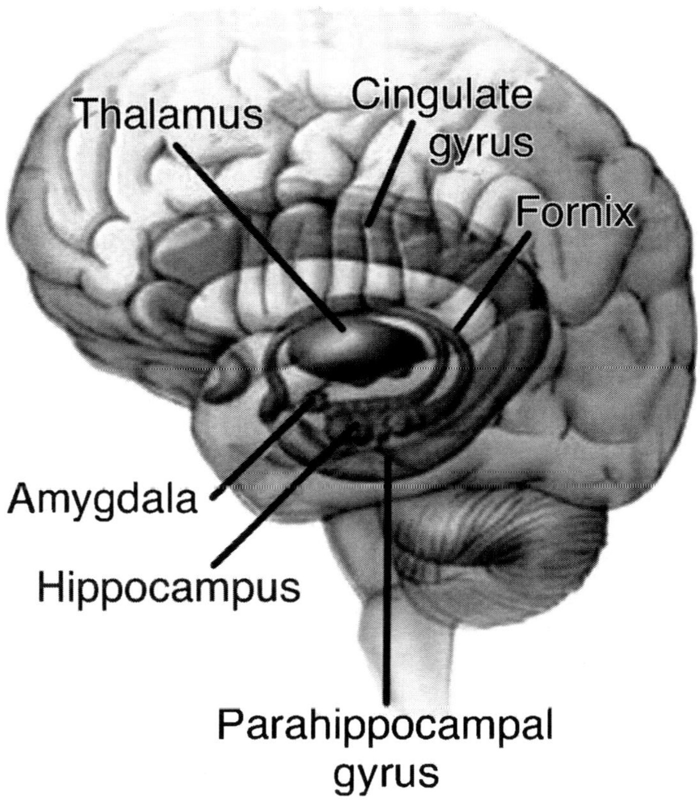

Figure 4.2. The Limbic System.

PERCEPTUAL, COGNITIVE, AND BEHAVIORAL DISTORTIONS DURING AN OIS/DFE

All of the above neurophysiological response mechanisms occur in life-threatening emergencies on a millisecond (thousandth of a second) to millisecond basis, enabling the person to mobilize the fight-or-flight response in order to survive. But, as we've discussed, law enforcement officers in a deadly force encounter must do more than just fight, flee, and survive. An officer's sworn responsibility is to control the scene, preserve life, and furthermore, to act safely, rationally, and lawfully in doing so—all in the moments where he or she could be instantly killed. Consequently, many officers who have been involved in a deadly force shooting episode have described one or more alterations in perception, thinking, and behavior that occurred during the event (Table 4.2). These responses may be interpreted as natural adaptive defensive reactions of a nervous system that is conserving energy

Table 4.2.
PERCEPTUAL, COGNITIVE & BEHAVIORAL PHENOMENA DURING AN OIS/DFE

(↑) = more common, (↓) = less common

Time: Time perception slows down (↑); time perception speeds up (↓).

Vision: Visual hyperfocus ("tunnel vision") (↑); reduced peripheral visual acuity or focus (↑); overall diminished visual acuity or focus (↓).

Audition: Auditory volume attenuation (↑); auditory volume enhancement (↓)

Perception: Threat magnification or misidentification (exact frequency unknown).

Action: Response automaticity ("autopilot") (↑); freezing-immobilization (↓).

Dissociation: Feelings of unreality (exact frequency unknown).

Stress: Relatively calm during event, significant stress reaction following event (↑); significant stress reaction during event (↓).

Memory: Diminished or distorted memory for some portions of event (↑); enhanced memory for other portions of event (↑); complete recall or complete amnesia for all or most of the event (↓).

Note: several of these phenomena may be experienced simultaneously or sequentially by an officer during the course of an OIS/DFE.

and allocating resources under extreme cognitive and emotional demand (Addis & Stephens, 2008; Artwohl, 2002, 2003, 2018; Artwohl & Christensen, 1997, 2019; Bohrer, 2005; Fyfe, 1986, 1988; Geller, 1982; Geller & Scott, 1992; Honig & Roland, 1998; Honig & Sultan, 2004; Klinger, 2001, 2006; Klinger & Bruson, 2009; Lewinski, 2008; Miller, 2005a, 2006a, 2006e, 2013b, 2015a, 2017, 2019b; Loughlin & Flora, 2017; Remsberg, 2008; Ross et al., 2012; Ryan, 2013).

TIME

The most common perceptual alteration during an OIS/DFE critical incident is a distortion in time perception. Paradoxically, this can assume two, seemingly opposite, patterns. Many officers recall isolated events of a shooting episode as occurring in slow motion ("the guy's gun hand just seemed to float up towards me"). At the same time, the whole episode, from start to finish, may seem to have lasted for a much briefer time period than it actually did ("they said it took ten minutes, but it seemed like just a few seconds to me").

In another expression of this phenomenon, officers will describe a surreal sense of perceptual time expansion, as in being able to see the rounds emerge from their gun and strike the suspect, causing the suspect's clothing to dart and twist with each impact. This perceptual time dilation effect is frequently correlated with visual hyperfocus, or "tunnel vision," described below. In potentially life-threatening situations, it is obviously adaptive for your brain to allow you to zero in on a threat in exquisite moment-to-moment detail, and with as few distractions as possible. There is also the possibility that officers may be unconsciously conflating their memories of the event with their re-evocation of slow-motion movie images of darting and dancing clothing in response to cinematic gunshot impacts.

ATTENTION, CONCENTRATION, AND PERCEPTION

Attention is what allows you to focus on a situation or task so that sensory input can proceed in a consistent and meaningful pattern. **Concentration** is the ability to consciously and purposefully keep several items in mind at once and direct and maintain your attention to a particular object, goal, or activity over time. As will be discussed later, this capacity is also sometimes subsumed under the rubric of **working memory**. By concentrating, you make an effort to avoid distractions that could disrupt your performance. At the same time, it is important to be able to switch attention to another object or situation when necessary, and even maintain different types, levels, and targets of attention and concentration as needed at any given time, either sequentially or simultaneously. A third term, **awareness**, refers to the sum total of moment-to-moment information about your current surroundings afforded by attention, concentration, perception, and access to background knowledge.

Effortful concentration, especially if prolonged, requires a great deal of mental energy and can be fatiguing (Baumeister, 2002, 2014). Accordingly, it is important to be able to produce a match between the often-changing demands of a critical situation and the precise level and direction of attention and concentration needed on a moment-to-moment basis; you don't want to squander attention by trying to focus on too many things at once. Some officers and emergency personnel modulate attention and concentration automatically and instinctively. For most, like any other critical skill, it requires some degree of training and practice (Miller, 2008d, 2008i).

Attention and the Brain

Control of attention and concentration is vital to the accurate perception of a threat and to carrying out the most adaptive behavioral response to it. As noted earlier, the **reticular formation** consists of a complex meshwork of neurons and fibers that connect the basic sensory modalities (vision, hearing, touch, pain, smell, taste, temperature, balance, and others) with the arousal, emotional, motivational, and thinking centers of the brain. In this way, what we experience through our senses is automatically coordinated with the proper perception of, and response to, the rapidly changing environment around us. Individuals who have suffered significant damage to the reticular formation may have eyes and ears that work fine, but the perceptions they take in have no significance to them; they are essentially unresponsive, even though the primary sensory pathways are intact. Thus, they may appear unaware of, or unengaged with, their surroundings, but they are not sleeping or in a coma–they don't respond because the sensory information that enters their nervous system "just doesn't register."

The closest any of us gets to this state in normal life is when we fail to hear someone right next to us talking in our ear because we're so focused on a second person's conversation, riveted by a TV show, engrossed in a social media interaction, or internally preoccupied with a troubling thought. An observer might say we're "distracted" or that our "mind is elsewhere." In fact, it may take an unexpected stimulus, such as a jabbing finger or a loud "helloooo . . ." to refocus our attention on the person trying to capture it. But our *ability* to focus attention is still intact, no matter where it may be directed at the moment. The neuropsychological bottom line is that we have a limited ability to focus attention on more than a few things at a time, whether on ourselves or in the environment. This ability becomes even more constricted in an emergency scenario.

Dimenstions of Attention

A number of authorities (Asken, 1993; Cohen, 2013; Doss, 2007; Hardy et al., 1996; Hays & Brown, 2004; Miller, 2008i; Nideffer, 1985; Nideffer & Sharpe, 1978; Ward, 2004) have conceptualized the faculty of attention as lying along two interrelated dimensions: breadth of focus and direction of focus.

Breadth of focus describes how narrow or wide the beam of attention is. When first encountering an unknown scene, officers typically don't want to overlook something important, so they set the attentional scan relatively wide to take in as much information as possible, much like using the wide angle lens setting of a surveillance camera. But if something critical is identified, then the focus narrows, like looking through a rifle scope, to concentrate on the target and eliminate peripheral distractions. Now, all of the officer's attention is trained on the task at hand, at the calculated expense of losing ambient perceptual input.

In other words, in a DFE, the officer's brain is deliberately inducing tunnel vision, because that's what's needed right now for the specific task of acquiring a dangerous target and neutralizing it. In fact, many critical situations require a person to flexibly shift concentration from broad to narrow and back again, or even to maintain a kind of divided consciousness, intently focusing on a particular subject of interest while simultaneously keeping a portion of the attentional beam in a scanning mode so as not to overlook existing or emerging threats.

Another attentional dimension is **direction of focus**, which can be internal or external. **External focus** is the most obvious, as it is important to be able to maintain awareness of the events taking place around you during a critical situation. But it may be just as important to maintain **internal focus** on what is taking place mentally and physically within your own mind and body during the critical incident. This includes your own arousal level, physiological functioning, balance, energy reserves, fear and anxiety, presence or threat of injury, or basic requirements like need for air, or, in prolonged crises, taking a meal or bathroom break. In fact, individuals who are especially high in the ability to scan their internal states, called **interoception**, show superior performance in a variety of functions and tasks, including decision making, memory, and empathic responding (Chua & Bliss-Moreau, 2016; Ernst et al., 2013; Kandasamy et al., 2016; Werner et al., 2009). Again, flexibility is the key, and during a critical incident, attention should monitor back and forth between internal and external, coordinating thought, feeling, and arousal with optimum task performance.

Attention and Perception in Critical DFE Scenarios

Consistent with the role of the brain's reticular formation in guiding perception to survival-relevent stimuli, and the cerebral cortex's role in making sense of the incoming information, sensory and perceptual distortions are frequently noted during DFEs. Most common is **visual hyperfocus**, or **tunnel vision**, in which the officer sharply tunes in to one particular aspect of the visual field, typically the suspect's gun or weapon (**weapon focus**), while blocking out almost everything in the periphery, including, sometimes, the perpetrator's face, his clothing, his race, the surrounding environment, or the actions of other officers or civilians at the scene. One research report (Ross et al., 2012) cites as much as a 70 perception reduction in peripheral vision during these critical incidents.

Similarly, **auditory exclusion**, or "**tunnel hearing**," may occur when the officer's attention is tuned exclusively to a particular set of sounds, most commonly the suspect's voice, while background noises are muted or excluded. Sounds in general commonly seem muffled and, in some cases, officers report not hearing their own or other officers' gunshots, or hearing them as faint pops. On the other hand, some sounds may seem magnified: this usually happens with voices or firearms sounds, but one officer recalled that "I could hear the guy's blood drip" (Ret. FDLE Agent James D. Sewell, personal communication). Of course, as noted earlier, in such unusual cases, one must try to distinguish enhanced perception from imagined perception or from distorted recall of the event, which we will discuss in Chapter 6.

In a sense, all perception is tunnel perception because nobody can be aware of everything at once, and true divided consciousness or simultaneous multitasking does not exist. In situations where we must deal with more than one challenge at a time, what we actually do is rapidly and sequentially allocate our attention from one task to another and back again. But, in doing so, we may lose data or proficiency in one or both tasks in the process—just try to follow two conversations at the same time and see what happens, or try to keep reading this page while someone is talking to you.

And even with no major interruptions, while you're reading this very page, you probably didn't notice the items on your desk or the background hum of your air conditioner, because your reticular formation is directing your vision and cognition to the material in this text. Under normal circumstances, we call this **selective attention**. What happens in a life-and-death emergency is similar, only the selection of what gets attended to is more concentrated and extreme (Lewinski, 2008; Lewinski & Redmond, 2009; Mack, 2003; Niedenthal & Kitayama, 1994; Sharps, 2010; Shornstein & Yantis, 2004; Simons, 2000; Vickers, 2007).

Lewinski & Redmond (2009) provide a practical example of this in a high-stress OIS/DFE scenario. An officer who is perceptually and cognitively preoccupied with the technical aspects of getting a clear line of sight so he can direct his fire on target will likely zero in on the relationship between his front firearm barrel sight and the target, thereby perceptually tuning out just about everything else going on around him—including, perhaps, the target's own actions, such as gesturing, turning, running, yelling, and so on. Upon later review of the entirety of the scene, it may be "obvious" to post-hoc third party observers that the target was holding a cell phone, not a gun, or that he was turning away from the officer or already on the ground, when he was shot, or that fellow officers were shouting, "he's down, he's down!" from the shooting officer's left side. The officer's focusing on the suspect's weapon or other perceived threat may also siphon off attention to, perception of, and later recall of, such additional "obvious" features as the subject's clothing, body type, or facial features (Sharps, 2010).

The vast majority of firearm crimes in the United States are committed with handguns; however, long guns, i.e., rifles, many with large magazine capacities and semiautomatic capability for rapid firing, are increasingly employed by perpetrators of gun violence (Herrera et al., 2015), especially in mass shooting incidents (Flannery, 1995; Langman, 2009; Miller, 2007e, 2008g, 2012; Schouten, 2006). With heightened danger in such scenarios comes a heightened probability for perceptual mistakes. To take just one example (cited in Herrera et al., 2015), in 2013, in Santa Rosa, California, a 13-year-old boy, wielding a pellet-gun replica of an AK-47 assault rifle, was shot and killed by sheriff's deputies, who claimed that they perceived the object to be a lethal firearm. Public outcry against the police was intense, probably related in no small part to the young age of the decedent, but also in part because the police "should have known" that the gun was only a pellet gun (as if such weapons cannot be dangerous in themselves). In fact, the pellet gun in question was specifically designed to look as much as possible like a real AK-47. The boy, whose age may not have been obvious to the deputies at the time, wielded the weapon like a real rifle, refused repeated orders to drop it, and raised it in the direction of the deputies before he was shot.

To study these perceptual phenomena systematically, Herrera et al. (2015) showed volunteers photographs of a realistic crime scene in which a male assailant aimed a long gun at an innocent victim. One of three weapons was depicted for each participant: (1) a bolt-action rifle, (2) a lever-action rifle, or (3) a BB gun. The researchers employed a **shoot/don't shoot (S/DS)** paradigm (discussed more fully in Chapter 5), in which subjects are presented with a visual depiction of a potentially dangerous or potentially harmless person, object, or situation, and must make the rapid decision to "shoot" or not, most commonly in the form of pressing one button on a console for shooting, and another for not shooting.

In the present study, subjects were asked to make a timed S/DS decision about the weapon scenario, based on their assessment of deadly threat to the portrayed victim. They were then asked to identify which type of weapon they had seen, and to describe as many of its features as they could. Subjects correctly identified the bolt-action rifle more frequently than the lever-action rifle, and both rifles were more often correctly identified than the BB gun. Nevertheless, the same number of participants made the rapid decision to "shoot" at the subjects holding the bolt-action rifle, lever-action rifle, and BB gun, and there was no difference in the amount of time each participant took to take that action, despite later being clearly able to distinguish the weapons.

That is, accurate identification in hindsight was unrelated to these subjects' response to the immediate threat.

Other research (Sharps et al., 2007) has shown that the weapons encountered in simulated S/DS scenarios don't even have to be weapons. Subjects were shown video depictions of officers responding to a "must-shoot" situation, in which the officer felt compelled to fire at an armed assailant in order to save the life of a potential victim. Approximately 80 percent of subjects concurred with the officer's decision to shoot an assailant depicted as wielding a handgun. However, almost as many subjects supported the officer's firing when the assailant was holding a power screwdriver that the study subjects mistook for a handgun. That is, in this study, the average person, under conditions of optimal lighting and unobstructed viewing conditions, could not tell a 9mm Beretta handgun from a power screwdriver, even when the tool had a clearly visible screwdriver bit and orange bit-collar, and with the word "Craftsman" embossed on the side in large silver letters.

Of course, in real-world circumstances, officers are expected to make near-instantaneous distinctions between objects of varying lethality, including telling the difference between a real gun and a toy one. These split-second perceptual judgments are typically made under rapidly evolving tactical conditions and where perception of the weapon or object may be obscured by poor lighting, the suspect's body position, or other environmental features (Aveni et al., 2003; Sharps, 2010; Sharps et al., 2007).

As discussed in Chapter 1, aggressive citizens have been known to deploy an impressive variety of both common and unusual objects against law enforcement officers, sometimes positioning these objects as if they were firearms. Just a few examples include pellet guns, dart guns, nail guns, power drills, other power tools, plastic toy guns, toy rockets, garden hose spray nozzles, and footwear (Sharps, 2010). Thus, in understanding the dynamics of a given deadly force encounter, it is important to distinguish whether an officer's decision to shoot is based on a *mis*perception of a common implement as a firearm or on the *correct* perception that even a deceptively benign object like a power drill, hand-held screwdriver, kitchen knife, barbeque fork, or hammer can be deployed to deadly effect in hostile hands.

However, most citizens mistakenly shot by police are not wielding power tools or toy weapon facsimiles; often the misinterpreted "weapon" turns out to be a genuinely harmless object like a wallet or cell phone, in which case the seeming senselessness or callousness of the shooting is highlighted in the public's mind; two examples of wallet-for-gun misidentification are the cases of Amadou Diallo in New York in1999, and Michael Davidson in Alabama in 2014. S/DS research with police officers has generally shown that the ability to make correct discriminations between weapons and harmless objects improves with greater skill, training, and experience of officers (Johnson et al., 2014; Suss & Ward, 2012; Tashman et al., 2006; Vickers & Lewinski, 2012; Ward et al., 2007, 2011), and that, in simulation studies, untrained civilians are better able to discriminate weapons from nonweapons when the objects are drawn from the front than from the back and when less of the object is concealed (Suss & Raushel, 2019). In addition, as discussed in Chapter 2, a myriad of situational factors, from reduced ambient illumination to the encounter occurring after a spirited chase, can heighten the perceived threat of a nonweapon object.

RELATIONSHIPS AMONG ATTENTIONAL, PERCEPTUAL, AND COGNITIVE PHENOMENA IN DEADLY FORCE ENCOUNTERS

As noted in Chapter 1, the U.S. Supreme Court in *Graham v. Connor* (1989) held that determinations about the constitutional justifiability of police use of force—deadly or not—must be "judged from the perspective of a reasonable officer on the scene, rather than with the 20/20 vision of hindsight." Much of the narrative and empirical research reviewed thus far has identified a range of perceptual and cognitive phenomena that can influence an officer's response to a deadly force encounter. These reactions—tunnel vision, sound attenuation, etc.—are typically described as isolated phenomena, yet in the real world of OIS/DFEs, these reactions are likely to occur together in various combinations that will be determined by multiple individual factors, including the officer's specific neuropsychological reaction pattern, the behavior of the suspect, and the actions of others at the scene. Still, it would be valuable to determine whether common, normative interactive patterns of psychological response to DFEs and other emergencies could be discerned and could be of practical utility for individual case analysis and reconstruction, as well as for training purposes.

One approach to this integrative analysis of deadly force psychology has been undertaken by Klinger and Brunson (2009), who analyzed the detailed narrative accounts of 80 police officers' recollections of what they experienced during a total of 113 incidents in which they shot citizens. The researchers examined not just the individual interaction patterns of cognition and perception phenomena during the shootings, but also took account of how different patterns of mental phenomena might unfold over the time frame of a shooting scenario, from priming and preparation for the encounter, to the deadly force encounter itself, to post-shooting recall of the events. The general finding was that officers often experience multiple perceptual alterations during a single OIS/DFE incident.

The most common perceptual distortion during a DFE was sound attenuation, which was reported in 82 percent of cases. Consistent with previous research, a significantly smaller number of officers, 20 percent, reported that some sounds seemed excessively loud. Tunnel vision was reported in 51 percent of cases, and having a heightened sense of visual detail was noted in 56 percent. Again, largely consistent with prior research and anecdotal reports, significantly more officers experienced events occurring in slow motion (56%) than speeded up (23%).

The researchers also examined changes in various modalities of cognition and perception across the time frame of the DFE, which revealed that cognitive and perceptual alterations may shift over the course of the event, illustrating how unique and individualized each officer's reaction can be. For example, some officers experienced a perceptual change, such as tunnel vision, occurring prior to firing, which then ceased once firing had begun, while other officers experienced the opposite, i.e., tunnel vision beginning upon firing.

Changes in time perception appeared to be relatively stable across the DFE event span. Nevertheless, for those officers who experienced normal time perception until they began to fire (12), twice as many experienced a shift to slow-motion (8) than to fast-motion (4) once they had fired their weapon. For those officers whose experience of slow-motion began prior to initiating fire (17), time returned to normal in 9 of them, moved to fast-motion in 7, and one officer perceived time both slowing down and speeding up in the post-shooting time period. For officers who experienced fast motion prior to firing (6), post-firing time perception moved to slow motion in five of them, and was experienced as both slow and fast in the one remaining case.

Distortions in visual perception were only slightly less stable than those for time perception. Officers experienced normal visual perception throughout the shooting scenario in 20 cases, tunnel vision both prior to and during firing in 22 cases, heightened visual acuity both prior to and during firing in 28 cases, and both tunnel vision and a heightened acuity at both points in time in 6 cases. Most intriguing was the sheer diversity of individualized changes in perception over time from pre-shooting to during shooting. These included shifts from normal vision to tunnel vision; normal vision to heightened visual acuity; either tunnel vision or enhanced acuity back to normal vision; tunnel vision to heightened acuity; tunnel vision to heighted acuity added to the initial tunnel vision; heightened acuity to normal vision; heightened acuity to tunnel vision; both tunnel vision and heightened acuity to heightened acuity only; both tunnel vision and heightened acuity to normal vision. Read this again if you have to, but you get the idea about the impressive range of perceptual phenomena experienced by officers during an OIS/DFE.

As noted earlier, accounts of extraordinarily enhanced perception in any modality need to be interpreted with caution because it cannot be ascertained if what subjects are retrospectively reporting reflect their actual perception at the time of the event or their recollective reconstruction of the experience, perhaps subliminally influenced by other officers' accounts, confabulatory jumbling of events, or even by intrusion of images from TV and movies. For example, Klinger and Brunson (2009) describe the case of two SWAT officers who fired at a murder suspect who had pointed a handgun at them, and later both reported that they saw some of their rounds strike the suspect, causing "his shirt to pop up off his body" with each successive bullet impact.

While this may well be an accurate recollection, and has been reported by other officers during OIS/DFE incidents, the resemblance to Hollywood stylized depictions of fluttering clothing recoiling in slow motion from bullet impacts was pointed out earlier. But, while this may represent a form of unconscious retrospective confabulatory recall, it may also reflect the enhanced time dilation effects that are known to occur during such a life-and-death emergency.

In Klinger and Brunson's (2009) study, the least stability across time frames seemed to occur for auditory perceptions. The most common change was a shift from normal hearing pre-firing to auditory attenuation during firing, in most cases involving muffled perception of the officers' own gunshots. Even the volume and quality of the sound perception varied across individual officers, some describing their own gunshots as like a toy "cap gun," others reporting a normal gunshot sound, except at a significantly lower volume. Still others heard no shots at all.

Again, these perceptual attenuations and distortions can be idiosyncratically selective, as in the case reported by the authors of another SWAT officer who failed to hear the burst of rounds from the automatic machine gun he was firing, yet clearly perceived the click-clack of the weapon's slide ejecting spent casings and delivering fresh rounds to the breech. A third SWAT marksman expressed confusion as to why his rounds did not sound as "deafening" as they should have. In my own post-shooting interviews with officers, a number of them have reported that they either did not hear their own or other officers' gunshots, or experienced them as greatly muffled, yet after the episode was over, their ears were ringing, suggesting that, during a critical emergency, the cerebral cortex may be actively suppressing conscious awareness of distracting auditory and other sensory stimuli.

Another indicator of response individuality and multiplicity in this study was the finding that, while no officer experienced all six possible permutations of visual, auditory, and temporal alterations either prior to or during shooting, most officers did experience several distortions at each time point. Prior to firing, officers reported experiencing at least two distortions in 66 percent of shootings, three or more in 36 percent, and four in 5 percent of the cases, which translates to a mean of 1.95 perceptual distortions per shooting in the pre-firing period. During firing, the mean number of distortions was even greater, at 2.65, with officers reporting at least two distortions in 75 percent of cases, three or more in 56 percent, and four or more in 9 percent of cases. Further, most of these multiple distortions were not just variations of the same modality, e.g., heightening or lowering of visual acuity or time perception, but represented distortions in separate modalities, for example, auditory attenuation plus tunnel vision plus shortened time perception.

Finally, Klinger and Brunson's (2009) research shows that the association of perceptual anomalies is not random, and that certain combinations are more likely than others. The strongest positive correlations (although not particularly high from a statistical standpoint) were between the pre-firing and during-firing measures of distortions in the same perceptual modality, which were, in descending order, for heightened visual detail, tunnel vision, slow motion, and fast motion.

Across different perceptual modalities, it thus appears that perceptual changes typically occur in the same direction, i.e., higher or lower. For example, when officers experience fast motion prior to firing, they are more likely to experience auditory amplification, both prior to and while firing. Similarly, officers who experience fast motion while firing are somewhat more likely to perceive an intensification of sound, both prior to and while firing. Conversely, when officers experience auditory attenuation prior to firing, they are more likely to experience slow motion, both prior to and while firing. Other correlations include: tunnel vision with reduced sound while firing, slow motion with auditory attenuation prior to firing, and fast motion prior to firing with intensified sound while firing.

Certain perceptual anomalies are less likely to occur in the presence of others, usually involving changes that have opposite valences. For example, increased and reduced auditory acuity prior to firing, slow and fast motion prior to firing, tunnel vision and increased visual acuity prior to firing, and tunnel vision with increased visual acuity while firing are all less likely to occur together.

Thus, the overall results of Klinger and Brunson's (2009) study indicate that, under life-threatening conditions, the human nervous system characteristically tunes its perceptual states across different modalities in the same general direction, toward either amplification and enhancement or diminution and restriction. In an OIS/DFE scenario, this means that slow motion prior to firing, slow motion while firing, and diminished sound prior to firing all tend to go together, as do fast-motion prior to and during firing and sound amplification prior to and during firing–but not always.

A question for further research concerns what kind of situational and individual factors determine these perceptual variations. That is, do different types of officers, in terms of cognition, temperament, personality, and/or experience, show differing reaction patterns during emergencies, or are the response patterns revealed in this study more universal across personality types, but perhaps vary by type of critical incident? What are the implications for assessing reasonableness of deadly force in these mercurial scenarios (Engel & Smith, 2009)? Also, while Klinger and Brunson's (2009) research explains the relationship among different types of perceptual and cognitive distortions under the critical stress of a DFE, there is one more factor to consider: how much stress? That is, does perceived intensity of stress make a difference in whether such perceptual phenomena occur, and if so, to what extent and in what combinations?

With regard to the latter question, using police officer subjects in virtual simulator scenarios, Ross and colleagues (2012) measured the officers' stress response subjectively through self-report, as well as objectively via salivary cortisol assays, and discovered a dose-response relationship between perceived level of stress and perceptual distortions. That is, perceptual accuracy decreased as both the frequency and intensity of the stressors increased. Combined with Klinger and Brunson's (2009) research, this suggests that, in any complex real-life DFE, explaining a given officer's experience and response must take into account the effects of type, number, frequency, and intensity of extant stressors on the type, number, interaction, and severity of perceptual and cognitive distortions, giving the analysis of such cases another whole dimension. We will return to stress effects later.

DISSOCIATION AND AUTOMATIC RESPONDING

Dissociation refers to a mental state where one's self or the surrounding environment is experienced as unreal or dreamlike. Some form of perceptual dissociation is reported fairly commonly by people who have survived an extreme emergency such as a natural disaster, vehicle crash, or sexual assault (Miller, 1994a, 1998b, 2015f), and a similar phenomenon may occur with police officers during a critical DFE (Miller, 2000, 2006e, 2013b, 2015d, 2019b). In rare instances, officers have described feeling as though they were standing outside the scene, observing it "like it was happening to someone else."

An even more common perception is often described as "going on automatic," where the officer experiences himself responding to the emergency, but with a diminished sense of conscious volition or personal agency, "like it was happening by itself," or "my body just knew what to do," or sometimes, "my training must have kicked in because it didn't even feel like it took any effort." In my clinical interviews with officers, this is where I archly ask them to reflect on all the times they moaned about those "unnecessary" required training and qualification exercises. In fact, the automatized kicking-in of his or her training at this critical moment is precisely what allows the officer to carry out whatever actions are necessary to survive the encounter and control the situation without being overwhelmed.

Dimensions of Automaticity

Most of the officers I've interviewed describe the automaticity response as occurring in relatively normal consciousness; much less commonly, it may be accompanied by a dissociatively unreal state described as akin to dreaming or hypnosis. In still other instances, the officer perceives himself carrying out his actions with a sense of unnatural calm, an almost robotic detachment, while a smaller number of officers report that they felt nearly overwhelmed by adrenalized panic, but were somehow nevertheless able to hold back the fear and "do what I had to do." Artwohl (2002) states that a minority of officers report intrusive distracting thoughts during the incident, often involving loved ones or other personal matters, but, in my experience, these reflections are more likely to be reported if the critical incident had been inordinately prolonged in some way, as in extended hostage-barricade scenarios (Miller, 2005c).

The trauma literature indicates that, unlike dramatic Hollywood portrayals, prolonged, disabling psychological impairment syndromes are the exception rather than the rule for most individuals who have experienced almost any kind of traumatic event (Bowman, 1997; Everstine & Everstine, 2006; Miller, 2015f). Research shows that individuals vary to the extent that they show **peritraumatic dissociation**, that is, a dissociative response occurring at the time of the traumatic event itself. Experiencing such a reaction is correlated with the development of **acute stress disorder (ASD)** shortly following the incident, and more severe and persistent symptoms of **posttraumatic stress disorder (PTSD)** in the ensuing weeks, months, or years. The same appears to apply to police officers involved in OIS/DFE scenarios (Artwohl, 2002; Fagan et al., 2006; Klinger & Brunson, 2009; Marmar et al., 1998; Martell et al., 2002; Novy, 2012; Reiser & Geiger, 1984). Estimates of the rate of peritraumatic dissociation during OIS/DFEs range from 39 percent (Artwohl, 2002) to 90 percent (Martell et al., 2002). However, longstanding psychological disability from any single traumatic event is rare.

A sense of confusion and/or helplessness may transiently occur during the DFE, but this is probably underreported due to the potential stigma attached to the appearance of "folding under pressure." A very small proportion of officers report that they "froze" at some point during the event; however, in most of these cases, Artwohl (2002) conceptualizes this supposed fear-immobilization response as actually representing an adaptive **action-reaction gap** in which the officer intuitively hesitates from shooting until the suspect has clearly posed a threat, a controlled response which actually requires quick and flexible thinking and works in favor of a nonlethal outcome. A number of officers, especially those relatively new on the job, have stated that it took a moment for their police authority to kick in.

With regard to the perceived automaticity of behavior during a DFE, Lewinski (2008) cites G. Miller et al.'s (1960) observations on stored unconscious memory programs for most well-practiced neuromotor skills that enable a person to carry out well-learned tasks without the cognitive redundancy of conscious deliberation. This would account for an officer's ability to seamlessly access the behavioral programs necessary to perform a critical task in a high-threat situation to the point that it might seem "automatic." It would also explain why the officer might have trouble recalling the precise details of the event, since he or she was not paying conscious attention to the entire sequence of actions as they were carried out, any more than I'm paying conscious attention to any particular keystroke while I'm typing this page, or you pay conscious attention to any particular pedal press or wheel turn when you're driving.

As with all such well-practiced activities, we decide what we want to type or where we want our car to go, and our brains and bodies take over from there. Also, as will be discussed in chapter 6 on memory, this would account for why, following an OIS/DFE or other critical incident, officers are frequently unable to remember exactly what happened or what they did: they cannot recall these experiences and events because they were never really attended to and processed in the first place.

Automatic Responding and the Brain

Most commentators speak of dissociation and automatic responding as if it always represents an anomalous, even pathological, reaction pattern, in contrast to conscious, willfully directed action, which we like to think of as a direct product of our personal agency and sense of control. But what if automatic responding is a perfectly natural, evolutionarily adaptive neuromechanism that we share with many creatures, and that helps us get out of rapidly unfolding crises when hesitation and cogitation might prove fatal?

Ohman (2005) and colleagues (Morris et al., 1998, 1999, 2001; Ohman & Mineka, 2001; Ohman & Wiens, 2003; Ohman et al., 2000) have used **functional brain imaging** to study the cerebral systems involved in the human stress response that may be activated by frightening stimuli, even those the person remains consciously unaware of. The researchers presented subjects with visual stimuli of fearful objects (spiders, snakes) or fear-inducing human faces (angry, threatening), in either a conscious condition (subjects were able to remember and describe what they saw that made them afraid), or in a "masked" condition (images were manipulated so that subjects could not consciously perceive and describe them).

The results suggested that sensory information activates the fear response in the human amygdala under both conditions, but that this may take place by different routes (Anderson et al., 2003; Armony & LeDoux, 2000; LeDoux, 1996, 2000). In the conscious processing mode, visual pathways from the **retina** of the eye project to the **lateral geniculate nucleus** of the thalamus, to the **visual cortex** in the occipital lobe, and thence to the **insular cortex** in the inferior temporal lobe where conscious recognition takes place, and finally to the amygdala for emotional processing of that percept's emotional meaning. Meanwhile, other cortical structures than inhibit and modulate amygdalar responding, such as the **anterior cingulate cortex** and **orbitofrontal cortex**, exert a top-down control of emotional responding, so that the emotional reaction and the resulting behavioral response remain modulated and proportional to the situation.

However, in many extreme emotional states, a parallel, subcortical, "fast-track" visual pathway bypasses more complex but more time-consuming cortical processing by projecting from the retina to the **superior colliculi** in the brainstem, to the thalamic **pulvinar nucleus**, and thence straight to the amygdala for emotional recognition and response via motor systems (see Chapter 5). Conscious processing may catch up a few fractions of a second later, or the individual may have already begun to act and only then realize what, through a combination of instinct and learning, he was able to accomplish "without realizing it."

No, class, the neuroanatomy lesson will not be on the exam. But it is important to understand that the neural principle of simultaneous multilevel emotional-sensory-motor processing is ubiquitous throughout the nervous system and is responsible for the numerous adaptive things we do to keep ourselves safe. Here's one example that almost everyone is familiar with. You inadvertently touch a hot or sharp surface and reflexively jerk your hand away, only to feel the actual pain about a half-second later. What? How could you pull your hand away if you didn't yet "know" it was burning or bleeding? Because Mother Nature was smart enough to not leave it up to your bulbous cerebral cortex to stand there and slowly reason out what to do while your hapless appendange is cooking or exsanguinating.

Neurophysiologically, it takes about 500 milliseconds (half a second) for the multisynaptic sensory message to get from finger to spinal cord, to brainstem, to thalamus, to primary somatosensory cortex, to perceptual recognition cortex, and from there to the motor cortex, subcortical motor structures, brainstem, to spinal cord motoneurons, and finally to the muscles that retract your injured limb. But the withdrawal reflex that nonconsciously pulls your hand away has only to traverse the various spinal cord centers below the level of the brain itself. This involves far fewer synapses and takes far less time to save your pinkie (only about 50-100 msec). Meanwhile, the cortical processing centers catch up a half-second later to let you know you've been singed or sliced.

Back to shooting. Police officers who seem to "go on automatic" may not be zoning out or taking tactical shortcuts in responding to a life-threatening emergency; quite the opposite. Their training has assimilated itself into the automatic perception and response cycle, allowing them to act constructively without having to multisynaptically "think about it." Of course, the more unfamiliar, complex, and challenging the situation is, the more the officer may have to enlist higher cortical centers to develop and execute novel and innovative survival action patterns. That's why any response to a stressful, complex situation is likely to involve a combination of short-path and long-path brain processing.

This may explain the phenomenon of an officer reporting that he was "watching himself" carry out the necessary actions. The automatic aspects of the tactical response being adequately handled by the short neurobehavioral pathway frees up his cerebral cortex to scan about for additional information. A similar thing happens to skilled athletes or musicians who describe the sensation of "flow" in which their performance takes on a "life of its own" and they execute their skill with a feeling of effortless mastery and automaticity (Csikszentmihalyi, 1990; Hays & Brown, 2014). On a more prosaic level, the same thing happens when you "unconsciously" drive a familiar route while engaged in conversation with a passenger or cell phone; later, you are "amnesic" for all the little details of starting, stopping, slowing, and turning that made it possible for you to get home without thinking about it. Thus, for trained exponents of any skill, these flexible patterns become baked into the corpus of their overall expertise, to be accessed and utilized when needed.

RECOGNITION-PRIMED DECISION MAKING

The development of accurate and efficient responding as a goal of training is a topic that has a long history of study in cognitive psychology and neuroscience, especially examining how effective decision makers operate under conditions of stress, danger, and confusion. When time and urgency are less important, complex decisions can be made by a careful, logical, step-by-step process: first access all the relevant information, then weigh the evidence carefully, and finally come up with a balanced analysis of risks and benefits to guide the appropriate action. But in the real world of emergency crisis management, decision makers have to think and act quickly, and hesitation can be fatal. Decision making in such naturalistic critical settings is characterized by several important features.

First, the circumstances are typically ill-defined and the tasks poorly structured. When arriving on the scene of an unfolding crisis, or having one thrust upon you, it is rarely immediately clear what the correct action to take should be. Instead, important pieces of information may be missing, and what is available may be incomplete, ambiguous, or just wrong. This is what transpires in the first few moments of a natural disaster, transportation accident, criminal assault, or DFE, many of which seem to unfold quickly or erupt instantaneously.

Second, the conditions and requirements of the situation are usually not static, but typically shift from moment to moment, as the crisis continues to unfold and more data flood in or trickle down from diverse sources and at different rates. This requires the responder to make rapid adjustments and course corrections to changing circumstances in real-time, with perception and action reciprocally influencing one another in a moment-to-moment time frame.

Third, complicating perceptual input and response output are the high adrenalin and cortisol levels, and other physiological effects of stress inherent in emergency situations. The stakes are often life and death, and the time pressure is intense, as decisions must be arrived at, implemented, or changed at a moment's notice.

Converging sources of research data and practical experience have identified a process called **recognition-primed decision making (RPDM)**, which is concerned with rapid decision making in complex, naturalistic, real-time settings. RPDM has been studied in fields as diverse as emergency medicine, disaster response, sports performance, hostage negotiation, civil disturbance management, chess competition, and military operations (Flin, 1996; Hardy & Kroenig, 2016; Kienan & Friedland, 1996; Klein, 1989, 1993, 1996, 1998; Klein & Crandall, 1995; Klein et al., 1986; Orasanu & Backer, 1996; Orasanu & Connolly, 1993; Regehr & Bober, 2004; Ross et al., 2004; Spaulding, 2005).

The RPDM model recognizes that, in critical circumstances, expert decision makers are able to invoke a cognitive strategy that does not require the kind of algorithmic, trial-and error deduction that is typically taught in formal courses on logical reasoning and analysis. Instead, by virtue of having accumulated a comprehensive storehouse of knowledge through extensive training and experience, called **domain knowledge**, experts in any field come to rely on an almost instantaneous, holographic, at-a-glance kind of decision making that usually results in the automatic and efficient application of an effective strategy for the challenge at hand. That is, seasoned experts think and act fast, and almost always get it mostly right. During crises, when there is a lot of activity and potential for confusion, RPDM is vital, and most well-trained, experienced responders employ it intuitively. RPDM no doubt contributes to the "automatic" responding that occurs during DFEs or other critical incidents (Artwohl & Christensen, 1997; Lewinski, 2008; Pinizotto et al., 2004; Vickers & Lewinski, 2012)–another argument for ongoing training and practice in diverse scenarios.

The actions that flow from RPDM, then, are "automatic," not in any spooky trance sense, but as the result of optimal training and experience that allows a competent professional–in this case, a police officer–to quickly grasp the demands of a critical situation and act accordingly. It is not "going with my gut" or "shooting from my hip," but a streamlined process of analysis, response, and course correction based on sold knowledge and expertise.

SUMMARY AND CONCLUSIONS

To operate smoothly in our respective physical and social environments, we naturally perceive our everyday experience as a coherent whole. Whether physiological or psychological, we only appreciate the complexity of any seemingly unitary function when one or more links in its complex underlying chains and meshworks break down and reveal the heretofore unseen intricacies of that particular process. For digestion, you hardly give your stomach a second thought until an infectious bug, toxic allergen, or overspiced foodstuff sends you racing for the commode and the Pepto. And for perception, you assume the world around you is just as it seems until a critical stressor disarticulates your sensory, attentional, and interpretive faculties, placing you in an unfamiliar and potentially destabilizing cognitive bubble.

Human resilience being what it is, most people in most emergency situations marshall their prior experience and current powers of analysis to figure out how to handle the predicament and survive, even to prevail against an adversary, whether it be an avalanche or an assailant. Police officers in a life-and-death OIS/DFE may be forced to overcome their fragmented and distorted perceptual worlds and to rely on their training and ingenuity to preserve life by taking a life. In the processes, certain perceptual anomalies are common, and some may lead to misperceptions and magnifications of threat and danger that impel a deadly force response which may have appeared reasonable and justifiable through the strained perceptual lens of the officer at the scene, but then later be judged to be excessive by observers and evaluators who's assessment and analysis is enhanced by access to the totality of the incident, only fragments of which were known to the officer at the time.

The research reviewed in this chapter should spur a program of further study and law enforcement education into the neurocognitive foundations of perception during all critical incidents, but especially OIS/DFEs, where the outcome necessarily carries a tremendous personal and societal weight. Even in the smallest activity, however, perception cannot be dissociated from action, to which we now turn.

Chapter 5

DEADLY FORCE COGNITION II: ACTION

Destiny is a name often given in retrospect to choices that had dramatic consequences.

J.K. Rowling

Exercising self-restraint can be depleting, yet it can also be ennobling.

Daniel Akst

Perception, accurate as it may be, is only useful if it contributes to effective action in an OIS/DFE or other critical emergency. When an officer's response is criticized following a DFE, it is rarely on the basis of what that officer thinks he saw or heard, but on what he *did,* albeit based on those reported perceptions. Thus, it is important to understand how the brain allows you to behave in the real world, in commonplace circumstances and extraordinary ones.

LEARNING, TRAINING, MEMORY, AND ACTION

Research into the neuropsychology of learning, memory, and performance has provided insight into how training affects the development of skills and how those skills become refined, automatized, and efficiently utilizable in a wide range of situations (Doyon & Ungerleiter, 2002; Eysenck, 1998; Kanazawa, 2012; Klein, 1998; Sokol et al., 2013; Sternberg, 2002; Storfer, 1990). This information may also partially provide the neuropsychological underpinnings for the RPDM model described in Chapter 4.

For anything to be learned, one's experiences must be processed in the brain (see also Chapter 6), and this ordinarily begins via the various senses. Through a brain structure called the **thalamus**, perceptual data is routed to various sites within the **sensory cerebral cortex** in the **occipital**, **tempo-**

ral and **parietal lobes** that process and integrate vision, hearing, touch, pain, and other modalities (except for smell, which has an extra-thalamic pathway more linked to limbic emotional and motivational structures; see below).

Information from these sensory areas is ultimately sent to the behavioral planning centers in the **frontal cortex** to determine the precise pattern of actions necessary to deal with the situation on a moment-to-moment basis. From there, the intended actions are broken down and sequenced by the **primary** and **secondary motor cortices** into the actual muscle movements that will be needed to carry out the specific activity (e.g., drive a car, fire a gun). There is a constant ongoing reciprocal feedback relationship between motor (frontal lobe) and sensory (parietal and temporal lobe) areas, such that what the person does is constantly being analyzed in terms of what effects those actions are having, so that moment-by-moment course corrections can occur as circumstances continuously shift.

With regard to the response patterns themselves, several additional brain structures are involved. The **cerebellum** fine-tunes and coordinates muscular movements so that each action is carried out in a smooth and efficient manner, and facilitates the progressive sharpening of motor skills with increasing length and depth of training. At the same time, a system of brain structures collectively known as the **basal ganglia** is responsible for managing the background stabilizing movements and postural adjustments that enable the skilled activity to take place. The basal ganglia are also important for providing just the right amount of motivational impetus for carrying out the action, determining if the activity (driving a vehicle, loading a weapon) is carried out lackadaisically or energetically (Figure 5.1).

Motivation is important, because *how* an activity is carried out means little if the person doesn't understand or care why he's doing it. Emotion and motivation are the province of another set of brain structures, the **limbic system**, especially the structure we've identified earlier as the **amygdala**, which continuously scans and analyzes the environment to determine the emotional valence, or meaning, of any given situation in terms of its survival value for the person. Through its interaction with the basal ganglia, the limbic system sets just the right emotional tone and motivational thrust that will prompt the most adaptive response to the situation (see a friend, feel pleasure and approach; see a foe, feel fear and withdraw—or feel anger and confront).

The limbic system is vital for another aspect of skilled practice and training: memory (see also Chapter 6). It makes adaptive sense that similar brain structures are utilized for emotion, motivation, and memory, because if an experience doesn't make an emotional impression, good or bad, why remember it? Experience only helps an individual learn, adapt, and survive if it can be stored, accessed, and utilized in future circumstances. For memories to be formed, information must, again, first be perceived and interpreted through the perceptual systems of the brain. Then, another limbic structure, the **hippocampus**, processes and consolidates learned skills and memories in a neurophysiological format that can be stored in appropriate brain areas and called into action when needed.

When first engaging any new skill, whether learning to play a complex lead guitar solo or speed-load and fire a handgun, the relevant sequence of actions are novel, and carrying them out has a forced, clumsy quality to it. That's because, without much past experience to go on, diverse and multiple areas of the brain are firing away, trying to figure out the most effective configuration of neuronal discharges and synaptic connections to master this new task. With increased practice and training, overall brain activity devoted to this task actually decreases because the various neural structures and networks become more streamlined and efficient in mediating the skill and in setting just the right emotional and motivational tone (alert and vigilant, but not enraged or panicked) to carry it out effectively.

In other words, reduced brain redundancy equals increased skill efficiency. That is why, when we see someone perform a complex skill in a smooth and seemingly effortless manner–the guitarist playing a blues riff or the handgunner pinging multiple bullseyes–we often marvel that he "makes it look so easy." But it's *not* easy; that person has practiced and practiced the skill over and over again, to a level where it is now soldered into his brain wiring and can be speedily evoked and executed when needed. Furthermore, additional training in a diverse variety of scenarios gives these responses the necessary flexibility to adapt to a wide range of shifting circumstances.

This may be one mechanism underlying the automatic responding reported by many officers in OIS/DFE confrontations. As discussed in Chapter 4, it is not "automatic" in any instinctive or magical sense; rather, it is the result of continued practice and refinement of the skill in question. Perhaps what appears to give these experiences their ethereal quality during a critical incident is the fact that they happen to occur in association with other perceptual phenomena described in Chapter 4, such as dissociative detachment, tunnel perception, time distortion, and so on. An officer who perceives himself to have acted efficiently and constructively amid a swirl of weird and unfamiliar cognitive experiences, may himself be astounded that he could have responded as well as he did. In fact, his RPDM-enhanced training was precisely what got him through the encounter successfully, and for that he should be grateful. However, even in the best of circumstances, errors are sometimes made.

TO SHOOT OR NOT TO SHOOT: COGNITION AND ACTION

As we've discussed, accurate perception does little good if it is not coordinated with proper responding. In fact, most police excessive force cases revolve around whether an officer fired too soon or how many rounds were fired, i.e., whether the force used was reasonable or "more than necessary." Crucial to many of these cases is the question of what were the neurocognitive bases of an officer's decision to fire his weapon and, just as importantly, his decision to hold fire or cease fire (Table 5.1).

Neuropsychology of Action and Reaction

Every goal, plan, intention, and action you wish to carry out ultimately depends on a precise and coordinated sequence of stopping and starting movements of the skeletal muscles of your body. In essence, each bit of voluntary behavior you emit is sculpted out of the infinite range, variety, and combinations of movements your body could be making at any given moment.

As discussed above, broad plans and intentions are elaborated by the anterior regions of the frontal lobes, the **prefrontal cortex**. The arrangements of body movements that will carry out those intentions are laced together by the **premotor areas** of the frontal cortex, and then sent to the **primary motor cortex** for the precise pattern of muscle contractions that will execute the task. The motor cortex transmits this information to the **motor neurons** in the brainstem and spinal cord, which, in turn, send axons to synapse on the particular muscles involved in that action. Meanwhile, col-

Table 5.1
FACTORS INVOLVED IN DECISION TO SHOOT

Perceptual accuracy: Is the danger correctly identified (see Chapter 4)?

Reasonableness standard: Is the shooting justifiable, based on the totality of the circumstances?

Reaction time: Can the officer shoot in time to neutralize the danger?

Cease fire: Can the officer stop shooting when the danger has been neutralized?

Working memory capacity: Can the officer deal with the complexity and speed of the OIS/DFE scenario?

Optimum arousal level: Is the officer under- or over-stimulated during the incident?

Ego depletion: What are the effects of officer stress and fatigue on his/her response to the OIS/DFE scenario?

lateral processes from the premotor and motor cortices communicate with the **basal ganglia** to coordinate the background posturing that will support the particular action, and with the **cerebellum** to gyroscopically coordinate the precise rapid execution of movements that will optimize the skilled activity. Feedback from these structures is sent back to the motor cortex, which also receives input from the sensory areas of the brain which are perceptually analyzing the effects of those actions on the real world.

Thus, on a millisecond-to-millisecond basis, the brain's motor cortex is receiving information on the effects of its activities from diverse internal and external sources, to assure that each momentarily intended behavioral activity is carried out appropriately. And for any skilled action sequence, it is just as important to be able to cease or shift a response pattern as it is to initiate the action in the first place.

For example, throwing a ball to your friend requires you to judge the distance and positioning between he and you, draw your throwing arm back just far enough and contract your arm, shoulder and chest muscles just strongly enough and rapidly enough to give the ball its proper force and trajectory so that it reaches its target, but doesn't overshoot it. But wait–your friend shifts to one side just as you're about to release the ball, so now, mid-pitch, you have to instantaneously recalibrate distance, position, and trajectory, and adjust your throw accordingly. But wait again–just as you're about to complete your throw, you realize your friend is standing right in front of a plate glass store window, so you now have to abruptly abort your ongoing action in mid-throw and halt the pitch entirely.

Can you do it? It depends on which stage in the sequence you're at when you become aware of the need to cease throwing and make the conscious decision to desist and recalculate. If your perception of the window and your conscious decision to abort the throw is unable to overcome the neuromuscular momentum of your arm swing, a shattered storefront, wholly unintended, is the unfortunate result.

Next day, you put on your uniform and go on shift as a patrol officer. During the course of your patrol, you are forced to confront an armed assailant who is potentially threatening you and civilians with a gun. Ignoring orders to drop the weapon, he raises his arm, points his gun, and looks like he is about to shoot, so you draw down, punch out, and begin to pull the trigger. But wait–he lowers his weapon and makes his way down the street, raises his weapon again, but this time he's standing in front of a group of citizens waiting for a bus, so you hold your fire and look for cover. He then moves to an isolated area, still threatening you with his weapon, but affording you a clean shot, and now you have to make that fateful choice. But wait again–at the last second, he wheels around and sprints away, just as you begin pulling the trigger of your gun. As the subject turns and flees,

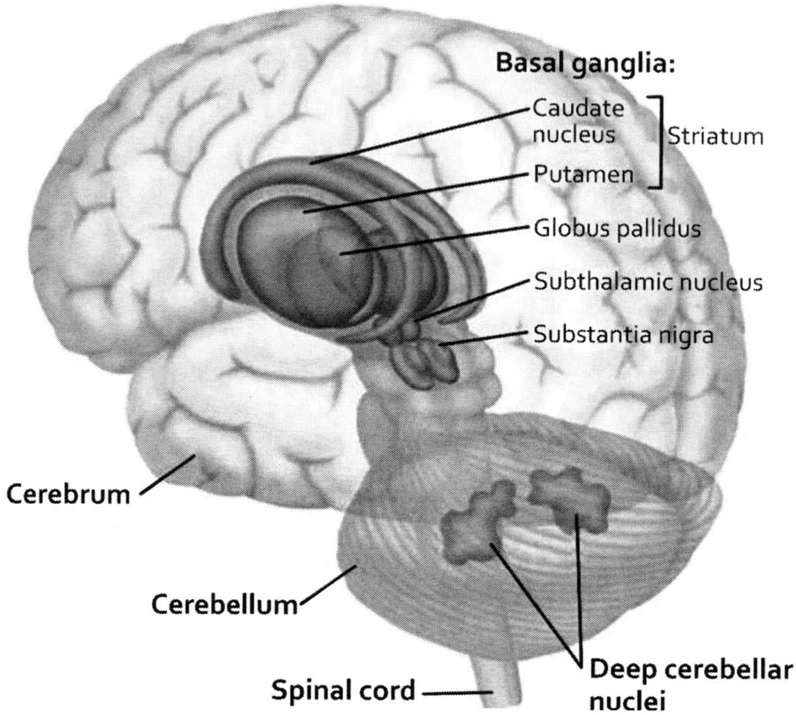

Figure 5.1. Subcortical Motor Systems: Cerebellum & Basal Ganglia.

you instinctively squeeze off several rounds in rapid succession before you realize he's turned away from you, and before you're able to cease your trigger pulls. Later, it is determined by investigators that your adversary has been "shot it the back."

There are some differences between the ball throw and gun firing examples, one of which is that each ball throw is a singular event, whereas firing one's weapon in a OIS/DFE usually involves repetitive trigger pulls. But you can think of other examples from ordinary life: repetitively pushing the button on a delayed-arriving elevator, or making a series of staccato key strokes on your sluggishly responding laptop, causing you to over-erase items that you wanted to save. Thus, proper response to any situation, especially one with critical consequences, involves the ability to both initiate and cease action, often rapidly and over short time frames.

Reaction Time and Deadly Force

The intricate and reciprocal relationship between perception and action described above also can be used to explain what, as noted in Chapter 4, is often interpreted as a premature reaction or overreaction on the part of officers who appear to literally "jump the gun" and fire at a subject who, in retrospect, had not yet posed a clear-cut deadly threat. In these cases, the involved officers are often pilloried as itchy-fingered cops who "shoot first and ask questions later." But are they justified in shooting first?

To begin with, remember that the reasonableness standard described in Chapter 1 does not expect officers to wait until the suspect has already attacked them, with a gun or any other weapon, before taking protective action; that is, the suspect is not entitled to a "free shot." Blair et al. (2011) point out that, in an armed confrontation between an officer and a criminal gunman, where each may be holding a firearm and contemplating their next move, it might seem that the two opponents are equally matched, i.e., that this is a "Mexican standoff."

However, radically different agendas and intentions are operating in the brains and minds of these two antagonists. The fact that he is holding a gun (and refusing commands to drop it and surrender) shows that criminal has already decided that he is willing to kill an officer in order to get what he wants, typically to escape. There are no pesky rules of engagement for the suspect to consider, and all he has to do to complete his action is make the decision to raise his arm, pull the trigger, and indiscriminately blast away: ""If this cop don't let me go, I'm gonna kill the motherfucker."

For the officer, meanwhile, things are more complicated. He must perceptually and cognitively assess the scene, consider the presence and position of the suspect, other officers, and civilians, weigh the appropriateness of using deadly force, and, even as the situation may rapidly change from moment to moment, come to a summary judgment about the entire scenario, then make the decision to fire his weapon, and finally pull the trigger, while at the same time continuing to perceptually assess the outcome of his actions: "If this suspect doesn't drop his weapon, I have to carefully observe his movements, interpret his actions, consider both the immediate and long-term results of my menu of possible responses, make a decision if, when, and how to fire, and then aim and pull the trigger to effectively and definitively neutralize the extant danger posed by the motherfucker."

So, even if the two individuals are standing there with guns trained on each other, the neurocognitive decision-making loop will necessarily involve many more synaptic pathways, and therefore extend many-fold the time between perception of danger and actual deadly force response (trigger pull), providing the suspect a distinct advantage, because in a deadly force encounter, even a few hundred milliseconds (a few tenths of a second) can make a life-or-death difference.

To study this, Blair et al. (2011) utilized a realistic experimental paradigm wherein sworn police officers abruptly confronted a volunteer "suspect" who role-played a criminal armed with a gun, pointed down and not yet aimed at the officer, whereas the officer had his gun pointed directly at the suspect and ordered him to drop the weapon. In one version of the experiment, the suspect surrendered; in the other version, he raised his arm to fire at the officer. Reaction times of both sets of participants were recorded.

Results showed that police officers and suspects took about the same time to fire. That is, despite the physical advantage of having already drawn down and punched out against an adversary who had to raise his gun to firing position, the officers fired simultaneously with, or later than, the suspect 61 percent of the time. Even in those cases where the officer was faster, the time difference was a negligible 0.2 seconds, which, even if the officer shot with 100 percent accuracy, would still allow the suspect to squeeze off at least one round before being hit. That is, the duration of neurocognitive processing called into play to determine the officers' final response effectively cancelled out the presumed physical advantage of gun position.

To be fair, not all suspects in an armed confrontation will have predetermined their intent to fire at an officer from the get-go, and a given suspect may well agonize over whether to give it up or to fight it out, knowing that the latter alternative will almost inevitably be the last decision he ever makes. But, for the study authors, their results illustrate why what seems like an impulsive or premature deadly force action may often really be the only reasonable response in a life-or-death scenario where milliseconds count.

Unintentional Discharges

In some cases, the shooting response may not even be a voluntary decision, and officers will claim that they discharged their weapons unintentionally or accidentally due to a variety of circumstances and influences. As noted in Chapter 2, being startled, losing one's balance, or other unanticipated events may induce an involuntary trigger pull (Artwohl, 2003; Enoka, 2003).

For most species of primate, including humans, the **grasp reflex** is a response that appears early in life to help infants cling to their mothers and, later, to retain wanted items securely. In babies, this is an involuntary response to tactile stimulation of the hand, which comes under increasingly greater voluntary and inhibitory control as the child's nervous system matures. Even in adults, however, states of panic associated with actual or perceived danger can elicit this reflex, as when a person trying to escape a burning building "can't let go" of the ladder rung, even though remaining in place may result in their immolation. Even our language reflects such manual metaphors, as when we "grasp" a concept, "grab" headlines, "cling" to power, fold in the "clutch," or "punch through" an obstacle.

In their study of involuntary discharges during deadly force encounters, Messina and colleagues (Messina, 1994, 2000; Messina & Czarnecki, 2002) invoke a similar concept in their description of the **fist reflex**, a response which occurs when an individual psychologically associates making a fist with a high stress confrontation. Indeed, in circumstances where displays of strength or resolve are called for, "making a fist" to emotionally drive home a point is a common response.

These authors point out that the fist reflex is often explicitly reinforced by sports such as boxing and martial arts, and through military or law enforcement training in fisted defensive tactics. Messina and Czarnecki's (2002) research has found that a high percentage of law enforcement officers who report involuntary discharges have in fact studied martial arts systems that emphasize making a fist under stress, with boxing being the most common sport in this category.

Many law enforcement trainers, such as Grossi (2003), tactically endorse the **universal cover mode**, i.e., keeping the finger off the trigger and outside the trigger guard, as a standard procedure in a non-immediately threatening situation. Of course, the utility of this practice hinges on each officer's perception of just how "immediate" a given threat may be. As we've seen, even in the same situation, individual officers can have very different perceptions of the extant danger, and one officer's response may influence the perception and action of others at the scene.

Shoot/Don't Shoot Research

As noted in Chapter 4, in the **shoot/don't shoot (S/DS)** paradigm, a research subject is presented with some form of visual depiction of a potentially dangerous or potentially harmless person, object, or situation, and the subject must make the rapid decision to "shoot" or "don't shoot," most commonly in the form of pressing one button on a console for shooting, and another for not shooting. In other variations of this technique, subjects are issued facsimile weapons and asked to actually go through the motions involved in firing or withholding fire. The advantage of the latter technique is that it more closely replicates what officers in an OIS/DFE actually do with their hands and bodies. The push-button methodology, while artificial, has the advantage of allowing the precise electronic recording of the subject's response latency, that is, how many milliseconds it takes for the subject to respond to the stimulus under varying conditions.

Sharps and colleagues (Sharps, 2010; Sharps & Hess, 2008) describe a series of studies in which a group of college student volunteers were informed that they were about to be shown situations that might or might not involve a crime or a source of danger, and that they could intervene to protect themselves or others "if you see an individual holding a weapon." They were then shown realistically staged videotaped scenarios, one depicting a male assailant pointing a 9mm Baretta handgun at a female victim in what was clearly an armed assault, the other depicting a repairman waving a power screwdriver at a woman in what might be construed as a vigorous argument over a home repair, but without an actual attack. Both scenes were presented in good lighting and without anything obscuring the view. In different versions of the experiment, volunteers could "shoot" by pressing a button, or alternatively, by firing a toy rubber-tipped dart gun. Findings showed that 88 percent of these college respondents fired at the armed perpetrator when he was aiming a handgun at the victim, and 85 percent also shot the repairman holding the power screwdriver.

But perhaps these results were due to the inexperience and lack of training on the part of these civilian volunteers, many of whom may never before have held a weapon or faced a dangerous assailant. Aren't sworn police officers specifically trained to hone their perceptual and response skills so they can discern true deadly firearms from less lethal objects? Also, what roles do such factors as environmental visual clarity (lighting, obstructions) and perceived time to respond (immediate lethal threat requiring instantaneous action versus unclear danger with time to further assess) play in a shooter's perception and response?

Recall that, in the Hererra et al. (2015) study cited in Chapter 4, civilian college student volunteers in a button-push shoot/no shoot paradigm, took about the same brief amount time to "shoot" depicted images of perpetrators wielding rifles versus BB guns, despite later being able to describe the actual differences between the weapons. These researchers repeated the procedure, but this time with actual trained police officers, and also varied the time constraints to respond. As might be expected, under conditions that gave the officers time to evaluate and assess the scene, they were significantly more accurate than the students in distinguishing the real rifle from the BB gun and adjusting their firing rates accordingly. But where circumstances forced an immediate decision, that is, where they had to act *now,* there was no significant difference in identification accuracy between officers and civilians.

It thus appears that training is indeed effective in sharpening discriminatory accuracy, until it strains the limits of the human nervous system's ability to perceive and respond in real-time. That is, all the training in the world won't enable even the strongest athlete to bench-press a two-ton weight because this is simply more than the human musculoskeletal system can tolerate. In the same way, you can't train even the keenest sharpshooter to make perceptual discriminations faster that the human eye can neurophysiologically transmit a visual signal to the brain (Clifford & Richards, 1977; Grossman, 1996; Grossman & Christensen, 2007; Hope et al., 2012; Sharps, 2010). Even for experienced personnel, the faster the response has to be made, the greater the likelihood of perceptual and response errors.

Stop Shooting

As discussed earlier, in many alleged excessive force cases, the criticism relates to whether the actual danger posed by the suspect justified an officer's initiating deadly force in the first place. But almost as many such cases revolve around the *amount* of force used, often quantified as the number of rounds fired at the suspect versus the number that a post-hoc evaluator–civilian witness, forensic examiner, or media pundit–believes should have been necessary to neutralize the threat, i.e., the "hail of bullets" critique discussed in Chapter 1. For example, in contested OIS/DFE cases, police dash cam or civilian cell phone videos have shown what looks like an officer continuing to fire at a subject when he is already on the ground, has begun to run away, or otherwise appears to no longer present an immediate threat to the officer or others.

In analyzing any of these cases, the question becomes: to what extent did an officer's continued firing represent his or her perception of the need to neutralize an ongoing threat, or to what extent was it due simply to neuromuscular momentum–that is, the officer kept pulling the trigger because that was the automatic response until the magazine was empty? Thus, as important as it is to understand when and why officers initiate lethal force, it is just as important to understand when and why they cease.

Lewinski & Redmond (2009) have reviewed the literature on what they aptly term the **stop shooting problem**, and have identified several key variables. For one thing, it appears that the longer the delay between the decision to begin firing and the decision to desist, the harder it is to stop the sequence. That is, the more rounds an officer has repetitively fired over a greater span of time, the more difficult it is to inhibit that reaction and the greater the time frame required to cease firing. Actually, this component may need to be parsed into two sub-elements: the actual time span covering the shooting response, and the number of trigger pulls that establish the repetitive pattern. This problem of **response perseveration** is a common one, as when, in the examples cited earlier, we keep rapidly pressing an elevator button or keyboard letter beyond the point necessary to achieve the desired result, indeed, even to the point where it unintendedly sabotages the action itself.

One neurophysiological explanation for this phenomenon is that stop and go processes–the brain mechanisms responsible for initiating and desisting from an action–appear to operate independently (Heilman et al., 1997;

Logan & Cowan, 1984). That is, as long as an organism is alive, no behavior ever involves *not* doing something, so the cognitive-motor processes to initiate the inhibitory cease-firing movements must compete with and override the cognitive-motor processes to maintain firing. In the case of movement, different patterns of **agonist** and **antagonist muscles** (those that contract to move a body part and those that relax to permit that movement) in the fingers and hands must be activated for weapon firing versus ceasing to fire. Even at the spinal cord level, when the muscles of one movement (e.g., contracting one's finger for a trigger pull) are activated, the muscles of the opposing movement (extending the finger to take pressure off the trigger) are inhibited; the reverse occurs when the decision to stop shooting is made.

Of course, in a real-life deadly force encounter, there is never just one thing going on at one time. That is, an officer is focused on the target, while assessing not just the extant threat from the suspect, but the effect of his own actions, the actions of other officers and civilians at the scene, the availability of cover, varying and changing potential sources of danger, his own internal thoughts and emotions, and any additional relevant ongoing events. This is the phenomena in cognitive psychology known as **divided attention**, which has been shown to slow down reaction times to each of the many alternate tasks being undertaken in a given situation (Johnson & Proctor, 2004).

Stop Shooting, by the Numbers: The Cognitive Psychology of DFEs

Lewinski and Redmond's (2009) research on the stop-shooting response in police officers has utilized a standard duty-issue, semiautomatic, short-trigger stroke handgun, such as a Glock. They have found that, if an officer is firing at a perceived deadly threat, and the perception abruptly changes so that officer now perceives the threat to have ended, the quickest he or she can cease firing is approximately .35 to .60 seconds, which, for most officers, translates into the completion of two trigger pulls, resulting in two rounds being fired *after* the moment the officer has made the conscious decision to stop shooting.

But that's just for the response itself. As noted in Chapter 4, total time from active-firing to cease-firing has to take into account the perceptual and cognitive processes that contribute to the officer's decision to cease fire. Through a review of their own and others' (Lewinski & Hudson, 2003a, 2003b; Vickers, 2007) research, Lewinski and Redmond (2009) arrive at the following calculations for elements of the stop-shooting decision and response: (1) perception that the threat level has changed = .25 seconds; (2) ascertainment and confirmation that a deadly force response is no longer required = .25 seconds; (3) decision and formation of the intent to stop firing = .25 seconds to .50 seconds; and (4) actual cessation of the motor response of firing = .25 to .33 seconds. Summing the perception times, decision times, and response times yields a minimum of about 1.5 seconds between an officer's perception of reduced threat and his actually ceasing to fire his weapon. If trigger pulls take an average of .25 seconds apiece, the officer may have thus fired four to six rounds *after* he has perceived the threat to have stopped.

And even that's assuming the officer is just focusing on the threatening suspect and nothing else. As discussed in Chapter 4, tunnel vision or weapon focus takes place in a large proportion of shooting scenarios, but in other cases, the officer's perception and response time will be further reduced by his attention being divided between the threatening suspect and a wide range of ambient sights and sounds. Again, doing the math, Lewinski and Redmond's (2009) and others' (Crevits et al., 2000) research has concluded that the human eye requires about 0.4 seconds to **saccade** (shift back and forth) from one side of a person's field of vision to the other. Assuming an officer who has begun firing at a perceived deadly threat is now scanning the peripheral environment while trying to discern any change in threat level, that length of eye movement time accounts for up to two additional trigger pulls, added to the totals above.

As noted earlier, in many contested OIS/DFE cases, officers may be accused of continuing to fire at a subject who witnesses claim, or videos seemingly show, to have already been rendered helpless and harmless. As an empirically validated response to at least some of these charges, Lewinski and Redmond's (2009) research suggests that officers may fail to suppress up to six rounds after the threat has objectively ended, but before that officer's nervous system has had a chance to process the change. And at least three of those rounds may continue to be automatically fired after the officer has made the conscious decision to stop shooting.

Individual Differences in Shooting Control: Working Memory Capacity

Many accounts portray police officer shooting behavior as if all officers were the same. But as the current volume has tried to make clear, officer personalities, attitudes, social skills, and cognitive styles vary across the psychological spectrum, probably somewhat narrower than that of the general population, but wide enough to expect differing responses to similar circumstances. One area that will be discussed later relates to individual differences in emotional processing during a critical incident, and Chapter 4 has outlined the myriad varieties and combinations of perceptual distortions that may occur during an OIS/DFE. A further dimension involves how individual differences in officer cognition relates to actual shooting behavior in a potentially deadly confrontation.

One such variable is called **working memory capacity (WMC)** which has been well studied in the broader field of cognitive psychology, and is defined by Brewer et al. (2016) as "a limited-capacity adaptive system for maintaining task-relevant information in an active and accessible state for the purpose of completing complex cognitive and behavioral tasks." Huh? In other words, working memory is what we ordinarily regard as our ability to concentrate and voluntarily focus attention on things we have to think about at a particular moment to solve a particular problem (Barkley, 2012; Brewer et al., 2016; Carver et al., 2013; Engle, 2002; Unsworth & Engle, 2007; Unsworth et al., 2014; Waters & Tucker, 2013).

WMC is typically measured using **span tasks** that require the subject to remember longer and longer strings of digits or more and more complex spatial sequences. It turns out that WMC correlates with a wide variety of adaptive cognitive skills, such as judgment, analytical reasoning, problem-solving, even general intelligence. These abilities, in turn, are thought to be mediated by the frontal-cortical, limbic, striatal, reticular, and other brain structures discussed in these chapters.

The higher a person's working memory capacity, the greater number and complexity of items they can "juggle" in their mind at any one time and, consequently, the greater their ability to focus and direct attention, solve immediate and ongoing problems, maintain goal-directed self-control of otherwise impulsive and automatic responding, and overcome distractions–all obviously valuable skills for an officer facing an OIS/DFE. Thus, it would seem that both the concept and experimental methodology of WMC should lend itself to the study of police officer shooting behavior in S/DS research. Does higher WMC predict more accurate and situationally appropriate shooting in OIS/DFE scenarios?

This question has been addressed in a series of studies (Kleider & Parrott, 2009; Kleider et al., 2011, 2016) which first measured volunteer subjects' WMC by means of a complex span task, then had them undergo an S/DS procedure. The researchers also added another variable of inducing negative emotion in half of the subjects prior to the task by forcing them to watch a police training video in which an officer is shot and killed; the other half of the subjects watched a similar video that ended peacefully. The study found that the lower the level of a subject's WMC (as assessed by the span task), the more likely they were they to shoot at unarmed targets. For reasons that are not entirely clear, one study in this series found that video-induced negative emotion seemed to increase shooting errors still further, whereas in the other study, emotion had no additional effect.

Brewer et al. (2016) asked 186 college students to complete a series of complex span tasks to measure their WMC, then had them rate a series of unpleasant photographs for level of subjective aversiveness, and finally put them through a computerized S/DS task in which the subjects were shooting in 20 percent, 50 percent or 80 percent of the trials. Results showed that all subjects showed a greater likelihood of shooting inappropriately (i.e., at an unarmed target) as the percentages of shooting trials increased. But, overall, subjects high in WMC shot more accurately than low-WMC subjects in all three conditions. That is, high-WMC subjects were able to adjust their shooting criteria to match the perceived level of legitimate (i.e., armed) targets, whereas low-WMC subjects tended to shoot more indiscriminately, netting them a greater number of false hits.

As with all research on individual differences, implications of studies like these are not just theoretical. If these findings can be replicated, should cognitive measures of working memory and other capacities be incorporated into officer screening protocols, perhaps especially for special unit assignments where gunplay is more likely, such as street crimes, gang interdiction, or drug trafficking assignments?

TO SHOOT OR NOT TO SHOOT: STRESS AND EMOTION

But officers are not just cognitive computers. As noted in Chapter 4, a variety of emotional reactions may occur in the course of an officer-involved shooting, from numbing to panic. In Lewinski and Redmond's (2009) study, the most common reason for a delayed reaction time in firing cessation was the officer's reaction to the immediate threat to his or her life (see also Lewinski, 2008). The **risk-averse bias** of human threat perception dictates that a given officer will inevitably take more time than the absolute neurocognitive limit to assure himself that the threat to his life has ended. In real OIS/DFE scenarios, the officer is not firing based on some abstract formula of optimally timed threat neutralization: he's shooting to save his life.

Under such emotionally charged conditions, that officer's criterion for ceasing to fire is not the absolute minimum number of rounds that might be needed to reduce the threat, but the reasonable number of rounds it will take to make that officer feel safe. This threat mode is likely to drastically degrade the perception of danger cessation signals that might seem obvious to a nonthreatened observer at the scene or retrospectively to investigators. In post-OIS interviews, officers will commonly report that "I emptied my mag because that's the procedure," when the very rationale for that policy is that, in any given situation, there is no way to be sure how many rounds will cumulatively provide the stopping power needed to neutralize what appears to be a deadly threat, so when in doubt, pop to drop (see Chapter 1).

Stress and Shooting Performance: Ego Depletion

As discussed above, in some of the WMC research, experimentally induced stress appears to further degrade shooting accuracy, while in others it doesn't. But since not everyone reacts to ostensibly stressful circumstances in the same way, an important trait factor that varies among individual is how much actual stress and arousal is actually experienced by a given person in a given crisis. Psychologists who regularly debrief officers following OISs or other critical incidents are impressed by the range of responses reported (presumably honestly) following such events. So, individual differences in stress reaction and coping may affect shooting behavior during an OIS/DFE.

Further, the two variables are likely to interact; that is increased stress may affect WMC and WMC may affect the individual's ability to cope with stress and keep behavior situation-appropriate. For example, special forces candidates exposed to a police stress scenario in which an officer entered a house containing a potentially violent suspect showed higher cortisol secretion and made poorer judgments, indicating greater subjective distress and reduced WMC, than subjects in more benign scenarios (Traverniers et al., 2010).

Stress also interacts with fatigue, in that sharp decision making skills that may be a function of WMC and other neurobehavioral self-control capacities are commonly felt to deteriorate as mental energy reserves are depleted, in which case, emotional factors may increasingly come to influence shooting decisions (Klukkert et al., 2009; Ma et al., 2013; Macrae et al., 1994). Thus, differences in the ability to perceive, analyze, conceptualize, and respond in a controlled, moderated way during an OIS/DFE or any other critical scenario way may represent **state** as well as **trait factors**. That is, officer A's WMC and other cognitive control skills may be constitutionally better than officer B's, but not when A has just handled a bunch difficult calls over a 10-hour shift, while B is just coming back to work after a refreshing weekend off.

Everyday experience informs us that we are better at dealing with most tasks and situations when we're not physically and emotionally exhausted, drained, wilted, fried, burned out, bummed out, wrung out, or any of the other terms we use to describe that tired-but-wired feeling when we're twanging on our proverbial last nerve. Psychologists who study this phenomenon refer to the concept of **ego depletion**, which has been found to exert a powerful influence on WMC and other self-control skills (Baumeister, 2002, 2014; Baumeister & Heatherton, 1996; Baumeister et al., 1998; Dang, 2018; DeWall, 2007; Finkel et al., 2009; Heatherton & Baumeister, 1996; Kashdan & Rottenberg, 2010; Muraven & Baumester, 2000; Reynolds & McCrea,

2016; Stucke & Baumeister, 2009; Vohs & Heatherton, 2000; Vohs et al., 2005, 2011).

According to the ego depletion model, each of us, at any given time, possesses a finite quantum of mental energy that fuels our ability to monitor, sustain, motivate, regulate, and control our emotions, thoughts, impulses, and behaviors. If demands on mental control are particularly high, or if this motivational fuel tank has already been tapped out by recent sustained self-regulatory activity, and especially if both conditions exist–i.e., high demand, low energy–then the ability to handle the next difficult situation will be impaired. Thus, challenges that may be well within your ability when you are fresh and rested are likely to evoke a cry of, "This is not a good time!" when you are ego-depleted. In this conceptualization, your depleted cognitive control capacity is seen as akin to a drained battery that needs recharging or an over-pumped muscle that needs a rest between workouts. Further, individuals vary as to how much of this mental energy reserve they naturally possess, and also the actual supply at any particular moment will vary depending on the situation and the person's recent history.

In the lab, ego-depletion is typically produced by having one group of subjects engage in some cognitively challenging task, like mental arithmetic or difficult puzzles, or by a physical stressor like vigorous exercise or something called the **cold-pressor task**, i.e., keeping your bare arm immersed in ice water till you can't stand it anymore (I've done this: trust me, it hurts). A control group is given a more pleasant, or at least neutral, activity to do for an equivalent length of time, like watching a video or playing a game. Then, a subsequent cognitive or interpersonal task is presented and the performance of the two groups is compared.

Research, some of which replicates observations of everyday behavior, suggests that exerting self-control on one task reduces the ability to regulate emotion or behavior on a subsequent task. A common example is feeling "hangry," i.e., feeling especially irritable after having skipped a meal; or having particular difficulty focusing at work when you've been dealing with unpleasant family members at home. Ego-depleted individuals have been found to be more susceptible to aggressive behavior, including domestic violence, when previously exposed to interpersonal stress at work or home. Essentially, ego-depleted individuals are more likely to displace or "take it out on" targets that may or may not be the source of the original stress.

So, now let's get back to imagining our two officers confronting the same OIS/DFE scenario, one just coming on duty with shiny shoes, the other drag-assing himself through the end of a long shift in which he has had to hold it together through multiple traffic stops, fractious citizen encounters, perhaps some physically demanding work (helping the little old lady change her tire), and maybe a few scuffles and arrests. Even assuming equivalent baseline self-control skills, which officer is more likely to be running on ego-fumes at this point, and how will his response differ from the officer who just topped off his cognitive-emotional tank?

Staller et al. (2018) studied this systematically by subjecting a group of German State Police officers to a cognitive suppression task (mental stress) and a cold pressor task (physical stress). A control group of officers engaged in some benign activity during that time. Then, the subjects were placed in a role-play scenario in which the officer had to prevent an intruder from entering a restricted area–not necessarily a deadly force scenario, but one potentially requiring some degree of vigorous physical restraint. Following the cold-pressor task, but not the cognitive suppression task, officers tended to use more forceful and aggressive behavior, and to use it earlier, than the unstressed control group. The authors theorize that ego depletion from trying to control the painful response to the cold-pressor task weakened the officers' ability to modulate their aggression in the intruder scenario. If we can extrapolate this to OIS/DFE scenarios, it really seems as if the difference between life and death in many such encounters may hinge on where that officer has been and what he has been doing in the hours preceding the confrontation.

Optimum Arousal Level, Threat Magnification, and Shooting Accuracy

Okay, stress and fatigue are important factors, but how much stress and what kind? We know from everyday experience that, with fully charged egos or ones with the power light blinking, a little jolt of arousal can be useful to get us going for a sports event, performance gig, or work project, often aided and abetted by a caffeinated beverage or other stimulating medicament. This enthusiastic, pumped-up, good feeling has been termed **eustress**, in contrast to the **distress** we feel when the pressure gets too great and the level of physiological and mental overstimulation begins to degrade performance, instead of enhancing it. This phenomenon relates to what is arguably one of the most robust findings in virtually every field of stress research: the **inverted U-shaped curve**, sometimes referred to as the **optimum arousal level**, or **OAL** (Flin, 1996; Hays & Brown, 2004; Klein, 1996; Miller, 2008i; Rodgers, 2006).

Essentially, the OAL principle (Figure 5.2) states that too little arousal yields low motivation, low effort, and therefore weaker performance on whatever task or function is being measured. Higher arousal yields better performance until an optimum peak is reached. Thereafter, as arousal increases, anxiety and agitation tend to predominate and performance begins to deteriorate. Students often grasp this concept by referring to their study behavior around exam time: a little fear-o'-God while preparing for the test

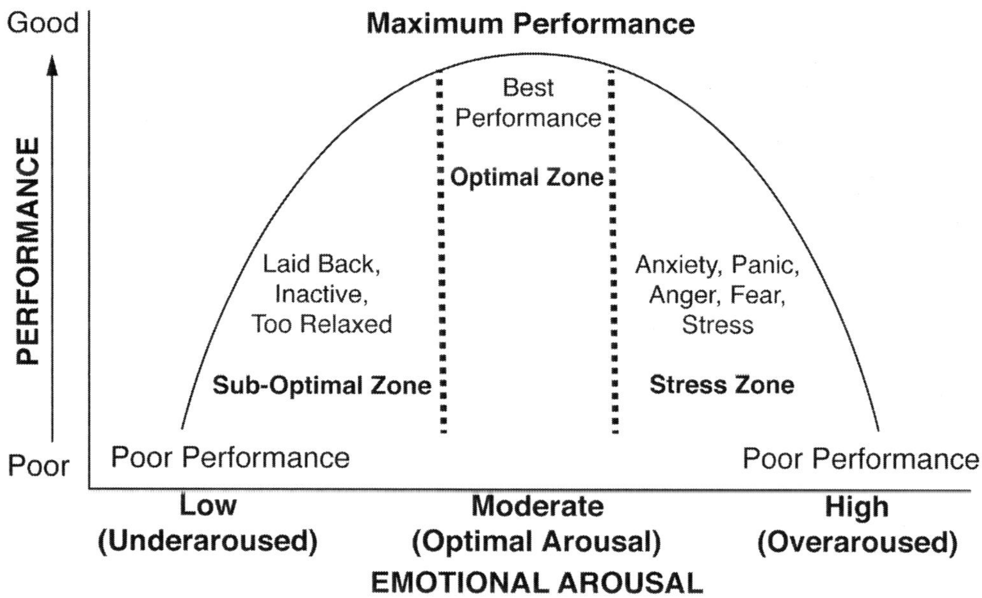

Figure 5.2. Optimum Arousal Level.

gets you pumped and motivated, but too much anxiety just freaks you out and makes it harder to concentrate and retain the material.

Neurophysiologically, we've already discussed the amygdala's role in assessing the valence of ongoing environmental input in terms of approach, avoidance, or challenge, as well as the reciprocal relationship between amygdala activation and frontal lobe modulation, in order for situations to be dealt with adaptively. Under states of significant stress, amygdala activation results in the release of biochemicals such as cortisol and norepinephrine which have further feed-forward activation effects and can hijack frontal lobe control mechanisms, leading the individual to experience a perceptually and cognitively enhanced version of the ambient danger (Amir, 2003; Bishop, 2007; Bishop et al., 2004; Eysenck et al., 2007; Verhage et al., 2018), sometimes referred to as **threat magnification**.

A series of shooting studies with sworn police officers used live actors and paint bullets (Nieuwenhuys et al., 2010, 2011). When an adversary appeared to be firing at the officers, the officers tended to focus longer and more frequently on the head and weapon of the opponent, shot earlier, and, significantly, were more likely to overlook their opponents' attempts to surrender, ending up shooting them anyway. Later analysis revealed that the highly stressed officers experienced a magnified expectation of threat, leading them to fire sooner and, in many cases, technically unnecessarily. Thus, in a real-life OIS/DFE scenario, extreme stress may cause the involved officer to mistakenly interpret a given confrontation as a deadly threat, whereas uninvolved witness or subsequent investigators may later fail to perceive a "reasonable" basis (Chapter 1) for the officer's decision to use deadly force.

In most of the contested shooting cases I've served on, the involved officer claims to have perceived a level of threat that justified deadly force, when witness accounts or video images fail to corroborate the officer's version of events. Somc examples include suspects on the ground appearing to rise up; immobile or barely moving suspects appearing to reach for or wield a weapon; nonweapon objects perceived as deadly weapons; standing stationary suspects appearing to move forward; and in two cases, a suspect running away appearing to be running toward the officer (see also Chapter 4).

Thus, stress and arousal may have a binary effect on shooting performance. Too little arousal, and the officer may fail to properly address an extant threat, zero in, and neutralize it effectively. Too far over into the red-zone side of the OAL curve, and the threat level may be overinterpreted at the same time as shooting accuracy decreases.

The importance of officers being in the "Goldilocks zone" of arousal during a shooting scenario seems to have been demonstrated by a study (Akinola & Mendez, 2012) who induced social stress in a sample of police officer volunteers by having them participate in a role play task involving dealing with a disgruntled citizen. The officers then had their cortisol levels measured and subsequently engaged in a simulated shooting task. Results showed that higher levels of cortisol were associated greater accuracy in shooting, which the authors interpret as the effects of stress on officer wariness and heightened vigilance to the target.

Higher levels of stress did not appear to degrade shooting accuracy in this study, which may be because the stress levels in the simulated role play and shooting conditions still did not approach the level which would occur in a real life-and-death confrontation. In those cases, under extreme threat, attention diverted to the source of the danger may be siphoned away from that necessary to accurately execute a shooting response, leading to a degradation of shooting accuracy (Nieuwenhuys & Oudijans, 2011; Nieuwenhuys et al., 2008; Shipley & Baransky, 2002). Further, in any given real-life OIS/DFE scenario, what will be the combined effect on involved officers of individual differences in stress level, OAL, WMC, ego-depletion, suspect behavior, and other internal and situational factors? How do these complex variables (and others) influence a particular officer's varying responses at the scene and, in contested cases, how does this figure into the justifiability and perceived reasonableness of his or her deadly force actions? Systematic research is just beginning in these areas, and hopefully will contribute to more accurate and fair assessments of individual cases.

SUMMARY AND CONCLUSIONS

You can't do nothing. Even standing still, lying down, or fast asleep, as long as your body is alive, you're engaged in some behavior. You're never not doing something, you're simply doing something else–except it's never simple because every action from an eye roll or finger twitch to a rock concert or military campaign involves a combination of conscious and unconscious choice points, feedback effects, and decision matrices, all operating at a time scale of milliseconds. A police officer not firing his weapon at a suspect is making just as determinative a choice as the one who opts to fire. The input guiding either decision is coursing in from each officer's perception of the environment, their cognitive, emotional, and intuitive appraisal of the moment-to-moment changing requirements of the situation, and the internal analysis of their own thoughts, feelings, and actions.

Viewed from outside, or judged from witness reports or available videographic evidence, it might seem that an officer made a snap decision to shoot or withhold fire, or that the officer's actions were ill-advised or excessive for the circumstances. But as is the case with perception described in Chapter 4, fair judgment of an officer's actions in an OIS/DFE scenario must be based on our empirically inferred knowledge of what that officer's brain might have been doing during the encounter.

The tough part is, we can never know everything because some internal states happen just too fast or occur too subliminally to register consciously in that officer's mind during the encounter. And even if an officer is cognizant of some or most of his thoughts and actions during the confrontation, the vagaries of memory processing and recall, especially under stress, suggest that what is later reported may contain gaps, elisions, reconstructions, distortions, and confabulations, as the officer and others work to piece together a coherent narrative of event. This is what we turn to in Chapter 6.

Chapter 6

DEADLY FORCE COGNITION III: MEMORY

The secret of a good memory is attention, and attention to a subject depends upon our interest in it. We rarely forget that which has made a deep impression on our minds.

Tryon Edwards

You don't remember what happened. What you remember becomes what happened.

John Green

Quick–what's the capital of France? What was your mother's maiden name? Show me how to access the Uber app on your smartphone. Where were you the first time you learned to do that?

Right before you read this, were you thinking of any of these things? Probably not. Yet you were instantaneously able to sift through the gazillions of information bits in your head to come up with just the right answers to these questions. How? Because your brain is a learning and memory machine–and, for that matter, so is virtually every cell in your body. Your immune system learns to recognize a flu virus you got as at age seven, so it can start pumping out antibodies if your grandchildren give you the same bug when you're seventy.

But the cells that are specifically designed for retaining and recalling information are your **neurons**, 86 billion of which reside in the average adult human brain, and each of which can receive information from up to thousands of other neurons, making the number of possible connections in your brain virtually incalculable. While some of the brain structures formed by these neurons are devoted to perception, action, emotion, thinking, and language, others are specialized for the learning, retention, and recall of information that all organisms, from paramecia to people, need to survive. And, as we've seen in previous chapters, with all such increasingly complex bioinformational processing systems comes an increasing susceptibility to *mis*information.

To our point: among the varied bones of contention being picked through during the examining of a contested OIS/DFE, what the officer remembers–or claims to remember–is a frequent source of investigative frustration. Commonly, officers will claim to have incomplete or distorted memories of an OIS/DFE or other critical incident, which can take a variety of forms. At one extreme is the officer who reports flawless recall of the entire event; however, as discussed below, the verifiable accuracy of such memories may not match their perceived clarity. At the other extreme is the officer who claims near-total amnesia for the episode, being unable to recall what happened or what he did, including such complex activities as securing cover, exchanging fire, switching ammo magazines, calling for backup, issuing commands to the suspect, aiding civilians, or communicating with other officers and first responders at the scene. When confronted with eyewitness accounts or video recordings of the event, this officer will express bafflement at his inability to summon his own independent memories of what happened.

More commonly, OIS/DFE-involved officers will recall some events, but be fuzzy about others. As noted in the discussion of perception in Chapter 4, heightened sensitivity to danger may result in some of these recollections being particularly vivid, i.e., "flashbulb memories," where other events may be absent from recall or emerge in distorted form. On the practical side, investigators may express skepticism that "something so important could just be forgotten," and may assume that the officer is feigning amnesia to cover up wrongdoing. Thus, in order to understand how and why memory distortions take place in critical incidents, it is important to know something about the cognitive neuropsychology of memory itself.

TYPES OF MEMORY

Like perception, memory is a complex process composed of a number of interlaced subcomponents (Table 6.1). Based on studies of patients with varying types of brain injuries and experimental research with healthy subjects under controlled conditions, cognitive psychology and neuroscience have been able to classify memory processes along several key dimensions (Butters & Miliotis, 1985; Curran & Shacter, 1997; Gazzaniga, 2014; Mayes, 2002; Miller, 1993; Zillmer et al., 2008; Zola, 1997; see Table 6.1, Figure 6.1).

Table 6.1.
TYPES OF MEMORY

Short-term memory: Seconds to minutes to hours. Memories retained for immediate use, then either discarded or stored.

Long-term memory: Hours to days to months to years to a lifetime. Memories consolidated, stored, and integrated with other memories for future use.

Verbal Memory: Memories for material that can be encoded and expressed in language. Includes most academic material, things we're told in words, or read on a page or screen.

Spatial Memory: Memories that are encoded and expressed in images or other nonverbal representations. Includes directions, mental maps, skills that require navigation through space.

Procedural Memory: Memory for skills and activities, such as driving a car, playing a sport, aiming a weapon. Includes motor memories that can be carried out automatically and "unconsciously."

Declarative Memory: Memories we can consciously recall and describe. Includes:

> **Semantic Memory:** Memory for facts and actions, without necessarily recalling where and when we learned them.
>
> **Episodic Memory:** Memory for events, experiences, and autobiographical facts.

Working Memory: Number of items we can hold in conscious awareness at any given time; often used synonymously with "concentration."

Implicit Memory: Memories we employ "without thinking," e.g., remembering a familiar parking space or the sequence of our morning routine. Usually involves familiar and overlearned material.

Note: The above categories of memory can occur in various combinations.

Short- and Long-Term Memory

Short-term memory is usually measured in seconds to minutes, sometimes hours, and generally concerns recall of material that needs to be utilized for a specific, immediate, one-time purpose but not necessarily stored for later use. Examples include remembering a telephone number to call someone later that day or remembering the events at a crime scene to relate to investigators when they arrive. Some short-term memories may find their way into long-term storage if they are especially vivid, pleasant, traumatic, or otherwise significant.

Long-term memory may persist for hours to decades. This is memory for material that will need to be recalled later or that will be used repeatedly by the person. It can either occur spontaneously and automatically in the case of vivid or important information, or may require active learning, continued practice, and repeated rehearsal for complex skills or bodies of information. Examples include applying classroom or field training knowledge to real-life tactical interventions. It also includes autobiographical memories, i.e., things you know about your own personal history.

Verbal and Visuospatial Memory

Verbal memory involves material that is learned via language and can be expressed in language. Examples include stories, conversations, and most academic subjects.

Visuospatial memory is memory for material that is learned via images and may be expressed in images. Examples include traveling routes and people's faces. Verbal and visuospatial memories can sometimes be cross-expressed, as when a police sketch artist reconstructs a suspect's facial image from a witness's verbal description, or a neighborhood resident draws a map to help a lost driver because "one picture is worth a thousand words."

Procedural and Declarative Memory

Procedural memory involves memory for skilled motor activities like riding a bike, batting a ball, or fixing an engine. The person can carry out the task without necessarily being able to describe the component processes: "I just know how to do it; it's automatic."

Declarative memory involves knowledge you can explain or demonstrate in some form. Declarative memory is further subdivided into semantic and episodic memory.

Semantic and Episodic Memory

Semantic memory includes information you can relate or teach to another person; for example, what are the precincts in your district? How do you drive a car, bandage a wound, or load a handgun?

Episodic memory is memory for personal events: When was the first time you learned your district map? Who was with you when you first passed your firearms qualification? What were you doing in the moments immediately before you got the shots-fired call over the radio? Semantic and episodic memories often go together ("I remember the funny instructor in the firearms class at the Academy where I learned to speed-load my weapon"), but are also commonly dissociable, i.e., you're able to recall a vast number of things without necessarily knowing when and where you first learned them ("Who remembers where I first learned about the district map?–I just know I know it"). Training in most complex tasks contains elements of both procedural and declarative memory, and is sometimes accompanied by episodic memory, especially if the training has been repetitive and has occurred over long periods of time.

Working and Implicit Memory

As discussed in Chapter 5, **working memory** involves how many mental data bits you can juggle in your conscious mind at one time as you attempt to solve a problem or carry out a task; it is usually described as focused concentration, as when an officer is searching for a concealed suspect while checking his own safety and that of nearby civilians, and at the same time is trying to recall the new code for backup assistance. **Implicit memory** usually requires no conscious effort to recall information, as when you come out of a store and "just remember" where your car is parked (doesn't always work if you're distracted), or you're able to answer a random question and bemusedly reflect, "Gee, I wonder how I know that?"

In daily life, these memory types continuously interact in different combinations (e.g., recalling the information in this book requires verbal, long-term, semantic memory), and, as will be discussed below, they can also be subject to a variety of distortions and disruptions.

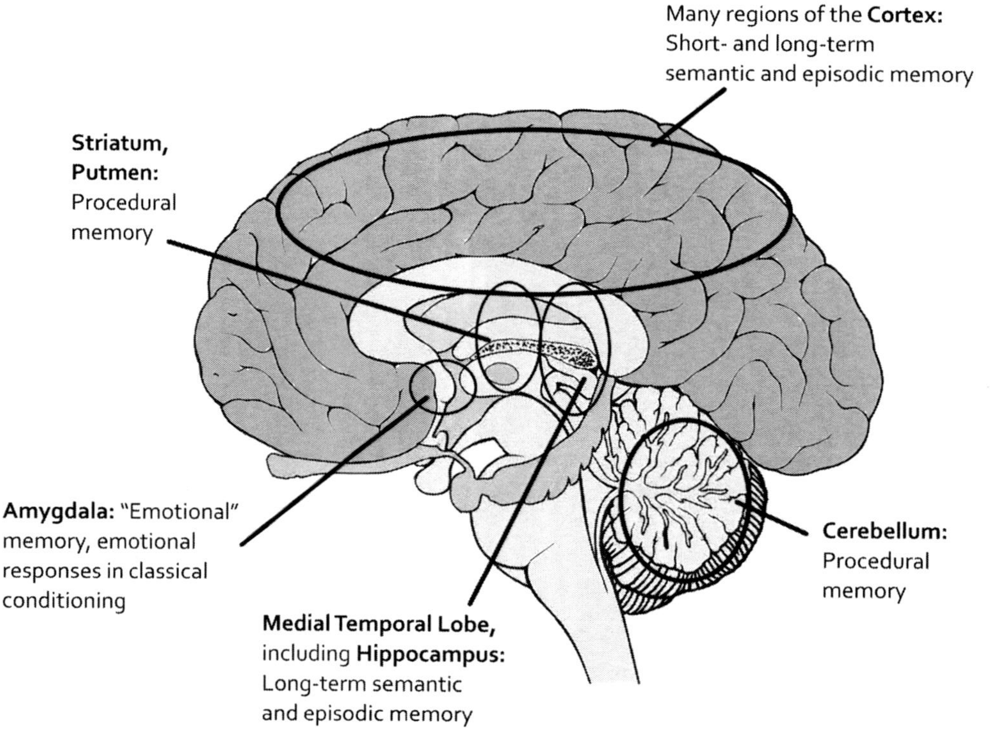

Figure 6.1. Different Structures in the Brain Handle Different Kinds of Memory..

Table 6.2.
STAGES OF MEMORY AND THE BRAIN

Input: Information gets into the brain via the sensory systems, directed by the reticular formation.

Consolidation: Amygdala assesses importance of information; hippocampus formats the data for storage in the brain.

Storage: Information is stored in various parts of the cerebral cortex, linked with similar material from past and present, to create an integrated storehouse of knowledge.

Retrieval: Frontal lobes and reticular formation search the memory store for information that is relevant to ongoing situational needs.

STAGES OF LEARNING AND MEMORY

Just as there are different types of memory, there are a number of stages a given bit of information needs to go through in order to enter the brain, be stored appropriately, and be available for later recall (Table 6.2). These stages are conceptualized by cognitive psychologists and neuropsychologists into four main categories: (1) input; (2) consolidation; (3) storage; and (4) retrieval.

Input: Pay Attention

In daily neuropsychological practice, patients sometimes complain of frequent memory problems, while psychometric testing reveals that the real difficulty is in paying attention to the material closely enough for it to register in the first place. This illustrates a fundamental point: you can't remember something you never learned. And you can't learn something if you don't pay attention to it.

For information processing, input consists of two main components (see also Chapter 4). From a neuropsychological perspective, **perception** is the process by which sensory data enters your nervous system, and may do so through a variety of sensory modalities: vision, hearing, touch, smell, and taste, often via several modalities simultaneously. Each of these modalities has its own neural pathways in the brain, which process the information in increasingly complex forms to give each perception a particular meaning and link it up with perceptions from other modalities.

For example, in vision, photonic energy (light) is captured by specialized cells in the retina and is conveyed via the optic nerve and optic tract to subcortical thalamic processing centers, such as the **lateral geniculate nucleus** of the thalamus, and from there to the **visual cortex** for making sense of what you see. Further brain processing links the visual environment with perceptual data coming from the other senses along their respective channels at a cortical site known as the **intersensory processing area**, so that at any given moment, what you experience is a coherent, integrated perceptual world: what you see corresponds to what you hear and feel, and so on. Meanwhile, a parallel visual system involving the **superior colliculus** in the brainstem allows you to make quick orienting movements to the source of a visual stimulus, even before you consciously become aware of it.

But, even under the best circumstances, you never perceive everything around you. At noted in Chapter 4, perception is actually quite selective and at any given moment, you're only aware of a fraction of the ambient sensory environment. And that's a good thing, because otherwise you'd quickly be overwhelmed by the sheer totality of the stimulus-filled world. As discussed previously, what governs what actually gets into your brain through the sensory channels at any given moment is the process of attention, a cognitive function mediated by the brain's **reticular formation**, consisting of a network of neurons diffusely distributed throughout the nervous system. Attentional processes usually function automatically, so that what you are aware of at any given moment corresponds to what you have to do at that moment. If you're engrossed in this book, you may not hear a person in the next room calling your name; if you're drawing down on an active shooter, you may not perceive the big, red Burger King sign standing right behind him.

In fact, in many cases where officers who have survived an OIS or other DFE say that they "can't remember," the reason may well be that the information was denied initial entry into the brain by the perceptual exclusion mechanisms described as tunnel vision. What does manage to work its way into the sensory systems of the brain may do so in diminished or distorted fashion.

Attention can operate in various forms and typically shifts from one mode to another over the course of a given activity. As noted earlier, attention can be wide and diffuse, as when patrolling a quiet street and just casually "taking everything in." Or it can be narrow and focused, as when trying peek through a crack to discern if that suspicious movement inside the grocery store was a burglar or a raccoon. Attention can be directed externally, as you pay close attention to what's going on in the store, or internally focused, as you monitor your own cognitive and emotional state and try to figure out what to do next. Again, tunnel vision, or tunnel perception more broadly, is a prime example of intensely externally focused attention. Bear in mind that, even with 20/20 eyesight, if your reticular formation is causing your visual system to zoom in on the immediate threat, you may not be able later to describe the gunman's clothing (or the Burger King sign), not because you can't remember it, but because, you didn't register it in the first place even though, to an observer, it was obvious that "it was standing right in front of you."

Thus, what we ordinarily regard as our normal perceptual world, in calm states or alarmed ones, is actually a small fraction of all the information buzzing around us; the brain, from moment to moment, sculpts out of this perceptual melange just that pattern of inputs relevant to what we need to focus on right now, often described as **selective attention**. Finally, most of the time, you can enlist your brain's frontal lobes in voluntarily modulating and directing your reticular formation to purposefully focus your faculties on a subject of particular interest for a sustained period of time, which we call **concentration**.

Consolidation: If It Feels Good or Bad, Remember It

Okay, eyes and ears–check. Reticular formation–check. Now, what? Even with all systems go, memories don't just slip into the brain like folders in a file cabinet. Assuming your perceptual and attentional systems are all operating flawlessly, what determines why you pay attention to one thing and not something else? What we focus on at any given moment is what is emotionally and motivationally important to us at that point in time. Importance usually falls across a binary dimension of something good or attractive to approach or engage (hot meal, hot date, hot investment) or something bad or dangerous to avoid or confront (unhealthy, unfriendly, unprofitable). The network of brain structures that enables us to assess the motivational valence of experience and determine what needs to be retained for future reference is called the **limbic system**, two of whose structures that we've encountered before are especially important for our present discussion of memory.

Recall that the **amygdala** sits within the anterior portion of the brain's temporal lobes, and is the neural structure most responsible for making continuous, rapid, on-line judgments about how good (pleasurable and survival oriented) or bad (unpleasant and harmful) each moment-to-moment experience is. Not surprisingly, the amygdala is most active at the extreme ends of the experience spectrum, i.e., when something is very good (hot date) or very bad (hot gun). Information from the amygdala is transmitted to diverse brain regions responsible for quick action (fight or flight), judgment and reasoning, and stored knowledge.

If the ongoing experience is worth remembering, the amygdala signals a brain structure immediately behind it, called the **hippocampus**, whose function is to format incoming information into a template that can facilitate its filing and cross-referencing in the brain, similar to how your computer formats an incoming file so it can be planted on your hard drive.

Note that the hippocampus is not where memories are actually stored; it is the structure that allows experiences to become memories in the first place, the vividness and permanence of which are based on input about their emotional importance coming from the neighboring amygdala. It is also important to realize that hippocampal processing takes time, several seconds to several minutes, and occurs progressively from moment to moment, so that what you are experiencing right now will not be fully encoded and formatted until a few minutes into the near future, and what you can clearly recall right now was encoded at least several seconds to minutes ago.

The hippocampus is very sensitive to electrical, mechanical or chemical disruption, which is why an individual who sustains a concussion, seizure, or drug overdose may not recall events that occurred immediately prior to the injury. Even if they were still conscious for those events, the physical blow has disrupted memory consolidation, and those experiences never had a chance to be stored in the brain for later recollection—a syndrome known as **retrograde amnesia**. Finally, memory consolidation of any given experience, skill, or bit of knowledge is not a one-time event; it is ongoing throughout the life of the person. Every time you learn or experience something—which is all the time—each memory you form is linked up with other, related memories already stored in your brain, creating a rich, integrated mnemonic gestalt, so that even memories you haven't consciously thought of in years are instantly recallable—albeit not always accurately, as we'll soon see.

Brains take time to recover, so even in a consciously awake person, prolonged hippocampal disruption from a prior blow or shock to the nervous system can continue to impair the hippocampus's ability to retain new information and form new memories for some time following the injury, the syndrome known as **anterograde amnesia**. Here, the person will typically have access to information that was formatted and stored prior to the impact, but has inordinate difficulty learning and remembering anything new that occurs post-injury. In most cases, impairment is only temporary, so hippocampal functioning will usually return to relatively normal, but those experiences that occurred during the time period of hippocampal shutdown will not have been properly formatted and imprinted, therefore the person will not be able to remember them because they were never completely inputted and consolidated in the first place. Thus, where the individual had not actually lost consciousness, examiners may be skeptical of the person's inability to recall information that was going on around him at the time of the incident.

For practical purposes, most officers in a DFE do not suffer physical injury to the brain, but here's the important point: even without a physical injury, severe psychological stress or trauma can divert reticular attention and suppress hippocampal memory consolidation, thereby resulting in an individual's impaired recall of events. This will be discussed in more detail below.

Storage: The More You Use It, the Better It Gets

In general, memory storage in the brain occurs within the cerebral cortex and is mostly modality-specific; that is, visual memories are stored around the visual cortex (occipital lobes), auditory memories are stored around the auditory cortex (temporal lobes), and somesthetic memories around the somatosensory cortex (parietal lobes). Complex memories that combine perceptual and motor elements are stored in the intersensory cortices, the **angular** and **supramarginal gyri**, that connect and integrate the various individual modality processing sites. But it is important to realize that memory traces are multiply represented throughout the brain; that is, the brain is a hologram when it comes to most memory functions, so that even patients with severe damage to one memory modality area may still be capable of some recall of those events by accessing interconnected brain networks, as long as those memories were processed intactly in the first place.

An important principle of memory storage is that it is progressive, integrative, and cumulative. In other words, last hired, first fired: the longer a given datum of memory is retained in the brain, the more linkages it acquires, and the more resistant it is to decay and forgetting. As noted above, memory consolidation of any complex experience or broad domain of knowledge is not a one-time event; it is ongoing throughout the life of the person. Every time you learn something or have an experience, each memory you form is linked up and reworked with related memories already stored in your brain, so that each recollection strengthens–and may potentially distort–the whole memory network related to that subject.

Retrieval: Come Back to Me

Input, consolidation, and storage of memories, no matter how intact, do you little good without the ability to recall them when necessary, that is, to pull them out of cortical storage and utilize them for a particular adaptive purpose. This is a function that largely falls to other structures in the limbic system memory circuit, the **hypothalamus**, the **anterior thalamus**, the **cingulate gyrus**, and the **dorsolateral frontal cortex**, as well as crucially involving the **reticular formation** to focus and direct the search process. These are the networked brain structures that enable you to "reach back" into your memory files and flexibly recall diverse bits of information, even those you may not have thought of in quite some time.

But, in fact, memory is never actually just recalled. That is, memories are not stored like static images in a video camera, but are holographically and multiply represented throughout the brain, memories for some things interconnected with memories for other things, and so on. Thus, in recalling any particular bit of information, your brain actually cobbles together the elements of that event or activity to produce the final product that you consciously remember and report. That is, memory is not recollective, but *reconstructive,* which is why one's memory for a given event may change with subsequent recalls: each time you "remember" something, your brain is piecing it together in a slightly different way, depending on the present context in which you are calling forth that particular recollection (Butters & Miliotis, 1985; Curran & Shacter, 1997; Hope et al., 2016; Schacter, 1999).

Not only that, but memory, like perception, abhors a vacuum, and if the person cannot locate the proper mnemonic elements to reconstruct the memory accurately, he or she will fill in the memory gaps with whatever that person's brain thinks comes closest, a phenomenon called **confabulation**. This is not lying; it is a largely unconscious process the brain employs to give us a sense of coherence, continuity, and consistency—"wholeness"—about our experiences, even if accuracy may be sacrificed in the process.

Motor Memory: An Exception?

One form of learning actually seems to occur independently of the hippocampal system: learning of motor programs. What is often referred to as "muscle memory" has little to do with the muscles themselves, but rather relies on the **basal ganglia** and **cerebellum**, along with the motor regions of the cerebral cortex, which we've encountered earlier. Recall that the cerebellum is the motor gyroscope of the brain, fine-tuning and coordinating voluntary movements into complex sequences of skilled actions, while the basal ganglia provide the postural and motivational support for complex activities. Much of what was described earlier as procedural memory is learned through these channels without necessarily recalling when and how you learned it, e.g., "like riding a bike."

There is evidence that these motor structures may learn and remember action programs independently of the other brain structures described above (Cohen, 1984; Gonzales & Burke, 2018; Graf & Schacter, 1985; Herzfeld et al., 2014; Mishkin et al., 1984; Scoville, 1968; Squire, 1994). For example, a few rare patients who have suffered severe bilateral damage to the hippocampus are unable to learn and recall any new information. Having lost the ability to consolidate new input, they essentially live in a "perpetual present," although they can recall information learned prior to the brain injury. However, if taught a motor skill like putting together a puzzle or negotiating a maze, their skill in this task will improve with each session—even though they will deny ever having encountered this task before. That is, their procedural memory (how to do the maze) is working, even though their episodic memory ("did I see this before?") is absent. During a DFE, if states of extreme stress temporarily inhibit hippocampal episodic memory formation, then this might account for an officer executing a sequence of adaptive responses to the crisis, yet having little or no recall of the event later. So, let's talk about stress. Can an acute stressor act like a bonk on the head to impair memory for an event?

STRESS AND MEMORY

Most memory research is conducted with volunteer subjects under relatively controlled and nonthreatening conditions. But the essence of an OIS/DFE is the fear and hyperarousal that such an encounter entails, and understanding this requires accessing our own knowledge of the human stress response system, as described earlier.

Recall that the amygdala's role in threat perception encompasses the moment-by-moment evaluation of the emotional and motivational valence of experiences; in other words, it assesses how important a given situation is to approach, avoid, or confront, and then remember. Under high-stress, potentially lethal circumstances, even a remarkable organ like the human brain can't do everything at once and, in such circumstances, it will channel its neurophysiological resources to where they are needed most. When the stakes are life and death, accurately recording an experience for later recall won't do you much good if you're already dead, so, under these conditions, reacting adaptively trumps remembering accurately.

That's why, in an acute life-threatening emergency, the hippocampal memory encoding process may get hijacked by the amygdala's rerouting of perceptual information directly to the behavioral programs enabling the individual to act quickly to survive and, if need be, control the situation as rapidly as possible. This probably accounts for the "going on automatic" experience of many officers during an OIS/DFE, where the motor programs for seeking cover, aiming, and firing seem to operate virtually independently of the officer's thinking and emoting systems. The rapid bypassing of the encoding and storage process by the perception-response express link also explains why, when later queried, the officer may not recall certain salient events because his hippocampus was on standby mode during the emergency.

But in an emergency, that's not all that's happening. Recall that, during an acute crisis of any type, neural systems such as the reticular formation narrow the perceptual field to allow the individual to focus and respond to just those features of the environment that will ensure survival. Also recall that the amygdala stimulates the **locus coeruleus**, to secrete **norepinephrine**, a chemical cousin of adrenalin, putting the entire brain and body into a physiologically hyperaroused emergency mode, aided by the release of large amounts of epinephrine, or adrenalin, from the **adrenal medulla** above the kidneys. Meanwhile, the **hypothalamic-pituitary axis (HPA)** energizes the hormonal system to stimulate the secretion of **cortisol** from the **adrenal cortex**, which has anti-inflammatory and energy-enhancing effects throughout the body and also acts on the hippocampus to suppress memory formation by binding to specialized receptors on hippocampal neurons.

All of this means that, like perception, memory processing during an OIS/DFE or other life-threatening event is narrowed, re-channeled, and prioritized in the best interests of immediate survival. This is why, in a DFE or other critical incident, the responding officer may not perceive events in the normal manner and therefore may not remember them normally, later.

In his research on attention and memory in deadly force shooting scenarios, Lewinski (2008) appears to be describing a similar process in relating how a complete neuromotor program, including significant amounts of stored motor memory, such as pointing and shooting a gun or maintaining cover while in the middle of a high-stress encounter, can occur with little or no conscious effort at all, except for the officer's instantaneous decision to engage the correct behavioral program to control the scene—an action which

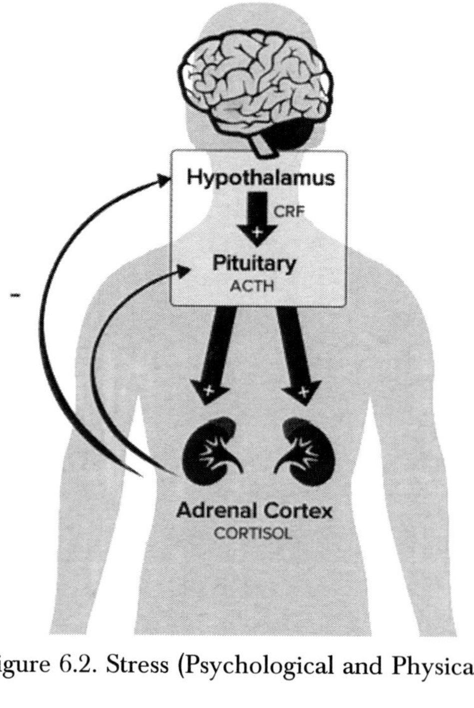

Figure 6.2. Stress (Psychological and Physical).

may seem intuitive or "instinctual," but is actually based on repetitive practice and training.

However, the very automaticity of that action means that the exact sequence of events by which it occurred will likely not be processed in the officer's memory, like the examples cited earlier of me typing this page without later being able to recount the particular order in which each sentence was written or revised; or you driving home from work while having an animated conversation with a passenger, and later being unable to recall the details of everything that happened on the road while en route. In fact, much of the "dissociation" reported during DFEs may actually involve the kind of non-hippocampal neuromotor cerebellar-mediated procedural memory described above.

If the to-be-remembered information has made it through this sensory-perceptual gauntlet and into the memory store, the retrieval of that particular information from among the countless items of stored data is an active cerebral process which requires intact attention and cognition involving the brain's frontal lobes, temporal lobes, and reticular formation (Squire & Schacter, 2003; Zillmer et al., 2008). As previously discussed, we don't just passively recall information, like replaying a video recording; we actively reconstruct it by reaching back into our brains to search for it, retrieve the elements of it, and then stitch the pieces together in as accurate a form as possible.

For most people, this usually seems effortless, but even under low-stress conditions, think back to all the times you got stuck on a "tip-of-the-tongue" phenomenon, really a "tip-of-the-brain" glitch, where your efforts to recall something were frustrated even though you "knew you knew it." Now imagine trying to recall already choppy memories formed incompletely under conditions of extreme stress while you're still in the aftermath of a traumatic event, with cortisol, adrenalin, norepinephrine, and other stress chemicals surging through your brain and body, and you're being asked to provide a detailed, point-by-point description of events by multiple skeptical investigators.

Memory Distortions Associated with an OIS/DFE

These facts about memory formation may make it easier to understand why up to a third of officers involved in OISs report some disturbance in their recollection of events (Artwohl, 1997, 2002; Grossman & Siddle, 1998; Honig & Roland, 1998; Klinger, 2001), This may involve impaired recall for particular events during the shooting episode or for all or part of the officer's own actions; the latter, as already noted, may be associated with the "going-on-automatic" response that is frequently reported. More rarely, probably due to reticular formation-based perceptual narrowing (tunnel perception), other aspects of the scene may be recalled with unusually clarity—a "flashbulb memory."

As with on-scene perception (Chapter 4), in any given OIS/DFE, what a particular officer does or does not remember may be quite individualized for that person, although several categories of memory lapses are more common. Up to a third of officers may not recall how many rounds they fired or, more rarely, may not remember having fired their weapon at all (Artwohl, 2003; Klinger, 2001). In fact, evidence suggests that there may be an inverse relationship between the actual number of rounds fired and the accuracy of an officer's recall of that number. Klinger (2001) studied 113 cases of OIS and found that the greater number of rounds fired, the poorer an officer's recall: with five or less rounds, 81 percent of officers accurately reported the number; with six to nine rounds, the accuracy figure shrank to 29 percent, and with 13 or more rounds, the recall rate plunged to 0 percent.

In my experience, number of rounds fired is frequently misremembered due to another factor not directly related to neurophysiology per se, but to the particular agency's shooting policy, particularly the "pop-to-drop" protocol. That is, these officers may not make much conscious effort to keep track of their trigger pulls because, having made the deadly force decision, they will just keep firing until they perceive the threat to have been neutralized, so it is almost irrelevant how many rounds it took—until someone starts questioning the shooting's justification. Then, the number of rounds may be used to argue that the level of force used ("hail of bullets") was excessive, and that the officer's lack of numerical recall either betrays a callous disregard for the slain suspect's life or represents the officer's slippery attempt to evade culpability by playing dumb.

In still other cases, an officer may show a combination of effects, that is, some narrow, isolated aspects of the deadly force scenario are recalled vividly, while others are hazy, distorted, or completely forgotten, or more likely, never encoded, for reasons discussed above. Thus, over a third of cases involve not so much a total loss of recall as a distortion of events, to the extent that the officer's account of what happened differs markedly from the report of other observers at the scene, or from videos recorded during the event. Variations in memory recall may interact with the kinds of multiple, shifting perceptual distortions described by Klinger and Brunson (2009; see Chapter 4), and a similar research program focused on memory would be enlightening.

The deleterious effect of an acutely stressful emergency scenario on subsequent memory for the event is hardly unique to law enforcement critical incidents. Survivors of transportation accidents and natural disasters, military personnel exposed to death and dismemberment, victims of physical and sexual assault, and even witnesses to a violent crime all may suffer impaired and/or distorted memory for the event, with many features of the incident forgotten or misremembered, while other memories are searingly sharp and persistent. Indeed, disorders of recollection, often involving a combination of overly vivid, disturbingly vague, and confusingly distorted memories make up one of the key diagnostic criteria for **posttraumatic stress disorder (PTSD)** (APA, 2013; Koopman et al., 1994; Morgan et al., 2004; Roemer et al., 1997; Scott et al., 2014; Southwick et al.,1997)–which, to be clear, the overwhelming majority of officers involved in an OIS/DFE *don't* have (Miller, 2005a, 2006d, 2008d, 2013b, 2015d, 2019a).

Memory distortions need not involve emergency situations. For example, research on the cognitive psychology of eyewitness memory (Benton et al., 2006; Conway, 2012; Loftus, 1996; Loftus et al., 1989; Morgan et al., 2004) has shown that this type of recall, too, is typically selective and reconstructive, and that one's subjective confidence and self-reported vividness of recall is often uncorrelated with the factual accuracy of the remembered event; that is, how clear a memory seems to be or how certain the person is about what he or she recalls may bear little relationship to what actually happened: it is common for rememberers to feel certain, but be wrong.

Thus, following a law enforcement OIS/DFE, Internal Affairs supervisors, grand jurors, and other investigators who are unfamiliar with the cognitive psychology of memory under stress may listen to an officer's spotty recollection of what the evaluators think ought to be a vividly memorable event ("how could you forget something like this?"), or they may hear an account by the officer that conflicts with the testimony of other observers, or with the images on cell phones and cameras, and mistakenly conclude that the officer is deliberately distorting facts or covering up events. In fact, many officers do not fully realize the extent of their own memory and perceptual gaps and distortions until confronted with the factual evidence, often in post-shooting operational debriefings, Internal Affairs investigations, or legal actions. The lesson for investigators is that discrepant accounts among eyewitnesses to a shooting scene do not automatically mean that someone must be lying, but may well represent honest differences in perception and recall (Artwohl, 2002, 2003).

Stress, Arousal, and Memory

One of the most important questions in both research and practice on stress and memory is the precise relationship between level of emotional arousal and accuracy of recall in diverse situations, whether law-enforcement-related or otherwise (Davis & Loftus, 2009; Hope et al., 2013, 2016; Leach & Ansel, 2008; Leach & Griffith, 2008; Meyerhoff et al., 2004;

Morgan et al., 2004, 2013; Morley & Farr, 2012; Payne et al., 2006; Safer et al., 1998). The explanations are often framed in the context of what we are now familiar with in the areas of perception and action: the concept of the **optimum arousal level**, or **OAL** (Flin, 1996; Hays & Brown, 2004; Klein, 1996; Miller, 2008i; Rodgers, 2006; also Chapter 5).

In the case of memory for officer-involved shootings, the OAL would be that which best enables the officer to focus his attention and concentrate on the task confronting him, allowing him to utilize his skills and also to remember the events clearly. In this case, the greater the arousal (ascending arm of the inverted-U; see Figure 5.1), the better the consolidation and recall of experience. But at some point past the OAL, higher arousal causes most functions, including memory formation, to degrade (descending arm of the inverted-U) and the officer's recollection would be expected to be less clear and accurate.

Research into the physiology of the stress response seems to support this concept (Adophs et al., 2005; Banks et al., 2014; De Kloet et al., 1998; Dequervain et al., 2000; Gal-Or et al., 1985; Kuhlman et al., 2005; Lupien & LePage, 2001; McGaugh, 2013; Miller, 2008; Phelps, 2006; Roozendaal, 2000; Schoofs et al., 2000; Traverners et al., 2013; Wolf et al., 2001). Threat-induced activation of the amygdala may enhance hippocampal coding of episodic memory at moderate levels of stimulation, but at higher levels, tends to inhibit it. Secretion of cortisol, in response to HPA-activation under stress, may likewise enhance cognitive processing at moderate levels, but at higher levels is known to have a suppressive effect on hippocampal functioning. In addition, high levels of stress impair frontal lobe executive function modulation of arousal, emotion, and behavior, so that the officer's split-second judgment and decision making are more vulnerable to disruption, and so is the memory for those events.

But even this is a simplistic explanation because, like other cognitive processes, memory for a stressful event is also influenced by a host of individual and contextual factors, including the individual's innate response pattern, the typicality versus novelty of the scenario compared to what he or she has trained for, and, importantly, what role the officer played at the scene, that is, was he directly confronted by the armed assailant or was he simply providing backup? Was he merely an observer of events, primed to respond if necessary, but not actually engaged in the encounter? As we've discussed, OIS/DFE investigators are often confoundd by, or skeptical of, differing accounts given by on-scene responding officers, observing officers, and civilian witnesses, often raising suspicions of deliberate memory fabrication, because, supposedly, officers should all be telling the same story since they all saw the same thing. But did they?

A study by Beehr et al. (2004) manipulated the stress level of a sample of officer volunteers by assigning them to three groups: (1) participating in a live-fire training simulation; (2) viewing a video of another officer going through the live-fire training; and (3) viewing a video with no shooting in it. They found that the subjects' recall for stressful simulation events was more accurate for simulated suspects portrayed as being armed than for unarmed suspects, which the researchers attribute to a **threat-focus effect**. In addition, memory was enhanced when the subjects had a chance to rehearse their recollections. Finally, overall accuracy of recall was unrelated to subject confidence; that is, subjects who were certain they were remembering events clearly were no more accurate than those less sure of their mnemonic prowess.

The work of Hope and colleagues (Hope et al., 2013, 2016) has highlighted the role of an officer's level of incident involvement on his or her memory encoding and recall of that event. This would seem to make intuitive sense: an officer who is zeroed-in on an assailant's weapon and trying to gauge if he will momentarily be killed might be expected to have a different perception, and later recall, than another officer who is covering the first officer, but who may not be actively threatened or directly engaging the assailant.

Hope et al. (2016) studied the behavior and recall of a simulated DFE in a sample of police officers, linked in pairs. One officer in each pair was designated an **operational active witness**, who was armed and was instructed to respond to the scenario, based on his experience and training, just as he would in a real operational setting. The other officer was a **nonoperational nonactive observer witness**, whose task it was to simply monitor the scenario as it unfolded. All officers in both groups underwent a preliminary briefing in which basic facts and information about the simulated scenario were discussed, similar to what officers might glean from a dispatcher or supervisor on the way to an actual call.

One item of information discussed in the briefing was the fact that the perpetrator was armed with a gun. A key feature of the scenario occurred in the final sequence when the role-play perpetrator turned suddenly to face the officers, throwing his hands out in front of him, however, with the gun remaining in his waistband throughout the critical phase of the encounter. Stress levels during the scenario were measured physiologically by monitoring both average heart rate and heart rate variability. Following the scenario, the event recall of all officers was surveyed via two formats: a free narrative report and a series of closed questions, similar to what might take place in a forensic or other investigative interview (Geiselman & Fisher, 1997; Geiselman et al., 2018).

At baseline, physiological readings for the two groups were equivalent. However, in the simulated shooting scenario, the active witnesses showed significantly elevated heart rates, indicating an increased physiological stress response, compared with the nonactive observer witnesses. Both groups correctly recalled similar amounts of information from the pre-scenario briefing. On free recall of the critical response phase of the scenario, however, the active witnesses remembered overall fewer details than the inactive witnesses, but the accuracy rate of these memories was no different than those of the inactive witnesses. In other words, the active witnesses recalled less information, but what they did remember was as accurate as the greater amount of information recalled by the inactive observers. As one possible explanation for these findings, the researchers speculate that trained law enforcement personnel may learn to adopt a **conservative reporting bias**; that is, they would rather not report something they're not sure of than go out on a limb and describe a fuzzy memory that could later be proven wrong.

Finally, the amount of information recalled by the active witnesses was negatively correlated with heart rate and heart rate variability; that is, the higher the level of stress-induced physiological arousal, the less information recalled, consistent with the idea that greater mobilization of brain systems to confront an extant threat leaves less cerebral capacity devoted to memory input and consolidation.

When it came to the closed-question recall format, accuracy rates were low for both active and observer officers, with just over half of questions answered correctly. Across subject groups, almost one-fifth of officers incorrectly reported that the perpetrator had pointed a weapon at them; however, the active officers were significantly more likely to make this error than observer officers, again apparently highlighting the effects of increased stress-induced arousal on amount and accuracy of information recalled in a simulated DFE scenario.

According to Hope et al. (2016), the effects of stress-induced arousal on memory recall make perfect sense in light of the inverted-U OAL paradigm. That is, the moderately elevated arousal level in the inactive observer officers (as indicated by an average heart rate of 110 bpm) may correspond to the ascending arm of the inverted-U curve, where increased arousal sharpens and focuses perception and recall. However, the extremely elevated arousal level (average of 126 bpm) in the active officers slides them down the descending arm of the OAL curve, where initial encoding of information to be remembered becomes degraded or distorted due to excessive stress.

The finding that 18 percent of the study's police officer sample erroneously remembered that the perpetrator pointed a weapon at them is cited by the researchers as consistent with a similar rate of misperceiving and misremembering weapon threat that occurs in military samples (Morgan et al., 2013), so that a **default threat bias** appears universal in responders who face critical decision-making in deadly threat situations (Grossman & Christensen, 2007; Lamme, 2006).

That is, with greater arousal comes a greater likelihood of overestimating danger at the scene and recalling greater level of danger when the crisis is over, which we have previously subsumed under the concept of **threat magnification**. In such high-stress scenarios, the expectation of a weapon wielded by an assailant, followed by failure to detect said weapon in a rapid initial visual sweep, may unconsciously activate the default threat response mechanism, leading the officer to the near-instantaneous conclusion that, "maybe the reason I don't see a weapon is not because it isn't there (an assumption that could get me killed), but because I'm just not picking it up fast enough, so I'd better neutralize the threat while I still can (better safe than sorry)." If this is the way it appeared to the officer at the scene, then this is the way he will remember it.

In line with the above, all officers in Hope et al.'s (2016) study who mistakenly reported seeing a weapon pointed at them responded by firing their own weapons in the scenario. Of course, in real-life contested OIS/DFE cases, an added complication is the possibility of unconscious or deliberate self-serving fabrication or distortion of memories by officers under investigation (see Chapter 9), or officers might just feel embarrassed by a possible overreaction that they believe would reflect poorly on their self-image of being able to keep sharp in a dire encounter: "I'm not the kind of cop who shoots somebody for no reason, so there must have been a deadly threat present, and, yeah, that's how I remember it."

As with perception, additional examples of mnemonic threat magnification include officers perceiving a grounded or immobilized subject as rising to attack them, misinterpreting nonthreatening objects as weapons (as in the S/DS research discussed in Chapter 4), or even perceiving subjects who are moving away from the officer as actually closing in.

Hope et al.'s (2016) research begins to weld the scientific study of stress psychophysiology with the existing knowledge base on the neuropsychology of emergency response cognition, emotion, action, and memory. Future studies will hopefully expand the range of physical and psychological measures used to develop a psychophysiological typology of the human stress response that can be applied to a wide range of military, law enforcement, and civilian applications. For practical purposes, these findings mean that, in investigating a police DFE, different modes of interrogatory information gathering (e.g., open narrative vs. closed question, etc.) may be optimally utilized for different officers with different on-scene experiences, and varying time periods following the incident.

SUMMARY AND CONCLUSIONS

Memory can be a precision tool or a blunt instrument. Memory for a given event is always a reconstructive process that can be mostly accurate, partly distorted, or just plain wrong, and how confident we are in the accuracy of our recollection may bear scant relationship to reality. "I forgot" can mean: (1) I never processed it in the first place; (2) I recall some of the event, but other parts are a blank; (3) I think I remember it, but I might be confusing it with something else; (4) I don't understand why what I remember is differently from what others claim they saw happen; or (5) I want to believe I did the right thing, so that's how I'll remember it.

The limbic brain mechanisms for emotion and memory evolved together because what you remember is determined by what is important to the survival of yourself and your species. Stressful circumstances induce physiological and psychological arousal which, depending on the severity, may either enhance or inhibit memory formation, sometimes both, affecting different aspects of remembering the same critical incident, so that some recollections are crystalline, others gauzy, still others nonexistent.

The vagaries of memory mean that some police officers who claim amnesia for some but not all events during a critical incident may be telling the truth, as are officers who remember events in a way that is discrepant from what others recollect or from stark video evidence. But some officers may be lying to cover themselves (see Chapter 9) and others may be unintentionally confabulating events, i.e., filling in their memory gaps with material that "seems right" or "makes sense" based on what they now know, post-incident. As with all topics discussed in this book, encouraging OIS/ DFE-involved officers—or any party or witness to any event—to profer as accurate and truthful a narrative as possible necessitates a careful approach to forensic information gathering informed by cognitive science as it continues to evolve.

Part III

DEADLY FORCE: PRACTICE AND POLICY

Chapter 7

POLICE DEADLY FORCE AND RACE

We are not going to let up until we see a strengthening of the trust and a strengthening of the accountability that exists between our communities and our law enforcement.

President Barak Obama,
presentation to White House
Tribal Nations Conference,
December 3, 2014

When you see these towns and when you see these thugs being thrown into the back of a paddy wagon, you just see them thrown in, rough, and I said, "Please don't be too nice."

President Donald Trump,
presentation to International
Association of Chiefs of Police,
July 7, 2017

We've danced around the topic long enough, resulting in too many needless deaths on both sides and so much unnecessary bitterness between citizens and police. A few pages won't resolve the whole issue of race and law enforcement, but in this chapter, I want discuss the points most relevant to the assessment and adjudication of OIS/DFE cases.

POLICE RACIAL BIAS: THE "FERGUSON EFFECT" AND BEYOND

The "Ferguson Effect" gets its name from the shooting of Michael Brown by Officer Darren Wilson in the city of Ferguson, Missouri on August 9, 2014. The phrase was first coined by St. Louis Metropolitan Police Chief Sam Dotson in 2014 to explain the perception of escalating crime rates as police supposedly pulled back from their interdiction efforts, allowing criminals to grow more emboldened. This was preceded and followed by a series of highly publicized police shootings of reportedly unarmed black citizens in American cities such as Baltimore, MD, North Charleston, SC, and Chicago, IL, among others (Dye & del Carmen, 2017; Wolfe & Nix, 2016).

Although the name is new, the effect of community condemnation of police on their subsequent laxity of response to neighborhood crime has been reported over the past century of North American police-community relations, including police strikes or work slow-downs in Boston in 1919, Montreal in 1969, Baltimore in 1974, Los Angeles in the 1990s, and others (Cook, 2015). In each case, the perception was that local police were holding back in their crime fighting efforts for fear of being accused of and prosecuted for racial profiling and bias, sometimes referred to as "de-policing" (Oliver, 2017). In some, more sinister, interpretations, police were allegedly permitting crimes to take place in retaliation for citizens' unfairly maligning the officers' efforts, or in some cases, for reporting the officers and/or cooperating with authorities who were investigating them, i.e., to "teach them a lesson." To some commentators (e.g., Wolfe & Nix, 2016), this has resulted in a critical challenge to the fundamental premise of police authority among many citizens, especially minority citizens.

Technology often drives and supports social movements, and widespread access to smartphone video recording, along with near-instantaneous social media dissemination, have exponentially expanded the average citizen's ability to surveil, monitor, and record police actions, then transmit them to virtually limitless numbers of people. Police officers, it is argued, who feel that their actions are misunderstood, or deliberately distorted and manipulated, will consequently be motivated to restrain their crime interdiction efforts in order to avoid being turned into public pariahs or prosecuted as felons. Former FBI director James Comey described the chilling consequences of this **viral video effect** on police motivation to assertively and proactively fight crime in the face of suspicion and hostility from the very public they are struggling to protect. A growing narrative among many community members is that *any* use of force by police against minority citizens is automatically excessive and illegitimate (Dye & del Carmen, 2017).

In a survey of almost 8,000 police officers, Morin et al. (2017) found that up to 93 percent of officer respondents believe that interactions between police and black citizens have generally become more tense, that, in particular, deadly force encounters between police and black citizens have made policing harder, and that, as a result, officers are now more concerned about their safety on the job. Consequently, officers have become more reluctant to use even necessary and justifiable force in crime interdiction, and many are less likely to stop and question citizens who behave suspiciously. That is, officers may forgo the use of even legitimate police tactics that might deter potential criminal activity.

To be fair, few officers will deliberately overlook an obvious and serious crime in progress, such as an armed robbery, sexual assault, or active shooter scenario, where the officer's aggressive interdiction efforts would be clearly understood. But they may not so readily hop out of their patrol car to approach a group of young males who are huddling together and perhaps planning a burglary or drug sale. Or they may wait to respond to a reported domestic violence incident in progress until sufficient back-up arrives, in order not to be baited into a tussle with a family member. In fact, published accounts (Dye & del Carmen, 2017) and my own experience suggest that most officers want to patrol and protect their areas effectively, because making a positive community impact is a primary source of pride and professional identity and one of the main reasons many of them went into policing in the first place.

What they *don't* want is to exert these efforts and then be reviled by the very citizens they are trying to protect or, worse, treated with suspicion by their own departmental superiors for what they perceive to be the brass's self-serving political agendas. In fact, studies have documented the corrosive effect on officers' morale and motivation that perceived loss of law enforcement authority and legitimacy can have when it comes both from the communities they patrol and from within their own agencies (Cook, 2015; Dye & del Carmen, 2017; Wolfe & Nix, 2016).

IS RACISM ENDEMIC TO POLICING?

The demographic facts are clear: most U.S. police officers are white; the citizens they confront in their law enforcement activities are disproportionately minorities. Does this mean that in American law enforcement, racial bias is inevitable? Some commentators (Chaney & Robertson, 2013; Hall et al., 2016; Tonry, 2011) go so far as to assert that American police identity and enculturation actively encourage racial bias, and that whites in general characteristically excuse (and thereby effectively encourage) police brutality against blacks because of the endemic racism in American society. In most surveys, black citizens experience themselves as unequally targeted by police use of force and other police actions. Police officers, for their part, experience interactions with black citizens as potentially more dangerous than with other citizens (Smith & Holmes, 2003).

For example, one large-scale study (Tonry, 2011) involving 1,010 black and 978 non-Hispanic white participants revealed a significant divergence of attitudes between the two groups concerning the criminal justice system. In this survey, 38 percent of whites and 89 percent of blacks viewed the criminal justice system as biased against blacks. Additionally, 56 percent of whites, compared to 8 percent of blacks, saw the criminal justice system as treating blacks fairly, and 68 percent of whites versus 18 percent of blacks expressed confidence in law enforcement as a whole. Another study (Elicker, 2008) found white citizens to be significantly more accepting than black citizens of police use of force when a citizen was attempting to escape custody.

Surveys (Brunson & Miller, 2006a, 2006b; Brunson & Weitzer, 2008; Rojek et al., 2012) of black citizens and police officers involved in alleged incidents of excessive force demonstrate that—no surprise—the two sides frequently see things from opposite polarities. Police officers typically regard their struggles with citizens as a skewed street fight in which all the constraints and regulations fall on the officer, but where there are no rules for the citizen. They view their forceful actions as reasonable and necessary to maintain safety, control the scene, and enforce the law. For their part, most black citizens understand, in a general way, the need for a law enforcement presence in a community, but interpret many officers' actions as unnecessarily dismissive, demeaning, coercive, and physically abusive.

A recent analysis (D'Souza et al., 2019) examined U.S. Department of Justice investigations of reported police misconduct and civil rights violations in four cities: Baltimore, Chicago, New Orleans, and Ferguson, Missouri. The reports consistently showed that black citizens were disproportionately impacted by several types of police misconduct: (1) racist and sexist language; (2) failure to de-escalate confrontations and even deliberate provoking of tensions with citizens; (3) using physical force as intimidation, punishment, or retaliation for a citizen's perceived disrespectful attitude; (4) inappropriate display or use of firearms or less-lethal weapons for intimidation, coercion, or to force compliance; (5) use of canines for intimidation, coercion, or punishment on adults and children, and often involving insufficiently trained or noncertified dogs; (6) pursuit of a citizen leads to officer shooting; (7) mistreatment of mentally ill citizens.

Other studies (Basehart & Cox, 1993; Patton et al., 2017; Sharps et al., 2019) have found that officers who use excessive profanity with citizens are more likely to be later judged to have used excessive force or at least to have acted unprofessionally, even if the outcome of the encounter (e.g., lawful arrest) is not disputed.

Question: is a society wherein the majority group overwhelmingly approves of police actions that are considered abusive by a minority group going to be willing to do anything substantive to curtail perceived police brutality against those minorities?

POLICE USE OF FORCE AND RACE

While there is scant agreement on causes, a convergence of research and anecdotal observation, from diverse locales and different time periods, largely concurs that police officers do apply force, including deadly force, proportionately more frequently with black citizens, and to a variable extent, other minorities such as Latinos, than with white citizens (Brown & Langan, 2001; Geller, 1982; Hall et al., 2016; Ho, 1993; Jacobs & O'Brien, 1998; Kobler, 1975; Meyer, 1980; Robin, 1963; Sherman, 1979; Sorenson et al., 1993; Takagi, 1974), although this opinion is not unanimous (Johnson et al., 2019).

While police deadly force and other serious use of force encounters are rare with any ethnic group (Chapter 1), more common are other types of police actions, such as surveillance, searches, traffic stops, ticketing, and arrests, and these, too, are more likely to occur with minority citizens (Gellman et al., 2007; James et al., 2016; Lange et al., 2005; Lundman & Kaufman, 2003; Meehan & Ponder, 2002; Rinehart et al., 2011; Terrill & Mastrofski, 2002). Even fellow officers are not immune: of 14 officers in New York State who were killed by other officers in mistaken-identity shootings over a 15-year period, 10 of the slain officers were racial minorities.

U.S. Department of Justice (DOJ) statistics (Alpert & Dunham, 2010; Brown & Langan, 2001; Cooper & Smith, 2011; FBI, 2015; Fox & Zawitz, 2006; Greenfield et al., 1999; Langan et al., 2001; Ross & Brave, 2018) indicate that less than 2 percent of police-citizen encounters result in any use of force, and only a fraction of these develop into police shootings. Ninety-eight percent of citizens killed by police are young males of any race. Since 1978, the proportion of black U.S. citizens killed by police has been declining, from 49 percent in 1978 to 35 percent in 1998, a 22 percent decline. Over the same time period, the number of white males killed by the police has increased by 21 percent. In absolute numbers, a white male, aged 16 to 29, is currently twice as likely as a black male and three times as likely as any other race to have any kind of police force used or threatened.

These are absolute numbers, but bear in mind that the proportion of black citizens in the general U.S. population is about 13 percent, which means that, in relative terms, a proportionately far greater number of black citizens are still being killed by police than white citizens. Conversely, during that same time period, young black males killed police officers at a proportional rate almost six times that of young white males. In 64 percent of the shooting incidents, the citizen attacked the police; in 24 percent, he or she fled or resisted the officer; and in 16 percent, the circumstances were undetermined.

A study commissioned by the *Washington Post* (Shane et al., 2017) found that, overall, the most common age of subjects shot and killed by police was 31, with over half of them between ages 20–39. Subjects were more than 95 percent male and over half were white, in absolute numbers. About two-thirds of subjects were attacking police when they were killed, and over 90 percent were armed. Six types of weapons accounted for over 90 percent of objects wielded by slain subjects. About two-thirds of these were guns; the others were knives, vehicles, toy weapons, a machete, and a sword. The authors recommend that future research focus not only on demographics, but on the individual characteristics of each encounter.

Worrall et al. (2018) surveyed the real-life OIS experiences of sworn police officers at a large municipal police department in the Southwestern United States. Replicating the DOJ data, they found that black suspects were one-third as likely to be shot as other-race suspects (although, again, consider this against racial proportionality in the general population). Importantly, suspect behavior was found to be a far greater predictive variable than race: displaying a weapon increased a suspect's chances of being shot seven-fold, and making direct aggressive threats against a police officer made it 29 times more likely that the suspect would be fired upon.

With regard to officer characteristics, in this study, patrol officers were significantly less likely to shoot a suspect than SWAT team members, and shooting was more likely to occur where multiple officers responded to the scene. The probability that an officer would shoot a suspect was correlated with the number of citizen complaints filed against that officer in the previous year. In this study, number of years of education did not correlate with an officer's propensity to shoot; however, as noted in Chapter 2, it is not the absolute amount of classroom time that accounts for the education effect on an officer's propensity to use or withhold force, but the traits of perseverance and self-control that allow an officer to complete a college degree, traits that appear to be associated with greater restraint and thoughtfulness in stressful confrontations.

If these data are to be believed, over the last three decades in the United States, police officers have been killing a declining number of young black males in absolute numbers, but still a population-proportionately greater number of young black males than young white males. At the same time, young black males have been killing a growing number of police officers. So, the bad news is that both sides may be right: if you are a young black male, you are proportionately more likely than any other demographic group member to be killed by a police officer; if you are a police officer, you are proportionately more likely to be killed by a young black male than by any other demographic group member.

Finally, it appears that we are not yet close to unanimity in confirming a race-based bias in OISs. Using a comprehensive database of fatal OISs, Johnson et al. (2019) recently found no evidence of anti-black or anti-Hispanic bias in police shootings. In fact, what emerged was an association of

Table 7.1.
FACTORS ASSOCIATED WITH POLICE USE OF FORCE AND RACE

Race of officer: No consistent relationship.found.

Environment: Low SES communities have higher levels of adverse police-citizen interacton of any kind.

Behavioral vicious cycles: Mutual mistrust between citizens and officers leads to higher incidences of provocation and escalation of adverse confrontations.

Shoot/don't shoot (S/DS) research and race:

Untrained civilians make more false-positive shooting errors (misidentify nonthreatening black target images as threatening, and fire at target).

Trained law enforcement officers make fewer false-positive errors and more false-negative errors (withhold fire from threatening black target images)

Brain recordings show that both civilians and officers experience conflict in responding to black target images and may actually try to suppress implicit race-biased response tendencies.

Training: Focused on teaching officers to make shooting decisions based on behavioral variables, not racial characteristics. Success has been mixed, especially where racial identity has become a cognitive heuristic for dangerousness.

crime rate with likelihood of being fatally shot. That is, in locales where minorities committed higher rates of violent crime, they were about three times as likely to be shot and killed by police; criminal violence, not race per se, was the salient factor. This, however, may be a distinction without a difference if police come to associate minority status with increased risk for criminal violence, as will be discussed later in this chapter.

FACTORS RELATED TO FORCE, DEALY FORCE, AND RACE

Few things are as simple as they superficially appear, and the search for explanations for a purported race-based police bias must try to carefully consider all the variables that contribute to police deadly force use in general (see Chapters 1 and 2), and with minority citizens in particular (Table 7.1).

Neighborhood Variables and Officer Race

This book has emphasized the importance of taking seriously, albeit not accepting uncritically, officers' perceptions and accounts of the worlds they live and work in. Police who have patrolled a particular area for any length of time get to know their territory and its inhabitants intimately and have learned that some neighborhoods, even some particular streets or individual addresses, may pose a higher risk than others for criminal activity and compromised officer safety (Cox et al., 2014; Stroshine et al., 2008). If officers' hypervigilant "cop radar" is tuned up higher in certain patrol areas, the likelihood for action–and overreaction–to a threat or challenge increases commensurately.

One important variable may be the race of the police officer him- or herself. A number of studies (Cox et al., 2014; Donohue & Levitt, 2001; Katz & Greenbaum, 1963; Page-Gould et al., 2008; Plant & Devine, 2003; Thompson & Sekaquaptewa, 2002; Trawalter et al., 2009) suggest that black officers who patrol areas with greater numbers of like-race citizens have fewer use-of-force incidents and make fewer arrests. Black officers are also more likely to proactively try to resolve citizen conflicts and to provide supportive community policing-type services, whether or not these are officially mandated by their agencies. An intuitively obvious explanation would be that an officer is likely to feel more affinity with, empathy for, and allegiance to, citizens of similar background, and therefore might be more inclined to "go easy" on them.

However, isn't it just as plausible that such similarity and familiarity might simply reduce the common fear and suspicion that people feel in unfamiliar contexts, thereby serving to lower the overall tension level of any given police-citizen encounter? That is, where black officers make fewer arrests and have fewer adverse encounters with black citizens, this may have less to do with any sort of racial favoritism, but rather with the overall lower emotional temperature that attends interactions with persons they more fully understand and feel comfortable with.

Nevertheless, commonality of race and culture does not guarantee less conflict. Other evidence suggests that black officers may be disproportionately more likely than white officers to shoot citizens, to be killed by citizens, and to use coercive actions with citizens (Brown & Langan, 2001; Friedrich, 1980; Fyfe, 1981; 1988; Geller & Karales, 1981; Geller & Scott, 1992; Jacobs & O'Brien, 1998; Mastrofski et al., 1995; Sorenson et al., 1993; Sun & Payne, 2004; Terrill & Mastrofski, 2002; Terrill & Reisig, 2003; Worden, 1995). Part of this difference in findings may relate to the demographics of deployment: in some agencies, black officers may be disproportionately assigned to minority neighborhoods where crime rates are highest. In such circumstances, a more reactive and aggressive policing style may be called for, regardless of citizen or officer race. In more placid communities, officers of any race can afford to lighten up and emphasize a more preventive and problem-solving approach to law enforcement.

In other words, in whatever patrol community they find themselves, black officers may be more likely to be invested in, involved in, and engaged with their neighborhoods, more likely to want to "own the beat" (see Chapter 1). Even here, however, individual officer attitude makes a difference. In a given neighborhood, officers, black or white, who adhere to a traditional law-and-order model of patrol policing are more likely to garner excessive force complaints than those trying to apply a more community policing-style approach. Finally, in any given encounter, individual citizen behavior (e.g., cooperative vs. belligerent) is a far more reliable predictor of police action than officer or citizen race, per se.

Demographic Variables

In their attempts to dodge accusations of blaming the victim, most researchers and theorists (many of whom are employed by universities or public agencies and may fear public censure or career damage) have steered clear of identifying suspect behavioral variables that might make police more likely to use force and deadly force with minority citizens. Putting it bluntly, what if police are more likely to kill black suspects because they believe that black suspects are more likely to kill them? As noted above, research from diverse locales and different time periods suggests that areas characterized by a greater proportion of black citizens being shot *by* police are also characterized by a greater proportion of black citizens shooting *at* police (Brown & Langan, 2001; Fyfe, 1982; Inn, 1977; James et al., 2013; MacDonald et al., 2001; Meyer, 1980; White, 2002).

Where such confrontations appear to single out black citizens, research suggests this may be explained by the factors of: (1) higher likelihood of violent criminal conduct by community members, especially young males; (2) lower level of overall community cooperation with law enforcement; (3) greater likelihood of residents being armed with firearms; (4) high-population urban areas with low socioeconomic status of the community; and (5) the perception by community members that the police are already biased and engaged in the continued repression of minority residents, creating a vicious cycle of hostility and recrimination (Black, 1971; Fyfe, 1982a; Jacobs & O'Brien, 1998; McElvain & Kposawa, 2008; Robin, 1964).

Again, part of this may be due to the demographics of many high-crime communities, which typically have a predominantly white police department and a predominantly minority citizenry. In these communities, young black males are more likely to be affected by deadly force encounters because young males of any race or ethnicity are disproportionately involved in illegal activity and aggressive confrontations of any sort (Cooper & Smith, 2011; Fox & Zawitz, 2006; Langan et al., 2001; Ross & Brave, 2018). In majority-white neighborhoods, it will be young white males who are most likely to be involved; in majority-black neighborhoods, it will be young black males; same with Latino communities, Asian communities, and so on.

Consciously or unconsciously, many officers will profile young males, including young black males, engaged in certain types of suspicious actions because the cops' instinct, training, and experience have taught them that these situations carry a high risk for potential illegal activity and danger. However, in the absence of suspicious behavior, there is little evidence that white officers systematically target minority citizens for their race alone (McElvain & Kposawa, 2004, 2008). Of course, the very definition of what constitutes "suspicious" behavior may be shaded by an officer's pre-existing prejudices or by his or her own real-world experience in dealing with citizens of varying ethnicities, while the citizens' perception of categorically unfair treatment makes them more likely to react to even neutral police contact with animosity, creating yet another vicious cycle of mutual acrimony and mistrust.

As noted above, violent environments often make for violent policing, and jurisdictions in which police officers kill civilians at higher rates are also those locales where civilians kill police officers, as well as one another, at higher rates (Garner et al., 1995; Griffin & Bernard, 2003; Lester, 1982, 1984). However, it may not always be clear where this vicious cycle begins, since some police officers may initially presume or come to believe that the entire community is more hostile to them than is actually the case, especially with less educated officers who may harbor pre-existing prejudices (Crawford, 1973; Lersch, 1998). Because they stay off the cops' radar (literally and figuratively), the silent majority of law-abiding citizens of any race, in any neighborhood, are rarely encountered by police on a daily basis, as officers deal mainly with lawbreakers, troublemakers, and their victims. It is thus easy for officers to have their perceptions of an entire community skewed in the direction of cynicism and hostility.

When an encounter ensues, many police officers will first try to use verbal and behavioral de-escalation strategies with all citizens before resorting to any kind of force, much less deadly force–if they think it will work. One situation where minority citizens may be unequivocally more likely to be subject to use of force than white citizens is in the presence of large crowds, especially where one or more minority citizens have initiated disrespect or outright aggression toward the police, and officers are fearful of being overwhelmed by sheer force of numbers (Mastrofski et al., 2002). Especially with the contagion effect that characterizes agitated groups of any type, white officers may believe, or have learned from experience, that groups of black citizens are less likely to take the officers' peacemaking efforts seriously, especially if these citizens have had frequent, unpleasant experiences with police in the past.

RESEARCH ON RACIAL BIAS IN POLICE SHOOTINGS

Of course, in addition to the quotidian indignities of unjust harassment, racial bias in policing becomes a deadly serious issue when it expresses itself in a differential rate of OIS/DFEs with racial minorities, if the primary factor is race alone. Through the use of improved technology and more informed theoretical conceptualizations, some researchers are attempting to subject the issue of police racial bias in OIS/DFEs to the cold light of scientific examination.

Shoot/Don't Shoot and Race

In Chapters 4 and 5, we encountered the **shoot/don't shoot (S/DS)** research paradigm. Recall that, in one version of these studies, volunteers are presented with a pair of keyboard buttons and told to press one button for a shoot response and the other for a don't-shoot response. Subjects are then shown photos or videos depicting either dangerous or neutral scenarios, and must make a S/DS decision as quickly as possible. As we've seen, this research has identified the fact that both untrained civilians and experienced police officers frequently mistakenly "shoot" suspects later revealed to have been depicted holding non-firearm objects, such as toy guns or power tools.

A number of researchers have applied the S/DS methodology to the study of race effects on decisions to shoot (Amodio et al., 2003, 2004; Correll et al., 2001, 2002, 2006; 2007a, 2007b; Cox et al., 2014; Eberhardt et al., 2004; James et al., 2013; Ma et al., 2013; Payne, 2001; Payne et al., 2002; Plant & Peruche, 2005; Plant et al., 2005; Sim et al., 2013). In most of these paradigms, the researchers cross-vary the combinations of race of the suspect with dangerousness of the scenario. For example, four depicted possibilities might be: (1) armed white suspect (wielding firearm); (2) unarmed white suspect (holding cell phone or work tool); (3) armed black subject (firearm); and (4) unarmed black subject (phone or tool). In many of these studies, an intriguing divergence of results has appeared, depending on the method of presentation.

With still images (photographs), civilians show a clear bias toward mistakenly shooting unarmed black suspects more frequently than unarmed white suspects, and correctly shooting armed black suspects more quickly than armed white suspects. Police officers show a less consistent pattern, but the trend is still toward shooting depicted black suspects more often than white ones, although formal training seems to somewhat attenuate this race bias effect. However, when the study methodology employs more realistic video sequences, a reverse race bias is seen, with both civilians and officers slower to shoot armed black than armed white suspects, and more often mistakenly failing to shoot armed black than armed white suspects. That is, with more realistic animated portrayals of shooting scenarios, both civilians and police officers are more likely to hold their fire with black suspects in an ambiguously dangerous situation.

Recalling the above discussion of neighborhood factors in influencing an officer's perception of danger, one study (Correll et al., 2001) varied the setting of the depicted black or white suspects by embedding their images in either a "threatening" environment (closed, dark alleyway) or a "neutral" one (open, sunny park). The participants, who were college students, not police officers, showed a racial bias only in the neutral environments, not the threatening ones. That is, subjects were more likely to mistakenly shoot depicted unarmed black subjects than unarmed white suspects in the park setting, but were just as likely to mistakenly shoot suspects of either race when they were portrayed as skulking in the dingy alleyway, implying that, in a tense situation, environmental creepiness outweighs race as the salient danger factor. However, an alternative explanation might be that the study subjects shot more unarmed black targets in the park than in the alley because of an implicit bias (see discussion below) that the black images "didn't belong" in the bright open spaces as much as the white images.

More recent research on shooting bias has focused on active police officers and utilized advances in S/DS technology and methodology. As noted in Chapters 4 and 5, a number of investigators (Cox et al., 2014; James et al., 2013, 2016) have criticized the pushbutton paradigm by pointing out that, while shooting requires a series of positive actions, such as raising a weapon and pulling the trigger, *not* shooting, by definition, implies lack of action or at least a different response in actively suppressing the shooting motion. Thus, pressing a second button or keyboard key for the don't-shoot choice is anomalous for the response an officer actually would be expected to make in a deadly force encounter, which is to refrain from pulling the trigger.

Accordingly, some researchers have devised more true-to-life experimental scenarios, with study subjects utilizing realistic weapon facsimiles and acting within the same kind of immersive virtual reality environments that are used in many law enforcement training curricula. Aside from their knowledge that this is a simulation, the subjects are operating in an S/DS scenario that is as close to the real thing as one can get. For the purposes of the race-biased shooting research discussed here, the task then becomes to incorporate the variations in the simulated suspects' race x weapon paradigm.

Using this type of immersive methodology, Cox et al. (2014) found that active-duty police officers made very few shooting errors with depicted suspects of any race. In fact, the most common type of error was either failing to shoot an armed suspect of any race when the officers would have been justified in doing so, or not responding fast enough to neutralize the simulated threat, which in a real-life DFE would have left themselves and others vulnerable to a lethal attack. In addition, the experimenters varied the environmental context of the scenarios and found that when officers were in simulated versions of other-race neighborhoods (e.g., white officer patrolling black neighborhood), they were more likely to mistakenly not shoot armed suspects of any race.

James et al. (2013) found similar results with police, military, and civilian subjects; that is, in realistic simulations, all three groups were significantly slower to shoot portrayed black suspects than white or Latino suspects, and significantly more likely to fail to shoot armed black suspects than white or Latino ones. Far from indicating an inherent anti-black bias on the part of police officers, the study's authors view their results and those of others as supporting a bias in *favor* of black suspects when it comes to their risk of being shot by police.

As for why, James et al. (2013, 2016) offer several speculative explanations: (1) modern police may be swiftly evolving toward greater cultural sensitivity; (2) modern police may be experiencing an "administrative effect," in which they make a special effort not to shoot minority suspects for fear of disciplinary and legal repercussions; and/or (3) the subjects in these studies may still harbor their secret prejudices, but are making a deliberate effort to appear unbiased in front of the experimenter, i.e., they're being deceptively restrained during the study, which may not reflect their real behavior on the street.

The study's authors note that none of these explanations is entirely satisfactory. It is unlikely that there has been a sudden national wave of sociocultural enlightenment influencing police officers' behavior toward racial minorities. The administrative effect, that is, fear of departmental censure, would not apply to the civilian participants in this study, although perhaps somewhat more so to the military service members. In fact, many officers who have been involved in noncontested OIS/DFEs have related to me in follow-up evaluations that they might have hesitated a little bit before firing at a minority citizen for fear of the potential backlash. Others have stated that there were previous incidents where they withheld or delayed fire because of a suspect's minority status. Although by far the exceptions (most officers report responding to the actual threat as they perceive it), these anecdotal reports may have serious implications for officer safety in such encounters.

Not wanting to be seen as racist by the experimenters could explain some of the effect, but let me suggest a fourth, more psychodynamic explanation, which is actually an extension of the third. That is, the officer participants may have wanted to convince *themselves* that they are fundamentally unbiased: "See, when I had the chance to shoot a black suspect (in the experiment), I held back and gave him the benefit of the doubt–that *proves* I'm not a racist, no matter what else I might do out there on the street."

Related to the above, there is apt to be somewhat of a self-report bias in recounting one's decision-making in either a simulation study or actual OIS/DFE; that is, it is highly unlikely that an officer would state that he was *more* motivated to shoot a suspect because of that suspect's minority status, even if it were true. And, in fact, the reverse race bias found is these studies is not universal: other simulation studies (e.g., Correll et al., 2007a, 2007b) have found both police and civilian participants to show a distinct racial bias toward shooting armed black suspects more quickly than armed white ones. Further research will hopefully clarify the individual factors of officer personality and departmental enculturation that account for these differences in outcomes.

Why at least some sworn police officers should show less of a shooting bias toward black targets than civilian volunteers may have a lot to do with training, according to Correll et al. (2011). In this view, continued practice in shooting simulations would allow officers to develop the kind of working memory capacity (WMC) and cognitive control discussed in Chapter 5, which, in turn, would enable them to override any prepotent response bias they may have toward black targets, simulated or real-life. At the same time, a component of such training involves learning how to control emotional and physiological responses to critical stress, so trained officers may be more capable of maintaining the optimum arousal level (OAL) discussed in Chapter 5 and, correspondingly, be less susceptible to the effects of ego-depletion. Yet, they're not immune. Other research shows that progressively increasing cognitive load can override the cognitive control benefit of training, allowing race bias to re-emerge in S/DS tasks. This speaks to the need for realistic training scenarios that replicate the kinds of intense police-citizen confrontations that occur in the real world (Beilock & Carr, 2001; Correll et al., 2014).

But, as Correll et al. (2011) point out, training cannot be the whole story and is certainly not a panacea for race-biased shooting. Special unit officers who work gang and street crimes details certainly get as much, if not more, tactical firearms and other combat training than patrol officers, yet these special unit officers show a greater race-based shooting bias than patrol officers, about equivalent to that of untrained civilians (Sims et al., 2013). The clue may lie in the populations these officers deal with. Patrol cops spend most of their time dealing with ordinary citizens; few civilians are paragons of virtue, but fewer are hard-core thugs, and most are just people. Special unit cops spend virtually all their professional time dealing with a particularly dangerous and relentless type of criminal. If a large proportion of the suspects they encounter are racial minorities, these officers will predictably have developed a perceptual and cognitive template equating minority status with violent criminality. In their experience, minority status has become a marker for potential high danger, warranting commensurate high vigilance, suspicion, and forceful response, and additional training is unlikely to disabuse them from a "bias" that they believe is essential to keeping them alive. The effects of training on race-biased shooting will be discussed further below.

Cognitive Heuristics and Implicit Biases

For police officers—or anyone, really—who might prefer not to think of themselves as overtly racist, **implicit biases** (Amodio & Devine, 2018; Dovidio et al., 2002; Hall et al., 2016; Payne, 2005), which can be partly or wholly unconscious, may influence our perceptions of people and our actions that flow from those perceptions. As noted above in the case of special unit police, these biases emerge out of experiences that may selectively mold one's impressions and opinions about a particular group of people because those experiences only represent one subset of that population, not the whole range. It's as if you grew up in a firehouse and then naturally assumed that all vehicles are red. So even if you emerge one day and see a blue or gray car, you might automatically assume it must be red underneath. In a similar way, if police officers' patrol experiences teach them that the offenders they encounter are disproportionately black, they may form a **cognitive heuristic**, or mental shortcut, that black equals trouble, because they less frequently come into contact with the majority of ordinary, law-abiding black citizens in any community.

In fact, in daily life, heuristics are part and parcel of efficient, adaptive human cognition because they streamline decision-making processes in familiar circumstances. Heuristics are useful because, on average, they enable us to make quick decisions based on experience, without having to engage in laborious chains of reasoning for each individual circumstance (Kahneman, 2011); this may form one foundation for RPDM discussed in Chapter 5. Problems arise, however, when the bases for a given set of heuristics are incorrect or incomplete and thereby result in unfair and unnecessary harm to people.

Mears et al. (2017) have described how several classes of cognitive heuristics may lead to the formation of implicit biases in police with regard to race.

Recency bias. Here, you form an impression about a group based on the last experience you had with one of them. An officer has just had an annoying or dangerous confrontation with a group of disrespectful young, black males. Now, he encounters another group of young blacks just standing around talking, and he thinks, "Oh-oh, here we go again," then primes himself for a confrontation that need not happen.

Availability bias. You form a quick conclusion based on the most salient information available, i.e., what's immediately "at the top of your mind." An officer receives a roll call briefing about adult gang members using minors as drug mules, then observes what looks like a dad walking his 6th-grader to school, and the officer wonders, "Hmmm, what if that tyke is carrying some swag in his innocent-looking backpack–maybe I should investigate. . . ."

Confirmation bias. With a dominant idea or opinion uppermost in your mind, you perceptually cherry-pick the evidence that supports your preconception and tune out information that contradicts or modifies it. A field training officer (FTO) stewards a new hire through a shift with many innocuous police-citizen interactions, but then ending with a fractious dialogue involving a pair of black youths, and subsequently tells the trainee, "See, I told you they were all like that."

It's easy to see how these three heuristic biases (and there are others not discussed here) can coalesce and mutually harden an officer's view of minority citizens. An officer has a bad experience with a black male. This is fresh on his mind when he encounters another group of young black males (recency bias) and triggers the salient stereotype of blacks as troublemakers (availability bias), causing him to tense up and project a condescending or hostile attitude toward the youths, which elicits a correspondingly pissy response from the group, leading the officer to think, "Well, what do expect from these people?" (confirmation bias). Further, these biases are reinforced through communication among fellow officers and general departmental lore, so eventually they become set in cognitive and cultural concrete, making them exceeding difficulty to change.

But it works both ways. Citizens, too, may commonly form these biases where, for example, a nasty cop gratuitously demeans a black citizen and, next day, the citizen is pulled over for a simple expired-tag traffic stop by a perfectly calm and courteous officer. But, yesterday's harassment still fresh in his mind, the citizen lashes out at the stunned patrolman who, then, fearing the worst, attempts to forcefully control the scene, which makes the citizen even angrier, eventuating in the most vicious of cycles, and leading to a needless injury or fatality. And of course, word (and sometimes cell phone videos) will get back to others in the community, amplifying still more the us-versus-them enmity between police and citizens.

Again, as emphasized repeatedly in this book, attention and respect must be paid to both officers' and citizens' perceptions of their worlds, because these biases are only biases if they exceed the realities of the various parties' actual experience, not if they're mostly true (Bolger, 2015; Jetelina et al., 2017; Lawton, 2007). If officers' impressions about the dangerous nature of certain communities, and the necessity of using appropriate levels of force, is borne out by practical experience, then expecting them to relax their vigilance just because somebody thinks "you're biased," will only heighten their cynicism and probably lead to even greater self-protective efforts which involve either a Ferguson-like neglect of criminal enforcement or an even more heavy-handed approach to citizen interactions, or both.

Same with citizens. Telling communities to trust and cooperate with local police will seem like a sick joke to citizens whose only interaction with cops have involved abuse, humiliation, or just incivility. The challenge, then, is for both police and community leaders to carefully analyze the reality-based factors that contribute to unnecessary friction between police and citizens, and then use this core of experiential validation as the basis for developing credible strategies to debunk the parts that are myths and improve the parts that are facts.

Finally, prejudice apparently does not discriminate. That is, implicit bias extends beyond race and may even be influenced by situational and historical factors. Following the September 11, 2001 terrorist attacks, Unkelbach et al. (2008) employed the S/DS paradigm depicting identical target faces (tan-complexioned, Caucasian-looking young male) holding either a pistol or a clearly harmless item such as a soda can. The only variation was that, for some presentations, the target was depicted as wearing a turban, which the researchers assumed made him look more "Muslim" (in itself, a bit of stereotype profiling), so the experimental matrix consisted of: (1) turban-gun; (2) turban-soda can; (3) bare head-gun; (4) bare head-can. Results showed that the civilian volunteer subjects experimentally shot both the gun- and can-wielding turbaned target more often than his bare-headed gun- and can-wielding twin, presumably reflecting the enculturated bias against Muslims provoked by the 9/11 attacks. Of course, we don't know what the results of this study might have been pre-9/11.

POLICE SHOOTING BIAS AND THE BRAIN

We've discussed research showing that subjects in S/DS experiments are quicker to press the "shoot" button when presented with a displayed still image is of a black person holding a harmless object, that is, they are more likely to identify the black image as threatening, although the relationship seems to reverse when more realistic moving images are shown. While one must be extra-cautious about proferring simplistic neuroscience explanations for complex perceptual, cognitive, and behavioral processes (Satel & Lilienfeld, 2013; Sternberg, 2010), some investigators have attempted to apply the principles and techniques of neuroscience research to the study of decision making under stress.

Brain-Based Bias?

Building on prior work in neuropsychology (Botvinick et al., 2001; Nieuwenuis et al., 2001), Amodio and colleagues (2004) have described two brain systems that are important for the quick detection and resolution of competing response tendencies. The first they term the **conflict-detection system**, which monitors one's ongoing responses to surrounding events, especially competing response tendencies to a given situation (e.g., fight or flight), and generally operates out of conscious awareness, much like a computer program that runs in the background, off-screen. Neuroanatomically, this system is hypothesized to involve the **anterior cingulate cortex**, which generally serves as a conflict/error-detecting mechanism in the brain, and is especially active when a quick, automatic response tendency is about to interfere with the individual's competing consciously intended response–that is, it assists you in looking (and thinking) before leaping.

When a discrepancy is detected, the conflict detection system alerts a second **regulatory system**, whose task it is to generate the intended response, while inhibiting competing responses. This system may be at least partially conscious, as it may require directed attention to implement both initiation and suppression mechanisms, and this is thought to involve the **prefrontal cortex** which generally mediates judgment and decision making.

A standard research methodology for measuring cerebral functioning is recording the brain's electrical activity. Most people are familiar with the **electroencephalogram (EEG)** used for the clinical diagnosis of neurological disorders, such as epilepsy. A more specialized measure is called the **event-related potential**, or **ERP**, a normal electrical brain wave pattern which may be evoked by a variety of environmental stimuli. Measuring the ERP allows researchers to study how the brain reacts to a wide range of perceptual and cognitive tasks. A subcomponent of the ERP is called the **error-related negativity component**, or **ERN**, which originates in the brain's anterior cingulate cortex, and is especially sensitive to conflicts which result in errors due to impaired behavioral control.

Amodio et al. (2004) asked 44 white female volunteers to look at a computer monitor display, while their ERNs were recorded. A brief image of either a black or white male was presented, followed by an image of either a handgun or a hand tool, such as a wrench. The participants were instructed to classify the second image as either a gun or a tool by pressing a corresponding button, and they had only 500 msec (half a second) to do it. Thus, the possible pairings were: (1) white face-gun; (2) white face-tool; (3) black face-gun; and (4) black face-tool. The presentations were repeated over multiple trials.

Results showed that participants took the most time (that is hesitated the longest) to respond correctly to the black-tool pairings, and these responses also showed the largest ERN recordings, suggesting that the subjects' brains were experiencing the greatest conflict over their implicit race bias in associating black faces with danger, and that their anterior cingulate cortices were working overtime to resolve the conflict and control the response. In fact, those subjects with the largest ERNs to race-based responses showed the highest levels of error-correction control throughout the task; that is, following errors, they tended to respond more slowly (risking exceeding the 500 msec safe response window), but more accurately. In other words, they appeared to be deliberatively self-correcting for their implicit race bias, and their brain readings reflected this.

But the subjects in Amodio et al.'s (2004) study didn't actually have to *shoot* anyone, even by simulation. Utilization of brain electrical activity technology as a gauge of racial bias was taken to the next level by Correll et al. (2006), who measured subcomponents of the ERP brain wave, called P200 and N200, within a shoot/don't study paradigm. The **P200** wave indicates activity of the anterior cingulate cortex in detecting conflict, while the **N200** indicates the prefrontal cortex's active inhibition of a prepotent (most likely to occur) response.

In this study, participants (a mixed-sex and mixed-race sample of college students) played a video game in which they were asked to make rapid (less than one second to respond) S/DS decisions, in this case using the push-button modality, in response to images of armed and unarmed targets, half of whom were white, half black. As in earlier studies, four combinations of stimuli were possible: armed whites, unarmed whites, armed blacks, unarmed blacks. To provide extra motivation for correct responses, a point system of credits and demerits was instituted, whereby correctly shooting an armed target or not shooting an unarmed target earned points, but incorrectly shooting an unarmed target or not shooting an armed target cost points. Prior to the procedure, a subset of study participants completed questionnaires designed to assess personal and subcultural racial biases, particularly with regard to racial stereotypes about aggressiveness and dangerousness.

Results showed that participants shot (by push button) armed blacks more quickly than armed whites, and suppressed firing at unarmed whites more quickly than at unarmed blacks. This was reflected in the neurophysiological data, with larger P200 (greater threat perception) and smaller N200 (reduced response inhibition) seen with images of black versus white targets. But the behavioral and neurophysiological response bias in this direction was even stronger for those participants whose questionnaire responses indicated a pre-existing stereotype of increased dangerousness of blacks. Thus, Correll et al.'s (2006) study suggests that a personal or cultural stereotype of blacks as more dangerous than whites could be something that, in some people—a few of whom may someday become police officers—might be neurodevelopmentally baked into the synaptic structure of their brains from an early age, resulting in their anterior cingulate cortex more quick to assess threat for black targets and their prefrontal cortex more slow to inhibit a preemptive strike.

We are thus left trying to make sense of these sets of findings. Where the white female subjects in Amodio et al.'s (2004) study have to classify the images of black or white males as dangerous (armed) or not (holding tool), they appear to harbor greater conflict and hesitancy in labeling blacks as a threat, and thereby take longer to make their decision, possibly as a way of unconsciously counteracting their implicit race biases. But when the task involves actually shooting to neutralize that threat, albeit in push-button format, and with a point-incentive added to the mix, Correll et al.'s (2006) mixed-sex, mixed-race subjects seem to have much less conflict and respond faster in shooting the black images, especially if they have already indicated by questionnaire that they harbor pre-existing racial biases.

We don't yet have the data, but it would be instructive to see what role is played by the race of the study participants in these results; for example, are black male volunteers more likely or less likely to experience conflict and inhibit their shooting response to black images than, say, white females? What role is played by pre-existing bias in each of these groups? What about age and profession? If study subjects include 40-year-old civilians, or young adult police or military service members, in addition to young adult college students, will we get different results? Often neglected in these kinds of studies are differences in cognition, temperament, and experience, even among individual members of a given identified group. That is, just as not all police officers have the same attitudes and personalities (Chapter 3), probably neither do all college students, all men or women, all blacks or whites, all younger or older people, and so on.

Meanwhile, similar findings have been obtained using **functional neuroimaging**, which allows scientists and clinicians to view patterns of brain activity in real-time, based on differential rates of metabolism (energy utilization) in different brain regions. Recall from the research discussed in Chapter 4, that "masked" aversive visual stimuli that bypass cortical processing may nevertheless elicit a fear response from the amygdala, even though the subject is not consciously aware of seeing the images (Ohman, 2005).

Cunningham et al. (2004) showed images of black and white faces to a group of white civilian volunteers who previously attested that they bore no racial prejudices. In one condition, the stimuli were clearly presented and in another condition they were masked, so that the subjects could not cortically process–that is, consciously perceive–the racial features of the images.

These white subjects were found to show greater amygdala activation, i.e., more fear, to the presentation of the black images, but only in the masked condition, that is, when they were consciously unaware of what they were seeing. In the unmasked condition, that is, when they were able to consciously identify the images, the amygdalar activation was accompanied by greater activity in the anterior cingulate cortex, orbitofrontal cortex, and dorsolateral prefrontal cortex, all structures that modulate and attenuate amygdalar activity.

In other words, for these self-proclaimed bias-free, white study subjects, exposure to black faces in the masked condition appears to have activated a conditioned prejudicial fear response that the subjects could dissociate from their self-protective bias-denial identity because they literally did not know what was making them afraid. But when experimental conditions allowed such awareness to kick in, i.e., when they could see the races' faces, they quickly and automatically activated the fear suppression mechanisms of the cerebral cortex to shush their panicking amygdalae and squelch their implicit biases, allowing them to continue to consciously assert that "I'm not a racist." (Aha, but your brain doesn't lie!)

Again, a confounding factor in all correlational studies examining behavior differences among groups (e.g., civilians vs. police officers) is the problem of individual variation. That is, even within a designated group, subjects are likely to have a range of personalities, temperaments, and cognitive styles. For example, responses of the brain's thalamus, insula, amygdala, basal ganglia, and cingulate cortex to images of fearful faces or dangerous scenarios have been found to be significantly heightened in subjects with anxious temperaments or diagnosed anxiety disorders (Anders et al., 2004; Demenescu et al., 2013; Fonzo et al., 2015; Holtz et al., 2012; Kilgore et al., 2014; Kim et al., 2012; Whalen et al., 2001). More subtle differences in neural processing no doubt exist within the normal variation of human personality (Buss, 2012; Miller, 1990, 2003a, 2003b; Millon & Davis, 2000; Sperry, 1995).

The range of personality types among sworn law enforcement personnel is likely to be narrower than that of the general population, partly because the police profession would be expected to select for individuals of tougher emotional fiber who would choose to go into this field of work. However, every law enforcement manager knows that different officers may respond differently to a variety of both routine and emergency scenarios, i.e., there is no one "police personality" (see Chapter 3). Therefore, differences in temperament, attitude, threat-sensitivity, and experience will likely play a role in any given officer's propensity to use force, including deadly force, with white or black citizens. It would be nice to see what EEGs and functional neuroimaging scans of Andy and Barney would look like in the S/DS implicit bias research paradigm, but I don't think many minorities lived in Mayberry.

Police Training and Racial Bias: Upside

Well, okay, police officers have brains, too (stop laughing), and if racial bias is hard-wired into an officer's neural software, is there any hope for reducing this bias in police OIS/DFEs, not to mention in law enforcement and society as a whole? If the brain is programmed for prejudice, is there anything we can do about it?

There are several general answers to this question. To begin with, as fascinating as the emerging neuroscience research may be, one need not invoke the brain to support an already existing large body of empirical and phenomenological findings on the psychology of racial bias and deadly force response, some of which has been reviewed in this chapter. Second, even if appealing to neurobiology, one thing we know about the brain is that it is characterized by a certain degree of plasticity: people can and do learn from experience (Gazzaniga et al., 2014; Kandel, 2012; Mitchell, 2018; Pascual-Leone et al., 2011; Plomin, 2018; Stiles, 2000; Weyadt, 2019). Yes, by dint of genetic blueprinting or early enculturation, it may be harder for some individuals than others to relearn and change old habits, but people do it all the time, albeit with various degrees of success. However, learning new attitudes and orientations is a lot more complex than learning specific new skills and action patterns, so the latter is probably where most first responder training should begin.

Many of the subjects in the previously described studies were volunteer college students in simulated scenarios. What about police officers whose training and experience may influence their pre-existing racial stereotypes, which in turn may have real life-and-death consequences for the citizens in their patrol communities? Employing the S/DS research paradigm with sworn police officers, recall that Correll et al. (2007a) found that their responses were similar to those of civilians in more quickly responding to images of armed black targets (shoot) and unarmed white targets (don't shoot), and more slowly to images of unarmed black targets (don't shoot) and armed white targets (shoot). But unlike the college students, who shot unarmed black targets more frequently than unarmed white targets, the police officers in that study were no more likely to shoot unarmed black targets than unarmed white targets, even though, similar to the civilians, it seemed to take the officers longer to decide to not-shoot the unarmed black targets.

This last point is important because it seems to suggest is that, in making their split-second decision to shoot or not shoot (at least in the experimental push-button paradigm), professional law enforcement training and experience may confer upon police officers the ability to either consciously overcome the automatic stereotypes that influence their reaction time, or to focus their attention and base their response on situation-relevant features (what is actually in the target's hand and what he's doing with it) rather than on race per se. For some commentators (Sim et al., 2013), this suggests an important role for training and experience in facilitating officers' ability to overcome the racial stereotypes that influence untrained civilians–for the present, in experimental S/DS scenarios; in the future, hopefully, in real-life police-citizen confrontations.

We ordinarily think of racial bias as something that is inculcated over a lifetime of exposure to derogatory stereotypes of certain groups, infused through family lore, the media, and the general culture. According to the theory of **stereotype accessibility** (Devine & Elliott, 1995; Hall et al., 2016; Sim et al., 2013), individual indoctrination and societal enculturation serve to link images of blacks, particularly young, black males, to the stereotype of danger, especially in the minds of white citizens, some of whom eventually become police officers. Even individuals who would like to think of themselves as unprejudiced may have these negative stereotypes floating just below the rim of consciousness, waiting for the right stimulus to flush them to the surface, maybe not as blatant discrimination or abuse per se, but in the form of more subtly different behavior toward people of certain groups. In a sense, stereotype accessibility may be one of the mechanisms that activates implicit bias, discussed earlier.

Indeed, just how easy it is to deliberately manipulate this type of racial stereotype accessibility was shown in a study by Correll et al. (2007b) who gave civilian volunteers newspaper articles to read describing violent crimes committed by either black or white perpetrators, prior to the volunteers' participation in a S/DS experiment. Following their reading of the white criminal stories, subjects showed no shooting bias between the presented white or black, armed or unarmed, targets. However, after reading about black criminals, subjects showed a distinct trend toward higher shooting rates for black versus white targets.

If this priming response in civilians also generalizes to police officers, minority readers at this point might well be wondering if their chances of surviving their next traffic stop depends on what this cop happened to read that morning while sitting on the can before heading off to work. It also may depend on what particular mood that cop is in. Research with civilian volunteers (Johnson & Fredrickson, 2005) has shown that experimental induction of a positive mood eliminates the white participants' **own-race bias**

(ORB), that is, the tendency to be less able to distinguish different members of another race compared to individuals from one's own race. This is not a trivial point, because viewing members of another group as homogenized caricatures of one another ("They all look alike to me") implicitly robs them of their individual identities as distinct autonomous human beings deserving of the same respect as you or I. If humor-induced reduction of ORB is associated with a feeling of greater individuality, humanity, and affinity toward other groups, then maybe this might translate into more courteous and cooperative police-citizen interaction. Maybe. In the meantime, comedy break at roll call, anyone?

Some cause for optimism comes from a study by Sim et al. (2013) in their own application of the newspaper article paradigm. They found that, for college student novices with no prior training or experience in S/DS scenarios, reading stories about black criminals prior to their push-button sessions was associated with a significantly higher racial bias, i.e., they shot more black images than white ones. In contrast, students who had participated in and already practiced the S/DS paradigm in previous trials, as well as a sample of actual active-duty police officers, were uninfluenced by the articles, suggesting that race-neutral training and real-life experience facilitate one's ability to ignore or override race-salient cues and focus on task-relevant cues—that is, to progress from racial profiling to behavioral profiling, responding to the actual level of threat, no matter who is creating it. So, maybe that newspaper-reading constipated cop won't be so hard on you, after all.

The corollary, however, is that formal training will probably not counteract impressions and characterizations that have grown out of officers' own repeated unpleasant race-related experiences on the job, and in these cases, attempts to "train them out of" their putatively bias-based stereotypes may backfire. That's because, for officers whose daily, real-life experiences regularly reinforce an association between blacks and danger, race itself has becomes a task-relevant cue for facilitating weapon detection and heightening the perception of threat (Sim et al., 2013).

In fact, officers with such adverse experiences who participated in anti-bias training predictably showed reductions in questionnaire assessments of racial bias following such training, and in some cases may have even convinced themselves that they were less biased, but in a simulated shooting study (Correll et al., 2007b), they still showed faster reaction times to black targets. For these officers, the training appears to have indeed made them more sensitive to racial cues, but this may have had the paradoxical effect of activating the very race-based stereotypes that the training was supposed to overcome.

Sim et al. (2013) nevertheless suggest that training may be effective in attenuating racial bias in police shootings, even if it does little to change basic attitudes. If officers believe it is within their practical interest to act in a nonbiased way, then heightened awareness of race may elicit a compensatory effort at **cognitive control**. That is, so long as safety is not compromised, an officer may make a conscious, deliberate effort (you can count on those good old frontal lobes) not to overreact to an experience-dependent, race-based perception of heightened danger, in order to preserve both the practice and appearance of fairness. Indeed, this has been shown to be the case in several of the studies cited earlier.

In neurophysiological terms, Sims et al. (2013) see this as the anterior cingulate cortex's threat response triggering the prefrontal cortex's s response-inhibition mechanism, consistent with Amodio et al.'s (2004) ERP findings of better cognitive control of behavior in subjects with superior conflict-detection skills. As noted above, training may not have to eliminate or reduce all bias in order to have a beneficial effect, if it at least results in officers consciously choosing to suppress racially biased responding in a real-life OIS/DFE or other use of force action: "Whether I like this citizen or not, these are the rules we have to follow."

Of course, as discussed in Chapter 5, effortful control of behavior will be made more difficult by a variety of factors that may operate before and during a real-world OIS/DFE, including time constraints, sleep deprivation, fatigue, environmental factors (lighting, obstructions), situational ambiguity, OAL, and ego depletion, as well as individual officer variables, such as intelligence, education level, temperament, attentional capacity, emotional reactivity, self-control, concurrent professional and personal stresses, and the emotionally arousing nature of the life-and-death encounter itself. Under these circumstances, effortful control would be expected to more quickly deteriorate, and officers may fall back on more ingrained perceptual and response biases (Baumeister, 2002, 2014; Baumeister & Heatherton, 1996; Beilock, 2010; Bodenhausen, 1990; Fridell & Binder, 1992; Govorun & Payne, 2006; Lambert et al., 2003; Sims et al., 2013; Villa et al., 2000).

What we seem to be able to conclude thus far is that a racial bias against black citizens–implicit or overt–is hardly inevitable in either civilians or police officers, at least in realistically simulated OIS/DFE scenarios. If these studies tell us anything, it is that at least as many subjects effortfully try (or at least their brains do) to suppress racial bias as expressed it in these experimental scenarios. So the stereotype of all cops inevitably singling out black citizens for extraordinarily abusive treatment appears to be as noxiously corrosive to police-community relations as stereotypes about the inherent danger of all minorities themselves. Why do some people, including police officers willingly succumb to their biases, while others seem able to defy their own prejudices, even at a risk to their own long-cherished ideas and sometimes even to their own lives? Is there an optimum middle point, a psychological bias-free zone between force-heavy cyncism and pollyannish disregard for safety? Importantly, can minds be changed? How? Again, only a scientifically objective and forthright approach to this line of research can yield realistic and workable answers to these important questions.

Police Training and Racial Bias: Downside

Recall from Chapter 2 that certain behavioral indicators have been found to predict a suspect's impending assault on officers, and many of these pre-attack indicators are taught in police training modules that prepare officers to deal with confrontations, some of which may involve deadly force (Johnson, 2015, 2017, 2019, Johnson & Aaron, 2013; Worrall et al., 2018). But what if some of these behavioral red flags that purportedly portend imminent danger are, for some citizens, merely signs of fear and concern about being falsely labeled as dangerous in the first place?

According to the theory of **stereotype threat** (Steele, 1997), members of marginalized groups, such as black Americans, have learned from experience that others, such as white police officers, may often regard them with suspicion and hostility, or at least be more likely to leap to an unfavorable judgment about them (remember those heuristics), so interactions with these authority figures are likely to induce anxiety, physiological arousal, and nervously impaired cognitive processing and communications skills. According to a survey by Kahn et al. (2018), some of these very responses of stereotype threat are erroneously being taught to police as reliable indicators of imminent suspect aggression, including: (1) fast breathing, nervous trembling, sweating, and facial flushing: (2) empty stare, fast blinking, looking around, and avoiding eye contact with the officer; (3) scratching or self-touching, jaw and other muscular tightening, clenching fists or alternately opening or closing fists, shifting weight, or other "unnecessary" movements; and (4) hesitant or partial responses to officer questions, repeating phrases or comments, and general confusion or befuddlement.

All of the training modules reviewed by Kahn et al. (2018) described these behavioral characteristics–typically with little empirical verification, and based primarily on personal experience and street lore–as sure-fire predictors of suspect danger, and none of the training curricula discussed stereotype threat or offered any alternative explanation for these citizen behaviors. Thus, an innocent minority citizen who is scared of offending or provoking an officer may display fear symptoms that the officer has been trained to interpret as harbingers of attack, thus escalating the potential for a violent and potentially deadly confrontation–yet another vicious cycle that can quickly spin out of control.

It should be noted that other, more explicit, pre-attack behaviors, such as assuming a bladed stance or verbal confrontation, may in fact be accurate pre-attack indicators (see Chapter 2). Again, this is not an either-or issue: depending on the situation, some citizen behaviors will portend trouble brewing, while others will carry no such dire prognostication, and the same type of behavior may mean different things for different citizens. Perhaps more so than for any other topic in this book, anyone serious about productively addressing improved police-minority relations must endorse an empirical approach to research, practice, and policy in this area.

SUMMARY AND CONCLUSIONS

I'm a racist and so are you, so deal with it. Racism with a small r—feeling more comfortable with people most like us and wary of those who are different until proven otherwise—is cooked into our human nature as an evolutionary self-preservative tribal instinct that, like our appendix and pinkie toe, may seem to have outlasted its functionality in modern multicultural societies that make any pretense to calling themselves civilized. Racism with a big R—willfully denying someone an otherwise deserved opportunity, or maliciously persecuting someone because of their ethnicity—is the more malignant mutation of this trait, and the one most people invoke when they complain about bias in policing, whether overt use of force or just daily interactions with citizens.

But natural doesn't mean inevitable. As human beings, we best use our intelligence and insight, not to deny or rationalize away the natural ills that beset us, but to examine their root causes and devise ways to counteract them or mitigate their effects. Infectious diseases are natural, but we employ sanitation and antibiotics to preserve lives. Hurricanes are natural, but we devise warning systems and evacuation strategies to save as many people as possible. Hunger is natural, but we improve agriculture and food distribution to ward off starvation. Mental illness is natural, but we utilize pharmacological agents and psychotherapies to alleviate suffering.

We can be an atrocious species, but we can also be a wise and benevolent one; this is the maddening duality of our natures. Racism is not a disease that can be cured by a pill, therapy, or trite cultural prescription. Although progress has been made and good people abound, ours is still a partially racism-infused society and there are still racist police officers, just as there are racist doctors, racist judges, racist politicians, and racist clergy. But, as this chapter has shown, many police officers do make an effort—sometimes conscious and deliberate, sometimes out of awareness and revealed only by the signals we hack from their brains—to override their prejudices and deploy deadly force and other law enforcement actions based on their perception of the exigencies of the situation, not the color or background of the citizen in question. If you're serious about alleviating racism in policing, start by respecting the real-life experiences and perspectives of both officers and citizens, and then support the research that earnestly looks for causes and solutions.

In the meantime, as a beat cop or police manager, strive for **professionalism**, which means you embody the maturity and integrity to fulfill your established role according to the accepted standards of your vocation (more Andys needed). A doctor will not like all patients, a lawyer will not like all clients, a waiter will not like all customers, and a police officer will not like all community members. The minimum we citizens have a right to expect, however, is that these professionals will treat us responsibly and fairly because that is the job they have signed up to do. Give respect to get respect; that way, if you must take ultimate step of depriving a citizen of their life, your actions may be better understood.

If a law enforcement agency identifies bad cops—racist or otherwise—who cannot or will not conform their behavior to the requirements of their policing duties, that agency owes it to the public they serve, not to mention to the rest of their officers' credibility and safety, to identify and assertively deal with those members who willfully abuse their authority. By the same token, community leaders must take a role in addressing the gratuitously provocative behavior of some citizens who delight in baiting and instigating cops. Police and community members should be collaborators, not adversaries, in the goal of community safety. Displaced citizen anger should not be used as a pretext for maligning and persecuting officers for doing their jobs, and collegial blue-wall solidarity should not be an excuse for shielding departmental assholes.

Please spare the Kumbaya music. This problem won't be solved overnight, and it will take more than good intentions. But we can start by detoxifying the poisonous media-fueled mythology of two monolithic groups, The Police and The Blacks as natural enemies, like a cobra and a mongoose. Most community members want the police to protect them, not hurt them. Most police officers want their service communities to not make their jobs more difficult than necessary. Any constructive solutions will take time, effort, and commitment. Start with acknowledging people's reality and having the respect to listen before you argue. Do the hard work of reasoning through and articulating your point. You think I couldn't understand? Help me understand. *Make* me understand. That goes for both sides, and if we can start to do that, with hard empirical research and a dollop of human compassion on our side, then maybe one day we'll all feel a little safer.

Chapter 8

DEADLY FORCE ENCOUNTERS: PSYCHOLOGICAL EFFECTS

If you have made mistakes, even serious ones, there is always another chance for you. What we call failure is not the falling down but the staying down.

Mary Pickford

Most of this book has focused on the psychological and situational factors that occur prior to and during the deadly force encounter itself. But the effects of an OIS/DFE on the officer do not end when the shooting stops. For most officers, there will be at least some period of time during which they confront their mortality and cope with the impact and implications of the actions they have carried out.

PSYCHOLOGICAL AFTEREFFECTS OF AN OIS/DFE

As we've discussed in previous chapters, the response of all people, including police officers, to any kind of potentially life-threatening incident will combine the characteristics of **universality** and **diversity**. That is, there are a few general principles of critical incident response and recovery that most people share (Table 8.1), but how these factors are expressed in any given case will vary according to the unique personality, temperament, cognitive style, life history, job experience, concurrent stressors, and existing support systems of each individual officer (Miller, 2000, 2005a, 2006a, 2006e, 2007g, 2013b, 2015d, 2017, 2019b).

Table 8.1.
PSYCHOLOGICAL EFFECTS FOLLOWING AN OIS/DFE

Physical symptoms: Can affect any organ system, but most common are cardiac, gastrointestinal, and sleep disturbances. In uncontested cases, symptoms are usually temporary.

Psychological symptoms: May include anxiety, confusion, survivor exhilaration, regret, obsessive rumination, posttraumatic symptoms. In uncontested cases, symptoms are usually temporary.

Symptoms in contested OIS/DFE cases: May include any of the above, as well as fear, anger, helplessness/hopelessness, recklessness/revenge, guilt, and clinical syndromes, such as depression, suicidal ideation, and PTSD.

Stages of Post-OIS Psychological Response

As just noted, although the post-incident psychological reaction to an OIS/DFE will necessarily be influenced by the individual personality and experience of the involved officer, certain common factors seem to underlie this response, and some authorities (Nielsen, 1991; Williams, 1991) have divided the post-shooting reaction into four basic phases. These should be conceptualized flexibly, as not all officers will show this precise sequence in just this precise order; nevertheless, certain elements of this pattern appear to be quite common, both in literature reports and in my own clinical practice. The exact sequence, timing, and intensity of these phenomena will of course be modified by the officer's age, personality, experience and time on the job, and the number of prior OIS/DFEs, if any. Note that these reactions may be observed in noncontested OIS/DFEs, non-fatal OISs, and non-firearm use of force cases. Where the officer is being investigated, disciplined, litigated, and/or prosecuted, additional stresses and challenges may arise (see below and Chapter 9).

In this schema, the post-OIS/DFE cycle often begins with an immediate **impact phase**. For officers who have just shot a suspect during a dangerous confrontation, there may be an initial sensation of relief and even exhilaration at having survived the encounter. But later, feelings of doubt or self-recrimination may surface, especially where the decision to shoot was less than clear-cut or where the suspect's actions essentially forced the hand of the officer into using deadly force, such as in botched robberies, domestic disputes, mental illness calls, or suicide-by-cop incidents (Grossman, 1996; Kennedy et al., 1998; Lindsay & Dickson, 2004; Miller, 2006c; Mohandie & Meloy, 2000; Pinizzotto et al., 2005). Or the officer may simply be confronting the fact that, however justified the response, he or she has nevertheless just taken a human life (Henry, 2004; Loughlin & Flora, 2017; Nhan, 2019; Remsberg, 2008; Ryan, 2013).

During the second **recoil phase**, the officer may seem detached and preoccupied, spacily going through the motions of his job duties, and operating on behavioral autopilot. At the time when all he wants to do is put the event out of his mind, he will typically be barraged with questions from investigators and from his peers, the latter due to the obvious strong identification factor among officers, each one wondering, "What would *I* have done under those circumstances?" He may also be sensitive and prickly to even well-meaning attaboys by his peers ("Way to go, Supercop–you got the guy"), and especially to accusatory-like interrogation and second-guessing from official investigators or the media ("Officer Jackson, did you really believe you were in fear for your life from a confused teenager?"). This will be discussed further below and in Chapter 9.

As the officer begins to come to terms with the shooting episode, a **resolution phase** ensues, wherein he assimilates the fact that the use of force action was necessary and justified in the battle for survival that often characterizes law enforcement DFEs. This resolution process may be complicated by departmental discipline, ongoing investigations, impending criminal prosecution, or civil litigation (see Chapter 9). However, even in uncontested cases, resolution may be partial rather than total, and psychological remnants of the experience may continue to resurface periodically, especially during future times of crisis. But overall, especially if the OIS has been administratively cleared, the overwhelming majority of officers are soon able to return to work with a reasonable level of confidence.

In the worst case, rare in my experience, sufficient resolution may never occur, and the officer enters into a prolonged **posttraumatic phase**, which may potentially impede or derail his or her law enforcement career. One factor in this kind of adverse reaction lies in the emotional disconnect between some officers' expectations of a heroic, armed confrontation (they watched TV cop shows as kids, too) and the gritty reality of most actual shooting scenarios, which typically involve petty criminals, mentally disordered subjects, domestic violence escalations, or the posturings of young-and-dumb juveniles. In less severe cases, a period of temporary leave allows the officer to decompress, possibly seek counseling, eventually regain his or her emotional and professional bearings, and ultimately return to the job. Still other officers return to work right away, but continue to perform marginally until their actions are brought to the attention of superiors.

Note that the timing of these phases, or the intervals between them, may vary widely among officers, from days to months, and that many officers will show some of these phases, but not others; still other officers may phase in and out in any order and may cycle back and forth among phases until a resolution is achieved. In my experience, the vast majority of officers cleared in justified DFEs or nonlethal OISs return to work within a few days or weeks without complication. Most of those with more adverse traumatic reactions can eventually get back on the job if provided with the proper psychological intervention and departmental support (Miller, 1995, 2006e, 2007b, 2007g, 2008d, 2008e, 2013b, 2015d, 2019b).

Individual and Incident-Specific Factors in Post-OIS Response

As noted in Chapter 3, some commentators have written about a prototypical "police personality;" however, as we've seen, research and clinical practice indicate that individual officers may show a range of temperamental, cognitive, and personality patterns. Combined with their personal experience and departmental enculturation, these variations will influence a given officer's professional activities, including his or her response to an OIS/DFE or related critical incident stressor (Miller, 2003b, 2004, 2006i; Twersky-Glasner, 2005). However, certain commonalities in response pattern and content have emerged from systematic study and clinical experience in this area (Anderson et al., 1995; Blum, 2000; Cohen, 1980; Geller, 1982; Honig & Sultan, 2004; Rudofossi, 2007, 2009; Russell & Beigel, 1990; Williams, 1999).

Some of these responses represent general posttraumatic reactions familiar to psychological trauma workers (Bowman, 1997; Gilliland & James, 1993; Greenstone & Leviton, 2001; Miller, 1998b, 2006i, 2008k, 2015f; Regehr & Bober, 2005), while others seem to have a more specific law enforcement line-of-duty shooting focus. Most of these reactions are transient and resolve over a matter of days and weeks, although they may persist longer in a smaller number of involved officers, and they may occur across the full range of psychological reaction stages described above.

Physical symptoms. These may include headaches, stomach upset, nausea, weakness and fatigue, cardiovascular symptoms, muscle tension and twitches, and changes in appetite and sexual functioning. Some form of temporary sleep impairment is nearly universal, including insomnia, frequent awakenings, and/or disturbing dreams.

Rumination. Officers commonly can't stop "replaying the tape" of the incident in their minds, at least for a few days following the incident; in part, this may be what is keeping them up at night. In some instances, rumination represents a self-search quest for reassurance ("Did I do the right thing?" "What could I have done differently?"). Where the OIS/DFE is under investigation or in litigation, rumination may extend into fears for the future ("What will happen to me now?" "Is my career over?" "Am I going to jail?").

Even in justified use of force cases, the stark confrontation with death can deliver an existential smack in the face, often prompting obsessive reflection on the officer's mortality and heretofore suppressed realization of the dangers of the job ("Holy shit–I came this close to being killed!"). Where injury or death of fellow officers, innocent civilians, or even police canines has occurred, ruminative self-recrimination may be magnified exponentially, as the officer gropes for some philosophical self-exculpatory trapdoor, or at least some comprehensible explanation for the episode that he can wrest a lesson from in order to avoid such a dire outcome in the future (Bernhard, 2019; Miller, 2007c).

Posttraumatic and other psychological reactions. While a full-blown PTSD syndrome following an OIS/DFE is rare, isolated and transient posttraumatic symptoms may include intrusive imagery and flashbacks, along with premonitions, distorted memories, and feelings of déjà vu. Some degree of anxiety and depression may occur, sometimes accompanied by panic attacks. There may be unnatural and disorienting feelings of helplessness, fearfulness, and vulnerability, along with self-second-guessing and guilt feelings. Substance abuse may complicate the picture, especially if this has been a coping mechanism in the past.

In the case of ambiguously resolved shootings, where the officer has been administratively cleared to return to work, but doubts linger about the circumstances among peers, supervisors, and/or the general public, the officer may manifest a pervasive agitation, irritability, and low frustration tolerance, along with fluctuating overt anger and resentment toward the suspect, the department, unsupportive peers and family, or civilians in general. Part of this may be a reaction to the conscious or unconscious sense of vulnerability that the officer experiences after a shooting incident. Sometimes, this is projected outward as a smoldering hostility, or as just a low-level but persistent grumpiness that makes the officer's every interaction with peers or citizens a grating source of stress and conflict. Combined with an increased hypervigilance and hypersensitivity to threats of all kinds, this reaction pattern may result in overaggressive policing, leading to further abuse-of-force complaints and possibly referral for a fitness-for-duty evaluation (Miller, 2004, 2007d, 2013b; Rostow & Davis, 2004).

Undetected and untreated, this pattern may spiral into a vicious cycle of angry and fearful isolation, withdrawal, and the spurning of potential sources of peer, family, and professional support. At the same time, some officers may become overly protective of their families, generating an alternating **control-alienation syndrome** (McMains, 1986b, 1991) in which they veer erratically between intrusively restrictive overprotectiveness and angry recrimination of family members for their perceived lack or empathy and support, which may only serve to aggravate already existing family stresses (Miller, 2007i). All this, combined with emotional lability ("I just get mad or cry at the drop of a hat;" "The slightest thing sets me off") and sometimes cognitive symptoms of impaired concentration and memory, may lead the officer to fear that he or she is "going crazy."

Situational Factors

Apart from the common reactions and individual personality and history of the officer, certain factors inherent in the particular OIS/DFE incident itself can affect the severity, persistence, and impact of post-shooting symptoms and reactions (Allen, 2004; Anderson et al., 1995; Blau, 1986; Bohrer, 2005; Honig & Sultan, 2004; Loughlin & Flora, 2017; McMains, 1986a, 1986b).

One obvious factor is the **degree of threat to the officer's life**, which can operate in two ways. First, the officer who feels that he or she was literally about to die may be traumatized by the extreme fear involved, but may nevertheless feel quite justified and guilt-free in having used deadly force on a suspect with clearly murderous intent. But where the danger was more equivocal and the suspect's actions harder to interpret, even with the benefit of 20/20 hindsight, there may be less of the fear factor and more second-guessing about what degree of force was actually necessary. Police officers pride themselves on their ability to manage a tense situation, control their reactions, and perform well under pressure, so they may experience a gnawing sense of doubt and self-recrimination where the situation abruptly got out of their control and turned deadly.

For example, at one extreme is the armed bank robber who, having been duly warned and ordered to surrender, brazenly draws down on the officer or points a gun at a civilian. In such a case, there is likely to be universal agreement that the officer had no choice–indeed, was duty-bound–to fire on the perpetrator in order to save innocent lives. At the other extreme is the obnoxiously inebriated high school punk who is pulled over on a dark street for a traffic violation, exchanges a few nasty words with the officer, and is shot for refusing to drop an object in his hand that turns out to be a cell phone. A related example is the schizophrenic homeless person who has heretofore been known only as a noisy neighborhood nuisance, but now is threateningly waving around a hammer or a kitchen knife and is shot while lunging at the officer.

In such ambiguous cases, a common reaction by the involved officer is anger at the suspect himself for forcing the officer's hand in taking the citizen's life. Inasmuch as rage and guilt are often intertwined, paradoxically greater anger may be shown toward a relatively more "innocent" suspect who's careless and stupid behavior resulted in a totally unnecessary shooting, e.g., the psychotic street person or the drunk kid with the big mouth, than at a suspect who more clearly "deserves" to get shot, e.g., the armed robber who fires at the officer first. Much of this officer's anger may smolder below the surface and emerge as general irritability and clashes with authority, the public, and family members.

Another situational factor is the **amount of preparation and warning** that existed prior to the shooting and the length of time the dangerous incident had persisted, which also may have varying effects (Askey et al., 2018). On the one hand, officers caught off guard are unlikely to have even a brief interval to think through their decision to shoot and may later perceive themselves, or be perceived by others, as having reacted out of fear or anger, no matter how justified the shooting is later officially judged to be. At the other extreme, where the shooting followed a prolonged stand-off, with lots of back-and-forth negotiating and maneuvering, as in hostage-barricade or suicide-by-cop scenarios, the extended period of time the officer spent deliberating over the decision to use deadly force may later take its own psychological toll, especially if the officer feels he tried and failed to verbally resolve the crisis (McMains & Mullins, 1996; Miller, 2005c, 2006c).

All of the above factors relate to two important dimensions: the amount of **control** the officer feels he or she had over the situation and degree of **conflict** that exists over the decision to take a human life. Generally, the less control and the more conflict the officer has experienced during and following the event, the more severe the psychological impact is likely to be (Miller, 1998b, 2006e, 2013b, 2015d, 2019a, 2019b).

Responses of Supervisors and Peers

Issues around control and conflict extend to the post-shooting phase, and will typically involve the amount and kind of attention the officer receives from his administration, peers, the community, and the media. While supervisors and administrators are understandably concerned about the public relations aspect of an OIS/DFE, most are generally supportive of their involved personnel (Blau, 1994; Bohrer, 2005; Garner, 2009, 2011, 2012; Henry, 2004; Klein, 1991; Russell & Biegel, 1990; Rynearson, 1988, 1994, 1996; Rynearson & McCreery, 1993; Sewell, 1986; Sprang & McNeil, 1995).

However, a department's efforts to appear objective and unbiased to the public and media may at times make it seem that the authorities are coming down especially hard on their own officer. Indeed, officers who believe that their agency's decision to launch an investigation or other adversarial action is based on politics and public relations will have a particularly hard time dealing with the feeling of having been "stabbed in the back" (see also Chapter 9).

Reactions of the officer's peers may help or harm his attempts to cope with the situation. As noted above, at first the officer may reap accolades from his cop buddies for surviving, protecting life, and "getting the job done." Because of the powerful mutual identification factor, police peers will typically want to hear all about the event, because someday they may be there too, and they want to believe that, in the breach, they will do the right thing. Many of these peers also hope that the officer's guts to pull the trigger will "rub off" on them should they encounter a similar situation. However, if the officer fails to regale them with an uplifting narrative of struggle and triumph, and instead reveals the conflict, doubt, and pain he or she is going through, the contagion effect may cause his fellow officers to denigrate or shun him.

This is because the implied psychological contract of such post-crisis mutual congratulatory rituals often involves a kind of blanket immunity against what Solomon and Horn (1986) call the **mark of Cain**, and Henry (2004) describes as the **death taint**. The descriptions of this peer-reaction process by some of the OIS/DFE-involved officers I've interviewed often sound similar, something along the lines of: "You have now made real for us the life-and-death situation we all fear. So you'd better show us how nobly and heroically you're dealing with this, throw us a positive spin, or all you've done is shove our frightening mortality up in our faces, and so to emotionally insulate and protect ourselves, we will scorn you and degrade you."

We want our armed societal protectors—police officers, soldiers—to be courageous and proficient, but we want them to be guardians, not killing machines, and many officers feel genuinely sad at having had to take a life, even if they objectively recognize that they had no choice in the situation and that the perpetrator's actions warranted a deadly force response. Human nature being what it is, even law enforcement professionals who are trained to kill cannot just automatically shed their familial, religious, and cultural upbringing when they don the uniform; a similar phenomenon is observed in military personnel (Grossman, 1996; Grossman & Christensen, 2007; Miller, 2008b). An officer may thus become irritated at his colleagues who want him to play the happy warrior, while they blithely disregard the turmoil he may be going through. Yet the officer is hurting and still needs all the support he can get, so, fearing total rejection, he may not want to burst his colleagues' bubble. Painful as putting up such a false front may be, it is still better than total isolation.

OFFICER REACTIONS TO A CONTESTED OIS/DFE INCIDENT

They all have that same look.

Law enforcement officers whom I have evaluated for court cases or treated clinically as patients, and who, for any length of time, have been under investigation or embroiled in legal actions related to their OIS/DFE experience, almost universally project a characteristically distinct facial expression which I can only describe as **beat down and burned out**. It is a blank, yet fraught mien, the fear and outrage encapsulated by time and fatigue behind drooped lids and pursed lips, the gaze focused into a murky distance haunted by unknown injuries and humiliations to come. The closest analogy I can invoke is the "thousand-yard stare" described in soldiers who have gone through a series of harrowing battles, with no clear end in sight. This is probably why a few of the police officers in such circumstances have told me, often in almost the eerily exact same words, "Sometimes, I think it would have been easier if I had just got shot."

Most of the stresses and challenges described in the previous sections are those facing officers who have survived an OIS/DFE or other use of force incident which has been administratively cleared and ruled justified. But when his actions are questioned, challenged, or condemned, it slams an additional tier of tectonic pressure onto the officer, as his entire self-concept and professional identity feel crushed and mangled, often by the very people he had always assumed he could count on to have his back.

Police officers are hardly the only professionals who are investigated, disciplined, terminated, prosecuted, and/or sued for allegedly unprofessional or illegal conduct. A nonexhaustive list includes federal agents, local police officers, corrections officers, firefighters, paramedics, medical and mental health clinicians, attorneys and judges, protective services and court personnel, clergy, airline and other transportation workers, corporate or government managers or executives, political figures, and military personnel (Miller, 2004, 2009b, 2011b, 2015b).

As noted in Chapter 1, what all of these professionals have in common is that they all occupy positions of high public authority and trust. Society places great power and responsibility in their hands and so we hold them to a higher standard of personal and professional conduct than other types of workers. Supervisors in these fields generally take the position that tolerating even a few bad apples can have drastic repercussions–practical, professional, political, financial–on their individual organizations and on their respective fields of practice as a whole. Hence, to preserve the honor and integrity of these professions and the public trust on which they rely, investigators may be especially zealous in pursuing those who are suspected of flouting the rules and tainting the name of the agency or organization in question.

That's why, in addition to everything an officer may go through in the aftermath of a cleared, justified OIS or other use of force incident, those facing additional adverse actions may experience any and all of the following (Miller, 2008f, 2009b, 2011b, 2015b).

Fear. Suddenly, the officer's career is on the line and with it, his or her whole sense of personal and professional identity, not to mention the prospect of loss of freedom and personal disgrace. Often, the biggest anxiety comes from not knowing what will happen next. As the crisis unfolds, there are good moments, when the officer is able to put it out of his mind and hope for the best, and bad moments when he or she is close to panic.

Anger. "I can't believe this is how I get treated for doing my job!" is a typical plaint. If the officer feels that his actions were really justified and that the department is making a big deal of this case because of politics, public relations, a personal vendetta, or just because the powers that be can't or won't listen to the officer's side of the story, he may be fuming. Even worse is when the officer believes that the discipline was meted out unfairly: "I know a dozen guys who've done the same thing as me–or far worse–and nothing happened to them!" Fear and anger typically alternate in a swirling spiral of emotions that may make it difficult for the officer to think rationally at just the time that clear-headedness may be vital.

Hopelessness/helplessness. Many investigated or charged officers go through periods during which they just crash into a wall of demoralization and defeat: "If this shit can happen, then what the hell's the point of anything?" Motivation is sapped, energy is drained, and the officer may shuffle around like the walking dead. Then, boom–some new crisis erupts and the anger and panic come flooding back. These kinds of roller-coaster emotional cycles prove debilitating over time and may lead to full blown depression and thoughts of suicide (Cummings, 1996; Miller, 2005b; Violanti et al., 2011).

Recklessness/revenge. Sometimes, as a reaction against feeling like an impotent victim, the officer will get the urge to act out is some way: "Fuck it, they think I'm a criminal, I'll show them how bad I can really be!" This is probably a subset of the angry response discussed above, but is far more dangerous. In these instances, it may be really hard to fight the temptation to figuratively stick a thumb in the eye of the officer's perceived tormentors, and it is here that the officer's family, legal counsel, and clinicians may struggle to help him maintain adaptive self-restraint.

Guilt. This is the real world where people are not perfect and, in some cases, as much as the officer hates to admit it, there may have been some ways he contributed to his own plight. In a few cases, it might have been outright illicit or criminal behavior, but more often it represents one of those "tipping point" moments when the officer made a choice to do one thing and not another. Perhaps a suspect jabbed the officer with a hidden syringe while he was trying to cuff him, so he gave the skell an extra thump as a thank-you. Or did he get overflirty with the cute college student at the auto accident scene and spent way too much time attending to her minor wounds, to the neglect of calling EMS quickly enough for the retiree in the other vehicle with a compound fracture? Great, now I've got a complaint of sexual misconduct and on-scene negligence.

Or, maybe–just maybe–I fired at the suspect when he was already on the ground after he gave me the finger, grinned, and tauntingly grabbed his crotch, but at the time, it sure looked like he was going for something in his waistband and getting up to lunge at me again." In such cases, fear, guilt, anger, and paranoia may all percolate and magnify the officer's distress: "What was I thinking?" "How could I have been so stupid?" "Everybody does it and I get screwed!" "I'll bet this was a set-up–they've had it in for me for a long time!"

Clinical syndromes. As noted earlier, these may be physical, such as headaches, muscle spasms, stomach problems, or sleep disruption: some souls scream with their bodies. Or the maladies may be psychological, including anxiety, panic disorder, depression, and (rarely) full-blown posttraumatic stress disorder (PTSD). Alcohol or substance abuse may be a risk (off-duty, on home confinement, plenty of time to sit around with nothing to do), further compounding the problem and possibly elevating the risk of suicidal behavior. It is usually around this time that the officer may begin to get so overwhelmed by the stress of the ongoing case that he or she is not able to function, and at that point, may ask for or, more commonly, be recommended by others, to seek professional help

PSYCHOLOGICAL INTERVENTION STRATEGIES FOR OFFICER-INVOLVED SHOOTINGS

We've seen that an officer's involvement in a contested OIS/DFE is likely to precipitate a cascade of events that can seriously impact his law enforcement career and his whole life. All police agencies take deadly force encounters seriously and most have specific policies in place to deal with them (Hatch & Dickson, 2007; IACP, 2009; Miller, 2011b, 2015b; Petrowski, 2002a, 2002b; Webb, 2011; see also Chapter 9).

But, regardless of the presumptive legitimacy and justifiability of the shooting or other use of force incident, *all* involved officers should be treated with the appropriate courtesy and respect due a responder whose professional responsibility has just placed him in a life-and-death scenario. A law enforcement agency's credibility and trust is best preserved by conducting its actions with their personnel, as well as with members of the public, in an unbiased and honorable manner. This applies from the first post-shooting moments, through investigations, administrative and disciplinary actions, to termination or prosecution, if it comes to that. Throughout the process, police agencies maintain their collective dignity by conferring appropriate dignity upon their individual members.

Presented here is a composite administrative and mental health model protocol for on-scene response to, and follow-up evaluation of, officers who

Table 8.2.
PSYCHOLOGICAL INTERVENTIONS FOR OFFICERS INVOLVED IN AN OIS/DFE

On-scene response: Assess officer's mental status, psychological fitness to make a statement, and plan for subsequent follow-up.
Post-critical incident psychological evaluation: Usually several days following the incident. Assess officer's mental state and readiness to return to duty. Vast majority of officers in uncontested cases return to work within a few days or weeks.
Specialized law enforcement counseling and psychotherapy: May be applied in a variety of contexts, but here is focused on working through any particularly disturbing and destabilizing aspects of the OIS/DFE, especially in contested cases.

have been involved in OIS/DFEs, as well as non-fatality shootings and other critical incidents. This protocol is culled and amalgamated from a variety of sources (Baruth, 1986; Blau, 1994; IACP, 2009; McMains, 1986a, 1986b, 1991; Williams, 1991), as well as my own experience with law enforcement, public safety, special unit, military, and other first responder and civilian agencies (Miller, 1994a, 1995, 1998b, 1999a, 1999b, 2000, 2005a, 2006a, 2006d, 2006e, 2006i, 2007b, 2007e, 2007f, 2007g, 2008b, 2008g, 2008h, 2009a, 2011b, 2013a, 2013b, 2015c, 2015d, 2017, 2019b, 2019c). This model can be adapted and modified to the needs of an individual police agency, and how this protocol is carried out in practice can make a tremendous difference in the later psychological adjustment of the involved officers and in department-wide morale (Table 8.2).

Officer-Involved Shooting: On-Scene Response

Not all agencies have an on-scene critical incident response policy. For those that do, the typical protocol is that, immediately following an OIS, designated personnel will respond to the shooting scene. In smaller departments, this may include the police chief or sheriff; in larger jurisdictions, it is usually the precinct captain or district undersheriff. Other responding personnel may include back-up officers, administrative officials, departmental investigators, peer support staff, mental health professionals, departmental attorney, media spokesperson or Public Information Officer (PIO), and others.

If the involved officers do not require medical care, a detailed **walk-through** may be carried out, where they take the investigators step-by-step through the event while it is still fresh in their minds. This is often video-recorded and may take several hours, especially where the scenario is a complex one and there are multiple officers involved. However, for reasons of practicality and liability, some jurisdictions have phased out the walk-through.

Reassurance to the involved officer should be provided by departmental authorities from the outset. This should simply communicate an understanding and appreciation of what the officer has just been through, and the assurance that the department will support him or her as much as possible throughout the process. Especially at this psychologically sensitive stage, the officer should be given the benefit of the doubt and treated with respect by departmental authorities.

At the scene, the officer should be provided on-scene access to legal counsel and, if possible, to a mental health professional. In most jurisdictions officers may refrain from speaking with investigators at the scene until an attorney is present and, in some departments, until they have been assessed as mentally fit to make a statement by a qualified mental health professional. This protects the officer's rights and at the same time makes it difficult for the officer to later challenge any on-scene statements on the basis of their having been made under mental duress or investigative coercion.

The weapon fired by the officer will almost always be impounded. This is a fairly standard on-scene policy, but the way it is carried out can make a big difference in how the officer adjusts to the post-shooting aftermath. In the worst case, the officer is unceremoniously stripped of his sidearm in full view of his colleagues, the media, and jeering bystanders, and forced to parade around with an empty holster, the epitome of emasculatory humiliation. In the best case, the weapon is turned over in private, and in many instances a replacement weapon is provided or the empty holster removed while the on-scene investigation proceeds.

As just noted, at many shooting scenes, involved personnel may remain at the site for hours in order to carry out the investigation and walk-through. However, no one should hang around the area longer than necessary and the officer should be released from the scene as quickly as possible and driven home or back to the police station by a supervisor or a pair of colleagues, to await further action. When taken home, the peers should accompany the officer to his door and leave only when it is assured that he is safe in the care of his family or otherwise stable enough to leave by himself.

Even if everybody is still on-scene, the officer's family should be notified of the shooting as soon as possible; family members should not be left to first hear about the incident on their radio, TV, or cell phone, or get a call from a neighbor who's seen or heard the story. If the family is out of town, every effort should be made to locate them, preferably through direct contact with a law enforcement agency in that location. Media requests should be handled by the agency's Public Information Officer.

On-Scene Psychological Assessment and Intervention

At least 30 years ago, almost all large departments and over two-thirds of small and medium-sized departments were providing some professional mental health support for officers involved in an OIS or other critical incident (McMains, 1986a; 1986b); hopefully, fiscal restraints and other considerations have not appreciably evaporated that support since then. As part of the on-scene call-out team, if you are the responding police psychologist or other licensed mental health clinician responder, you have a specific but important role to play. Note that, in most professional interactions with a licensed mental health professional, privacy and confidentially are protected by the Supreme Court ruling in *Jaffee v. Redmond* (1996), and clinicians are advised to familiarize themselves with the parameters and limitations of this standard (also see below and Chapter 9).

First, when the call comes in, try find out as much as possible about the nature of the incident. When arriving at the scene, check in with the on-scene supervisor, identify the involved officer, and try to find a comfortable place to conduct the interview. "On-scene" doesn't necessarily mean standing next to the crime scene tape or pacing back and forth in front of the news cameras. As long as the officer stays inside the established perimeter and can be found by authorities when needed, he or she is still technically on-scene. Many such interviews take place inside a police vehicle or command bus.

Next, determine the officer's mental status. This may range from extremes of panic, confusion, and disorientation–rare, in my experience–to unnatural calmness and stoic denial ("I'm okay; no problem")–a far more common response. Sometimes, emotions will swing back and forth at the scene. Validating these reactions as normal stress responses is an important part of on-scene intervention.

For the visibly upset officer, use calming and distraction techniques to bring his or her mental state into a more rational and receptive mode. For the defensive, sealed-over officer, what is often helpful is an individualized version of the critical incident stress management procedure known as **defusing**, which follows a basic tripartite structure (Miller, 1999a, 2006d, 2007f, 2013b, 2019b; Mitchell & Everly, 1996), as follows:

Ask the officer to tell you what happened. This will typically elicit a stiff, dry, detail-laden rendition of events, as if the officer were testifying before a review board or in court. Listen to the story until you have a good sense of the sequence of events. Then, ask the officer to describe "what was going on in your mind while it was happening," which can yield clues to the officer's cognitive and emotional state. Finally, provide factual information and support regarding any disturbing reactions the officer may be having at the scene. Remember that the goal of on-scene psychological intervention is not to conduct psychotherapy, but rather to allow the officer to loosen up just enough for the clinician to be able to assess his mental status and, if necessary, to use temporary mental strengthening techniques (Miller, 2006i, 2008d, 2008i) to help him keep it together until the immediate crisis has resolved.

Dr. Alexis Artwohl (personal communication) cites several legal experts in opining that officers at a post-shooting scene should not be asked by a mental health professional (MHP), or anyone else, to recount the events he or she has just experienced, until they have gone through at least one sleep cycle and, even then, any such communication should be only with, or in the presence of, the officer's legal counsel. I agree that a detailed exposition at the scene is unnecessary and even ill-advised, but in some cases, the officer is going to be asked questions anyway, so the main function of the on-scene MHP's query is precisely to assure that the officer is in a reasonably intact state to make coherent sense in his own behalf. As I emphasize in this chapter and the next one, during the course of any legal proceeding, the attorney is the boss and psychological advice or intervention does not supersede legal strategy or procedure. Accordingly, it goes without saying (so I'll say it) that, beginning at the shooting scene itself, all officer statements should be made in the presence of counsel. Years ago, when I did call-outs, I never experienced a problem with the on-scene attorneys, and most were glad that the department even cared enough to drag me out of bed to be there with their officer.

Follow-Up Psychological Services in an Officer-Involved Shooting

In some departments, the officer may be referred for a **post-critical incident psychological evaluation**, usually within a few days to a week following the incident, in order to assess for any residual adverse psychological disturbances. As noted earlier, normal short-term post-shooting reactions include heightened tension, impaired sleep, and ruminating and/or dreaming about the incident; these usually abate within a few days. If the shooting is administratively cleared and there are no psychological problems noted, the officer will usually be returned to service within a week or so. If the officer seems to be having an especially hard time coping, stress debriefing or psychological counseling may be recommended. For an otherwise healthy officer, this type of intervention is usually short-term and is typically followed by a second evaluation for return to duty. In high-profile or contested shootings, however, the psychological stress is likely to be far higher and officers may be out of service for prolonged periods of time (Miller, 2011b, 2015b; Rudofossi, 2007, 2009; Solomon & Horn, 1986).

Note that many departments utilize an on-scene intervention with no mandatory follow-up, while other departments do the reverse; a few still have no policy at all in this area. Of course, police psychologists should always consult with their departments regarding the protocols for such incidents–ideally, law enforcement managers, administrators, and mental health clinicians would be involved in collaboratively developing these protocols in the first place (Miller, 2006f, 2006h, 2006i).

PSYCHOLOGICAL TREATMENT OF OFFICERS INVOLVED IN AN OIS/DFE

Following the original shooting incident and the follow-up assessment session, some officers may request additional contact with a mental health clinician, while others may be referred or even ordered to go by their supervisors. To preserve objectivity, the clinician who performs the initial post-OIS evaluation typically should not be the one to conduct counseling and psychotherapy with the officer; however, in smaller departments, psychologists may have to play multiple roles. Certainly, the clinical psychological treatment of a police officer involved in a contested OIS/DFE case should be entirely separate from the forensic evaluation by an objective expert witness, which will be discussed in Chapter 9. The following clinical recommendations are directed toward the treating clinician and are synthesized and summarized from a variety of sources (Blau, 1994; Horn, 1991; Kirschman, 2007; Kirschman et al., 2014; McMains, 1986a, 1991; Miller, 1995, 1998b, 1999b, 2007g, 2013b, 2015d, 2017; Rudofossi, 2007, 2009, 2011; Wester & Lyubelsky, 2005; Wittrup, 1986; Zeling, 1986).

Psycholegal Issues

Several important issues may arise in the psychological treatment of officers embroiled in a contested OIS/DFE case. First, officers and their attorneys may be reluctant to engage such help for fear of confidentiality breaches. As noted above, the U.S. Supreme Court in *Jaffee v. Redmond,* 1996 (which actually involved a police shooting case) ruled that patient-psychotherapist communications enjoy the same degree of privilege as attorney-client communication. That means if you are a licensed psychotherapist engaged in the voluntarily self-initiated assessment or treatment of a police officer–or any patient, for that matter–your lips are sealed, and so are any records pertaining to your clinical treatment of that officer, including family members. Therefore, you cannot reveal any aspect of your interaction with your patient to anyone without express permission of that patient. In a psycholegal context, this also means that other parties in the litigation are barred from accessing your mental health records. But there are a few exceptions, and these are not specific to law enforcement officers, but apply to any patient under psychological care.

The first set of exceptions concern issues of safety regarding your patient and others. All states have **mandated reporting laws** that stipulate that if any state-licensed clinical treatment provider, who is a de facto **mandated reporter**, becomes aware that their patient is engaged in the physical or sexual abuse or neglect of a minor child, elderly person, or disabled person, that clinician is obligated to report it to that state's Department of Children and Families.

Some states have **duty-to-protect** laws that apply to mental health clinicians who become aware that their patient intends to harm a specific person; in other states, the law does not compel, but nevertheless allows, a clinician to breach confidentiality if it is in the service of preventing a credible threat from being acted out. Relatedly, all states provide for the **temporary involuntary commitment** of a person deemed by a qualified doctor or first responder to be a danger to self or others. In a clinical setting, this is usually invoked when the therapist believes that their patient is suicidal, whether this includes intended aggression against a third party or not.

In the above two circumstances, any information disclosed by the clinician would apply strictly to the reasons for the action, e.g., child abuse, suicidal crisis, or aggressive threat, and would not usually include unrelated clinical information. For example, where a distraught officer under investigation makes a suicidal gesture or credible threat against a supervisor or family member, information relevant to his treatment for nonemergency issues surrounding the original OIS/DFE event itself might well be irrelevant to the present crisis, and thereby would probably still be protected by confidentiality and privilege. (FYI: I've never actually had such an extreme case and don't know of any clinicians who have, because most of these officers endure their fates in quiet agony, but it is nevertheless reassuring that such a clinico-legal contingency exists.)

Ironically, fewer protections apply if an officer, or any patient involved in legal action, chooses to put his or her own mental state at issue in the case. For example, in a criminal case, if your officer-patient were to pursue a diminished capacity defense ("I was mentally impaired at the time of the shooting") and elects to use his treatment with you as evidence ("And the notes from my treatment sessions with Dr. Smith prove I was not in my right mind when I pulled the trigger"), then *all* the therapist's records may become discoverable, i.e., opposing counsel may subpoena virtually any part of your patient's chart since, in effect, your patient has opened the door.

While all mental health clinicians should prepare themselves for the possibility of these kinds of events, bear in mind that they are exceedingly rare in any kind of mental health practice, much less those involving police and public safety personnel. Nevertheless, it is important to understand that the rules surrounding confidentiality and privilege apply to the therapist, not the patient. That is, it is the clinician's professional responsibility to assure that no unauthorized information gets disclosed to any third party, excluding the exceptions noted above. Patients, however, are free to blab about their treatment to anyone they wish, usually to friends or family members. Again, while not common, an attorney may fear that any such outside-the-office revelations may not be protected by confidentiality and privilege, and if discovered by opposing counsel, may be used as evidence against the officer.

Therefore, out of an abundance of caution, some attorneys will instruct their clients to talk to no one, not even a mental health clinician, reasoning that, if any fragment of incriminating data finds its way into adverse evidence, all the therapy in the world won't do much good if their client is carted off to prison. Other attorneys are concerned that the information provided to the clinician by the officer may distort or conflict with the carefully crafted defense narrative the attorney and client are putting together. In still other cases, the clinical treatment may have begun after the OIS/DFE event, but before the decision was made to discipline, fire, prosecute, or sue the officer, which may have come weeks or months later. Now, the case is contested, the stakes in the outcome have increased, everyone gets more and more paranoid, and the lawyer may yank the officer out of treatment.

Conversely, where an attorney believes that his or her client is about to crack under the strain of a particularly prolonged and/or brutal adversarial process, the lawyer may actively enlist a mental health professional to help "keep the lid on," provide a confidential outlet for the officer to vent his fears and frustrations, and thereby deter the officer-client from unadvisedly talking to peers, friends, unvetted family members, or others. In my experience, most attorneys will take a hands-off approach to their client's mental health treatment, as long as they know they can communicate with the clinician when necessary, of course, with the permission and authorization of the officer-patient. Nevertheless, before beginning clinical treatment of any police officer, public safety worker, or military service member who is involved, or may become involved, in any kind of significant disciplinary or legal action, it is advisable to have a frank discussion with both the officer and his or her attorney, to clarify exactly what your role may or may not be.

The Treatment Process

Ideally, psychological intervention services should be accessible as soon after the shooting incident as possible; however, treatment is often delayed as officers may attempt to wait out, thaw out, or tough out the attendant strains and stresses on their own, until the pressure mounts and the need for outside help becomes apparent either to the officer himself or, more likely, to peers, supervisors, or family members. If an officer seems to be coping adequately on his own, or if he steadfastly refuses to become a "mental case" by seeing a shrink, this should never be forced, but clinical services should be available if he wants them.

In most cases, interventions should be short-term and be focused on supporting the officer through the present crisis. How narrow or broad the range of issues to be covered will be determined on a case-by-case basis, depending on how the incident has affected the officer, his family, colleagues, and others. But the general guideline is that post-shooting psychological intervention should be focused on managing the aftereffects of the critical incident in question.

Accordingly, a realistically positive atmosphere should prevail during the course of treatment. The guiding assumption should be that, in his own judgment, the officer acted properly, can successfully manage the current crisis with a little help, and will ultimately be exonerated and perhaps even return to active duty, if this is still an option and, if not, that the officer will ultimately find an alternative route to a satisfactory career and life. This does not mean sugar-coating the facts; indeed, as we'll soon see, a major component of the treatment process is to provide ongoing reality checks. But, in contested shooting cases, the psychologist's office may be the only place the officer does not feel like a hounded criminal, and the treating clinician must be able to compartmentalize his or her own feelings and opinions about the justifiability of the OIS/DFE if he or she is going to provide effective treatment. The treating clinician's role is thus always that of an *advocate of the officer's mental health,* regardless of the legal status of the case.

Treatment Guidelines

Most of these recommendations apply equally to officers in both cleared and contested OIS/DFEs, but for the latter, some special considerations may apply. On initial contact with the officer, the mental health clinician's role may replicate the basic intervention stages of a critical incident stress debriefing model (Bohl, 1995; Miller, 1999a, 2006d, 2007f, 2013b; Mitchell & Everly, 1996), applied, in this case, on an individual level, and focused, at least initially, on stabilization and restrengthening.

First, review the facts of the case with the officer. This allows for a relatively nonemotional narrative of the incident, and many of these officers may have already provided their rendition of events to a variety of investigators, often under skeptical, adversarial, or downright hostile circumstances. However, in the therapeutic context, this accounting of events serves a separate but related function. Precisely because of the cognitive and perceptual distortions that commonly occur in these kinds of incidents (see Chapters 4–6), what may be particularly disturbing to the officer is the lack of clarity in his own mind as to the actual nature and sequence of events. Just being able to review what is known about the facts of the case in a safe and supportive environment may provide a needed dose of mental clarity and sanity to the situation.

Solomon (1991, 1995) describes one such therapeutic application as a process of going over the incident "frame by frame," which allows the officer to verbalize the moment-to-moment thoughts, perceptions, sensory details, feelings, and actions that occurred during the OIS/DFE or other critical incident. This can help the officer become aware of, sort out, and understand what happened. Be sensitive, however, to the pacing and intensity of such recollections, so as not to retraumatize the officer or encourage him to misremember events that may have been incompletely processed in the first place or did not occur at all. The goal is recollection and consolidation, not fabrication or confabulation (see Chapter 6).

Next, review the officer's thoughts and feelings about the shooting incident, but don't expect everything to be sorted out at once. Remember, an OIS/DFE represents a special kind of critical incident, and it may take more than one attempt for the officer to productively untangle and reveal what's going on in his mind. Give him extra time or extra sessions to express his thoughts and feelings, and be sure to monitor the reactions so as not to encourage unproductive spewing or loss of control. One of the most important things the clinician can do at this stage is to help the officer modulate his or her emotional catharsis so that it comes as a relief, not a burden.

As science-based mental health clinicians, one of the most valuable contributions we can make is providing factual information about common psychological reactions to a shooting incident (Chapters 4-6). The kinds of cognitive and perceptual distortions that take place during an OIS, the post-traumatic symptoms and disturbances, and the sometimes off-putting and distressing responses of colleagues and family members, are likely to be quite alien to the officer's ordinary experience, and might be interpreted by him or her as signs of going soft or crazy (frequent comment: "I heard about these things, but I didn't think it would happen to me"). Normalize these responses for the officer, and try to give a realistic projection of what will come next. Often, just this kind of authoritative reassurance from a competent and credible mental health professional can mitigate the officer's anxiety considerably.

Finally, provide recommendations for follow-up services which may include additional individual sessions, family therapy, referral to departmental or community support services, possible medication consult, substance abuse programs, and so on (in contested cases, be sure to touch base with the officer's lawyer first). As with most cases of critical incident psychological intervention with public safety personnel, mental health treatment targeted to OIS reactions tends to be short-term, although additional services may be sought later for other problems partially related or even unrelated to the precipitating event. Indeed, successful psychological resolution of a critical incident sometimes serves as the stimulus to explore and deal with other troublesome aspects of an officer's life, such as family and relationship issues (Blau, 1994; Miller, 1998b, 2007i).

PSYCHOLOGICAL STRATEGIES FOR HELPING OFFICERS DEAL WITH THE STRESS OF AN INTERNAL INVESTIGATION OR LEGAL ACTION

As noted earlier, a contested OIS/DFE case bears all the stresses of an administratively cleared shooting, with the added burdens of traumatic life disruption, identity fragmentation, societal castigation, family dissolution, personal humiliation, and fear of onerous punishment. This ordeal can persist unabated for months or years. Some officers in these straights have stated, "I'd rather have cancer; then, at least, people would feel sorry for me." If this sounds extreme, consider: how would you deal with it if this were happening to you and you were in danger of losing everything you ever worked for? Right–you don't even want to think about it.

But as a mental health advocate for your officer, you have to think about it, because your role may span those of coach, therapist, teacher, parent-surrogate, cheerleader, anger-projection punching bag, toxic pain-absorber, crisis manager, and hand-holder. The following are some useful coping strategies that can be utilized and adapted to the unique circumstances and personality of an officer facing an adversarial action related to his or her involvement in an OIS/DFE or other critical incident. If you are the officer's mental health clinician–or, for that matter, attorney, peer supporter, supervisor, family member, or friend–the following are practical recommendations you can pass on to your officer to aid in his self-help efforts, to guide him in de-escalating from potential further trouble, and to encourage him to work productively with those who are trying to help (Miller, 2008f, 2009b, 2011b, 2015b, 2019b).

Don't Panic

I know, easy for me to say. If you're an officer under investigation, litigation, or prosecution, there's no way you can avoid carrying around a huge unwanted sack of anxiety from now until the case is resolved, one way or another. But the goal is to deal with it without becoming too overwhelmed by panic, or the phobic avoidance it engenders, in order to function as well as possible on your own behalf. *Clinician:* teach the officer a number of basic stress-management techniques and cognitive-behavioral coping strategies, to encourage the sense that he can at least control something, if only his own breathing or sleep schedule. Utilize whatever works: tapes and manuals or in-office relaxation or biofeedback exercises. Encourage the officer to practice these techniques at home, so that he or she can utilize them whenever necessary. *Attorney:* if your case strategy is to keep your client out of a shrink's office for now, at least enlist a mental health professional as a consultant to point you toward stress self-management techniques you can pass along that are safe, valid, and effective.

Strategize

Another good reason to control anxiety is to keep it from overwhelming productive thinking and problem-solving. At multiple points in time, you will have to sit down with your attorney so you both can figure out how to best handle your case. While a treating mental health clinician will rarely be invited to contribute directly to case strategy (the role of a retained psychologist expert witness may be a different story, which will be considered in Chapter 9), he or she can still facilitate this process by occasionally serving as a pair of auxiliary frontal lobes, sifting through the confusion, modeling rational thinking, and helping you rein in and work through counterproductive limbic-emotional impulses. More directly, an objective advisor can help you keep your focus on a constructive future, post-case. This longer-term game plan may be modified multiple times as new information comes in and contingencies change, but at least you'll *have* a game plan, an existential rope bridge across the abyss on whose banks you're currently teetering.

Ask Your Lawyer

The above discussion raises another important point. When involved in a stressful, confusing legal action, patients in general, and police officers in particular, may ask their mental health clinician, "What should I do about . . . ?" If the question relates more or less strictly to psychological issues—techniques for quelling panic attacks, how to deal with children's questions, ways to keep one's mind engaged during home confinement, and so on—clinicians should generally feel free to call upon their relevant skills and expertise to help the officer.

But if the question seems to touch on any matter of direct relevance to the case—e.g., should I drive my kids to school, even though I'm on house confinement?; should I answer a pesky reporter's continuing phone messages or tell her to leave me alone?—then, the rule in any litigation context is that legal precedes clinical, so "ask your lawyer first," should be the default response. In practice, I've found that, as long as the clinician's psychological advice is realistic, sensible, and in their client's best interest, most attorneys will pretty much agree with the clinician's psychological advice. But don't take this for granted–always ask first.

Keep A Low Profile

Speaking of advice, one near-universal recommendation in cases like these is for you, the officer, *not* to become the protruding nail head or squeaky wheel, begging to be hammered or greased. Especially where the case seems to drag on, and anxiety and suspicion continue to fester, you may begin to feel a great temptation to "take it to the streets," to publicize your trials and tribulations so that the whole world will rise up and denounce the cosmic injustice you have surely been dealt.

Don't. Remind yourself that, even if you were to spread the holy word far and wide, except for a few close family members and allies, most people's reaction will be somewhere between "who cares?" and "better you than me, sucker." Aside from this unsupportive response, turning the case into a crusade and acting like the poster-child for wrongful discipline or malicious prosecution will, in most cases, only backfire and damage your chances of being exonerated or reinstated by forcing the ultimate decision-makers into an us-versus-them contest of wills.

In the same way, be very wary of third parties who may want to make your case their own *cause célèbre,* because these "helpers" almost always have their own idiosyncratic political or social agendas, or just want to make a journalistic name for themselves, and may have little genuine concern for your overall welfare. You don't have to be overly cynical or paranoid, but always go back to the fundamental rule noted above: ask your lawyer first.

Keeping a low profile also means–duuuh–staying out of further trouble. During a paid leave or unpaid suspension, with too much free time on your hands and too much dysphoric rumination percolating in your head, you may be tempted to go out, have some fun, blow off some steam, and raise a little hell while you still can. Short answer: again, don't. From now until this case is resolved, you must comport yourself as if there were video and audio surveillance trained on you 24/7.

No, it may not be fair to be trapped in virtual (or real) house arrest, not working, not going out with family and friends, just pacing around like a caged animal and driving yourself and your loved ones nuts. But look at the big picture: would you want IA or the DA to be on the verge of cutting you a break, only to learn at the last minute that you were involved in further illegal, obnoxious, or just embarrassingly stupid behavior? *Attorneys and clinicians:* sometimes, you may have to forcefully communicate to your officer some version of, "don't be a schmuck." Encourage the officer to tough it out and collaborate with his small, but dedicated, cadre of allies in working productively toward a favorable resolution.

Work the Case

The opposite extreme from the crusader-for-justice syndrome is often dejected apathy, sometimes progressing to frank clinical depression. In these cases, positive action may be the best medicine. Where practical, and within the bounds of legality and case strategy, ask your attorney to give you some tasks that can move the case along–researching relevant resources, organizing and updating paper or computer files, preparing and rehearsing testimony–in order to help you "obsess constructively" and burn up some of that surplus nervous energy that might otherwise lead you to trouble. Just remember to check everything with your lawyer first, so as to be a helper, not a pest, and so the activity is empowering, not further deflating.

Don't Lie

This is crucial. Experienced attorneys and clinicians know that our clients and patients don't always tell us the truth–and we're trying to help them! Under the intense adversarial pressures of an investigation or legal charge, the temptation to bend the truth and spin the story will be extreme. But if the powers-that-be suspect you are lying, and certainly if you're caught in a direct fabrication, it could blow your whole case and lead to additional criminal charges. One of my saddest experiences as a forensic examiner and expert witness in all kinds of civil and criminal cases is to have to go back to the attorney who retained me and say, "Sorry, lawyer, but I think your client is full of beans." Even otherwise solid cases have been self-sabotaged by defendants stupidly prevaricating on matters that might have been inconsequential if only they had played it straight. As discussed in Chapter 9, even intendedly honest renditions of events can be distorted by the vagaries of memory formation and recall, but deliberate lying is far worse because, as every attorney knows, "it only takes one crumb of bullshit to stink up the whole room."

More commonly, officers may not flat-out conjure events from thin air (see Chapter 9), but, like most people, they will self-defensively spin their recollections to accord with the preferred interpretation of their actions; that is, they come to believe the stories they tell, frequently reinforced by multiple repetitions, because it paints them in a more positive light. Again, let your attorney and, if appropriate, your mental health clinician help you to process and relate the events in question until a consistent and comprehensible narrative emerges.

Have a Plan B

And, preferably, a C and a D, too. An important component of productive problem solving is contingency planning. When the smoke clears away, even if the worst case scenario of prison time is averted, chances are, your law enforcement career is effectively over, and it is vital to have some plans made ahead of time for what you're going to do in your new life. Understandably, this kind of advance planning is harder than it sounds because the mere acknowledgment of any alternate future plans will seem like a pessimistic capitulation to the possibility of failure. Nevertheless, let the people you still trust help you make these contingency plans for the same reason people buy medical or property insurance: you hope the big one doesn't hit, but if it does, you want to be ready, so you can recover and rebuild.

SUMMARY AND CONCLUSIONS

Psychologically helping police officers who have been involved in an OIS/DFE is a select but important part of police psychology practice. Human beings who have faced the imminent prospect of losing their life and, in response, have had to take a life, experience a special kind of challenge that shares some features with traumatic stressors in general, but also contains some unique features that may require specialized clinical skills to help them cope. When, in addition, those officers face the drastic life implosion created by a contested shooting or other use-of-force case, the pressures can be catastrophic and require mental health practitioners to expand their clinical roles and strategies in unique and productive ways.

One of these is the ability and willingness to operate within the legal system. While direct experience in forensic psychology is not a prerequisite for psychotherapeutic work with police officers, clinicians who want to serve this population should understand that cops and courts frequently go together and, although most interaction with the officer will occur in private and off the radar, occasionally the clinician may be called upon to consult with attorneys and/or testify on the officer's behalf. In addition, especially with officers facing contested OIS/DFE actions, the clinician may find him- or herself engaged in one of the most therapeutically demanding roles of their careers, often radiating out to include family members and others.

But taking on this clinical role in a contested OIS/DFE case also affords the mental health professional the opportunity to staunch the hemorrhage of an officer's self-respect and sanity amid what is arguably one of the most severe crises a human being can face: "I did something everybody thinks is wrong and they all hate me and want me to rot in hell." Forget about any Clarence-the-Angel happy ending fantasies: your clinical efforts will be a qualified success if you can help your officer hold onto some coarse, knotted rope line of dignity while he fights to get the pieces of his life back.

Chapter 9

DEADLY FORCE ENCOUNTERS: LEGAL CONSEQUENCES

Great services are not canceled by one act or by one single error.

Benjamin Disraeli

Justice consists not in being neutral between right and wrong, but in finding out the right and upholding it, wherever found, against the wrong.

President Theodore Roosevelt

The previous chapter dealt with the role of the police psychologist as mental health treatment provider and clinician-advocate for his or her patient. Another important role for police psychologists is serving as a retained expert witnesses in contested OIS/DFE and other law enforcement legal cases. The present chapter will provide a concise summary of the legal issues surrounding an officer's involvement in a contested OIS/DFE encounter, particularly from the perspective of the police psychologist who is involved in the case. For specific legal advice and services, readers are encouraged to consult and retain qualified and experienced legal counsel.

POSSIBLE CONSEQUENCES OF A CONTESTED OIS/DFE

Sometimes, a given OIS/DFE or other use of force case is controversial from the outset; other times, a considerable interval may elapse before disciplinary actions are taken, charges are files, or lawsuits are brought.

Table 9.1.
POSSIBLE OUTCOMES OF A CONTESTED OIS/DFE

Internal investigation: Officer typically on leave while investigation proceeds.

Career impairment: Reduction in rank, reassignment, suspension or removal from special unit.

Suspension: With or without pay, with or without restrictions.

Termination: Officer is fired.

Criminal prosecution: May include a range of charges.

Civil litigation: Officer is sued, usually along with the department, city, and anyone else connected to the incident.

Personal disruption: Adverse effects on the officer's health, family, and social status.

Internal Affairs or Outside Agency Investigation

The process of investigating a contested DFE incident typically begins with a departmental **Internal Affairs (IA)** probe, which can feel particularly abrasive to the involved officer because it comes from inside the tribe, from one's fellows and professional peers, from the folks who should understand. In fact, to avoid accusations of bias, many agencies are moving toward objective assessments by outside state and federal investigative agencies in conjunction with, or as an alternative to, an internal probe (for more comprehensive reviews of OIS/DFE investigation and management protocols, see Geiselman et al., 2018; Ross & Dunston, 2018; Webb, 2011). While the details vary from agency to agency, there are several possible outcomes of an internal investigation.

Exoneration/dismissal. The allegations are found to have an insufficient basis to sustain them, the officer is thanked for his or her cooperation, and is returned to duty.

Discipline. The investigative panel concludes that the officer did do something wrong, but not severe enough to be terminated, so he or she may be subject to a range of sanctions, from paid leave, to suspension without pay, demotion in rank, reassignment to other duties, removal from a special unit, verbal or written reprimand, or other measures. Many agencies have specific **progressive discipline** protocols that dictate the level of sanction for the type and number of infractions.

Termination. The charges are either serious enough in themselves, or the infractions show a recurring pattern, to warrant the officer being fired from the agency.

Criminal Prosecution

An OIS/DFE case may be deemed sufficiently questionable to be turned over to state or federal prosecutors for further investigation, which may lead to criminal assault or homicide charges being brought against the officer. Actually, in law, **homicide** is defined simply as the killing of one human being by another, without any particular attribution of blame or motive, whereas **murder** is the crime of *unlawfully* killing a person, with the willful intent to do so (Flowers, 2002; Miller, 2012; Palermo & Kocsis, 2005).

In fact, the law recognizes a variety of categories of homicide, each with their own attribution of psychological motive and responsibility, and each having a distinct legal definition with respect to adjudication and punishment (Flowers, 2002; Miller, 2012). Note that the key element in each charge is the precise motive and intent behind the actual act, based on the assessment and judgment of the prosecutor bringing the charge; the advice of forensic mental health clinicians is rarely sought in making these determinations. The following represents a general consensus of the criteria for each charge, but precise definitions and standards may vary across different jurisdictions, and readers are advised to consult competent legal counsel for their individual cases.

Homicide: The killing of one human being by another. Being killed by an animal, machine (unless directed by a person), disease, or act of nature, no matter how gruesome or tragic, is not homicide. Also, as noted above, homicide may or may not constitute a crime, depending on the circumstances.

Murder: The unlawful killing of one human being by another. In law, there are two basic types of murder.

First-degree Murder: Killing that is willful, deliberate, and premeditated. The killer plans to commit the unlawful homicide ("malice aforethought") and carries it out with full knowledge and intention of the act. Example: a police officer becomes angered by a citizen's disrespect and resolves to shoot him to "teach him a lesson." A more sinister example is a corrupt officer who kills another person as part of a larger pattern of criminal activity, e.g., drug dealing.

Second-degree Murder: Killing that is malicious and/or reckless without premeditation or necessarily with intent to kill. Example: during an encounter, an officer senses danger, but cannot confirm a lethal threat, but he makes the decision to shoot the suspect because "when in doubt, it's better to shoot first and ask question later."

Manslaughter: The unlawful killing of a human being without express or implied malice. There are two basic forms.

Voluntary Manslaughter: Killing that takes place in the heat of emotion and is not premeditated or committed with malice, the classic "crime of passion." Example: during an encounter, a citizen makes a move that angers or frightens the officer, and he impulsively fires at the citizen.

Involuntary Manslaughter: Killing of another person due to **negligence**, defined as: (1) failure to perform a legal duty expressly requested to safeguard human life; (2) commission of an unlawful act not otherwise considered a felony; or (3) resulting from the commission of a lawful act in a negligent or improper manner. Example: an officer fires at a threatening or fleeing suspect from an unsafe distance, and/or without proper consideration of backdrop and the surrounding environment, and unintentionally strikes and kills an innocent civilian.

There are also a number of types of homicide that don't ordinarily result in prosecution.

Justifiable Homicide: Killing that has legal justification. The most common example in law enforcement is an officer legitimately and lawfully firing to neutralize an extant threat to life, causing the death of the suspect. These incidents will usually be administratively cleared.

Excusable Homicide: A completely unintentional killing without blame or fault on the part of the killer, i.e., an accident. Example: during an otherwise legitimate and justifiable defense of life, a fired round ricochets off a wall and strikes a citizen around the corner, whom the officer could not possibly have known was there because the area is usually locked down and fenced off from intruders, yet this citizen managed to sneak in and hide there. These kinds of bizarre incidents are, in fact, exceedingly rare in law enforcement shooting incidents. A more common example would be an officer patrolling in his vehicle, going the speed limit, observing all traffic rules and safety measures, when a citizen on a bike abruptly shoots out between two parked cars, giving the officer no time to brake before striking the rider.

Other charges in contested OIS/DFE cases may include violation of civil rights, evidence tampering, aiding and abetting, assault and battery (in nonfatal shooting) and others. It is not uncommon for officers to be charged with multiple offenses simultaneously, as prosecutors attempt to get the officer to admit guilt and accept a plea or, alternatively, to help prospective jurors "shop" for a level of charge they will feel comfortable rendering a guilty verdict on. In some cases, prosecutors may even change or add charges midtrial, if the judge allows it.

Although I don't have statistics on this subject, my subjective impression is that police officers charged with criminal offenses are less likely to plea bargain than other defendants, probably because they are much less likely to believe, and therefore admit, that they committed a crime, and they are determined to specifically exculpate themselves from the practical legal consequences of the charges and to more broadly redeem themselves from the taint of any wrongdoing.

Civil Lawsuit

This is an action that may be taken by a second or third party who sues the officer, the law enforcement agency, the municipality, and possibly a range of other defendants for **compensatory** and **punitive damages**. Most commonly, in such **personal injury** or **tort** (Latin for "damages") cases, the plaintiff is either the injured party who claims to be the victim of an excessive force action, such as a police beating, Tasing, nonfatal shooting, or alleged sexual assault, or is the surviving family member of a deceased subject in a fatal police OIS/DFE. In such cases, lawsuits may be filed for any of the following causes of action.

Wrongful Death. The police officer's actions resulted in the unlawful and illegitimate death of the citizen, causing pain and suffering to the survivors.

Physical Injury. The officer's actions resulted in a broken shoulder, concussion, or nonfatal bullet wound, requiring medical and rehabilitative care, and causing physical impairment, pain, and suffering to the plaintiff.

Emotional Injury. The officer's actions resulted in the development of anxiety, depression, appetite or sleep impairment, PTSD, or other mental disorder or disabling psychological condition, causing emotional impairment, pain, and suffering.

Loss of Consortium. Due to physical and/or emotional injury, the plaintiff is unable to participate in intimate relations, causing distress to him/herself and his/her partner (yes, you can sue for that).

Financial Injury. The officer's actions resulted in the plaintiff incurring financial loss, including medical bills, mental health care, lost wages and future earnings, family relocation and housing expenses, and other losses. In cases where a young, male plaintiff–the most frequent target of a use of force or deadly force action–is critically injured and incapacitated, the size of the lawsuit may be considerable, incorporating anticipated medical costs and lost earnings over than plaintiff's entire future lifespan.

Insufficient Action or Negligent Performance of Duties. The officer's incompetence or neglect of procedure in protecting a subject, who may be a felon in custody or an uninvolved innocent bystander, led to that subject's injury or death. For example, improperly handcuffing or securing a suspect in a vehicle led to that suspect's broken wrist or spine. Or failing to heed a suspect's distress during a takedown led to his asphyxiation. Or failing to take a clearly psychotic or intoxicated subject to a hospital led to that subject's suicide, overdose, or assault of a civilian. Or a car chase of a fleeing felon results in the death of an innocent motorist or pedestrian (which is why many agencies now have a "don't-pursue" rule in such circumstances).

Where an employee of any public or private organization commits an actionable offense in the course of, or in connection with, the performance of his or her duties, it is standard litigation practice to sue just about everyone involved, including the employee, the organization, and any sponsoring or supporting parties. In this endeavor, civil tort law supplies a menu of legal rationales.

Negligent Hiring. "Officer Wayne's pre-employment psychological screening report listed his suitability for law enforcement work as 'marginal to poor,' and yet the Gotham Police Department hired him anyway."

Negligent Training. "Officer Wayne never received proper training in manual takedown tactics, and so he did not know how to properly apply the chokehold, resulting in the subject's death."

Negligent Policy. "The Gotham PD's policy of requiring patrol officers to request less-lethal ordnance from their shift sergeant made these devices unavailable during the confrontation, resulting in Officer Wayne unnecessarily shooting and killing the citizen."

Negligent Supervision or Negligent Discipline. "In the course of Officer Wayne's first two years of service, he accumulated a disproportionately high number of citizen complaints and departmental disciplinary actions, but no constructive efforts were taken to correct his dysfunctional work pattern."

Negligent Retention. "Knowing Officer Wayne was a dysfunctional employee, Gotham PD kept him in their employ longer than they reasonably should have."

The above list is not exhaustive, and even where a given officer or agency is not directly involved in a particular civil lawsuit or criminal case, that officer's personnel file and other records, or the officer's testimony, may be subpoenaed by plaintiff, prosecution, or defense counsel for use in the unrelated case. For example, in prosecuting a criminal defendant for sexual assault, or in the case of a citizen suing a hotel for stolen property, the on-scene officer's actions might be questioned and his records or testimony subpoenaed.

Finally, criminal charges and civil lawsuits against an officer may be brought simultaneously, and it is not uncommon for civil claims to be settled earlier, while criminal proceedings may drag on for years. It is also not uncommon for civil claims to run into the millions of dollars.

FORENSIC PSYCHOLOGICAL ASSESSMENT OF POLICE OFFICERS IN CONTESTED DEADLY FORCE CASES

Psychological evaluations for law enforcement encompass many different referral issues, ranging from pre-employment screening, to fitness for duty, to assessment for counseling and treatment. While a comprehensive ac-

Table 9.2.
PSYCHOLOGICAL EVALUATION OF AN
OFFICER IN A CONTESTED OIS/DFE CASE

Fiduciary relationship: Contrasts between objective psychological examiner and personal clinician.

Evaluation components: Review of records, interview of officer, interview of collaterals, specialized tests and measures, conclusions and recommendations.

Recommendations for officers: Be punctual, be courteous, ask appropriate questions, and, above all, be honest.

count of the full range of such assessments cannot be provided here, I want to present a brief outline of the evaluation process for officer-involved shootings, focusing on the role of the psychological expert witness in evaluating the state of mind of an officer who is being prosecuted and/or sued following a deadly force encounter. Attorneys who are involved in such cases may gain some insight into the evaluation process and subsequent testimony, while officers themselves ought to have an idea of what to expect from such an evaluation.

Many of the components of an OIS/DFE psychological evaluation are similar to those for forensic psychological evaluations in general (Blau, 1984; Drogin et al., 2011; Melton et al., 2018, Miller, 2012; 2013d,), while others relate specifically to police officers under legal charge (Miller, 2007d, 2011b, 2015b). Bear in mind that, as with all clinical and forensic procedures with real-life, complex human beings, the following model may be flexibly adapted to the needs of the individual officer in question.

Forensic versus Clinical Evaluations

As noted in Chapter 8, the role of the psychologist as forensic expert witness is different from that of the psychologist as clinical treatment provider in two main ways. First, a primary role of the mental health clinician is to be an advocate for their patient. As we've seen, this doesn't mean being unrealistic or untruthful, but that every intervention must address itself to what is in the best interests of the mental health of the officer. Sometimes a psychotherapist may be called upon to testify as a **treating expert**, always at the request of the patient and his or her lawyer where that client is a plaintiff in a civil case (personal injury or family law) or defendant in a criminal case (criminal competency or exculpatory mental state). But the understanding is that this is something the patient and his or her attorney has agreed to and, indeed, has requested because they believe the psychotherapist's input will further their case.

Second, and related to the first point, where a person voluntarily agrees to enter treatment with a mental health professional (or any clinician), the resulting **fiduciary relationship** exists between the therapist and the patient, and forms the basis of confidentiality and privilege discussed in Chapter 8. That means any notes, reports, or other products of the treatment relationship are essentially "owned" by the doctor and patient. However, in a forensic context, any psychological (or medical) evaluation of a defendant is typically ordered by the court, and so constitutes a **mandated referral**, not a voluntary one. Therefore, the results of that evaluation–clinical interview, case notes, psychological test data, written reports, etc.–are "owned" by the ordering entity, usually the court, by way of the attorney who got the court order to do the evaluation. Therefore, there is no expectation of privacy, and the evaluation results are potentially discoverable.

Taking the Case

Many psychologist expert witnesses do forensic work as one component of a general clinical practice, whereas others focus almost exclusively on working within the legal system. Contested OIS/DFE cases are comparatively rare (good!), so few forensic or police psychologists can fill an entire career with just these types of cases. Many expert witnesses advertise their services in print and online media or are listed with legal referral services.

An attorney in a contested OIS/DFE case will most likely contact a psychologist who has a track record of working with police officers and/or who has been involved in research, publication, teaching, or training in this area. Note that one requirement for an expert in this field is that he or she be prepared to testify, if needed, and often, to travel in order to do so.

If contacted by an attorney, first determine if this case is appropriate for you. I always try to set aside a certain amount of time for a phone conference to ascertain if this is a case I feel comfortable taking. Very few cases of any type sound perfectly good or perfectly bad when you first hear of them, so often I will request that the attorney send a concise packet of records that summarize the main case points and that will take me about an hour or two to review. If I then feel confident about the case, I will move on to the next step. If I don't, I will politely decline the case and charge the attorney for the record review time. When I do turn down a case, I try to offer as clear a rationale as possible for my decision, assuming the attorney even wants to hear that part before issuing a terse thank-you and moving on in their search for a more agreeable expert.

If I opt to take the case, we next discuss retention fees and what the attorney and I can expect from one another. Forensic experts and attorneys alike typically feel that everyone's professional role should be established as clearly as possible from the outset. For example, attorneys have to know that the expert will expect to be provided with all relevant case materials and information, will do a thorough and competent evaluation, will call it the way he or she sees it, and will not testify to anything he or she does not believe best represents that expert's carefully arrived at and honest conclusions and opinions.

Evaluation Setting

Many contested OIS/DFE cases will involve out-of-town officers, so the actual forensic evaluation may occur in one of three ways: (1) they come to you; (2) you go to them; (3) you use the miracle of modern technology to schedule an internet video interview. Several practical considerations may determine the choice of options. First, the officer may be in custody or forbidden to leave his jurisdiction as a condition of bail or house arrest, in which case options 2 or 3 apply. A face-to-face interview is usually preferable to a screen-to-screen encounter, but travel can be inconvenient for the psychologist and expensive for the client and attorney, so video may be the logical choice. For out-of-town cases, an added advantage of using electronic communication is that it is far more convenient to schedule one or more follow-up interviews through this medium, if these become necessary.

In many cases, the attorney will ask, and some will insist, that they be present during the evaluation of their client. I won't get into the full controversy around whether or not the presence of third parties can potentially contaminate the objectivity of any forensic psychological evaluation (see Boone, 2013; Otto & Kraus, 2009; Shealy et al., 2008), but if the attorney will be present, it is reasonable for you to ensure that he or she sits out of the officer's line of sight and remains silent unless spoken to. Doesn't mean they will, but at least you can so instruct. Conflicts over this issue most commonly arise where opposing counsel is the one requesting a second-opinion evaluation of your attorney's client. This kind of re-evaluation (and sometimes multiple evaluations) is common in many civil damages and criminal competency cases, but, in my experience, is rare in OIS/DFE cases, in which there is typically only the defendant's retained psychologist doing a full examination—although the prosecution may bring in their own experts to review and critique the psychologist's report and testimony.

In still other cases, the presence of their attorney during the evaluation can actually prove re-assuring and comforting to the examinee, who may then be more likely to speak freely to the examiner because he or she is not afraid of saying something that the attorney may later rebuke them for. Again, if you agree to this, instruct the attorney to keep quiet and stay out of sight. That goes for attorneys on either side of the case. Each case must be judged on its own merits, but the overriding principle is not to allow into the evaluation process anything that will unduly influence either the procedure or the results.

Finally, in highly adversarial settings, opposing counsel may convince a judge to order not just the presence of the client's attorney, but the use of a court stenographer and videographer. In these cases, it is the examining clinician's decision, but if he or she feels that this will markedly contaminate the examination process, the clinician should say so ahead of time and decline to conduct the evaluation under these conditions. I've only had a few of these situations (all in civil cases and none involving police officers), and for the most part, I didn't object, even finding the presence of this kind of "backup data" useful in formulating my own forensic conclusions and opinions. But you will make your own decision based on the totality of the circumstances in your case.

Evaluation and Report Components

The structure and content of the forensic evaluation, and the resultant report, in a contested OIS/DFE case will be similar to that of most forensic evaluations generally, except insofar as the exam addresses its specialized topic area. Attorneys will usually ask the psychologist to do a full evaluation of their client and integrate the findings with the relevant supporting case material (most U.S. cases, in my experience), whereas, in other cases, the expert will be given the opportunity to review pre-existing case materials and hold forth on the supporting psychological literature, but without interviewing, indeed, sometimes not even seeing, the officer, except in court if the expert is called to testify (more common in Canada, for example).

Upon completion of the evaluation, the psychologist will usually prepare a detailed written report which, if favorable to the retaining attorney's case, will be entered into the record as a **discoverable document** (available to both sides). In many cases, the attorney may want to have a conference with the psychologist prior to the expert's generating such a document to make sure its contents will conform to the lawyer' overall defense narrative in the case. If both psychologist and attorney have done their homework, it usually is, but on a few occasions, the assessment leads to conclusions that are discrepant from what the psychologist at first assumed, and the expert must be frank about what conclusions his or her work will and will not support. If the lawyer isn't happy, he or she will likely say, "Thanks, Doc," will settle any remaining accounts, and leave the report unwritten and the unfavorable findings undiscovered. So, while you may be the expert in psychology, it is the attorney who determines the case strategy.

Although structure and style vary from expert to expert, the forensic report, when completed, should contain all of the following basic elements that reconstruct the evaluation you carried out.

Identifying Information. Subject's name; age; sex; date of birth; law enforcement agency and jurisdiction; departmental ID number (if relevant); case number (if filed); date of incident; date(s) of evaluation; referral source (usually the attorney); and evaluator's name.

Reason for Referral. In a contested DFE case, this will usually be a summary description of the relevant case and the officer's purported role in the index incident.

Record Review. There may be dozens, hundreds, or thousands of printed pages, not to mention electronic documents, photographs, audio and video recordings, and even physical evidence, encompassing witness statements, crime scene analyses, autopsy reports, medical, psychological, and employment records, testimony transcripts, and much, much, much more. The expert's job is to wade through all of this material, sift and sort what is pertinent to the psychological part of the case, and ultimately explain how these relevant exhibits and data points contribute to his or her case formulation.

Record review should cover two basic areas: (1) **case history:** everything that has happened, from the time the buildup to the index incident began to unfold to the moment the officer sits down in front of you; (2) **background history:** everything about this officer's past that is relevant to your formulation, including family background, developmental history, medical records, level and type of education, employment record, and especially history of this subject's performance as a law enforcement officer.

Prior Evaluations. In many civil and criminal forensic cases where expert witnesses are retained, it is common for each side to have their own psychologist perform an independent examination of the client, and render their independent, and typically conflicting, reports and testimony. In contested OIS/DFE criminal cases, however, an opposing expert is less common, and when present, is usually retained by the prosecution to opine that the officer is exaggerating or misrepresenting his or her experiences during the OIS/DFE, or that the defense expert's conclusions are unwarranted or invalid. In some cases, the opposing expert will examine the officer in question, but in other instances, he or she will base their opinion on the defense psychologist's report and background materials.

In yet other circumstances, rare in contested police OIS/DFE cases, but not uncommon in routine criminal and civil personal injury cases, you may be retained to examine the defendant officer after a previously retained expert failed to deliver the strong case the retaining attorney was hoping for: in a less charitable conceptualization, this is called "doctor shopping." And you may not even be told, at least at first, that such a prior evaluation exists, especially if the previous expert's report, or untranscribed findings and raw data, were never entered into evidence and thereby never made discoverable.

Where it is clear that prior less-than-favorable evaluations have indeed taken place, prepare to be charmed and flattered by the attorney, who has now chosen you to be the "real" expert who is uniquely qualified to mine the hidden nuggets of exculpatory truth from the left-over dross of the prior exams. In any case, make sure you ask about prior psych evals and go over them carefully to see why expert number one (or two or three) wasn't willing to deliver what this attorney was hoping for.

Clinical Interview. This, of course, is the core of any forensic psychological evaluation, and can take a few hours or many days, sometimes spread out over periods of time, to allow the psychologist to garner as much information as possible from the officer himself. Interview styles and formats vary, but all successful interviews generally include some flexible combination of unstructured (free narrative), semi-structured (open-ended questions), and structured (close-ended questions or questionnaires) formats (Geiselman et al., 2018; Nesca & Dalby, 2013). In fact, reading a transcript or watching a video of a smoothly and skillfully conducted clinical-forensic interview will often give the impression of two people having just a friendly, if spirited, conversation.

Among all the information gleaned from the clinical interview, two important points to be covered include: (1) the officer's account, in his own words, of exactly what transpired, what events he experienced, what others did, what his internal thought processes were, what he found familiar or unusual about this incident, and what he has done and has been experiencing since the incident, up to the present time; (2) how his version of events compares to–or why it contradicts with–that of others at the scene, with records you have reviewed, and with the formal statements and documents of investigators, prosecutors, and witnesses on this case. Indeed, your own questioning of this officer may be quite pointed at times, as you play "devil's advocate" and grill the officer about issues that are sure to come up from the other side.

Collateral Information. This usually means interviewing others who witnessed the incident, before, during, and after the officer's involvement. In contested DFE cases, however, most of these individuals will be legally inaccessible to examining experts, and you will probably have to content yourself with the involved parties' formal statements as they appear in case records.

Psychological Tests and Measures. Ironically, as quantitatively driven as many forms of psychological evaluation often are (e.g., intelligence, personality, and neuropsychological testing), there really are no validated psychometric instruments that have been developed for the specific purpose of measuring perceptual and other distortions during OIS/DFEs (Chapters 4–6). Some general-purpose cognitive and personality tests are used with police officers in other contexts (e.g., pre-employment screening, fitness for duty), but may have little applicability in OIS/DFE assessments. In my experience, most OIS/DFE evaluations will involve little or no formal testing, unless unusual issues are raised in the case, e.g., adjudicative competency, insanity defense, or claims of mental impairment, which, so far, I have not encountered in a strictly law enforcement OIS/DFE case.

In other instances, the results of prior psychological testing may be used in an attempt to buttress one side of the case or the other (in one case, a personality test was cited as showing the officer had "psychopathic and Machiavellian traits," with little supportive context), and if the expert feels this data has been used inappropriately, he or she should so state. Whether or not to re-administer the test, or administer new ones, should be carefully considered, and only done if there is some specific clinical-forensic question that can be uniquely addressed by a specific test. Tests should never be deployed as randomly cast bait in "fishing expeditions" for potentially defensive or incriminatory data; you may catch more than you bargained for and then be faced with how to explain it.

Diagnostic and Forensic Conclusions. This is probably the most challenging part of the report to write, because the expert must now take all the envelopes, boxes, folders, paper reams, CDs, DVDs, flash drives, jpegs, mpegs, and pdfs of data and integrate them with information gleaned from the defendant-officer's interview and examination, in order to arrive at: (1) a cogent psychological description; and (2) a supportable legal theory of what that officer's mental state can reasonably be inferred to have been during the entire OIS/DFE event. This must be clearly and carefully articulated in the report, and will be the basis for your future expert testimony, if called upon.

MALINGERING

"But how do you know they're telling the truth?"

Every forensic psychologist has had their own "oh-shit" moment when we suspect we're being deceived or manipulated by the very client our lawyer has paid us good money to evaluate. More so than for most medical and clinical disciplines, the diagnostic data of psychology rely almost exclusively on a subject's self-report. There are no X-rays or blood tests to tell whether a subject is telling the truth, misremembering or jumbling otherwise factual events, or just flat-out lying. Not surprisingly, defendants in criminal cases (and plaintiffs in civil cases) may have powerful motives for spining the story in a way they think will best help them. Consequently, forensic psychologists have devoted considerable time and energy to devising strategies for determining the veracity of a subject's report, usually classified under the rubric of malingering detection.

Description and Prevalence of Malingering in Psychological Evaluations

Malingering is defined as the conscious and intentional simulation of illness or impairment for the purpose of: (1) obtaining financial compensation or other reward; (2) evading duty, responsibility, or obligation; or (3) being relieved of the consequences of one's criminal actions or other illicit behavior. In other words, there is a practical and sensible, albeit ill-intended, motive for the subterfuge and therefore it does not represent a mental disorder per se, although malingering may co-occur along with a variety of medical and psychiatric syndromes. In malingering, the subject is essentially lying for profit or to escape the consequences of his or her behavior.

Malingering occurs commonly in medical settings, especially in neurology and orthopedics (e.g., chronic pain, weakness, paralysis, amnesia, etc.), and is often seen in the context of insurance disability claims or civil lawsuits. Malingering is not to be confused with a variety or **somatoform disorders**, in which a subject also displays nonveridical signs and symptoms, but actually believes that he is ill or impaired, i.e., the patient is fooling himself as much as the doctors (Miller, 1984; Trimble, 2004). Examples include persisting anxious hypochondriacal health concerns in the face of repeated clean bills of heath, or patients who unconsciously, psychosomatically transform their fears and conflicts into physical symptoms.

In fact, malingering is not necessarily "abnormal," because we all sometimes do it–tell me you never called in sick to work when you really wanted to stay home and watch a ball game or go shopping. Thus, for any given case of suspected malingering, it is often the context that determines our assessment of the relative blameworthiness of the subject's motives and actions–occasional, harmless hooky-playing vs. trying to defraud an insurance company or weasel out of a serious felony.

In mental health settings, the incidence of malingering differs widely across various clinical and forensic settings and populations, with estimates widely ranging from 1 percent to 50 percent (DeViva & Bloem, 2003; Franklin & Thompson, 2005; Frueh et al., 2000, 2003, 2005, 2007; Resnick, 1995, 1997, 1999; Schretlen 1988). Many experts view malingering in terms of a continuum, based on the degree to which the subject is consciously aware of his actual motivation to deceive (Nies & Sweet, 1994; Travin &

Potter, 1984), and in any given subject, there may be a mélange of motivational factors. For example, most people don't like to think of themselves as liars, so even though they may be consciously feigning a particular mental state, they manage to convince themselves that they are really thinking what they're thinking, that is, they come to believe their own stories. Others, such as those with narcissistic and antisocial personality disorders, will have no qualms about making up their bullshit tales and may even take special delight in fooling experts, authorities, and almost anyone else, i.e., "lying for lying's sake"—only, it's not just for lying's sake, it's for the sake of feeling powerful by deceiving and manipulating other human beings.

What is Malingered in an OIS/DFE Case?

In civil cases, malingering in psychological disability claimants typically occurs where the traumatic event has led to a civil lawsuit for monetary damages against a third party or to argue for a greater military benefits or an employment disability award. In these cases, the more impaired the plaintiff appears, the greater the anticipated payoff. In criminal cases, a defendant may claim significant psychopathology to argue for incompetency to stand trial, exculpation (insanity defense) or a lighter penalty for a criminal charge or conviction (diminished capacity) (Bartol & Bartol, 2019; Costanzo & Krauss, 2018; Miller, 2012; Wrightsman, 2001).

But in contested OIS/DFE cases, officer-defendants rarely claim to suffer mental impairment at the time of the psych eval or during the trial; on the contrary, they commonly attempt to present themselves as paragons of mental health. If they are fudging about anything, it will be what they claim to have experienced during the OIS/DFE incident itself, that is, this might be a special form of **retrospective malingering**. No database yet exists on the extent and nature of malingering in OIS/DFE cases, but I will attempt to formulate criteria based on extrapolations from malingering research in other areas of forensic psychology (e.g., posttraumatic stress disorder, chronic pain, postconcussion syndrome, schizophrenia), along with my own clinical-forensic observations.

For the kind of retrospective mental state analysis needed for conceptualizing a contested OIS/DFE case, the database will necessarily consist of the subject's self-report, and the statements of others at the scene, as documented in written reports or testimony. Actually, a clear precedent for this kind of **retrospective diagnosis** in forensic psychology exists in the form of the **insanity defense** (Gutheil, 2002; Kane, 2006; Resnick & Harris, 2002; Sadoff & Dattilio, 2011). Here, the psychologist examines the subject in the present, but utilizes information about the subject's behavior at the time of the alleged offense, i.e., in the past, to form an impression of the subject's then-state of mind. A similar inferential assessment process occurs in conceptualizing the perceptual, cognitive, and behavior distortions that purportedly existed in the officer's mind at the time of the OIS/DFE, although rarely in the context of a diagnosable mental impairment syndrome; but rather, as discussed in Chapters 4-6, as an expectable reaction of an otherwise normal brain and mind to extreme life-and-death stress.

Indicators of Malingering in OIS/DFE Cases

Authorities on malingering detection agree that there are only two ways to determine malingering with absolute certainty: (1) the subject admits it; or (2) the subject is caught doing precisely what he claims he can't do (Larrabee & Berry, 2007; Stone & Boone, 2007; Sweet, 2009). Examples from clinical-forensic practice abound, some verging on the comical: A physical disability plaintiff with chronic pain who claims to be unable to lift more than 15 pounds on formal functional capacity testing is videotaped unloading large stone pavers from his pickup truck to construct a new deck patio. A brain injured subject who produces extremely low scores on neuropsychological tests of learning and memory takes college classes while officially disabled from work. A subject who claims she cannot drive to her jobsite due to severe phobic anxiety related a vehicle crash is observed operating an Uber cab in busy downtown traffic. A PTSD claimant who states that he isolates himself in his room 24 hours a day is photographed shopping at a mall and dancing at a club.

There are a plethora of psychometric tests and measures purported to detect malingering, many developed for assessing veridical versus feigned cognitive impairment in traumatic brain injury and other neuropsychological cases. But bear in mind that no single indicator is a sure-fire lie-detector—there is no "X-ray of the mind." Thus, in assessing the veracity of an officer's description of his or her mental state at the time of the OIS/DFE, we must rely on two main data sources: (1) the officer's account, and (2) collateral information.

Several chapters in this book have delineated the common types of perceptual and cognitive distortions reported by officers during OIS/DFEs, the overwhelming majority of these described by officers who have been administratively cleared and presumably have nothing to gain by making up symptoms. Indeed, many of these officers are reluctant to report or acknowledge any psychological disturbance for fear that it might make them seem weak or crazy, and therefore unfit for duty, so there is probably considerable *under*-reporting of these experiences in officers who have been involved in uncomplicated OIS/DFEs. But, although they are loathe to admit that these phenomena have happened to them, most officers are aware that they exist, through Academy training, continuing education, accounts of their fellow officers, internet searches, or information provided by their attorney. Thus, in a contested OIS/DFE case, an officer may now feel it is to his advantage to play up these symptoms for their presumed exculpatory value.

Thus, although there is no single sure-fire indicator to discern if an examinee is telling the truth, forensic clinicians follow the scientific literature and their own training and experience in searching for patterns of behavior, self-report, and test results that may yield clues to veracity. In fact, this is pretty much what police detectives do in evaluating their own cases.

With this in mind, extrapolating from the existing literature on malingering in other kinds of forensic psychology cases (Cima et al., 2004; Cunnien, 1997; Denny, 2008; Frueh et al., 2000; Hall & Hall, 2006, 2007; Hall & Poirier, 2001; Hartlage, 1998; Heath et al., 2003; Knoll & Resnick, 2006; Lowenstein, 2001; Lynn & Belza, 1984; Miller, 1993, 1998b, 1998c, 2001, 2015f; Resnick, 1995, 1997, 1999; Sparr, 1996; Sparr & Pankratz, 1983; Taylor, 2001; Williams, 1998), and using our knowledge of veridical OIS/DFE mental phenomena gleaned from research described in previous chapters and from our own experience with administratively cleared, non-contested police shooting cases, we may construct our clinical-forensic judgment in a contested case on two main pillars: **inconsistency** and **atypicality**, which frequently go together and can be further parsed into signs and symptoms reflecting **fabrication**, **exaggeration**, **extension**, and/or **misattribution** (see Table 9.3). These indicators include the following.

Too Many Symptoms. As reviewed in Chapter 4, research by Klinger and Brunson (2009) has documented that an officer may experience two or three, and as many as four or five perceptual and cognitive symptoms in a

Table 9.3.
TYPES OF MALINGERING IN PSYCHOLOGICAL EVALUATIONS

Fabrication: The officer has no symptoms or impairments resulting from the traumatic event, but fraudulently represents that he has. Least common form of malingering because it necessitates not only feigning symptoms, but often lying about one's role in the critical incident, which may later be refuted by other evidence and testimony.

Exaggeration: The officer has real symptoms or impairments resulting from the critical incident but represents them to be far worse than they really are.

Extension: The officer has experienced real symptoms or impairments resulting from the incident, and these have now recovered or improved, but he falsely represents them as continuing or even as having worsened over time.

Misattribution: The officer has symptoms or impairments that preceded, postdated, or are otherwise unrelated to the critical incident, but he fraudulently attributes them to that event.

given DFE incident. But malingerers commonly feel impelled to pile on an exaggerated number of symptoms, as if there were some direct incremental correlation between sheer volume of symptoms and reduced criminal culpability. An officer's recounting of a dozen or more such disturbances defies clinical credulity.

Overly Vivid, Dramatic, or Bizarre Symptoms. Some officers seem to conflate OIS/DFE perceptual-cognitive phenomena with accounts they're read or heard about florid symptoms in other psychiatric syndromes, such as schizophrenia, PTSD, dissociative disorders, or even somnambulism (sleepwalking). As such, the accounts they provide are unlike the typical cognitive distortions described in this book. One officer, apparently having heard of "dissociation" during DFEs, described a kind of out-of-body experience, where he described himself floating above the scene and watching himself confront the assailant, "like in another dimension." Another claimed to have hallucinated the voices of deceased relatives instructing him how to respond (note: always consider religious and cultural backgrounds when evaluating such cases). Yet another officer, who claimed near-total amnesia for the episode (not in itself unusual) also reported that he did recall "marching around like a robot, like I was sleepwalking" (was he awake, or asleep, or what?).

Again, this doesn't mean these unusual phenomena *can't* happen during a DFE, they're just highly unusual. It also might mean that an officer's hitherto undetected subclinical psychopathology (e.g., schizotypal personality disorder) may influence his or her reaction to the OIS/DFE in unusual and idiosyncratic ways (e.g., the officer who floated above the fray or the one receiving messages from beyond), which is why a thorough clinical examination and background assessment are always crucial to a comprehensive evaluation.

Narrative is Too Literal, Technical, or "Textbooky." Let's face it, if an officer wanted to learn how to feign a variety of realistic OIS/DFE cognitive-perceptual distortions, he could start by reading this book–or one of the many sources listed in the bibliography, or even the abundance of descriptions provided on police websites and trade magazines. But unless he is able to inject his own nuanced experiences and impressions into the narrative, it is likely to sound like it was mentally cut and pasted from one of these secondary sources. Sometimes combined with the too-many-symptoms maneuver described above, these officers will reel off a dry, technical, stilted shopping list of symptoms: "I experienced auditory exclusion and time dimension," said one officer, apparently misquoting a published passage on time dilation or time distortion. Another officer came in with a long list of symptoms in medical terminology, which he had written down, "so I won't forget them."

Another expression of this is the officer who misinterprets published descriptions of legitimate symptoms but may misunderstand them and relate them in an unrealistic way. For example, tunnel vision refers to the attentional and perceptual narrowing that allows concentrated focus on an object or situation of interest at the expense of peripheral awareness. But an officer whose knowledge of tunnel vision comes not from personal experience but from a misinterpreted secondary description, may describe this as akin to looking down an actual tunnel, "like someone was holding two paper towel tubes in front of my eyes," or "like I was looking through the wrong end of a telescope." The closest this comes to an actual physiological phenomenon would be an attack of optic neuritis that afflicts patients with multiple sclerosis–which, presumably, this officer did not have. In extreme cases, some of these descriptions–e.g., the scene "zooming in an out of focus"–sound more like Hitchcockian movie effects than real-life perceptual distortions, although the one or two latter such descriptions I've encountered were in non-police-related disability cases.

Unusual or Embellished Post-Shooting Reactions. Chapter 8 has described the types of typical post-incident physical and psychological reactions, immediate, delayed, and long-term, that can follow an OIS/DFE. Sometimes, in an apparent attempt to heighten the perceived severity of mental impairment at the scene, officers will exaggerate or embellish their accounts of what they experienced in the aftermath: "I was paralyzed for three days; I just lay on my bed, unable to move." Again, given the extremely wide range of normative post-incident reaction in officers of diverse personalities and experiential backgrounds, the examiner must be cautious in imputing nonveridicality to an officer's report just because it sounds bizarre.

Story Changes, Often in Response to Suggestion. Chapter 6 discussed how the vagaries of memory processing, even under normal circumstances, but especially under conditions of high stress, can distort an officer's recall of events, especially over the multiple retellings that he or she will inevitably have to provide in the course of an investigation or legal action. However, the core facts and themes of the recollected narrative, no matter how weird-sounding or discrepant from other accounts they may be, usually remain relatively consistent across retellings, because this is how the officer actually remembers it. With partial or complete memory gaps, the officer will typically say, "This part is fuzzy, but . . . ," or, "I don't know, that part is just a blank," and will go on to describe the rest of the incident he does recollect.

However, when the recalled facts seem to drift over successive retellings, especially in the direction the officer might believe has greater exculpatory credence, this may be sign that the recall is being adjusted to accommodate the examiner, whether a law enforcement investigator or psychologist, especially if that examiner subtly or overtly conveys that the present story doesn't add up. In such cases, the number and nature of on-scene cognitive distortions may change from retelling to retelling, and may even be transparently responsive to suggestion. For example, an officer who reports changes in perceptual clarity may be told by the examiner that this often co-occurs with gaps in memory. On a subsequent examination–guess what?–memory problems now figure prominently in the officer's account. This **narrative drift** may even be seen within a single evaluation session.

I've encountered this kind of narrative drift phenomenon in a couple of suspect-shot-in-the-back cases, where (as noted in Chapters 1 and 4), tactically and statutorily, the officer's actions may have been justified, but, because his judgment at the scene has become a core issue in the case, he feels the need to further excuse his actions by claiming perceptual or cognitive distortion. Fine. The problem arises when the distortions keep getting more and more distorted each time he tells the story. First, "I saw the suspect running to retrieve what I thought was a weapon, so I fired." Later: "I remember the suspect facing me with what I thought was a weapon, so in fear for my life, I fired." Even later: "I know the witness accounts and video recordings all indicate that the suspect was running away, but I really thought he was coming towards me when I fired." Note that any one of these misperceptions could have then been legitimately experienced and later recalled, but the inflationary trajectory of the story over time is what raises suspicion.

To be fair, this kind of narrative drift is quite common in other types of legal cases involving civil personal injury plaintiffs or criminal defendants, and may not necessarily represent a purposefully conscious intention to deceive. As noted earlier, most people don't like to think of themselves as fundamentally dishonest, and subjects of a legal action may subtly convince themselves that each successive version of their story is the true one. In such cases, the subject may express wounded outrage at the suggestion that he or she is deliberately faking, which often has the effect of poisoning the entire investigative process, each side now feeling that the other is fundamentally mendacious and untrustworthy.

Once again, before pouncing on any particular inconsistency or exaggeration, examiners should remember that a determination of malingering is tantamount to labeling the subject a liar and a potential perjurer, and therefore this label should–in police cases or in any forensic context–never be applied lightly and should not be based on just a single indicator, no matter how bright red that flag may be. Rather, such a conclusion should reflect the examiner's comprehensive analysis of the findings from clinical interview, subject history, known facts of the case, and collateral information. This includes the understanding that people may fail to tell the whole truth and nothing but the truth for a variety of intermixed reasons and motives, conscious or subconscious, ill-intended or self-protective, and that the impetus to bend such truths may be more likely the higher the stakes for a subject's physical, emotional, and vocational well-being. Indeed, who among us is always and completely honest–with others or ourselves? Does that make us liars and malingerers? Depends on the situation.

THE FORENSIC PSYCHOLOGICAL EVALUATION: RECOMMENDATIONS FOR OFFICERS

Great. One more pencil-twirling, clipboard-cradling, pointy-headed investigator-type you have to tell this whole story to all over again. But, wait–this time, your attorney *wants* you to talk to this egghead. As a cop, you've probably testified against a lot of criminal defendants. Maybe you've even interviewed witnesses and interrogated suspects yourself. But now, it's your head on the block, so what do you do to make the best impression and not look like a jerk? The following is a set of recommendations I would offer to police officers undergoing any type of psychological evaluation with me, but specifically for ones involving an officer's mental state during an OIS/DFE (Miller, 2008f, 2009b, 2011b, 2015b).

Don't Assume the Worst. I'm not your enemy. For that matter, I'm not your friend, either. My only job is to objectively evaluate your current and past mental status and retrospectively relate it to the specific legal questions revolving around the charges you're facing.

Come Prepared. If appearing in person, show up on time. Bring any records or other materials that were requested, if not already supplied by your attorney. Other commonsense recommendations include bringing reading glasses and having a good breakfast or lunch prior to a morning or afternoon exam. Accordingly, I'll make sure I'm ready at the appointed time and will be prepared to conduct the evaluation.

Don't be Afraid to Ask Questions. If you have a question about something I ask, or an instruction I give you is unclear, let me know. Bear in mind, however, that I'll probably have to defer many of your otherwise reasonable inquiries until your attorney is prepared to go over my report with you. That's because providing the answer at the present time could compromise the validity and objectivity of the evaluation as a whole. If I can't answer a particular question, I'll tell you so, but there's no harm in asking.

Be Honest. The entire validity of the evaluation hinges on the accuracy of the information you give me. Please don't try to snow me, play me, impress me, intimidate me, cajole me, or bullshit me. Describe everything that happened just as you remember it. If you lie to me, and that lie is immortalized in my report, and the other side seizes upon it, the worst that happens to me is maybe some temporary courtroom embarrassment during cross-examination. The worst that happens to you is the jury now thinks you made everything up, and off to prison you may go. Remember: normal, healthy, honest people can make imperfect judgments, can have legitimate memory gaps, and can do most things right and a few things wrong, but if you unrealistically try to oversell yourself or whitewash your thoughts or actions, it will probably backfire.

Even though it was your own lawyer who may have hired me, at various points in the interview, I'm going to ask you difficult, pointed questions, like I'm the worst adversarial prosecutor trying to burn you. That's because they're going to ask me the same tough questions in court, and I want to hear your story from you before they spin it for the jury. I want to pin you to the wall, and in so doing, thoroughly satisfy myself that we have an unimpeachable case that I can support and explain. Just tell it like it is.

What if I've been retained by the court or by opposing counsel and you feel like you're in enemy territory? Truth-telling still works in your favor, because the more believable I find you to be, the less likely I am to develop unwarranted suspicions and biases regarding your account of the facts. But if you try to keep me guessing at the outset, I'm going to err on the side of skepticism and will be prepared to challenge and refute almost anything you tell me after that.

Expect to be Treated Courteously and Behave Accordingly. No matter which side hired me, even as I'm endeavoring mightily to pokes holes and elicit inconsistencies in your story, you should never intentionally be made to feel demeaned, humiliated, or treated like a criminal suspect. Indeed, there is nothing to gain by making you squirm unnecessarily, because the more comfortable and less defensive you feel during the examination, the more open you're likely to be, and the more useful information I'll probably get from you. Likewise, I expect you to behave with reasonable respect and decorum. Both examiner and officer should keep in mind that we're both professionals who are each here to do a job.

ON THE SPOT: TESTIFYING IN COURT FOR POLICE OFFICER DEFENDANTS IN OIS/DFE CASES

Some police officers cite testifying in court as one of the most stressful aspects of the job, perceiving it (correctly) as an adversarial system, where they can be skewered by clever opposing counsel during hostile and aggressive cross-examination. Alternatively, court day may be seen as boredom purgatory, taking the officer away from "real" police work. Many patrol officers will have to testify only a few times in their careers, while for others,

Table 9.4.
TESTIFYING IN COURT FOR LAW ENFORCEMENT OFFICERS

Preparation: Know what you want to say and how to say it.

Attitude and demeanor: Confident, not cocky, polite, and respectful of judge and jury.

Communication style: Clear, to the point, think before answering questions, ask for repetition if necessary.

Dealing with cross-examination: Don't be baited into impulsive or angry responding, ask for clarification of any questions you don't fully understand.

General impression: Be the officer the jurors would want to call if they needed help.

such as traffic cops and detectives, court testimony is regular part of their work routine.

But, in a contested OIS/DFE case, it is now you, the accused officer, who is on the dock, and your role has switched from objective witness to the defendant on trial. You may be shocked and dismayed to realize that you're not afforded the same deference and respect you were accustomed to in your official police officer witness role, and the very criminal justice system you used to work *with* is now arrayed *against* you, trying, with all their persuasive zeal, to paint you, the one-time defender of the people, as just another skell. Your world has truly turned upside down.

Library shelves creak under the weight of learned tomes purveying the accumulated wisdom surrounding effective trial testimony, and this section can hardly purvey an exhaustive account of this subject. Rather, while the core principles of effective testimony are generalizable to defendants, victims, plaintiffs, fact witnesses, and experts (Barsky & Gould, 2002; Brodsky, 1991, 2004; Chambers, 1996; Findley & Sales, 2012; Griffith, 2005; Kressel & Kressel, 2002; Medina, 2012; Mogill, 1989; Posey & Wrightsman, 2005; Vinson & Davis, 1993), here I want to review some basic insights and observations gleaned from working with officers in trouble (2006g, 2009c, 2011b, 2015b). Always with attorney collaboration and assent, the following is a summary of testimony tips that I try to inform and reinforce with the officers I work with (Table 9.4). In large part, these recommendations also apply to testimony by psychologist expert witnesses.

Preparing for Testimony

Attorneys understand the importance of trial preparation and will usually do whatever they can to make their client's testimony most effective and persuasive to the jury.

Organize. One recommendation that applies to any kind of witness is to write down the gist of what you want to say, because writing out your thoughts in words is an excellent way to clarify, organize, and remember the points you will want to get across during your testimony. Draw pictures to help your description and to jog your memory, and remember to show everything you produce to your lawyer before trial.

Review Your Case. And review it again. In fact, there is no such thing as too much preparation. But this doesn't mean memorizing a script. Rather, the more thoroughly you know your facts and ideas about the case, the easier it will be to answer questions thrown at you from the proverbial left field because you won't be relying on rote memorization of individual answers to different questions; instead, your knowledge and recollection will comprise an organic, holistic narrative process that will be hard to trip up by clever cross-examination. You will probably have several pre-trial meetings with your attorney to go over your testimony. Ideally, the goal is not for the attorney to spoon-feed your words to you, but for both of you to clarify the substance of your testimony, to agree on a narrative theme and a terminology that will best express what you have to say, and to get a sense of what you will be asked by both sides.

Rehearse. Most of this will be mental rehearsal, going over the facts of the case and your testimony in your head. You might also rehearse out loud, while driving in your car, in front of a mirror at home, or with your attorney. Even if you have been a seasoned witness in your police career, there is still no substitute for adequate preparation, and many a veteran "expert" has let his or her overconfidence lead to loose ends which are then used by clever opposing counsel to hang them. Don't rehearse like reading from a script, but try to anticipate potential adversarial curve balls and prepare a range of carefully thought-out responses.

On the Stand

Certainly, most important aspects of courtroom demeanor cannot be programmed; every witness brings his or her own unique style to the stand. Nevertheless, there are a few principles of effective testimony that all witnesses can productively apply.

Attitude. To the average citizen, which also includes the average juror, a police officer is still a figure of authority and respect, so use this to your advantage. Maintain composure and dignity at all times. Your demeanor, while professional, should shade slightly more to the deferential side. This does not mean that you should bow and scrape to the jury, but your behavior should convey an attitude of mutual respect, with you and jurors as equal partners in resolving this very important issue. Recalling Chapter 3, be an

Andy on the stand: serious but not grim, confident but not cocky, humble but not humiliated. Be the cop the jurors would want to turn to if they were in trouble.

Body Language. Like your mother told you, sit up straight and don't slouch. If there is a microphone in front of you, sit close enough so that you don't have to lean over every time you speak. Keep any notes or presentation materials neatly organized in front of you, so you can find documents and exhibits when needed.

While testifying, look at the attorney while he or she is questioning you, then switch your eye contact to the jury while answering the question; it's them you have to establish a connection with, and jurors tend to find witnesses more credible when they "looked us in the eye." Visually engage, but don't glare, and don't be too concerned if you have a hard time reading the jurors' faces: as far as I know, there's no established correlation between juror behavior in court and ultimate verdict arrived at, although research does suggest that perceived credibility of both defendant and attorney favorably influence juror decision-making (Findley & Sales, 2012)–another reason to always tell the truth.

Communication Style. Be neither overly aloof nor overly intense. Open, courteous, and dignified are the communication watchwords to remember. Speak as clearly, slowly, and concisely as possible to be understood. Keep sentences short and to the point. Keep your voice steady and use a normal conversational tone. Don't mumble, shout, or waffle, but neither should you speak in a robotic monotone. Your general attitude toward the jury should convey a sense of collegial respect: you are there to present the facts as you know them to a group of mature adults who, you are confident, will make the right decision.

Listen carefully to each question from the attorney before you respond. If you don't fully understand a question, ask the attorney to repeat it or rephrase it. Don't be baited into giving a quick answer; if you need a couple of seconds to compose your thoughts, take them. Speak as clearly and concisely as possible. Answer the question completely, but don't overelaborate or ramble. Don't try to bluff your way out of a tricky question. Jurors will understand if you don't have a snappy counterpoint for every barb the opposing attorney lobs at you, so if you don't know the answer to a question, state plainly, "I don't know." If you try to make it up as you go along, opposing counsel will seize on the inevitable inconsistencies in your testimony to discredit you. Don't become cranky or defensive.

Above all, again, be honest. Like most people, jurors don't like feeling that they're being played, and the honorable police officer image you've tried so hard to cultivate will blow back in your face if they think you're lying, because you're not just some ordinary defendant trying to save his neck; now you're the rogue cop, the failed protector (Chapter 1) that we citizens all fear and loathe. It's true that sometimes jurors may think you're lying when you're not (and that's just what the other side wants them to think), but don't hand opposing counsel the ax to chop down your testimony.

Cross-Examination Tactics

Attorneys will commonly phrase questions in a way that constrains your answers in the direction they want you to go. If you feel you cannot honestly answer the question by a simple yes-or-no answer, say so: "Sir, if I limit my answer to yes or no, I will not be able to give factual testimony. Is that what you wish me to do?" Sometimes, the attorney will voluntarily reword the question. If he presses for a yes-or-no answer, at that point either your defense attorney will pop up to voice an objection or the judge will intervene. The latter may instruct the cross-examining attorney to allow you more leeway in responding, or to rephrase the attorney's question, or the judge may simply order you to answer the question as it has been asked, in which case that's what you do, with a resigned look on your face.

Another attorney ploy is to phrase questions in such a way as to force you to respond in an ambiguous manner, often prefacing your answer with such wishy-washy phrases, as: "I believe," "I estimate," "To the best of my recollection," "As far as I know," "What I was able to piece together," "I'm pretty sure that," and so forth. If the facts warrant it, be as definite about your answers as possible. If they don't, honestly state that this particular piece of your testimony may not be a clear perception or recollection, but continue to be firm about what you *are* sure about.

In general, try not to answer beyond the question. For example, if the attorney asks you to phrase your answers in precise measurements that are not relevant or that you cannot accurately recall, don't speculate, unless you're specifically to do so.

> *Attorney:* Officer Jackson, you said the deceased victim suddenly closed the distance between you while raising the knife over his head. How far away was he when you made the decision to shoot him?
>
> *Officer:* He was about half a block away when I ordered him twice to drop the knife. He kept coming, and when he was about a quarter of a block away, I fired.
>
> *A:* How many feet away was he when you fired?
>
> *O:* I don't know.
>
> *A:* Surely, officer, you can estimate the distance. Was it ten feet, twenty feet? A hundred?

> *O:* I really can't accurately estimate the exact number of feet. But on that block, between myself and the suspect, there was a liquor store, a dry cleaner, and the front steps of a post office. The suspect was a little closer to me than the post office, so I'd estimate fifteen to twenty feet.

A related ploy is for the attorney to ask you to estimate something reasonable, like the amount of time that has passed (which most people can roughly gauge in terms of seconds or minutes), and then switch to other topics, while maneuvering you to preserve the estimative mindset. Now, everything you say has become an "estimate" or something recalled "to the best of my recollection." Later, in his or her summation, opposing counsel will state something like: "And Officer Jackson really hasn't described anything solid has he? Everything is an estimate, a guess, an inference. Ladies and gentlemen of the jury, does a loose collection of "maybe's" and "I-guess-so's" suggest that Officer Jackson is giving us his truthful recollection of events?

This doesn't mean you should inject false surety into naturally iffy information, but try to emphasize that the ambiguity lies with the subject matter, not with your own perceptions and interpretations.

> *Attorney:* Officer Jackson, from your distance of twenty feet away, on a dark street at night, could you see exactly where the deceased victim was holding the knife? Couldn't he have been carrying it at his side? Or couldn't he have been raising his unoccupied hand to surrender?
>
> *Officer:* The suspect had the knife handle in his right hand, and I could clearly observe the blade above his head in the light of an overhead street lamp. Further, I could hear the suspect making a growling noise and I also saw him make a back-and-forth chopping movement with the knife as he ran towards me.

Again, if you don't know the answer to a question or don't recollect an event, just say you don't know. In many of these cases, an expert witness will testify as to the normative and expectable perceptual and memory distortions that occur in the course of an OIS/DFE, which will provide the jury with a scientific context for these gaps. Even without this, however, jurors will generally respect and appreciate honest ignorance of a few details far more than an apparent ad hoc attempt to make everything "fit in" with your testimony.

General Impression

One lesson of litigation is that no one is immune from manipulative cross-examination by crafty or aggressive opposing counsel. So, whether your inquisitor wields a scalpel or a chainsaw, try to maintain as much composure and dignity as possible. Again, easy for me to say, but I've endured my own share of testimonial torment from overly unctuous or combative cross-examination. Remember, an important part of trial testimony is the impression you make on the jury by your demeanor, language, and grace under pressure, so avoid either being cowed into submission or baited into an angry overreaction. Yes, easier said than done. But that's one more reason to go over your testimony before the trial: to anticipate challenges and become comfortable with the substance and narrative structure of your case.

Finally, again remember that most citizens, including most jurors, want to believe that the people they place their trust in–doctors, police officers, public officials–have their best welfare in mind. This means that they will usually try to give you the benefit of the doubt if you can give them a credible reason to do so. It also means that if you betray them through dishonesty or flagrant disrespect, they may come down on you especially hard for violating that trust. Prepare carefully for your case, be clear and honest in your testimony, maintain dignity and decorum, and hope that the system will work for you.

SUMMARY AND CONCLUSIONS

Justice. We all say we want it, but most of us have our own idiosyncratic notions of what it means. If people were all good, there'd be no need for courts and cops, and society would be a paradise on Earth. If people were all evil, an alternate Dantean hell on Earth would prevail and humankind would probably not have survived to this point. Frustratingly, even mostly nasty people may be capable of flashes of humanity; Hitler petted his dogs, after all. And even mostly good people can do the occasional shitty thing, by accident but well-intendedly, purposefully but ill-advisably, or deliberately and maliciously.

Police officers who have been involved in an OIS/DFE deserve our respect and consideration, even as we may objectively investigate their actions. For police to be a credible authority within their service communities, those communities must believe that truly bad law enforcement actors will not be coddled or shielded from justice. But for police managers and administrators to retain their own credibility among their constituent officers, those officers must believe that political expediency and other nonfact-based motives will not impel a slippery rush to thin justice for officers in trouble. As this book has hopefully made clear, science is vital to the fair adjudication of contested OIS/DFE cases. But for trust to prevail, all parties must be convinced that the science in question is utilized fairly, objectively, and with wisdom.

BIBLIOGRAPHY

Aamodt, M.G. (2004). *Research in law enforcement selection.* Boca Raton, FL: Brown Walker Press.

Addis, N. & Stephens, C. (2008). An evaluation of a police debriefing programme: Outomes for police officers five years after a police shooting. *InternationalJournal of Police Science and Management, 10,* 361–373.

Adlam, K.R. (1982). The police personality: Psychological consequences of being a police officer. *Journal of Police Science and Administration, 10,* 344–349.

Adolphs, R., Denberg,N.L. & Tranel, D. (2001). The amygdala's role in long-term declarative memory for gist and detail. *Behavioral Neuroscience, 115,* 983–992.

Adolphs, R., Tranel, B. & Buchanan, T.W. (2005). Amygdala damage impairs emotional memory for gist but not details of complex stimuli. *Nature Neuroscience, 8,* 512–518.

Aita, S.L, Hill, B.D., Musso, M.W. & Gouvier, W.D. (2018). Can we identify bad cops based on history? Base rates of historical markers in law enforcement pre-employment evaluations. *Journal of Police and Criminal Psychology, 33,* 201–208.

Akinola, M. & Mendez, W.B. (2012). Stress-induced cortisol facilitates threat-related decision making among police officers. *Behavioral Neuroscience, 126,* 167–174.

Allen, S.W. (1986). Suicide and indirect self-destructive behavior among police. In J.T. Reese & H.A. Goldstein (Eds.), *Psychological services for law enforcement* (pp. 413–417). Washington DC: USGPO.

Allen, S.W. (2004). Dynamics in responding to departmental personnel. In V. Lord (Ed.), *Suicide by cop: Inducing officers to shoot* (pp. 245–257). Flushing: Looseleaf Law Publications.

Alpert, G.P. & Dunham, R. (2004). *Understanding police use of force: Officers, suspects, and reciprocity.* New York: Cambridge University Press.

Alpert G.P. & Dunham, R. (2010). Policy and training recommendations related to police use of CEDs: Overview of findings from a comprehensive national study. *Police Quarterly, 13,* 235–259.

Alpert, G.P., MacDonald, J. & Dunham, R. (2005). Police suspicion and discretionary decision making during citizen stops. *Criminology, 43,* 407–434.

Alpert, G.P. & Smith, W.C. (1994). How reasonable is the reasonable man? Police and excessive force. *Journal of Criminal Law and Criminology, 85,* 481–501.

Alprin, G. & Wilson, J.V. (1974). Controlling police conduct: Alternatives to the exclusionary rule. In C.J. Weistart (Ed.), *Police practices* (pp. 44–45). New York: Oceana Publishing.

American Psychiatric Association (2013). *Diagnostic and statistical manual of mental disorders* (5th ed.). Washington, DC: Author.

Amir, N., Elias, J.,Klumpp, H. & Przeworski, A. (2003). Attentional bias to threat in social phobia: Facilitated processing of threat or difficulty disengaging attention from threat? *Behavior Research and Therapy, 41,* 1325–1335.

Amodio, D.M. & Devine, P.G. (2006). Stereotyping and evaluation in implicit race bias: Evidence for independent constructs and unique effects on behavior. *Journal of Personality and Social Psychology, 91,* 652–661.

Amodio, D.M., Harmon-Jones, E. & Devine, P.G. (2003). Individual differences in the activation and control of affective race bias as assessed by startle eyeblink response and self-report. *Journal of Personality and Social Psychology, 84,* 738–753.

Amodio, D.M., Harmon-Jones, E., Devine, P.G., Curtin, J.J., Hartley, S.L. & Covert, A.E. (2004). Neural signals for the detection of unintentional race bias. *Psychological Science, 15,* 88–93.

Anders, S., Lotze, M., Erb, M., Grodd, W. & Birbaumer, N, (2004). Brain activity underlying emotional valence and arousal: A response-related fMRI study. *Human Brain Mapping, 23,* 200–209.

Anderson, A.K., Christoff, K., Panitz, D., De Rosa, E. & Gabrieli, J.D.E. (2003). Neural correlates of the automatic processing of threat facial signals. *Journal of Neuroscience, 23,* 5627–5633.

Anderson, A.K. & Phelps, E.A. (2001). The human amygdala supports affective modulatory influences on visual awareness. *Nature, 411,* 305–309.

Anderson, W., Swenson, D. & Clay, D. (1995). *Stress management for law enforcement officers.* Englewood Cliffs: Prentice Hall.

Andreano, J.M. & Cahill, L. (2006). Glucocorticoid release and memory consolidation in men and women. *Psychological Science, 17,* 466–470.

Armony, J.L. & LeDoux, J.E. (2000). How danger is encoded: Toward a systems, cellular, and computational understanding of cognitive-emotional interactions in fear. In M.S. Gazzaniga (Ed.), *The cognitive neurosciences* (pp. 1067–1079). Cambridge, MA: MIT Press.

Arsenault, L., Moffitt, T.E., Caspi, A., Taylor, P.J. & Silva, P.A. (2000). Mental disorders and violence in total birth cohort: Results from the Dunedin study. *Archives of General Psychiatry, 57,* 979–986.

Artwohl, A. (2002). Perceptual and memory distortion during officer-involved shootings. *FBI Law Enforcement Bulletin,* October, pp. 18–24.

Artwohl, A. (2003). No recall of weapon discharge. *Law Enforcement Executive Forum, 3:2,* 41–49.

Artwohl, A. (2018). Memory and decision making under stress. In D.L. Ross & G.M. Vilke (Eds.), *Guidelines for investigating officer-involved shootings, arrest-related deaths, and deaths in custody* (pp. 96–115). New York: Routledge.

Artwohl, A. & Christensen. L.W(1997) *Deadly force encounters: What cops need to know to mentally and physically prepare for and win a gunfight.* Boulder, CO: Paladin Press.

Artwohl, A. & Christensen, L.W. (2019). *Deadly force encounters* (2nd ed.). Portland, OR: LWC Books.

Asken, M.J. (1993). *PsycheResponse: Psychological skills for optimal performance by emergency responders.* Englewood Cliffs: Regents/Prentice Hall.

Askey, A., Cowell, B., Burch, J. & Stephens, D. (2018). Insights on officer safety from officer-involved shooting and near-miss incidents. *The Police Chief,* May, pp. 42–45.

Aveni, T.J. (2003). *Officer-involved shootings: What we don't know has hurt us.* Spofford, NH: Police Policy Study Council.

Balko, R. (2014). *Rise of the warrior cop: The militarization of America's police forces.* New York: BBS Publishers.

Banks, J.B., Tarter, J.L. & Welhaf, M.S. (2014). Where's the impairment? An examination of factors that impact sustained attention following a stressor. *Cognition and Emotion, 28,* 856–866.

Barkley, R.A. (2012). *Executive functions: What they are, how they work, and why they evolved.* New York: Guilford Press.

Barrett, L.F., Tugade, M.M. & Engle, R.W. (2004). Individual differences in working memory capacity and dual-process theories of the mind. *Psychological Bulletin, 130,* 553–573.

Barsky, A.E. & Gould, J.W. (2002). *Clinicians in court: A guide to subpoenas, depositions, testifying, and everything else you need to know.* New York: Guilford Press.

Bartlett, C., Oliphant, H., Gregory, W. & Jones, D. (2016). Ego-depletion and aggressive behavior. *Aggressive Behavior, 42,* 533–541.

Bartol, C.R. & Bartol, A.M. (2019). *Psychology and law: Research and practice* (2nd ed.). Thousand Oaks, CA: Sage.

Baruth, C. (1986). Pre-critical incident involvement by psychologists. In J.T. Reese & H.A. Goldstein (Eds.), *Psychological Services for Law Enforcement* (pp. 413–417). Washington DC: USGPO.

Baseheart, J.R. & Cox, T.C. (1993). Effects of police profanity on a receiver's perceptions of credibility. *Journal of Police and Criminal Psychology, 9,* 9–19.

Baumeister, R.F. (2002). Ego depletion and self-control failure: An energy model of the self's executive function. *Self and Identity, 1,* 129–136.

Baumeister, R.F. (2014). Self-regulation, ego-depletion, and inhibition. *Neuropsychologia, 65,* 313–319.

Baumeister, R.F., Bratslavsky, E., Muraven, M. & Tice, D.M. (1998). Ego depletion: Is the active self a limited resource? *Journal of Personality and Social Psychology, 74,* 1252–1265.

Baumeister, R.F. & Heatherton, T.F. (1996). Self-regulation failure: An overview. *Psychological Inquiry, 7,* 1–15.

Beehr, T.A., Ivanitskaya, L., Glaser, K., Erofeev, D. & Canali, K. (2004). Working in a violent environment: The accuracy of police officers' reports about shooting incidents. *Journal of Occupational and Organizational Psychology, 77,* 217–235.

Beeson, J. (2107). Psychological and social factors in the use of force. In M.J. Palmiotto (Ed.). *Police use of force: Important issues facing the police and the communities they serve* (pp. 143–156). Boca Raton, FL: CRC Press.

Beigel, H. & Beigel, A. (1977). *Beneath the badge: A study of police corruption.* New York: Harper & Row.

Beilock, S.L. (2010). *Choke: What the secrets of the brain reveal about getting it right when you have to.* New York: Free Press.

Beilock, S.L. & Carr, T.H. (2001). On the fragility of skilled performance: What governs choking under pressure? *Journal of Experimental Psychology: General, 130,* 701.

Benton, T.R., Ross, D.F., Bradshaw, E., Thomas, W.N. & Bradshaw, G.S. (2006). Eyewitness memory is still not common sense: Comparing jurors, judges, and law enforcement to eyewitness experts. *Applied Cognitive Psychology, 20,* 115–129.

Berman, D.E. & Dudai, Y. (2001). Memory extinction, learning anew, and learning the new: Dissociations in the molecular machinery of learning in cortex. *Science, 291,* 2417–2419.

Bernhard, D. (2019). The human impact of line-of-duty deaths. *The Police Chief,* February, pp. 40–42.

Binder, A. & Scharf, P. (1980). The violent police-citizen encounter. *Annals of the American Academy of Police Science, 452,* 111–121.

Bishop, J.S. (2007). Neurocognitive mechanisms of anxiety: An integrative account. *Trends in Cognitive Sciences, 11,* 307–316.

Bishop, J.S., Duncan, J. & Lawrence, A.D. (2004). State anxiety modulation of the amygdala response to unattended threat-related stimuli. *Journal of Neuroscience, 24,* 10364–10368.

Bittner, E. (1970). *The functions of the police in modern society.* Rockville, MD: National Institute of Mental Health.

Bittner, E. (1978). The functions of the police in modern society. In P.K. Manning & J. Van Maanen (Eds.), *Policing: A view from the street* (pp. 32–50). Santa Monica: Goodyear Publishing.

Black, D. (1971). The social organization of arrest. *Stanford Law Review, 23,* 1087–1111.

Blair, J.P., Pollock, J., Montague, D., Nichols, T., Curnutt, J. & Burns, D. (2011). Reasonableness and reaction time. *Police Quarterly, 14,* 323–343.

Blake, M.J. & Miller, R.D. (2015). Ambushes on U.S. law enforcement officers. *The Police Chief,* August, .12–13.

Blau, T.H. (1984). *The psychologist as expert witness.* New York: Wiley.

Blau, T.H. (1986). Deadly force: Psychological factors and objective evaluation–A preliminary effort. In J.T. Reese & H.A. Goldstein (Eds.), *Psychological Services for Law Enforcement* (pp. 315–334). Washington DC: USGPO.

Blau, T.H. (1994). *Psychological services for law enforcement.* New York: Wiley.

Blum, L.N. (2000). *Force under pressure: How cops live and why they die.* New York: Lantern Books.

Bodenhausen, G.V. (1990). Stereotypes as judgmental heuristics: Evidence of circadian variations in discrimination. *Psychological Science, 1,* 319–322.

Bohl, N.K. (1991). The effectiveness of brief psychological interventions in police officers after critical incidents. In J.T. Reese, J.M. Horn & C. Dunning (Eds.), *Critical Incidents in Policing* (pp. 31–38). Washington DC: US Department of Justice.

Bohl, N.K. (1995). Professionally administered critical incident debriefing for police officers. In M.I. Kunke & E.M. Scrivner (Eds.), *Police psychology into the 21st century* (pp. 169–188). Hillsdale, NJ: Erlbaum.

Bohrer, S. (2005). After firing the shots, what happens? *FBI Law Enforcement Bulletin,* September, pp. 8–13.

Bohrer, S. & Chaney, R. (2010). Police investigations of the use of deadly force can influence perceptions and outcomes. *FBI Law Enforcement Bulletin,* January, pp. 1–7.

Bohrer, S., Kern, H.A. & Davis, E.F. (2008). The deadly dilemma: Shoot or don't shoot? *FBI Law Enforcement Bulletin,* March, pp. 7–12.

Bolger, P.C. (2015). Just following orders: A meta-analysis of the correlates of American police officer use of force decisions. *American Journal of Criminal Justice, 40,* 466–492.

Boone, K.B. (2013). *Clinical practice of forensic neuropsychology: An evidence-based approach.* New York: Guilford Press.

Botvinick, M.M., Braver, T.S., Barch, D.M., Carter, C.S. & Cohen, J.D. (2001). Conflict monitoring and cognitive control. *Psychological Review, 108,* 624–652.

Botvinick, M.M., Nystrom, L.E., Fissel, K., Carter, C.S. & Cohen, J.D. (1999). Conflicet monitoring versus selection-for-action in anterior cingulate cortex. *Nature, 402,* 179–181.

Bowman, M. (1997). *Individual differences in posttraumatic response: Problems with the adversity-distress connection.* Mahwah: Erlbaum.

Brandl, S.G. & Stroshine, M.S. (2012). The role of officer attributes, job characteristics, and arrest activity in explaining police use of force. *Criminal Justice Policy Review, 24,* 551–572.

Brandl, S.G., Stroshine, M.S. & Frank, J. (2012). Who are the complaint-prone officers? An examination of the relationship between police officers' attributes, arrest activity, assignment and citizens' complaints about excessive force. *Journal of Criminal Justice, 29,* 521–529.

Bremmer, J.D. (2006). Traumatic stress: Effects on the brain. *Dialogues in Clinical Neuroscience, 8,* 45–461.

Bresler, S., Scalora, M.J., Elbogen, E.B. & Moore, Y.S. (2003). Attempted suicide by cop: A case study of traumatic brain injury and the insanity defense. *Journal of Forensic Science, 48,* 190–194.

Brewer, G.A., Ball, B.H. & Ware, J.M. (2016). Individual differences in working memory capacity and shooting behavior. *Journal of Applied Research in Memory and Cognition, 5,* 185–191.

Brodsky, S.L. (1991). *Testifying in court: Guidelines and maxims for the expert witness.* Washington, DC: American Psychological Association.

Brodsky, S.L. (2004). *Coping with cross-examination and other pathways to effective testimony.* Washington, DC: American Psychological Association.

Brown, M.F. (1983). Shooting policies: What patrolmen think. *Journal of Criminal Justice, 12,* 277–288.

Brown, J.M. & Langan, P.A. (2001). *Policing and homicide, 1976–1998: Justifiable homicide by police, police officers murdered by felons.* Washington, DC: US Department of Justice.

Brunson, R. & Miller, J. (2006a). Gender, race, and urban policing: The experience of African American youths. *Gender and Society, 20,* 531–552.

Brunson, R. & Miller, J. (2006b). Young black men and urban policing in the United States. *British Journal of Criminology, 46,* 613–640.

Brunson, R. & Weitzer, R. (2008). Police relations with black and white youths in different urban neighborhoods. *Urban Affairs Review, 10,* 1–28.

Buss, A.H. (2012). *Pathways to individuality: Evolution and development of personality traits.* Washington, DC: American Psychological Association.

Butters, N. & Miliotis, P. (1985). Amnestic disorders. In K.M. Heilman & E. Valenstein (Eds.), *Clinical neuropsychology* (2nd ed.). New York: Oxford University Press.

Call, J.A. (2003). Negotiating crises: The evolution of hostage/barricade crisis negotiation. *Journal of Threat Assessment, 2,* 69–94.

Cancino, J.M. (2001). Walking among giants 50 years later: An exploratory analysis of patrol officer use of violence. *Policing, 24,* 144–161.

Carpenter, B.N. & Raza, S.M. (1987). Personality characteristics of police applicants: Comparisons across subgroups and with other populations. *Journal of Police Science and Administration, 15,* 10–17.

Carta, I., Chan, C.H., Schott, A.L., Dorizan, S. Khodakhah, K. (2019). Cerebellar modulation of the reward circuitry and social behavior. *Science, 363,* 248.

Carter, D.L. (1976). Police brutality. In A.S. Blumberg & E. Niederhoffer (Eds.), *The ambivalent force* (pp. 321–330). New York: Holt, Rinehart & Winston.

Carver, C.S., Johnson, S.L. & Joorman, J. (2013). Two-mode models of self-regulation and serotonergic functioning: Diverging manifestations of impulse and restraint. In B.W. Sokol, F.M.E. Grouzet & U. Muller (Eds.), *Self-regulation and autonomy: Social and developmental dimensions of human conduct* (pp. 255–278).

Cascio, W.F. (1977). Formal education and police officer performance. *Journal of Police Science and Administration, 5,* 89–96.

Chambers, D. (1996). Police-defendants: Surviving a civil suit. *FBI Law Enforcement Bulletin,* March, pp. 34–39.

Chaney, C. & Robertson, R.V. (2013). Racism and police brutality in America. *Journal of African American Studies, 17,* 480–505.

Charney, D.S., Deutsch, A.Y., Krystal, J.H., Southwick, S.M. & Davis, M. (1993). Psychobiologic mechanisms of posttraumatic stress disorder. *Archives of General Psychiatry, 50,* 294–305.

Chua, E.F.& Bliss-Moreau, E. (2016). Knowing your heart and your mind: The relationship between metamemory and interoception. *Consciousness and Cognition, 45,* 146–158.

Cima, M., Nijman, H., Merckelbach, H., Kremer, K. & Holnack, S. (2004). Claims of crime-related amnesia in forensic patients. *International Journal of Law and Psychiatry, 27,* 215–221.

Clagett, R. (2004). After the echo. *Police,* March, pp. 42–49.

Clifford, B.R. & Richards, V.J. (1977). Comparison of recall by policemen and civilians under conditions of long and short duration of exposure. *Perceptual and Motor Skills, 45,* 503–512.

Cloherty, J.J. (2004). Legal defense of law enforcement officers in police shooting cases. In V. Lord (Ed.), *Suicide by cop: Inducing officers to shoot* (pp. 85–150). Flushing: Looseleaf Law Publications.

Cohen, A. (1980). "I've killed that man 10,000 times." *Police, 3,* 4.

Cohen, N.J. (1984). Preserved learning capacity in amnesia: Evidence for multiple memory systems. In L.R. Squire & N. Butters, (Eds.), *Neuropsychology of memory* (pp. 122–139). New York: Guilford Press.

Cohen, R.A. (2013). *The neuropsychology of attention.* New York: Springer.

Conway, A.R.A., Kane, M.J., Bunting, M.F., Hambrick, D.Z., Wilhelm, O. & Engle, R.W.(2005). Working memory span tasks: A methodological review and user's guide. *Psychonomic Bulletin and Review, 12,* 769–786.

Conway, M.A. (2012). Ten things the law and others should know about human memory. In L. Nadel & W. Sinott-Armstrong (Eds.), *Memory and law* (pp. 359–372). New York: Oxford University Press.

Cook, P.J. (2015). Will the current crisis in police legitimacy increase crime? *Psychological Science in the Public Interest, 16,* 71–74.

Cooper, A. & Smith, E.L. (2011). *Homicide trends in the United States, 1980–2008.* Washington, DC: US Department of Justice, Bureau of Justice Statistics.

Correll, J., Hudson, S.M., Guillermo, S. & Ma, D.S. (2014). The police officer's dilemma: A decade of research on racial bias in the decision to shoot. *Social and Personality Psychology Compass, 8,* 201–213.

Correll, J., Park, B., Judd, C.M. & Wittenbrink, B. (2002). The police officer's dilemma: Using ethnicity to disambiguate potentially threatening individuals. *Journal of Personality and Social Psychology, 83,* 1314–1329.

Correll, J., Park, B., Judd, C.M. & Wittenbrink, B. (2007a). The influence of stereotypes on decisions to shoot. *European Journal of Social Psychology, 37,* 1102–1117.

Correll, J., Park, B., Judd, C.M., Wittenbrink, B., Sadler, M.S. & Keesee, T. (2007b). Across the thin blue line: Police officers and racial bias in the decision to shoot. *Journal of Personality and Social Psychology, 92,* 1006–1023.

Correll, J., Urland, G.R. & Ito, T.A. (2006). Event-related potentials and the decision to shoot: The role of threat perception and cognitive control. *Journal of Experimental Social Psychology, 42,* 120–128.

Correll, J., Wittenbrink, B., Park, B., Judd, M. & Goyle, A. (2011). Dangerous enough: Moderating racial bias with contextual threat cues. *Journal of Experimental Social Psychology, 47,* 184–189.

Costanzo, M. & Krauss, D. (2018). *Forensic and legal psychology: Psychological science applied to law.* New York: Worth Publishers.

Couture, R.T., Singh, M., Lee, W., Chahal, P., Wankel, L. & Oseen, M. (1999). Can mental training help to improve shooting accuracy? *Policing: An International Journal of Police Strategies and Management, 22,* 696–711.

Cox, W.T.L., Devine, P.G., Plant, E.A. & Schwartz, L.L. (2014). Toward a comprehensive understanding of officers' shooting decisions: No simple answers to this complex problem. *Basic and Applied Social Psychology, 36,* 356–364.

Crawford, C. & Burns, R. (1998). Predictors of police use of force: The application of a continuum perspective in Phoenix, *Police Quarterly, 1,* 41–63.

Crawford, T.J. (1973). Police overperception of ghetto hostility. *Journal of Police Science and Administration, 1,* 168–174.

Crevits, L., De Clerk, M. & Van Maele, G. (2000). Reliability of saccades. *Neuro-ophthalmology, 24,* 319–325.

Csikszentmihalyi, M. (1990) *Flow: The Psychology of Optimal Experience.* New York: HarperCollins.

Cummings, J.P. (1996). Police stress and the suicide link. *The Police Chief,* October, pp. 85–96.

Cunnien, A.J. (1997). Psychiatric and medical syndromes associated with deception. In R. Rogers (Ed.), *Clinical assessment of malingering and deception* (2nd. ed., pp. 23–46). New York: Guilford Press.

Cunningham, W.A., Johnson, M.K., Raye, C.L., Gatenby, J.C., Gore, J.C. & Benaji M.R. (2004). Separable components in the processing of black and white faces. *Psychological Science, 15,* 806–813.

Curran, T. (1997). Amnesia: Cognitive neuropsychological aspects. In T.E. Feinberg & M.J. Farah (Eds.), *Behavioral neurology and neuropsychology* (pp. 463–472). New York: McGraw Hill.

Dang, J. (2018). An updated meta-analysis of the ego depletion effect. *Psychological Ressearch, 82,* 645–651.

Davis, D. & Loftus, E.F. (2009). Expectancies, emotion and memory reports of visual events: Applications in the legal system. In J.R. Brockmole (Ed.), *The visual world in memory* (pp. 178–214). New York: Psychology Press.

Deane, M., Steadman, H., Rorum, r. Veysey, B. & Morrissey, J. (1999). Emerging partnerships between mental health and law enforcement. *Psychiatric Services, 50,* 99–101.

De Kloet, E.R., Vreugdenhil, E., Oitzl, M.S. & Joels, M. (1998). Brain corticosteroid receptor balance in health and disease. *Endocrine Reviews, 19,* 269–301.

De Leo, D., Bertolote, J. & Lester, D. (2002). Self-directed violence. In E.G. Krug, L.L. Dahlberg, J.A. Mercy, A.B. Zawi & R.Lorenzo (Eds.), *World report on violence and health* (pp. 185–212). Geneva: World Health Organization.

del Carmen, R.V. (1994). Criminal and civil liabilities of police officers. In T. Barker & D.L. Carter (Eds.), *Police deviance* (3rd ed., pp. 409–430). Cincinnati, OH: Anderson.

Demenescu, L.R., Kortegaas, R., Cremers, H.R., Renken, R.J., van Tol, M.J. & van der Wee, N.J.A. (2013). Amygdala activation and its functional connectivity during perception of emotional faces in social phobia and panic disorder. *Journal of Psychiatric Research, 47,* 1024–1031.

Denny, R.L. (2008). Negative response bias and malingering during neuropsychological assessment in criminal forensic settings. In R.L. Denny & J.P. Sullivan (Eds.), *Clinical neuropsychology in the criminal forensic setting* (pp. 91–134). New York: Guilford Press.

de Quervain, D.J., Roozendaal, B. Nitsch, R.M., McGaugh, J.L. & Hock, C. (2000). Acute cortisone administration impairs retrieval of long-term declarative memory in humans. *Nature Neuroscience, 3,* 313–314.

Devine, P.G. & Elliot, A.J. (1995). Are racial stereotypes really fading? The Princeton trilogy revisited. *Personality and Social Psychology Bulletin, 21,* 1139–1150.

DeWall, C.N., Baumeister, R.F., Stillman, T.F. & Gailliot, M.T. (2007). Violence restrained: Effects of self-regulation and it's depletion on aggression. *Journal of Experimental Social Psychology, 43,* 62–76.

Dezenhall, E. (2007). *Damage control: Why everything you know about crisis management is wrong.* London: Portfolio Books.

Dickerson, S.S. & Kemeny, M.E. (2004). Acute stressors and cortisol responses: A theoretical integration and synthesis of laboratory research. *Psychological Bulletin, 130,* 355–391.

Donner, C.M. & Jennings, W.G. (2014). Low self-control and police deviance: Applying Gottredson and Hirschi's general theory to officer misconduct. *Police Quarterly, 17,* 203–225.

Donohue, J. & Levitt, S. (2000). The impact of race on policing and arrests. *Journal of Law and Economics, 64,* 367–394.

Donahue, M.E. & Horvath,F.S. (1991). Police shooting outcomes: Suspect criminal history and incident behaviors. *American Journal of Police, 10,* 17–34.

Doss, W. (2007). *Condition to win: Dynamic techniques for performance-oriented mental conditioning.* Flushing, NY: Looseleaf Law Publications.

Douglas, K.S. & Skeem, J.L. (2005). Violence risk assessment: Getting specific about being dynamic. *Psychology, Public Policy and Law, 11,* 347–383.

Dovidio, J.F., Gaertner, S.L., Kawakami, K. & Hodson, G. (2002). Why can't we just get along? Interpersonal biases and interracial distrust. *Cultural Diversity and Ethnic Minority Psychology, 8,* 88–102.

Doyon, J. & Ungerleider, L.G. (2002). Functional anatomy of motor skill learning. In L.R. Squire & D.L. Schacter (Eds.), *Neuropsychology of memory* (3rd. ed., pp. 225–238). New York: Guilford Press.

Drogin, E.Y., Dattilio, F.M., Sadoff, R.L. & Gutheil, T.G. (2011). *Handbook of forensic assessment: Psycholgical and psychiatric perspectives.* Hoboken, NJ: Wiley.

D'Souza, A., Weitzer, R. & Brunson, R.K. (2019). Federal investigations of police misconduct: A multi-city comparison. *Crime, Law and Social Change, 71,* 461–482.

Ducrose, M., Smith, E. & Langan, P. (2007). *Contacts between police and the public 2005.* Washington, DC: Department of Justice, Bureau of Justice Statistics.

Dugan, J.R. & Breda, D.R. (1991). Complaints about police officers: A comparison among types and agencies. *Journal of Criminal Justice, 19,* 165–171.

Dunham, R. (2009). Officer and suspect demeanor: A qualitative analysis of change. *Police Quarterly, 12,* 6–21.

Dunham, R., Alpert, G., Stroshine, M. & Bennett, K. (2005). Transforming citizens into suspects: Factors that influence the formation of police suspicion. *Police Quarterly, 8,* 366–393.

Duran, P.L. (1999). *Developing the survival attitude: A guide for the new officer* (2nd ed.). Flushing, NY: Looseleaf Law Publications.

Durose, M., Smith, E. & Langan, P. (2007). *Contacts between police and the public, 2005.* Washington, DC: US Department of Justice, Bureau of Justice Statistics.

Dye, S. & del Carmen, A. (2017). The Ferguson Effect reinterpreted. *The Police Chief,* October, pp. 64–70.

Eberhardt, J.L., Goff, P.A., Purdie, V.J. & Davies, P.G. (2004). Seeing black: Race, crime, and visual processing. *Journal of Personality and Social Psychology, 87,* 876–893.

Eith, C. & Durose, M.R. (2011). *Contacts between police and the public, 2008.* Washington, DC: US Department of Justice, Bureau of Justice Statistics.

Elicker, M.K. (2008). Unlawful justice: An opinion study on police use of force and how views change based on race and occupation. *Sociological Viewpoints, 24,* 33–49.

Engel, R.S., Calnon, J. & Bernard, T. (2002). Theory and racial profiling: Shortcomings and future directions in research. *Justice Quarterly, 19,* 249–273.

Engel, R.S. & Serpas, R. (2017). Evidence-based use-of-force policy: How research could improve development and training. *The Police Chief,* April, pp. 28–36.

Engel, R.S. & Silver, E. (2001). Policing mentally disordered suspects: A reexamination of the criminalization hypothesis. *Criminology, 39,* 225–252.

Engel, R.S. & Smith, M.R. (2009). Perceptual distortion and reasonableness during police shootings: Law, legitimacy, and future research. *Criminology and Public Policy, 8,* 141–151.

Engel, R.S., Sobol, J. & Worden, R. (2000). Further exploration of the demeanor hypothesis: The interaction effects of suspects' characteristics and demeanor on police behavior. *Justice Quarterly, 17,* 235–258.

Engle, R.W. (2002). Working memory capacity as executive attention. *Current Directions in Psychological Science, 11,* 19–23.

Engle, R.W., Tuholski, S.W., Laughlin, J.E. & Conway, A.R.A. (1999). Working memory, short-term memory, and general-fluid intelligence: A latent-variable approach. *Journal of Experimental Psychology: General, 128,* 309–331.

Enoka, R. (1993). Involuntary muscle contractions and the unintentional discharge of a firearm. *Law Enforcement Executive Forum,* Vol. 3, No. 2.

Ernst, J., Northoff, G., Boker, H., Seifritz, E. & Grimm, S. (2013). Interoceptive awareness enhances neural activity during empathy. *Human Brain Mapping, 34,* 1615–1624.

Etzioni, A. (1975). *A comparative analysis of complex organizations.* New York: Free Press.

Eysenck, H. (1998). *A new look at intelligence.* New Brunswick, NJ: Transaction Publishers.

Eysenck, M.W., Derakshan, N., Santos, R. & Calvo, M.G. (2007). Anxiety and cognitive performance: Attentional control theory. *Emotion, 7,* 336–353.

Fazel, S. & Danesh, J. (2002). Serious mental disorder in 23000 prisoners: A systematic review of 62 surveys. *Lancet, 359,* 545–550.

Federal Bureau of Investigation (1992). *Killed in the line of duty: A study of selected felonious killings of law enforcement officers.* Washington DC: U.S. Department of Justice.

Federal Bureau of Investigation (1994). *Law enforcement officers killed and assaulted, 1994: Uniform Crime Reports.* Washington DC: US Department of Justice.

Federal Bureau of Investigation (1998). *Law enforcement officers killed and assaulted, 1997: Uniform Crime Reports.* Washington DC: US Department of Justice.

Federal Bureau of Investigation (2006). *Violent encounters: A study of felonious assaults on our nation's law enforcement officers.* Washington, DC: US Department of Justice.

Federal Bureau of Investigation (2015). *Law enforcement officers killed and assaulted, 1987–2014.* Washington, DC: US Department of Justice.

Feuer, A. (1998). Drawing a bead on a baffling end game: Suicide by cop. *New York Times,* June 21, p. wk–3.

Findley, J.D. & Sales, B.D. (2012). *The science of attorney advocacy: How courtroom behavior affects jury decision making.* Washington, DC: American Psychological Association.

Finkel, E.J., DeWall, C.N., Slotter, E.B., Oaten, M. & Foshee, V.A. (2009). Self-regulatory failure and intimate partner violence perpetration. *Journal of Personality and Social Psychology, 97,* 483–499.

Finn, M.A. & Stalans, L.J. (2002). Police handling of the mentally ill in domestic violence situations. *Criminal Justice and Behavior, 29,* 278–307.

Fisher, R.P. & Geiselman,R.E. (1992). *Memory-enhancing techniques for investigative interviewing: The cognitive interview.* Springfield, IL: Charles C Thomas.

Fishel, J., Gabbidon, S.L. & Hummer, D. (2007). A quantitative analysis of wrongful death lawsuits involving police officers in the United States, 1995–2005. *Police Quarterly, 10,* 455–471.

Fitzgerald, S.C. & Bromley, M.L. (1998). Surviving deadly force encounters: A case study. *Journal of Police and Criminal Psychology, 13,* 25–35.

Flannery, R.B. (1995). *Violence in the workplace.* New York: Crossroad.

Flin, R. (1996). *Sitting on the hot seat: Leaders and teams for effective critical incident management.* New York: Wiley.

Flowers, B.R. (2002). *Murder, at the end of the day and night: A study of criminal homicide offenders, victims, and circumstances.* Springfield, IL: Charles C Thomas.

Fonzo, G.A., Ramsawh, H.J., Flagan, T.M., Sullivan, S.G., Letamendi, A. & Simmons, A.N. (2015). Common and disorder-specific neural responses to emotional faces in generalized anxiety, social anxiety, and panic disorders. *British Journal of Psychiatry, 206,* 206–215.

Fox, J.A. & Zawitz, M.W. (2006). *Homicide trends in the United States: 2002 update.* Washington, DC: US Department of Justice, Bureau of Justice Statistics.

Frewen, P. & Lanius, R. (2006). Toward a psychobiology of posttraumatic self-dysregulation: Reexperiencing, hyperarousal, dissociation, and emotional numbing. *Annals of the New York Academy of Sciences, 1071,* 110–124.

Fridell, L.A. & Binder, A. (1992). Police officer decision-making in potentially violent confrontations. *Journal of Criminal Justice, 20,* 385–399.

Friedman, N.P. & Miyake, A. (2004). The relations among inhibition and interference on cognitive function: A latent variable analysis. *Journal of Experimental Psychology: General, 133,* 101–135.

Friedrich, R.J. (1980). Police use of force: Individuals, situations, and organizations. *Annals of the American Academy of Political and Social Science, 452,* 82–97.

Frueh, B.C., Hammer, M.B. & Cahill, S.P. (2000). Apparent symptom overreporting among combat veterans evaluated for PTSD. *Clinical Psychology Review, 20,* 853–885.

Fyfe, J.J. (1981). Who shoots? A look at officer race and police shooting. *Journal of Police Science and Administration, 9,* 367–382.

Fyfe, J.J. (1982). Race and extreme police-citizen violence. In J.J. Fyfe (Ed.), *Readings in police use of deadly force* (pp. 173–194). Washington, DC: Police Foundation.

Fyfe, J.J. (1986). The split-second syndrome and other determinants of police violence. In A.T. Campbell & J. Gibbs (Eds.), *Violent transactions* (pp. 258–281). Oxford: Blackwell.

Fyfe, J.J. (1988a). Police use of deadly force: Research and reform. *Justice Quarterly, 5,* 165–205.

Fyfe, J.J. (1988b). Defining the good cop. *Contemporary Psychology, 33,* 615–616.

Fyfe, J.J. (1996). Training to reduce police-civilian violence. In W.A. Geller & H. Toch (Eds.), *Police violence: Understanding and controlling police abuse of force* (pp. 165–179). New Haven: Yale University Press.

Fyfe, J.J. (2000). Policing the emotionally disturbed. *Journal of the American Academy of Psychiatry and the Law, 28,* 345–347.

Gallo, F.J. (2011). Police use of force. In J. Kitaeff (Ed.), *Handbook of police psychology* (pp. 323–343). New York: Routledge.

Gal-or, Y., Tenenbaum, G., Furst, D. & Shertzer, M. (1985). Effect of self-control and anxiety on training performance in young and novice parachuters. *Perceptual and Motor Skills, 60,* 743–746.

Garner, G.W. (1995). Street smarts: Safely handling intoxicated persons. *FBI Law Enforcement Bulletin,* December, pp. 10–13.

Garner, G.W. (2005). *Surviving the street: Officer safety and survival techniques.* Springfield: Charles C Thomas.

Garner, G.W. (2009). Surviving the circus: How effective leaders work well with the media. *The Police Chief,* March, pp. 52–57.

Garner, G.W. (2012). *Media relations for law enforcement leaders.* Springfield: Charles C Thomas.

Garner, G.W. (2016). *High-risk patrol: Reducing the danger to you* (3rd ed.). Springfield: Charles C Thomas.

Garner, G.W. (2018). *Why cops die (and how to prevent it).* Springfield: Charles C Thomas.

Garner, J.H., Buchanan, J., Schade, T. & Hepburn, J. (1996). *Understanding the use of force by and against the police.* Washington, DC: National Institute of Justice.

Garner, J.H., Schade, T., Hepburn, J. & Buchanan, J. (1995). Measuring the continuum of force used by and against the police. *Criminal Justice Review, 20,* 146–168.

Garner, J.H. & Maxwell, C.D. (1999). Measuring the amount of force use by and against the police in six jurisdictions. In *Use of force by police: Overview of national and local data* (NCJ 176330, October, pp. 25–44). Washington, DC: US Department of Justice.

Garner, J.H., Maxwell, C.D. & C. Heraux (2002). Characteristics associated with the prevalence and severity of force used by the police. *Justice Quarterly, 19,* 705–746.

Garner, J.H., Schade, T., Hepburn, J. & Buchanan, J. (1995). Measuring the continuum of force used by and against the police. *Criminal Justice Review, 20,* 146–168.

Gazzaniga, M.S., Ivry, R.B. & Mangun, G.R. (2018). *Cognitive neuroscience: The biology of the mind* (5th ed.). New York: W.W. Norton.

Geiselman, R.E. & Fisher, R.P. (1997). Ten years of cognitive interviewing. In D.G. Payne & F.G. Conrad (Eds.), *A synthesis of basic and applied approaches to human memory* (pp. 291–310). Mahwah, NJ: Lawrence Erlbaum.

Geiselman, R.E., Wilson, J.F. & Artwohl, A. (2018). Conducting the investigative interview. In D.L. Ross & G.M. Vilke (Eds.), *Guidelines for investigating officer-involved shootings, arrest-related deaths, and deaths in custody* (pp. 285–304). New York: Routledge.

Geller, W.A. (1982). Deadly force: What we know. *Journal of Police Science and Administration, 10,* 151–177.

Geller, W.A. & Karales, K.J. (1981). Shootings of and by Chicago police: Part I. *Journal of Criminal Law and Criminology, 72,* 1813–1866.

Geller, W.A. & Scott, M. (1992). *Deadly force: What we know.* Washington, DC: Police Executive Research Forum.

Geller, W.A. & Toch, H. (1996). Understanding and controlling police abuse of force. In W.A. Geller & H. Toch (Eds.), *Police violence: Understanding and controlling police abuse of force* (pp. 292–328). New Haven: Yale University Press.

Gellman, A., Fagan, J. & Kiss, A. (2007). An analysis of the New York City Police Department's "stop and frisk" policy in the context of claims of racial bias. *Journal of the American Statistical Association, 102,* 813–823.

Gentz, D. (1991). The psychological impact of critical incidents on police officers. In J. Reese, J. Horn & C. Dunning (Eds.), *Critical incidents in policing* (pp. 119–121). Washington DC: US Government Printing Office.

Gilboa, A., Shalev, A.Y., Laor, L., Lester, H., Louzoun, Y. & Chisin, R. (2004). Functional connectivity of the prefrontal cortex and the amygdala in posttraumatic stress disorder. *Biological Psychiatry, 55,* 263–272.

Gill, J. R., & Pasquale-Styles, M. (2009). Firearm deaths by law enforcement. *Journal of Forensic Sciences, 54,* 185–188.

Gilliland, B.E. & James, R.K. (1993). *Crisis intervention strategies* (2nd ed.). Pacific Grove, CA: Brooks/Cole.

Gonzales, C.C. & Burke, M.R. (2018). Motor sequence learning in the brain: The long and short of it. *Neuroscience, 389,* 85–98.

Gould, L.A. (2000). A longitudinal approach to the study of police personality: Race/gender differences. *Journal of Police and Criminal Psychology, 15,* 41–51.

Govorun, O. & Payne, K.B. (2006). Ego-depletion and prejudice: Separating automatic and controlled components. *Social Cognition, 24,* 111–136.

Graf, P. & Schacter, D.L. (1985). Implicit and explicit memory for new associations in normal and amnesic subjects. *Journal of Experimental Psychology: Learning, Memory, and Cognition, 2,* 501–518.

Graham v. Connor (1989). 490 US 386.

Grant, J.D. & Grant, J. (1996). Officer selection and the prevention of abuse of force. In W.A. Geller & H. Toch (Eds.), *Police violence: Understanding and controlling police abuse of force* (pp. 150–164). New Haven: Yale University Press.

Graves, W. (1996). Police cynicism: Causes and cures. *FBI Law Enforcement Bulletin,* June, pp. 16–20.

Greenfield, L.A., Langan, P.A. & Smith, S.K. (1999). Revising and fielding the police-public contact survey. In *Use of force by police: Overview of national and local data* (NCJ 176330, October, pp. 15–18). Washington, DC: U.S. Department of Justice.

Greenstone, J.L. (2005). *The elements of police hostage and crisis negotiations: Critical incidents and how to respond to them.* New York: Haworth Press.

Griffin, S.P. & Bernard, T.J. (2003). Angry aggression against police officers. *Police Quarterly, 6,* 3–21.

Griffith, D. (2005). What characteristics make a good chief? *Police,* June, p. 14.

Gross, J.P. (2016). Judge, jury, and executioner: The excessive use of deadly force by police officers. *Texas Journal on Civil Liberties and Civil Rights, 21,* 155–181.

Grossi, D.M. (1993). Unintentional discharges: A training concern. *The Police Marksman,* March/April, pp. 23–26.

Grossman, D. (1996). *On killing: The psychological cost of learning to kill in war and society.* Boston: Little, Brown.

Grossman, D. & Christensen, L.W. (2007). *On combat: The psychology and physiology of deadly conflict in war and peace* (3rd ed.). Mascoutah, IL: Warrior Science Publications.

Grossman, D. & Siddle, B.K. (1998, March). *Critical incident amnesia: The physiological basis and the implications of memory loss during extreme survival stress situations.* Milstadt, IL: PPCT Management Systems.

Grote, D. (1995). *Discipline without punishment: The proven strategy that turns problem employees into superior performers.* New York: Amacom.

Gutheil, T.G. (2002). Assessment of mental state at the time of the criminal offense: The forensic examination. In R.I.Simon & D.W.Shuman (Eds.), *Retrospective assessment of mental states in litigation: Predicting the past* (pp. 73–100), Washington, DC: American Psychiatric Publishing.

Gutheil, T.G. & Dattilio, F.M. (2008). *Practical approaches to forensic mental health testimony.* Philadelphia: Lippincott Williams & Wilkins.

Hafenback, J. & Nasiripour, S. (2005). Ex-NYPD officer killed in standoff. *South Florida Sun-Sentinel,* May 28, pp. 1A, 6A.

Haier, R.J. (2017). *The neuroscience of intelligence.* New York: Cambridge University Press.

Hails, J. & Borum, R. (2003). Police training and specialized approaches to respond to people with mental illness. *Crime and Delinquency, 49,* 52–62.

Hall, A.V., Hall, E.V. & Perry, J.L. (2016). Black and blue: Exporing racial bias and law enforcement in the killings of unarmed black male civilians. *American Psychologist, 71,* 175–186.

Hall, C., Votova, K., Heyd, C., Walker, M., MacDonald, S., Eramian, D. & Vilke, G.M. (2014). Restaint in police use of force events: Examining sudden in-custody death for prone and not-prone positions. *Journal of Forensic and Legal Medicine, 31,* 29–35.

Hall, H.V. & Poirier, J.G. (2001). Post-traumatic stress disorder and deception. In H.V. Hall & J.G. Poirer (Eds.), *Detecting malingering and deception: Forensic distortion analysis* (2nd ed.; pp. 171–204). Boca Raton, FL: CRC Press.

Hall, H.V. & Pritchard, D.A. (1996). *Detecting malingering and deception: Forensic distortion analysis.* Delray Beach, FL: St. Lucie Press.

Hall, R.C.W. & Hall, R.C.W. (2006). Malingering of PTSD: Forensic and diagnostic considerations, characteristics of malingerers, and clinical presentations. *General Hospital Psychiatry, 28,* 525–535.

Hall, R.C.W. & Hall, R.C.W. (2007). Detection of malingered PTSD: An overview of clinical, psychometric, and physiological assessment. Where do we stand? *Journal of Forensic Science, 52,* 717–725.

Hardy, W. & Kroening, D. (2016). *Recognition-primed decision making: Military training white paper.* Human Dimension Capabilities Development Task Force (HDCDTF), Mission Command–Capabilities Development and Integration Directorate (CDID)

Harper, T. (2000). Shoot to kill. *The Atlantic Monthly,* October, pp. 28–33.

Hartlage, L.C. (1998). Clinical detection of malingering. In Reynolds, C.R. (Ed.), *Detection of malingering during head injury litigation* (pp. 239–260). New York: Plenum.

Hatch, D.E. & Dickson, R. (2007). *Officer-involved shootings and use of force: Practical investigative techniques* (2nd ed.). Boca Raton, FL: CRC Press.

Hays, K.F. & Brown, C.H. (2004). *You're on! Consulting for peak performance.* Washington, DC: American Psychological Association.

Hays, T. (1994). Daily horrors take heavy toll on New York City police officers. *Boca Raton News,* September 28, pp. 2A–3A.

Hazelwood, R.R. & Warren, J. (1990). The criminal behavior of the serial rapist. *FBI Law Enforcement Bulletin,* February, pp. 11–16.

Heatherton, T.F.& Baumeister, R.F. (1996). Self-regulation failure: Past, present, and future. *Psychological Inquiry, 7,* 90–98.

Heath, W.P., Stone, J. Darley, J.M. & Granneman, B.D. (2003). Yes, I did it, but don't blame me: Perceptions of excuse defenses. *Journal of Psychiatry and Law, 31,* 187–226.

Heilman, K.M., Watson, R.T. & Rothi, L.G. (1997). Disorders of skilled movements: Limb apraxia. In T.E. Feinberg & M.J. Farah (Eds.), *Behavioral neurology and neuropsychology* (pp. 227–235). New York: McGraw Hill.

Helfgott, J.B., Hickman, M.J. & Laboissiere, A.P. (2015). A descriptive evaluation of the Seattle Police Department's crisis response team officer/mental health professional partnership pilot program. *International Journal of Law and Psychiatry, 44,* 109–122.

Henckens, M.J.A.G., Hermans, E.J., Pu, Z., Joels, M. & Fernandez, G. (2009). Stressed memories: How acute stress affects memory formation in humans. *Journal of Neuroscience, 29,* 10111–10119.

Henriquez, M.A. (1999). IACP national database project on police use of force. In *Use of force by police: Overview of national and local data* (NCJ 176330, October, pp. 19–24). Washington, DC: U.S. Department of Justice.

Henry, V.E. (2004). *Death work: Police, trauma, and the psychology of survival.* New York: Oxford University Press.

Herrera, M.R., Sharps, M.J., Swinney, H.R. & Lam, J. (2015). Deadly force or not? Visual and cognitive interpretation of rifles and BB guns in crime-scene context. *Journal of Police and Criminal Psychology, 30,* 254–260.

Herzfeld, D.J., Pastor, D., Haith, A.M., Rossetti, Y., Shadmehr, R. & O'Shea, J. (2014). Contributions of the cerebellum and the motor cortex to acquisition and retention of motor memories. *Neuroimage, 98,* 147–158.

Hickman, M.J., Piquero, A.R. & Garner, J.H. (2008). Toward a national estimate of police use of nonlethal force. *Criminology and Public Policy, 7,* 563–604.

Hillbrand, M. (2001). Homicide-suicide and other forms of co-occurring aggression against self and against others. *Professional Psychology: Research and Practice, 32,* 626–635.

Ho, T. (1993). Individual and situational determinants of the use of deadly force: A simulation. *American Journal of Criminal Justice, 18,* 41–60.

Hogan, R. (1971). Personality characteristics of highly rated policemen. *Personnel Psychology, 24,* 679–686.

Holman, M. & Vilke, G.M. (2018). Neck holds. In D.L. Ross & G.M. Vilke (Eds.), *Guidelines for investigating officer-involved shootings, arrest-related deaths, and deaths in custody* (pp. 163–186). New York: Routledge.

Holmes, M.D. (2000). Minority threat and police brutality: Determinants of civil rights criminal complaints in U.S. municipalities. *Criminology, 38,* 343–366.

Holtz, K., Pane-Farre, C.A., Wendt, J., Lotze, M. & Hamm, A.O. (2012). Brain activation during anticipation of interoceptive threat. *Neuroimage, 6,* 857–865.

Homant, R.J. & Kennedy, D.B. (2000a). Effectiveness of less than lethal force in suicide-by-cop incidents. *Police Quarterly, 3,* 153–171.

Homant, R.J. & Kennedy, D.B. (2000b). Suicide by police: A proposed typology of law enforcement officer assisted suicide. *Policing: An International Journal of Police Strategies and Management, 23,* 339–355.

Homant, R.J., Kennedy, D.B. & Hupp, R.T. (2000). Real and perceived danger in police officer assisted suicide. *Journal of Criminal Justice, 28,* 43–52.

Honig, A.L. & Lewinski, W. (2008). A survey of the research on human factors related to lethal force encounters: Implications for law enforcement training, tactics, and testimony. *Law Enforcement Executive Forum, 8,* 129–152.

Honig, A.L. & Roland, J.E. (1998). Shots fired: Officer involved. *The Police Chief,* October, pp. 65–70.

Honig, A.L. & Sultan, E. (2004). Reactions and resilience under fire: What an officer can expect. *The Police Chief,* December, pp. 54–60.

Hope, L., Blocksidge, D., Gabbert, F., Sauer, J.D., Lewinski, W. & Mirashi, A. (2016). Memory and the operational witness: Police officer recall of firearms encounters as a function of active response role. *Law and Human Behavior, 40,* 23–35.

Hope, L., Gabbert, F. & Fraser, J. (2013). Postincident conferring by law enforcement officers: Determining the impact of team discussions on statement content, accuracy, and officer beliefs. *Law and Human Behavior, 37,* 117–127.

Hope, L., Lewinski, W., Dixon, J., Blocksidge, D. & Gabbert, F. (2012). Witnesses in action: The effect of physical exertion on recall and recognition. *Psychological Science, 23,* 386–390.

Horn, J.M. (1991). Critical incidents for law enforcement officers. In J.T. Reese, J.M. Horn & C. Dunning (Eds.), *Critical incidents in policing* (rev. ed., pp. 143–148). Washington DC: Federal Bureau of Investigation.

Hudzik, J.K. (1978). College education for police: Problems in measuring component and extraneous variables. *Journal of Criminal Justice, 6,* 69–81.

Hughes, T. (2001). Police Officers and civil liability: "The ties that bind"? *Policing, 24,* 240–262.

Hunt, J. (1985). Police accounts of normal force. *Urban Life, 13,* 315–341.

Hutson, H.R., Anglin, D., Yarbrough, J., Hardaway, K., Russell, M., Strote, J., Canter, M. & Blum, B. (1998). Suicide by cop. *Annals of Emergency Medicine, 32,* 665–669.

International Association of Chiefs of Police (2005). *Use of force: Concepts and issues paper.* Alexandria, VA: IACP.

International Association of Chiefs of Police (2009a). *Officer-involved shooting guidelines.* Alexandria, VA: IACP.

Jacobs, D. & O'Brien, R.M. (1998). The determinants of deadly force: A structural analysis of police violence. *American Journal of Sociology, 103,* 837–862.

Jaffee v. Redmond, 518 U.S. 1 (1996),

James, L., Fridell, L. & Straub, F. (2016). Implicit bias versus the "Ferguson Effect": Psychosocial factors impacting officers' decisions to use deadly force. *The Police Chief,* February, pp. 44–51.

James, L., Klinger, D. & Vila, B. (2014). Racial and ethnic bias in decisions to shoot seen through a stronger lens: Experimental results from high-fidelity laboratory simulations. *Journal of Experimental Criminology, 10,* 323–340.

James, L., Vila, B. & Daratha, K. (2013). Results from experimental trials testing participant responses to White, Hispanic, and Black suspects in high-fidelity deadly force judgment and decision-making simulations. *Journal of Experimental Criminology, 9,* 189–212.

Jetelina, K.K., Jennings, W.J., Bishop, S.A., Piquero, A.R. & Gonzales, J.M.R. (2017). Dissecting the complexities of the relationship between police officer-civilian race/ethnicity dyads and less-than-lethal use of force. *American Journal of Public Health, 107,* 1164–1170.

Johnson, D.J., Tress, T., Burkel, N., Taylor, C. & Cesario, J. (2019). Officer characteristics and racial disparities in fatal officer-involved shootings. *Proceedings of the National Academy of Sciences, 116,* 15877–15882.

Johnson, K.J. & Fredrickson, B.L. (2005). "We all look the same to me." Positive emotions eliminate the own-race bias in face recognition. *Psychological Science, 16,* 875–881.

Johnson, R.R. (2011). Suspect mental disorder and police use of force. *Criminal Justice and Behavior, 38,* 127–145.

Johnson, R.R. (2015). Perceptions of interpersonal social cues predictive of violence among police officers who have been assaulted. *Journal of Police and Criminal Psychology, 30,* 87–93.

Johnson, R.R. (2017). Show me your hands! Police and public perceptions of violent interpersonal cues. *Journal of Police and Criminal Psychology, 32,* 289–299.

Johnson, R.R. & Aaron, J.L. (2013). Adults' beliefs regarding nonverbal cues predictive of violence. *Criminal Justice and Behavior, 40,* 881–894.
Johnson, R.R. & Morgan, M. (2013). Police officer development of suspicion: An international literature review. *Criminal Justice Studies, 26,* 99–114.
Johnson, R.R., Stone, B.T., Miranda, C.M., Vila, B., James, L. & James, S.M. (2014). Identifying psychophysiological indices of expert vs. novice performance in deadly force judgment and decision making. *Frontiers in Human Neuroscience, 8,* 512.
Johnson, W.D. (2018). Managing a deadly force encounter as a law enforcement leader. *The Police Chief,* December, p. 36–38.
Kahn, K.B., McMahon, J.M. & Stewart, G. (2018). Misinterpreting danger? Stereotype threat, pre-attack indicators, and police-citizen interactions. *Journal of Police and Criminal Psychology, 33,* 45–54.
Kahneman, D. (2011). *Thinking fast and slow.* New York: Farrar, Straus & Giroux.
Kaminski, R.J., Digiovanni, C. & Downs, R. (2004). The use of force between the police and persons with impaired judgment. *Police Quarterly, 7,* 311–338.
Kanazawa, S. (2012). *The intelligence paradox: Why the intelligent choice isn't always the smart one.* New York: Wiley.
Kandasamy, N., Garfinkel, S.N., Page, L., Hardy, B., Critchley, H.D., Gurnel, M. & Coates, J.M. (2016). Interoceptive ability predicts survival on a London trading floor. *Scientific Reports, 6,* 32986.
Kandel, E.R. (2012). *Principles of neural science* (5th ed.). New York: McGraw-Hill.
Kane, A.W. (2006). Psychology, causality, and court. In G. Young, A.W. Kane & K. Nicholson (Eds.), *Psychological knowledge in court: PTSD, pain, and TBI* (pp. 13–51). New York: Springer.
Kappeler, V.E. (1997). *Critical issues in police civil liability* (2nd ed.). Prospect Heights: Waveland.
Kappeler, V.E., Kappeler, S.F. & del Carmen, R.V. (1993). A content analysis of police civil liability cases: Decisions of the federal district courts, 1978–1990. *Journal of Criminal Justice, 21,* 325–337.
Kappeler, V.E., Sapp, A.D. & Carter, D.L. (1992). Police officer higher education, citizen complaints, and departmental rule violations. *American Journal of Police, 11,* 37–54.
Kashdan, T.B. & Rottenberg, J. (2010). Psychological flexibility as a fundamental aspect of health. *Clinical Psychology Review, 30,* 865–878.
Katz, I. & Greenbaum, C. (1963). Effects of anxiety, threat, and racial environment on task performance of Negro college students. *Journal of Abnormal and Social Psychology, 66,* 562–567.
Keinan, G. & Friedland, N. (1996). Training effective performance under stress: Queries, dilemmas, and possible solutions. In J. Driskell & E. Salas (Eds.), *Stress and human performance* (pp. 257–277). Mahwah, NJ: Erlbaum.
Kennedy, D.B., Homant, R.J. & Hupp, R.T. (1998). Suicide by cop. *FBI Law Enforcement Bulletin,* August, pp. 21–27.
Kesic, D., Thomas, S.D.M. & Ogloff, J.R.P. (2012). Analysis of fatal police shootings: Time, space, and suicide by police. *Criminal Justice and Behavior, 39,* 1107–1125.

Kesic, D., Thomas, S.D.M. & Ogloff, J.R.P. (2013). Use of nonfatal force on and by persons with apparent mental disorder in encounters with police. *Criminal Justice and Behavior, 40,* 321–337.

Killgore, W.D., Britton, J.C., Schwab, Z.J., Price, L.M., Weiner, M.R. & Gold, A.L. (2014). Cortico-limbic responses to masked affective faces across PTSD, panic disorder, and specific phobia. *Depression and Anxiety, 31,* 150–159.

Kim, J.E., Dager, S.R. & Lyoo, I.K. (2012). The role of the amygdala in the pathophysiology of panic disorder: Evidence from neuroimaging studies. *Biology of Mood and Anxiety Disorders, 2,* 20.

Kirschman, E.F. (2007). *I love a cop: What police families need to know* (rev ed.). New York: Guilford Press.

Kirschman, E.F., Kamena, M. & Fay, J. (2014). *Counseling cops: What clinicians need to know.* New York: Guilford Press.

Klahm, C.F. & Tillyer, R. (2010). Understanding police use of force: A review of the evidence. *Southwest Journal of Criminal Justice, 7,* 214–239.

Kleider, H.M. & Parrott, D.J. (2009). Aggressive shooting behavior: How working memory and threat influence shooting decisions. *Journal of Research in Personality, 43,* 494–497.

Kleider, H.M., Parrott, D.J. & King, T.Z. (2010). Shooting behavior: How working memory, arousal, and affect influence police officer shoot decisions. *Applied Cognitive Psychology, 24,* 707–717.

Kleider-Offutt, H.M., Clevinger, A.M. & Bond, A.D. (2016). Working memory and cognitive load in the legal system: Influences on police shooting decisions, interrogation and jury decisions. *Journal of Applied Research in Memory and Cognition, 5,* 426–433.

Klein, G.A. (1989). Recognition-primed decisions. In W. Rouse (Ed.), *Advances in man-machine systems research* (Vol. 5, pp. 47–92). Greenwich, CT: JAI Press.

Klein, G.A. (1993). A recognition-primed decision (RPD) model of rapid decision making. In G. Klein, J. Orasanu, R. Calderwood & C. Zsambok (Eds.), *Decision making in action* (pp. 79–103). New York: Ablex.

Klein, G.A. (1996). The effect of acute stressors on decision making. In J. Driskell & E. Salas (Eds.), *Stress and human performance* (pp. 49–88). Hillsdale: Erlbaum.

Klein, G.A. (1998). *Sources of power: How people make decisions.* Cambridge: MIT Press.

Klein, G.A., & Crandall, B.W. (1995). The role of mental simulation in problem solving and decision making. In P. Hancock, J. Flach, J. Caird & K. Vicente (Eds.), *Local applications of the ecological approach to human-machine systems* (pp. 324–358). Hillsdale: Erlbaum.

Klinger, D.A. (1995). The microstructure of nonlethal force: Baseline data from an observational study. *Criminal Justice Review, 20,* 169–186.

Klinger, D. A. (2001). *Police responses to officer-involved shootings.* U.S. Department of Justice,. Washington, DC: National Institute of Justice, U.S. Government Printing Office: NCJ 192286.

Klinger, D.A. (2004). *Into the kill zone: A cop's eye view of deadly force.* San Francisco: Josey-Bass.

Klinger, D.A. (2005). Social theory and the street cop: The case of deadly force. *Issues in American Policing, 7,* 1–15.

Klinger, D.A. (2006). Police responses to officer-involved shootings. *National Institute of Justice Journal, 253,* 21–24.

Klinger, D.A. & Brunson, R.K. (2009). Police officers' perceptual distortions during lethal force situations: Informing the reasonableness standard. *Criminology and Public Policy, 8,* 117–140.

Klockars, C.B. (1985). *The idea of police.* Beverly Hills, CA: Sage.

Klockars, C.B. (1996). A theory of excessive force and its control. In W.A. Geller & H. Toch (Eds.), *Police violence: Understanding and controlling police abuse of force* (pp. 1–22). New Haven: Yale University Press.

Klukkert,A., Ohlemacher, T. & Feltes, T. (2009). Torn between two targets: German police officers talk about the use of force. *Crime, Law, and Social Change, 52,* 181–206.

Knoll, J. & Resnick, P.J. (2006). The detection of malingered post-traumatic stress diorder. *Psychiatric Clinics of North America, 29,* 629–647.

Kobler, A. (1975). Figures (and perhaps some facts) on police killing of civilians in the United States 1965–1969. *Journal of Social Issues, 31,* 185–191.

Kolb, L.C. (1987). A neuropsychological hypothesis explaining posttraumatic stress disorders. *American Journal of Psychiatry, 144,* 989–995.

Koopman, C., Classen, C. & Spiegel, D. (1994). Predictors of posttraumatic stress symptoms among survivors of the Oakland/Berkeley California firestorm. *American Journal of Psychiatry, 151,* 888–894.

Kop, N. & Euwema, M.C. (2001). Occupational stress and the use of force by Dutch police officers. *Criminal Justice and Behavior, 28,* 631–652.

Kressel, N.J. & Kressel, D.F. (2002). *Stack and sway: The new science of jury consulting.* Cambridge, MA: Westview.

Kroll, M.W. & Brave, M.A. (2018). Taser: Conducted electrical weapons. In D.L. Ross & G.M. Vilke (Eds.), *Guidelines for investigating officer-involved shootings, arrest-related deaths, and deaths in custody* (pp. 246–271). New York: Routledge.

Kuhlmann, S., Piel, M. &Wolf, O.T. (2005). Impaired memory retrieval after psychosocial stress in healthy young men. *Journal of Neuroscience, 25,* 2977–2982.

Kurz, D. & Gibb, B.V. (2017). When less (force) is more: De-escalation strategies to achieve officer objectives and simultaneously reduce the use of force. *The Police Chief,* April, pp. 56–61.

Lacy, J.W. & Stark, C.E.L. (2013). The neuroscience of memory: Implications for the courtroom. *Nature Reviews: Neuroscience, 14,* 649–658.

Lambert, A.J., Payne, B.K., Jacoby, L.L., Shaffer, L.M., Chasteen, A.L. & Khan, S.R. (2003). Stereotypes as dominant responses: On the "social facilitation" of prejudice in anticipated public contexts. *Journal of Personality and Social Psychology, 84,* 277–295.

Lambert, K.G. & Kinsley, C.H. (2011). *Clinical neuroscience: Psychopathology and the brain* (2nd. ed.). New York: Oxford University Press.

Langan, P.A., Greenfield, L.A., Smith, S.K., Durose, M.R. & Levin, D. (2001). *Contacts between police and the public: Findings from the 1999 national survey.* Washington, DC: US Department of Justice.

Langman, P. (2009). *Why kids kill: Inside the minds of school shooters.* New York: Palgrave Macmillan.

Lawton, B. (2007). Levels of nonlethal force: An examination of individual, situational, and contextual factors. *Journal of Research on Crime and Delinquency, 44,* 163–184.

Leach, J. & Ansell, L. (2008). Impairment in attentional processing in a field survival environment. *Applied Cognitive Psychology, 22,* 643–652.

Leach, J. & Griffith, R. (2008). Restrictions in working memory capacity during parachuting: A possible cause of "no-pull" fatalities. *Applied Cognitive Psychology, 22, 147–157.*

LeDoux, J.E. (1996). *The emotional brain: The mysterious underpinnings of emotional life.* New York: Simon & Schuster.

LeDoux, J.E. (2000). Emotion circuits in the brain. *Annual Review of Neuroscience, 23,* 155–184.

Lee, H. & Vaughn, M.S. (2010). Organizational factors that contribute to police deadly force liability. *Journal of Criminal Justice, 38,* 193–206.

Lersch, K.M. (1998). Predicting citizen race in allegations of misconduct against the police. *Journal of Criminal Justice, 26,* 87–97.

Lersch, K.M. & Mieczkowski, T. (1996). Who are the problem-prone officers? An analysis of citizen complaints. *American Journal of Police, 15,* 23–44.

Lester, D. (1982). Civilians who kill police officers and police officers who kill civilians. *Journal of Police Science and Administration, 10,* 384–387.

Lester, D. (1984). The use of deadly force by police. *Police Journal, 57,* 170–171.

Lester, D. & TenBrink, W. (1985). Police solidarity and tolerance for police misbehavior. *Psychological Reports, 57,* 326.

Lewinski, B. (2000). Why is the suspect shot in the back? Finally, hard data on how fast the suspect can be in 11 different shooting scenarios. *The Police Marksman, 25,* 20–28.

Lewinski, B. (2008). The attention study: A study on the presence of selective attention in firearms officers. *Law Enforcement Executive Forum,* 8, 107–13.

Lewinski, B. & Hudson, B. (2003a). Time to start shooting? Time to stop shooting? The Tempe study. *The Police Marksman, 28*(5), 26–29.

Lewinski, B. & Hudson, B. (2003b). The impact of visual complexity, decision making, and anticipation: The Tempe experiments 3 and 5. *The Police Marksman, 28*(5), 24–27.

Lewinski, B. & Redmond, C. (2009). New developments in understanding the behavioral science factors in the "stop shooting" response. *Law Enforcement Executive Forum, 9,* 35–54.

Lilienfeld, S.O. & Lilienfeld, K. (2008). Science and pseudoscience in law enforcement: A user-friendly primer. *Criminal Justice and Behavior, 35,* 1215–1230.

Link, B., Andrews, H. & Cullen, F. (1992). The violent and illegal behavior of mental patients reconsidered. *American Sociological Review, 57,* 275–292.

Link, B.G. & Stueve, A. (1994). Psychotic symptoms and the violent/illegal behavior of mental patients compared to community controls. In J. Monahan & H. Steadman (Eds.), *Violence and mental disorder: Developments in risk assessment* (pp. 137–159). Chicago: University of Chicago Press.

Link, B.G., Stueve, A. & Phelan, J. (1998). Psychotic symptoms and violent behaviors: Probing the components of "threat/control override" symptoms. *Social Psychology and Psychiatric Epidemiology, 33,* 495–560.

Livingston, J.D., Desmarais, S.L., Verdun-Jones, S., Parent, R., Michalak, E. & Brink, J. (2014). Perceptions and experiences of people with mental illness regarding their interactions with police. *International Journal of Law and Psychiatry, 37,* 334–340.

Lobo, I., de Oliveira, L., David, I.A., Pereira, M.G., Volchan, E., Rocha-Rego, V., Figueira, I. & Mocaiber, I. (2011). The neurobiology of posttraumatic stress disorder: Dysfunction in the prefrontal-amygdala circuit? *Psychology & Neuroscience, 4,* 191–203.

Loftin, C., Wiersma, B., McDowall, D. & Dobrin, A. (2003). Underreporting of justifiable homicides committed by police officers in the United States, 1976–1998. *American Journal of Public Health, 93,* 1117–1121.

Loftus, E.F. (1996). *Eyewitness testimony.* Cambridge: Harvard University Press.

Loftus, E.F. (2005). Planting misinformation in the human mind: A 50-year investigation of the malleability of memory. *Learning and Memory, 12,* 361–366.

Loftus, E.F., Greene, E.L. & Doyle, J.M. (1989). The psychology of eyewitness testimony. In D.C. Raskin (Ed.), *Psychological Methods in Criminal Investigations and Evidence* (pp. 3–46). New York: Springer.

Logan, G.D. & Cowan, W.B. (1984). On the ability to inhibit thought and action: A theory of an act of control. *Psychological Review, 91,* 295–327.

Loo, R. (1999). Police suicide: The ultimate stress reaction. In J.M. Violanti & D. Paton (Eds.), *Police trauma: Psychological aftermath of civilian combat* (pp. 241–254). Springfield, IL: Charles C Thomas.

Lord, V.B. (2000). Law enforcement-assisted suicide. *Criminal Justice and Behavior, 27,* 401–419.

Lord, V.B. & Sloop, M.W. (2010). Suicide by cop: Police shootings as a method of self-harming. *Journal of Criminal Justice, 38,* 889–895.

Lorist, M.M. & Tops, M. (2003). Caffeine, fatigue, and cognition. *Brain and Cognition, 53,* 82–94.

Lough, T.A. (2018). Effective agency response to the media in use of force incidents. In D.L. Ross & G.M. Vilke (Eds.), *Guidelines for investigating officer-involved shootings, arrest-related deaths, and deaths in custody* (pp. 305–314). New York: Routledge.

Loughlin, J.K. & Flora, K.C. (2017). *Shots fired: The misunderstandings, misconceptions, and myths about police shootings.* New York: Skyhorse Publishing.

Lowenstein, L.F. (2001). Factors differentiating successful versus unsuccessful malingerers. *Journal of Personality Assessment, 77,* 333–338.

Lundman, R.J. (1974). Routine police arrest practices: A commonwealth perspective. *Social Problems, 22,* 127–141.

Lupien, S.J. & LePage, M. (2001). Stress, memory, and the hippocampus: Can't live with it, can't live without it. *Behavioral Brain Research, 127,* 137–158.

Lynch, G.W. (1986). Why officers need a college education. *Higher Education and National Affairs,* September, p. 11.

Lynch, G.W. (1987). Cops and college. *America,* April 4, pp. 274–275.

Lynn, E. & Belza, M. (1984). Factitious post-traumatic stress disorder: the veteran who never got to Vietnam. *Hospital and Community Psychiatry, 35,* 697–701.

Ma, D.S., Correll, J., Wittenbrink, B., Bar-Anan, Y., Sriram, N. & Nosek, B.A. (2013). When fatigue turns deadly: The effects of cognitive depletion and sleep-deprivation on the decision to shoot. *Basic and Applied Social Psychology, 35,* 515–524.

Mack, A. (2003). Inattentional blindness: Looking without seeing. *Current Directions in Psychological Science, 12,* 180–184.

MacDonald, J., Kaminski, R., Alpert, G. & Tennenbaum, A. (2001). The temporal relationship between police killings of civilians and criminal homicide: A refined version of the danger-perception theory. *Crime and Delinquency, 47,* 155–172.

Macrae, C.N., Milne, A.B. & Bodenhausen, G.V. (1994). Stereotypes as energy-saving devices: A peek inside the cognitive toolbox. *Journal of Personality and Social Psychology, 66,* 37–47.

Marmar, C.R., Weiss, D.S. & Metzler, T.J. (1998). Peritraumatic dissociation and posttraumatic stress disorder. In D. Bremnaer & C.R. Marmar (Eds.), *Trauma, memory, and dissociation* (pp. 216–242). Arlington VA: American Psychiatric Publishing.

Mastrofski, S.D., Reisig, M.D. & McCluskey, J.D. (2002). Police disrespect toward the public: An encounter-based analysis. *Criminology, 40,* 519–552.

Mastrofski, S.D., Worden, R. & Snipes, J. (1995). Law enforcement in a time of community policing. *Criminology, 33,* 539–563.

Mayes, A.R. (2002). Exploring the neural bases of complex memory. In L.R. Squire & D.L. Schacter (Eds.), *Neuropsychology of memory* (3rd. ed., pp. 24–34). New York: Guilford Press.

McCafferty, F.L. & McCafferty, M.A. (1998). Corruption in law enforcement: A paradigm of occupational stress and deviancy. *Journal of the American Academy of Psychiatry and Law, 26,* 57–65.

McCafferty, F.L., Souryal, S. & McCafferty, M.A. (1998). The corruption of a law enforcement officer: A paradigm of occupational stress and deviancy. *Journal of the American Academy of Psychiatry and Law, 26,* 433–458.

McLeod, L.C., Thomas, S.D.M.& Kesic, D. (2014). The frequency and nature of resolution of potential police provoked shooting encounters. *International Journal of Law and Psychiatry, 37,* 383–389.

McCluskey, J. & Terrill, W. (2005). Departmental and citizen complaints as predictors of police coercion. *Policing: An International Journal of Police Strategies and Management, 28,* 513–529.

McCluskey, J., Terrill, W. & Paoline, E. (2005). Peer group aggressiveness and the use of coercion in police-suspect encounters. *Police Practice and Research: An International Journal, 6,* 19–37.

McElvain, J.P. & Kposowa, A.J. (2004). Police officer characteristics and internal affairs investigations for use of force allegations. *Journal of Criminal Justice, 32,* 265–279.

McElvain, J.P. & Kposowa, A.J. (2008). Police officer characteristics and the likelihood of using deadly force. *Criminal Justice and Behavior, 35,* 505–521.

McGaugh, J.L. (2013). Making lasting memories: Remembering the significant. *Proceedings of the National Academy of Sciences of the United States of America, 110,* 10401–10407.

McGaugh, J.L. & Roozendaal, B. (2002). Role of adrenal stress hormones in the forming of lasting memories in the brain. *Current Opinion in Neurobiology, 12,* 205–210.

McKenzie, I.K. (2005). Suicide by cop. In L.E. Sullivan & M.R. Haberfeld (Eds.), *The encyclopedia of law enforcement* (Vol. 3, pp. 1316–1320). Thousand Oaks, CA: Sage.

McLeod, L.C., Thomas, S.D.M.& Kesic, D. (2014). The frequency and nature of resolution of potential police provoked shooting encounters. *International Journal of Law and Psychiatry, 37,* 383–389.

McMains. M.J. (1986a). Post-shooting trauma: Demographics of professional support. In J.T. Reese & H. Goldstein (Eds.), *Psychological services for law enforcement* (pp. 361–364). Washington DC: US Government Printing Office.

McMains. M.J. (1986b). Post-shooting trauma: Principles from combat. In J.T. Reese & H. Goldstein (Eds.), *Psychological services for law enforcement* (pp. 365–368). Washington DC: US Government Printing Office.

McMains, M.J. (1991). The management and treatment of postshooting trauma. In J.T. Horn & C. Dunning (Eds.), *Critical incidents in policing* (rev ed., pp. 191–198). Washington DC: Federal Bureau of Investigation.

McMains, M.J. & Mullins, W.C. (1996). *Crisis negotiations: Managing critical incidents and situations in law enforcement and corrections.* Cincinnati: Anderson.

Mears, D.P., Craig, M.O., Stewart, E.A. & Warren, P.Y. (2017). Thinking fast, not slow: How cognitive biases may contribute to racial disparities in the use of force in police-citizen encounters. *Journal of Criminal Justice, 53,* 12–24.

Medina, M.J. (2012). *Winning court testimony for law enforcement officers: The law, art, and science of effective court communication.* Flushing, NY: Looseleaf Law Publications.

Melton, G., Petrila, J., Poythress, N.G. & Slobogin, C., Otto, R.K., Mossman, D. & Condie, L.O. (2018). *Psychological evaluations for the courts: A handbook for mental health professionals and lawyers* (4th ed.). New York: Guilford.

Mendoza, S.A., Gollwitzer, P.M. & Amodio, D.M. (2010). Reducing the expression of implicit stereotypes: Reflective control through implementation intentions. *Personality and Social Psychology Bulletin, 36,* 512–523.

Menifield, C.E., Shin, G. & Strother, G. (2019). Do white law enforcement officers target minority suspects? *Public Administration Review, 79,* 56–68.

Messina, P. (1994). Involuntary discharge experiment. *International Defensive Tactics Journal,* January, pp. 2–3.

Messina, P. (2000). Ready when your gun goes "bang"? *American Police Beat,* October, p. 35.

Messina, P. & Czarnecki, F. (2002). Martial arts for cops: The dark side. *The Police Marksman,* January/February, pp. 16–17.

Meyer, M. (1980). Police shootings of minorities: The case of Los Angeles. *Annals of the American Academy of Political and Social Science, 452,* 98–110.

Meyerhoff, J.L., Norris, W., Saviolakis, G.A., Wollert, T., Burge, B., Atkins, V. & Spielberger, C. (2004). Evaluating performance of law enforcement personnel during a stressful training scenario. *Annals of the New York Academy of Sciences, 1032,* 250–253.

Miller, G.A., Galanter, E. & Pribram, K.H. (1960). *Plans and the structure of behavior.* New York: Holt, Rinehart & Winston.

Miller, J. & Fry, L. (1976). Reexamining assumptions about education and professionalism in law enforcement. *Journal of Police Science and Administration, 4,* 187–198.

Miller, L. (1984). Neuropsychological concepts of somatoform disorders. *International Journal of Psychiatry in Medicine, 14,* 31–46.

Miller, L. (1985). Neuropsychological assessment of substance abusers: Review and recommendations. *Journal of Substance Abuse Treatment, 2,* 5–17.

Miller, L. (1986). Conversion, paranoia, and brain dysfunction. *British Journal of Psychiatry, 148,* 481.

Miller, L. (1987). Neuropsychology of the aggressive psychopath: An integrative review. *Aggressive Behavior, 13,* 119–140.

Miller, L. (1990). *Inner natures: Brain, self, and personality.* New York: St. Martin's Press.

Miller, L. (1993). *Psychotherapy of the brain-injured patient: Reclaiming the shattered self.* New York: Norton.

Miller, L. (1994a). Civilian posttraumatic stress disorder: Clinical syndromes and psychotherapeutic strategies. *Psychotherapy, 31,* 655–664.

Miller, L. (1994b). Traumatic brain injury and aggression. In M. Hillbrand & N.J. Pallone, (Eds.), *The psychobiology of aggression: Engines, measurement, control* (pp. 91–103). New York: Haworth.

Miller, L. (1995). Tough guys: Psychotherapeutic strategies with law enforcement and emergency services personnel. *Psychotherapy, 32,* 592–600.

Miller, L. (1998a). Brain injury and violent crime: Clinical, neuropsychological, and forensic considerations. *Journal of Cognitive Rehabilitation, 16*(6), 2–17.

Miller, L. (1998b). *Shocks to the system: Psychotherapy of traumatic disability syndromes.* New York: Norton.

Miller, L. (1998c). Malingering in brain injury and toxic tort cases. In E. Pierson (Ed.), 1998 *Wiley Expert Witness Update: New Developments in Personal Injury Litigation* (pp. 225–289). New York: Wiley.

Miller, L. (1999a). Critical incident stress debriefing: Clinical applications and new directions. *International Journal of Emergency Mental Health, 1,* 253–265.

Miller, L. (1999b). Effective psychotherapeutic strategies with police and emergency services personnel. In L. Territo & J.D. Sewell (Eds.), *Stress management in law enforcement* (pp. 317–332). Durham, NC: Carolina Academic Press.

Miller, L. (2000). Law enforcement traumatic stress: Clinical syndromes and intervention strategies. *Trauma Response, 6*(1), 15–20.

Miller, L. (2001). Not just malingering: Syndrome diagnosis in traumatic brain injury litigation. *Neurorehabilitation, 16,* 109–122.

Miller, L. (2003a). Personalities at work: Understanding and managing human nature on the job. *Public Personnel Management, 32,* 419–433.

Miller, L. (2003b). Police personalities: Understanding and managing the problem officer. *The Police Chief,* May, pp. 53–60.

Miller, L. (2004). Good cop–bad cop: Problem officers, law enforcement culture, and strategies for success. *Journal of Police and Criminal Psychology, 19,* 30–48.

Miller, L. (2005a). Critical incident stress: Myths and realities. *Law and Order,* April, p. 31.

Miller, L. (2005b). Police officer suicide: Causes, prevention, and practical intervention strategies. *International Journal of Emergency Mental Health, 7,* 101–114.

Miller, L. (2005c). Hostage negotiation: Psychological principles and practices. *International Journal of Emergency Mental Health, 7,* 277–298.

Miller, L. (2006a). Critical incidents: Myths and realities. *Training Wheel,* January-March, pp. 46–47.

Miller, L. (2006b). Undercover policing: A psychological and operational guide. *Journal of Police and Criminal Psychology, 21,* 1–24.

Miller, L. (2006c). Suicide by cop: Causes, reactions, and practical intervention strategies. *International Journal of Emergency Mental Health, 8,* 165–174.

Miller, L. (2006d). Critical incident stress debriefing for law enforcement: Practical models and special applications. *International Journal of Emergency Mental Health, 8,* 189–201.

Miller, L. (2006e). Officer-involved shooting: Reaction patterns, response protocols, and psychological intervention strategies. *International Journal of Emergency Mental Health, 8,* 239–254.

Miller, L. (2006f). Command leadership under fire. *Command,* Fall, pp. 6–13.

Miller, L. (2006g). On the spot: Testifying in court for law enforcement officers. *FBI Law Enforcement Bulletin,* October, pp. 1–6.

Miller, L. (2006h). Psychological principles and practices for superior law enforcement leadership. *The Police Chief,* October, pp. 160–168.

Miller, L. (2006i). *Practical police psychology: Stress management and crisis intervention for law enforcement.* Springfield, IL: Charles C Thomas.

Miller, (2006j). Practical strategies for preventing officer suicide. *Law and Order,* March, pp. 90–92.

Miller, L. (2007a). Negotiating with mentally disordered hostage takers: Guiding principles and practical strategies. *Journal of Police Crisis Negotiations, 7,* 63–83.

Miller, L. (2007b). Stress management: The good, the bad, and the healthy. *Illinois D.A.R.E. Officers Association Newsletter,* March 30, p. 18.

Miller, L. (2007c). Line-of-duty death: Psychological treatment of traumatic bereavement in law enforcement. *International Journal of Emergency Mental Health, 9,* 13–23.

Miller, L. (2007d). The psychological fitness-for-duty evaluation. *FBI Law Enforcement Bulletin,* August, pp. 10–16.

Miller, L. (2007e). School violence: Effective response protocols for maximum safety and minimum liability. *International Journal of Emergency Mental Health, 9,* 105–110.

Miller, L. (2007f). Crisis intervention strategies for treating law enforcement and mental health professionals. In F.M. Dattilio & A. Freeman (Eds.), *Cognitive-behavioral strategies in crisis intervention* (3rd ed., pp. 93–121). New York: Guilford.

Miller, L. (2007g). Law enforcement traumatic stress: Clinical syndromes and intervention strategies. In L. Territo & J.D. Sewell (Eds.), *Stress management in law enforcement* (2nd ed., pp. 381–397). Durham, NC: Carolina Academic Press.

Miller, L. (2007h). Police personalities: Understanding and managing dysfunctional officers. In L. Territo & J.D. Sewell (Eds.), *Stress management in law enforcement* (2nd ed., pp. 473–486). Durham, NC: Carolina Academic Press.

Miller, L. (2007i). Police families: Stresses, syndromes, and solutions. *American Journal of Family Therapy, 35,* 21–40.

Miller, L. (2008a). When the best force is less force: Anticipating and defusing potential patrol perils. *ILEETA Use of Force Journal, 8*(1), 7–10.

Miller, L. (2008b). Military psychology and police psychology: Mutual contributions to crisis intervention and stress management. *International Journal of Emergency Mental Health, 10,* 9–26.

Miller, L. (2008c). The ultimate use of force: The psychology of killing. *ILEETA Use of Force Journal, 8*(2), 7–11.

Miller, L. (2008d). Stress and resilience in law enforcement training and practice. *International Journal of Emergency Mental Health, 10,* 109–124.

Miller, L. (2008e). Wounded warriors: Stress and crisis management for military and law enforcement personnel. *Crisis Management and Traumatic Stress Report, 1,* 11–22.

Miller, L. (2008f). Psychological survival tips for dealing with an excessive force investigation. *ILEETA Use of Force Journal, 8*(4), 18–22.

Miller, L. (2008g). Workplace violence: Practical policies and strategies for prevention, response, and recovery. *International Journal of Emergency Mental Health, 9,* 259–279.

Miller, L. (2008h). The practice of crisis intervention. In J. Krzyzowski (Ed.), *Emergency psychiatry: Concepts and principles* (pp. 69–90). Warsaw: Medyk.

Miller, L. (2008i). *METTLE: Mental toughness training for law enforcement.* Flushing, NY: Looseleaf Law Publications.

Miller, L. (2008j). *From difficult to disturbed: Understanding and managing dysfunctional employees.* New York: Amacom.

Miller, L. (2008k). *Counseling crime victims: Practical strategies for mental health professionals.* New York: Springer.

Miller, L. (2009a). Criminal investigator stress: Symptoms, syndromes, and practical coping strategies. *International Journal of Emergency Mental Health, 11,* 87–92.

Miller, L. (2009b). You're it! How to psychologically survive an internal investigation, disciplinary proceeding, or legal action in the police, fire, medical, mental health, legal, or emergency services professions. *International Journal of Emergency Mental Health, 11,* 185–190.

Miller, L. (2009c). Testifying in court: Practical strategies for public safety, emergency services, and mental health professionals. *International Journal of Emergency Mental Health, 11,* 263–269.

Miller, L. (2010a). On-scene crisis intervention: Psychological guidelines and communication strategies. *International Journal of Emergency Mental Health, 12,* 11–19.

Miller, L. (2010b). Managing problem employees: A model program and practical guide. *International Journal of Emergency Mental Health, 12,* 275–285.

Miller, L. (2011a). Suicide intervention: Basic processes and strategies. *International Journal of Emergency Mental Health, 13,* 37–41.

Miller, L. (2011b). Cops in trouble: Helping officers cope with investigation, prosecution, or litigation. In J. Kitaeff & K. Cather (Eds.), *Handbook of police psychology* (pp. 479–490). New York: Psychology Press.

Miller, L. (2012). *Criminal psychology: Nature, nurture, culture.* Springfield, IL: Charles C Thomas.

Miller, L. (2013a). Military and law enforcement psychology: Cross-contributions to extreme stress management. In L.Territo & J.D. Sewell (Eds.), *Stress management in law enforcement* (3rd ed., pp. 455–486). Durham, NC: Carolina Academic Press.

Miller, L. (2013b). Law enforcement traumatic stress: Clinical syndromes and intervention strategies. In L.Territo & J.D. Sewell (Eds.), *Stress management In law enforcement* (3rd ed., pp. 565–582). Durham, NC: Carolina Academic Press.

Miller, L. (2013c). Hostage negotiations. In B.A. Moore & J.E. Barnett (Eds.), *Military psychologists' desk reference* (pp. 86–90). New York: Oxford University Press.

Miller, L. (2013d). Psychological evaluations in the criminal justice system: Basic principles and best practices. *Aggression and Violent Behavior, 18,* 83–91.

Miller, L. (2015a). Why cops kill: The psychology of police deadly force encounters. *Aggression and Violent Behavior, 22,* 97–111.

Miller, L. (2015b). Police officers in the legal system. In Clevenger, S.M.F., Miller, L., Moore, B.A & Freeman, A. (Eds.), *Behind the badge: A psychological treatment handbook for law enforcement officers* (pp. 171–183). New York: Routledge.

Miller, L. (2015c). Special unit policing: Hostage negotiation, undercover, and sex crimes investigation. In Clevenger, S.M.F., Miller, L., Moore, B.A & Freeman, A. (Eds.), *Behind the Badge: A psychological treatment handbook for law enforcement officers* (pp. 184–201). New York: Routledge.

Miller, L. (2015d). Police officer stress: Syndromes and strategies for intervention. In Clevenger, S.M.F., Miller, L., Moore, B.A & Freeman, A. (Eds.), *Behind the badge: A psychological treatment handbook for law enforcement officers* (pp. 202–221). New York: Routledge.

Miller, L. (2015e). Managing mentally ill individuals: Recommendations for police officers. In Clevenger, S.M.F., Miller, L., Moore, B.A & Freeman, A. (Eds.), *Behind the badge: A psychological treatment handbook for law enforcement officers* (pp. 222–238). New York: Routledge.

Miller, L. (2015f). *Posttraumatic stress disorder and forensic psychology: Applications to civil and criminal law.* New York: Springer.

Miller, L. (2017). Shots fired: Stresses and strategies in officer-involved shootings. In R.J. Burke (Ed.), *Stress in policing: sources, consequences, and interventions* (pp. 115–133). New York: Routledge.

Miller, L. (2019a). Stress, traumatic stress, and posttraumatic stress syndromes. In L.Territo & J.D. Sewell (Eds.), *Stress management in law enforcement* (4th ed, pp. 7–30). Durham, NC: Carolina Academic Press.

Miller, L. (2019b). Police deadly force encounters: Psychological reactions and recovery patterns. In L.Territo & J.D. Sewell (Eds.), *Stress management in law enforcement* (4th ed, pp. 115–144). Durham, NC: Carolina Academic Press.

Miller, L. (2019c). Military and law enforcement psychology: Cross-contributions to extreme stress management. In L.Territo & J.D. Sewell (Eds.), *Stress management in law enforcement* (4th ed, pp. 211–238). Durham, NC: Carolina Academic Press.

Millon, T. & Davis, R. (2000). *Personality disorders in modern life.* New York: Wiley.

Mischel, W. (2014). *The marshmallow test: Mastering self-control.* New York: Little, Brown.

Mischel, W. & Gilligan, C. (1964). Delay of gratification, motivation for the prohibited gratification, and response to temptation. *Journal of Abnormal and Social Psychology, 4,* 411–427.

Miskin, M., Malamut, B. & Bachevalier, J. (1984). Memories and habits: Two neural systems. In G. Lynch & M.N. Weinberger (Eds.), *Neurobiology of learning and memory* (pp. 87–100). NewYork: Guilford Press.

Mitchell, J.T. & Everly, G.S. (1996). *Critical incident stress debriefing: Operations Manual* (rev. ed.). Ellicott City: Chevron.

Mitchell, K.J. (2018). *Innate: How the wiring of our brains shapes who we are.* Princeton, NJ: Princeton University Press.

Moffitt, T.E., Arsenault, L., Belsky, D., Dickson, N., Hancox, R., Harrington, H., Houts, R., Poulton, R., Roberts, B.W., Ross, S., Sears, M.R., Thomson, W.M. & Caspi, A. (2011). A gradient of childhood self-control predicts health, wealth, and public safety. *Proceedings of the National Academy of Sciences, 108,* 2693–2698.

Mogil, M. (1989). Maximizing your courtroom testimony. *FBI Law Enforcement Bulletin,* May, pp. 7–9.

Mohandie, K. & Meloy, J.R. (2000). Clinical and forensic indicators of "suicide by cop." *Journal of Forensic Science, 45,* 384–389.

Mohandie, K. & Meloy, J.R. (2010). Hostage and barricade incidents within an officer-involved shooting sample: Suicide by cop, intervention efficacy, and descriptive characteristics. *Journal of Police Crisis Negotiations, 10,* 101–115.

Mohandie, K., Meloy, J.R. & Collins, P.I. (2009). Suicide by cop among officer-involved shooting cases. *Journal of Forensic Science, 54,* 456–462.

Mollen Commission (1994). *Report of the Commission to Investigate Allegations of Police Corruption.* New York: Mollen Commission.

Morabito, E. & Doerner, B. (1997). Police use of less-than-lethal force: Oleoresin Capsicum (OC) spray. *Policing: An International Journal of Police Strategy and Management, 20,* 680–697.

Morabito, M.S., Socia, K., Wik, A. & Fisher, W.H. (2017). The nature and extent of police use of force in encounters with people with behavioral health disorders. *International Journal of Law and Psychiatry, 50,* 31–37.

Morgan, C.A., Hazlett, G., Doran, A., Garrett, S., Hoyt, G., Thomas, P. & Southwick, S.M. (2004). Accuracy of eyewitness memory for persons encountered during exposure to highly intense stress. *International Journal of Law and Psychiatry, 27,* 265–279.

Morgan, C.A. & Southwick, S. (2014). Perspective: I believe what I remember, but it may not be true. *Neurobiology of Learning and Memory, 112,* 101–103.

Morgan, C.A., Southwick, S., Steffian, G., Hazlett, G.A. & Loftus, E.F. (2013). Misinformation can influence memory for recently experienced, highly stressful events. *International Journal of Law and Psychiatry, 36,* 11–17.

Morin, R., Parker, K., Stepler, R. & Mercer, A. (2017). *Behind the badge: Amid protests and calls for reform, how police view their jobs, key issues, and recent fatal encounters between blacks and police.* Washington, DC: Pew Research Center.

Morley, J.E. & Farr, S.A. (2012). Hormesis and amyloid-beta protein: Physiology or pathology? *Journal of Alzheimer's Disease, 29,* 487–492.

Morris, J.S., DeGelder, B., Weiskrantz, L. & Dolan, R.J. (2001). Differential extra-geniculostriate and amygdala responses to presentation of emotional faces in a cortically blind field. *Brain, 124,* 1241–1252.

Morris, J.S., Ohman, A. & Dolan, R.J. (1998). Conscious and unconscious emotional learning in the human amygdala. *Nature, 393,* 467–470.

Morris, J.S., Ohman, A. & Dolan, R.J. (1999). A subcortical pathway to the right amygdala mediating unseen fear. *Proceedings of the National Academy of Sciences, 96,* 1680–1685.

Mumola, C.J. (2007). *Arrest-related deaths in the United States 2003–2005.* Washington, DC: US Department of Justice.

Muraven, M. & Baumeister, R.F. (2000). Self-regulation and depletion of limited resources: Does self-control resemble a muscle? *Psychological Bulletin, 126,* 247–259.

Nesca, M. & Dalby, J.T. (2013). *Forensic interviewing in criminal court matters: A guide for clinicians.* Springfield, IL: Charles C Thomas.

Nhan, J. (2019). *Issues and Controversies in Policing Today.* New York: Rowman & Littlefield.

Nideffer, R. & Sharpe, R. (1978). *Attention control training: How to get control of your mind through total concentration.* New York: Wideview Books.

Niedenthal, P.M. & Kitayama, S. (1974). *The heart's eye.* San Diego, CA: Academic Press.

Niederhoffer, A. (1969). *Behind the shield: The police in urban society.* Garden City: Doubleday Anchor.

Nielsen, E. (1991). Traumatic incident corps: Lessons learned. In J. Reese, J. Horn & C. Dunning (Eds.), *Critical Incidents in Policing* (pp. 221–226). Washington DC: US Government Printing Office.

Nieuwenhuys, S., Ridderinkhoff, K.R., Blom, J., Band, G.P.H. & Kok, A. (2001). Error-related brain potentials are differently related to awareness of response errors: Evidence from an antisaccade task. *Psychophysiology, 38,* 752–760.

Nieuwenhuys, A. & Oudejans, R.R.D. (2010). Effects of anxiety on handgun shooting behaviorof police officers: A pilot study. *Anxiety, Stress & Coping, 23,* 225–233.

Nieuwenhuys, A. & Oudejans, R.R.D. (2011). Training and anxiety: Short- and long-term effects on police officers' shooting behavior under pressure. *Cognitive Processes, 12,* 277–288.

Nieuwenhuys, A., Pijpers, J.R., Oudejans, R.R.D. & Bakker, F.C. (2008). The influence of anxiety on visual attention in climbing. *Journal of Sport Exercise Psychology, 30,* 171–185.

Nix, J., Campbell, B.A., Byers, E.H. & Alpert, G.P. (2017). A bird's eye view of civilians killed by police in 2015: Further evidence of implicit bias. *Criminology and Public Policy, 16,* 1–32.

Novak, K.J. & Engel, R.S. (2005). Disentangling the influence of suspects' demeanor and mental disorder on arrest. *Policing, 28,* 493–512.

Novak, K., Frank, J., Smith, B. & Engel, R. (2002). Revisiting the decision to arrest: Comparing beat and community officers. *Crime and Delinquency, 48,* 70–98.

Novy, M. (2012). Cognitive distortions during law enforcement shooting. *Activitas Nervosa Superior, 54,* 60–66.

Nowicki, D. (1999). Twelve traits of highly effective police officers. *Law and Order,* October, pp. 45–46.

Ohman, A. (2005). The role of the amygdala in human fear: Automatic detection of threat. *Psychoneuroendocrinology, 30,* 953–958.

Ohman, A., Flykt, A. & Lundqvist, D. (2000). Unconscious emotion: Evolutionary perspectives, psychophysiological data, and neuropsychological mechanisms. In R. Lane & L. Nadel (Eds.), *The cognitive neuroscience of emotion* (pp. 296–327). New York: Oxford University Press.

Ohman, A. & Mineka, S. (2001). Fears, phobias, and preparedness: Toward an evolved module of fear and fear learning. *Psychological Review, 108,* 483–522.

Ohman, A. & Wiens, S. (2003). On the automaticity of autonomic responses in emotion: An evolutionary perspective. In R.J. Davidson & K.R. Scherer (Ed.), *Handbook of affective sciences* (pp. 256–275). New York: Oxford University Press.

Oliver, M.M. (2017). Depolicing: Rhetoric or reality? *Criminal Justice Policy Review, 28,* 437–461.

Orasanu, J. & Backer, P. (1996). Stress and military performance. In J. Driskell & E. Salas (Eds.), *Stress and human performance* (pp. 89–125). Hillsdale: Erlbaum.

Orasanu, J. and Connolly, T. (1993). The reinvention of decision making. In G. Klein, J. Orasanu, R. Calderwood & C. Zsambok (Eds.), *Decision making in action* (pp. 127–166). New York: Ablex.

Ostrom, E., Parks, R.B. & Whitaker, G.P. (1978). *Patterns of metropolitan policing.* Cambridge: Ballinger.

Oswald, F., Mitchell, G., Blanton, H., Jacardi, J. & Tetlock, P. (2015). Using the IAT to predict ethnic and racial discrimination : Small small effect sizes of unknown societal significance. *Journal of Personality and Social Psychology, 108,* 562–571.

Otto, R.K. & Kraus, D.A. (2009). Contemplating the presence of third-party observers and facilitators in psychological evaluations. *Assessment, 16,* 362–372.

Page-Gould, E., Mendoza-Denton, R. & Tropp, L.R. (2008). With a little help from my cross-group friend: Reducing anxiety in intergroup contexts through cross-group friendship. *Journal of Personality and Social Psychology, 95,* 1080–1094.

Paoline, E.A. & Terrill, W. (2004). Women police officers and the use of coercion. *Women and Criminal Justice, 15,* 97–119.

Paoline, E.A. & Terrill, W. (2007). Police education, experience, and the use of force. *Criminal Justice and Behavior, 34,* 179–196.

Parent, R.B. (1998). Suicide by cop: Victim-precipitated homicide. *The Police Chief, 65,* 111–114.

Parent, R.B. (1999). Victim-precipitated homicide: Police use of deadly force. *Police Magazine,* September, pp. 22–26.

Parker, R.N. & Aurhahn, K. (1998). Alcohol, drugs, and violence. *Annual Review of Sociology, 24,* 291–311.

Parker, R.N. & Cartmill, R.S. (1998). Alcohol and homicide in the United States 1934–1995—or one reason why U.S. rates of violence may be going down. *Journal of Criminal Law and Criminology, 88,* 1369–1398.

Parker, R.N. (1998). Alcohol, homicide, and cultural context: A cross-national analysis of gender-specific homicide victimization. *Homicide Studies, 2,* 6–30.

Pascual-Leone, A., Freitas, C., Oberman, L., Horvath, J.C., Halko, M. & Eldaief, M. (2011). Characterizing brain cortical plasticity and network dynamics across the age span in health and disease with TMS-EEG and TMS-fMRI. *Brain Topography, 24,* 302–315.

Patton, C.L., Asken, M., Fremouw, W.J. & Bemis, R. (2017). The influence of police profanity on public perception of excessive force. *Journal of Police and Criminal Psychology, 32,* 340–357.

Patrick, U.W. & Hall, J.C. (2017). *In defense of self and others: Issues, facts, and fallacies—the realities of law enforcement's use of deadly force* (3rd ed.). Durham, NC: Carolina Academic Press.

Payne, B.K. (2001). Prejudice and perception: The role of automatic and controlled processes in misperceiving a weapon. *Journal of Personality and Social Psychology, 81,* 181–192.

Payne, B.K. (2005). Conceptualizing control in social cognition: How executive functioning modulates the expression of automatic stereotyping. *Journal of Personality and Social Psychology, 89,* 488–503.

Payne, B.K., Lambert, A.J. & Jacoby, L.L. (2002). Best laid plans: Effects of goals on accessibility bias and cognitive control in race-based misperceptions of weapons. *Journal of Experimental Social Psychology, 38,* 384–396.

Payne, J.D., Jackson, E.D., Ryan, L., Hoscheidt, S., Jacobs, J.W. & Nadel, L. (2006). The impact of stress on neutral and emotional aspects of episodic memory. *Memory, 14,* 1–16.

Peak, K.J. (2003). *Policing America: Methods, issues, challenges* (4th ed.). Upper Saddle River: Prentice-Hall.

Perrou, B. & Farrell, B. (2004). Officer-involved shootings: Case management and psychosocial investigations. In V. Lord (Ed.), *Suicide by cop: Inducing officers to shoot* (pp. 239–242). Flushing: Looseleaf Law Publications.

Petrowski, T.D. (2002a). Use-of-force policies and training: A reasoned approach (part I). *FBI Law Enforcement Bulletin,* October, pp. 25–32.

Petrowski, T.D. (2002b). Use-of-force policies and training: A reasoned approach (part II). *FBI Law Enforcement Bulletin,* November, pp. 24–32.

Phelps, E.A. (2006). Emotion and cognition: Insights from studies of the human amygdala. *Annual Review of Psychology, 57,* 27–53.

Phillips, T. & Smith, P. (2000). Police violence occasioning citizen complaint: An empirical analysis of time-space dynamics. *British Journal of Criminology, 40,* 480–496.

Pinizzotto, A., Davis, E.F., Bohrer, S.B. & Infanti, B.J. (2012). Restraint in the use of deadly force: A preliminary study. *FBI Law Enforcement Bulletin,* June, pp. 1–11.

Pinizzotto, A.J., Davis, E.F. & Miller, C.E. (1997). *In the line of fire: Violence against law enforcement.* Washington, DC: U.S. Department of Justice.

Pinizzotto, A.J., Davis, E.F. & Miller, C.E. (2000). Officers' perceptual shorthand: What messages are offenders sending to law enforcement officers? *FBI Law Enforcement Bulletin,* July, pp. 1–6.

Pinizzotto, A.J., Davis, E.F. & Miller, C.E. (2004). Intuitive policing: Emotional/rational decision making in law enforcement. *FBI Law Enforcement Bulletin,* February, pp. 1–6.

Pinizzotto, A.J., Davis, E.F. & Miller, C.E. (2005). Suicide by cop: Defining a devastating dilemma. *FBI Law Enforcement Bulletin,* February, pp. 8–20.

Phelps, E.A. (2004). Human emotion and memory: Interactions of the amygdala and hippocampal complex. *Current Opinion in Neurobiology, 14,* 198–202.

Plant, E.A. & Devine, P.G. (2003). The antecedents and implications of interracial anxiety. *Personality and Social Psychology Bulletin, 29,* 790801.

Plant, E.A., Goplen, J. & Kunstman, J.W. (2011). Selective responses to threat: The roles of race and gender in decisions to shoot. *Personality and Social Psychology Bulletin, 37,* 1274–1281.

Plant, E.A. & Peruche, B.M. (2005). The consequences of race for police officers' responses to criminal suspects. *Psychological Science, 16,* 180–183.

Plant, E.A., Peruche, B.M. & Butz, D.A. (2005). Eliminating automatic racial bias: Making race non-diagnostic for responses to criminal suspects. *Journal of Experimental Social Psychology, 41,* 141–156.

Plomin, R. (2018). *Blueprint: How DNA makes us who we are.* Cambridge, MA: MIT Press.

Pogrebin, M.R. & Poole, E.D. (1993). Vice isn't nice: A look at the effects of working undercover. *Journal of Criminal Justice, 21,* 383–394.

Praet, B.D. (2002). Suicide by cop or death by indifference? *The Police Chief,* July, pp. 14.

Reeves, F.B. & Bergum, B.O. (1972). Perceptual narrowing as a function of peripheral cue relevance. *Perceptual and Motor Skills, 35,* 19–24.

Reiser, M. & Geiger, S. (1984). The police officer as a victim. *Professional Psychology: Research and Practice, 15,* 315–323.

Reisig, M.D, McCluskey, J.D., Mastrofsky, S.D. & Terill, W. (2004). Suspect disrespect towards the police. *Justice Quarterly, 21,* 241–268.

Reiss, A.J. (1971). *The police and the public.* New Haven: Yale University Press.

Reiss, A.J. (1980). Controlling police use of force. *Annals of the American Academy of Political and Social Science, 452,* 122–134.

Remsberg, C. (2008). *Blood lessons: What cops learn from life-or-death encounters.* San Francisco: Calibre Press.

Resnick, P.J. (1995). Guidelines for the evaluation of malingering in posttraumatic stress disorder. In R.I. Simon (Ed.), *Posttraumatic stress disorder in litigation: Guidelines for forensic assessment* (pp. 117–134). Washington, DC: American Psychiatric Press.

Resnick, P.J. (1997). Malingering of posttraumatic stress disorders. In R. Rogers (Ed.), *Clinical assessment of malingering and deception* (2nd ed., pp. 130–152). New York: Guilford.

Resnick, P.J. (1999). The detection of malingered psychosis. *Psychiatric Clinics of North America, 22,* 159–172.

Resnick P.J. & Harris, M.R. (2002). Retrospective assessment of malingering in insanity defense cases. In R.I. Simon & D.W. Shuman (Eds.), *Retrospective assessment of mental states in litigation: Predicting the past* (pp. 101–134), Washington, DC: American Psychiatric Publishing.

Reynolds, J.J. & McCrea, S.M. (2016). The dual-component theory of inhibition regulation: A new model of self-control. *New Ideas in Psychology, 41,* 8–17.

Riksheim, E. & Chermak, S. (1993). Causes of police behavior revisited. *Journal of Criminal Justice, 21,* 353–382.

Robin, G.D. (1963). Justifiable homicide by police officers. *Journal of Criminal Law and Criminology, 54,* 225–231.

Robin, G.D. (1964). Police slayings of criminals. *Police, 8,* 32–35.

Robson, D. (2019). *The intelligence trap: Why smart people make dumb mistakes.* New York: W.W. Norton.

Roemer, L., Litz, B., Orsillo, S.M., Ehlich, P.J. & Friedman, M.J. (1998). Increases in retrospective accounts of war-zone exposure over time: The role of PTSD symptom severity. *Journal of Traumatic Stress, 11,* 597–605.

Rojek, J., Alpert, G.P. & Smith, H.P. (2012). Examining officer and citizen accounts of police use-of-force incidents. *Crime and Delinquency, 58,* 301–327.

Roozendaal, B. (2000). Glucocorticoids and the regulation of memory consolidation. *Psychoneuroendocrinology, 25,* 213–238.

Ross, D.L. (2000). Emerging trends in police failure to train liability. *Policing: An International Journal of Police Strategies and Management, 23,* 169–193.

Ross, D.L. (2012). Analyzing perceptions and misperceptions of police officers in lethal force virtual simulator scenarios. *Law Enforcement Executive Forum, 12,* 53–73.

Ross, D.L. (2018). Legal and liability issues surrounding the use of force. In D.L. Ross & G.M. Vilke (Eds.), *Guidelines for investigating officer-involved shootings, arrest-related deaths, and deaths in custody* (pp. 41–67). New York: Routledge.

Ross, D.L. & Brave, M. (2018). Vital statistics and arrest-related deaths. In D.L. Ross & G.M. Vilke (Eds.), *Guidelines for investigating officer-involved shootings, arrest-related deaths, and deaths in custody* (pp. 19–20). New York: Routledge.

Ross, D.L. & Dunston, M.S. (2018). Officer-involved incident investigation guidelines. In D.L. Ross & G.M. Vilke (Eds.), *Guidelines for investigating officer-involved shootings, arrest-related deaths, and deaths in custody* (pp. 116–148). New York: Routledge.

Ross, D.L. & Murphy, R. (2018). Stress, perceptual distortion, and human performance. In D.L. Ross & G.M. Vilke (Eds.), *Guidelines for investigating officer-involved shootings, arrest-related deaths, and deaths in custody* (pp. 68–95). New York: Routledge.

Ross, D.L., Murphy, R.L. & Hazlett, M.H. (2012). Analyzing perceptions and misperceptions of police officers in lethal force virtual simulator scenarios. *Law Enforcement Executive Forum, 12,* 53–73.

Ross, K.G., Klein, G.A., Thunholm, P., Schmitt, J.F. & Baxter, H.C. (2004). The recognition-primed decision model. *Military Review,* July-August, pp. 6–10.

Rostow, C.D. & Davis, R.D. (2002). Psychological fitness for duty evaluations in law enforcement. *The Police Chief,* September, pp. 58–66.

Rudofossi, D. (2007). *Working with traumatized police officer-patients: A clinician's guide to complex PTSD syndromes in public safety personnel.* Amityville, NY: Baywood.

Rudofossi, D. (2007). *A cop doc's guide to public safety complex trauma syndrome: Using the five police personality styles.* Amityville, NY: Baywood.

Rudofossi D. (2011). Police and public safety complex trauma and grief: An eco-ethological existential analysis. In J. Kitaeff (Ed.), *Handbook of police psychology* (pp. 437–468). New York: Routledge.

Russell, H.E. & Beigel, A. (1990). *Understanding human behavior for effective police work* (3rd ed.). New York: Basic Books.

Ryan, W. (2013). *Souls behind the badge: The real world of policing–an insider's view.* Saskatoon, Canada: Indie Ink Publishing.

Sadoff, R.L. & Dattilio, F.M. (2011). Criminal responsibility. In E.Y. Drogin, F.M. Dattilio, R.L. Sadoff & T.G.Gutheil (Eds.), *Handbook of forensic assessment: Psychological and psychiatric perspectives* (pp. 121–144). Hoboken, NJ: Wiley.

Safer, M.A., Christianson, S.A., Autry, M.W. & Osterlund, K. (1998). Tunnel memory for traumatic events. *Applied Cognitive Psychology, 12,* 99–117.

Sapolsky, R.M. (1996). Why stress is bad for your brain. *Science, 273,* 749–750.

Satel, S. & Lilienfeld, S.O. (2103). *Brainwashed: The seductive appeal of mindless neuroscience.* New York: Basic Books.

Savaser, D. & Chan, T.C.(2018). Positional and restraint asphyxia, In D.L. Ross & G.M. Vilke (Eds.), *Guidelines for investigating officer-involved shootings, arrest-related deaths, and deaths in custody* (pp. 149–162). New York: Routledge.

Schacter, D.L. (1999). The seven sins of memory. Insights from psychology and cognitive neuroscience. *American Psychologist, 54,* 182–203.

Schade,T.V. & Bruns, G.H. (1989). Police shooting performance in threatening environments. *American Journal of Police, 8,* 31–48.

Scharf, P. & Binder, A. (1983). *The badge and the bullet: Police use of deadly force.* New York: Prager.

Schoofs, D., Wolf, O.T. & Smeets, T. (2009). Cold pressor stress impairs performance on working memory tasks requiring working memory functions in healthy young men. *Behavioral Neuroscience, 123,* 1066–1075.

Schouten, R. (2006). Workplace violence: A overview for practicing clinicians. *Psychiatric Annals, 36,* 791–797.

Schouten, R. & Brennan, D.V. (2016). Targeted violence against law enforcement officers. *Behavioral Sciences and the Law, 34,* 608–621.

Schuck, A.M. (2004). The masking of racial and ethnic disparity in police use of physical force: The effects of gender and custody status. *Journal of Criminal Justice, 32,* 557–564.

Scott, J.C., Wrocklage, K.M., Crnich, C., Jordan, J., Krystal, J.H., Matt, G.E., Southwick, S.M. & Schweinsburg, B.C. (2014). A quantitative meta-analysis of neurocognitive functioning in posttraumatic stress disorder. *Psychological Bulletin, 141,* 105–140.

Scoville, D. (1998). FYI: Getting you to pull the trigger. *Police, 11,* 36–44.

Scoville, W.B. (1968). Amnesia after bilateral mesial temporal lobe excision: Introduction to case H.M. *Neuropsychologia, 6,* 211–213.

Scrivner, E.M. (1999). Controlling police use of excessive force: The role of the police psychologist. In L. Territo & J.D. Sewell (Eds.), *Stress management in law enforcement* (pp. 383–391). Durham: Carolina Academic Press.

Sewell, J.D. (1986). Administrative concerns in law enforcement stress management. *Police Studies: The International Review of Police Development, 9,* 153–159.

Sewell, J.D. (2007). Working with the media in times of crisis: Key principles for law enforcement. *FBI Law Enforcement Bulletin,* March, pp. 1–6.

Shane, J.M., Lawton, B. & Swenson, Z. (2017). The prevalence of fatal police shootings by U.S. police, 2015–2016: Patterns and answers from a new data set. *Journal of Criminal Justice, 52,* 101–111.

Shapiro, D. (1965). *Neurotic styles.* New York: Basic Books.

Sharps, M.J. (2010). *Processing under pressure: Stress, memory, and decision-making in law enforcement.* Flushing, NY: Looseleaf Law Publications.

Sharps, M.J. (2012). The mental edge: Effective cognitive processing in law enforcement. *The Police Chief, 79,* 100–105.

Sharps, M.J. & Hess, A.B. (2008). To shoot or not to shoot: Response and interpretation of response to armed assailants. *Forensic Examiner, 17,* 53–64.

Sharps, M.J., Hess, A.B., Casner, H., Ranes, B. & Jones, J. (2007). Eyewitness memory in context: Toward a systematic understanding of eyewitness evidence. *Forensic Examiner, 16,* 20–27.

Sharps, M.J., Torkelson, J.F., Hulett, D.L., Kuhn, M.L. & Sevillano, C.N. (2019). Police profanity and public judgments of guilt and effectiveness in officer-involved shootings. *Journal of Police and Criminal Psychology, 34,* 87–90.

Shaw, J. (1983). Post-shooting trauma. *FBI Law Enforcement Bulletin, 52,* 17–18.

Shealy, C., Cramer, R.J. & Pirelli, G. (2008). Third party presence during criminal forensic evaluations: Psychologists' opinions, attitudes, and practices. *Professional Psychology: Research and Practice, 39,* 561–569.

Sheets, J.J. & Sprouse, J.K. (2019). Ambushes and unprovoked attacks: New FBI study examines assaults on law enforcement. *The Police Chief,* February, pp. 26–29.

Sherman, L. (1979). Measuring homicide by police officers. *Journal of Criminal Law and Criminology, 70,* 546–560.

Sherman, L.W. (1980). Causes of police behavior: The current state of quantitative research. *Journal of Research in Crime and Delinquency, 17,* 69–100.

Sherman, L.W. (1993). Defiance, deterrence, and irrelevance: A theory of the criminal sanction. *Journal of Research in Crime and Delinquency, 30,* 445–473.

Shev, E.E. & Hewed, J.J. (1977). *Good cops, bad cops.* San Francisco: San Francisco Book Co.

Shin, L.M., Rausch, S.L. & Pitman, R.K. (2006). Amygdala, medial prefrontal cortex, and hippocampal function in PTSD. *Annals of the New York Academy of Sciences, 1071,* 67–79.

Shipley, P. & Baranski, J.V. (2002). Police officer performance under stress: A pilot study on the effects of visuomotor behavior rehearsal. *International Journal of Stress Management, 9,* 71–80.

Shomstein, S. & Yantis, S. (2004). Control of attention shifts between vision and audition in human cortex. *Journal of Neuroscience, 24,* 10702–10706.

Signorelli W.R. (2006). *The crisis of police liability lawsuits.* Durham, NC: Carolina Academic Press.

Silver, E., Felson, R.B. & Vaneseltine, M. (2008). The relationship between mental health problems and violence among criminal offenders. *Criminal Justice and Behavior, 35,* 405–426.

Silver, E. & Teasdale, B. (2005). Mental disorder and violence: An examination of stressful life events and impaired social support. *Social Problems, 52,* 62–78.

Sim, J.J., Correll, J. & Sadler, M.S. (2013). Understanding police and expert performance: When training attenuates (vs. exacerbates) stereotypic bias in the decision to shoot. *Personality and Social Psychology Bulletin, 39,* 291–304.

Simons, D.J. (2000). Attentional capture and inattentional blindness. *Trends in Cognitive Sciences, 4,* 147–155.

Sloane, C. & Vilke, G.M. (2018). Less lethal weapons, not including Taser. In D.L. Ross & G.M. Vilke (Eds.), *Guidelines for investigating officer-involved shootings, arrest-related deaths, and deaths in custody* (pp. 228–245). New York: Routledge.

Smith, B.W. & Holmes, M.D. (2003). Community accountability, minority threat, and police brutality: An examination of civil rights criminal complaints. *Criminology, 41,* 1035–1063.

Solomon, R.M. (1988). Post-shooting trauma. *The Police Chief,* October, pp. 40–44.

Solomon, R.M. (1990). Administrative guidelines for dealing with officers involved in on-duty shooting situations. *The Police Chief,* February, p. 40.

Solomon, R.M. (1991). The dynamics of fear in critical incidents: Implications for training and treatment. In J.T. Reese, J.M. Horn & C. Dunning (Eds.), *Critical incidents in policing* (pp. 347–358). Washington DC: Federal Bureau of Investigation.

Solomon, R.M. (1995). Critical incident stress management in law enforcement. In G.S. Everly (Ed.), *Innovations in disaster and trauma Psychology: Applications in emergency services and disaster response* (pp. 123–157). Ellicott City: Chevron.

Solomon, R.M. (1997). I know I must have shot, but I can't remember. *The Police Marksman, 21*(4), 48–51.

Solomon, R.M. & Horn, (1986). Post-shooting traumatic reactions: A pilot study. In J.T. Reese & H. Goldstein (Eds.), *Psychological services for law enforcement (pp. 383–393). Washington DC: US Government Printing Office.*

Somodevilla, S.A. (1986). Post-shooting trauma: Reactive and proactive treatment. In J.T. Reese & H. Goldstein (Eds.), *Psychological services for law enforcement* (pp. 395–398). Washington DC: US Government Printing Office.

Sorenson, J., Marquart & Brock, D. (1993). Factors relating to killings of felons by police officers: A test of the community violence and conflict hypotheses. *Justice Quarterly, 10,* 417–440.

Sousa, W., Ready, J. & Ault, M. (2010). The impact of Tasers on police use-of-force decisions: Findings from a randomized field-training experiment. *Journal of Experimental Criminology, 6,* 35–55.

Southwick, S.M., Morgan, C.A., Nicolaou, A.L. & Charney, D.S. (1997).Consistency of memory for combat-related traumatic events in veterans of Operation Desert Storm. *American Journal of Psychiatry, 154,* 173–177.

Sparr, L.F. (1996). Mental defenses and posttraumatic stress disorder: Assessment of criminal intent. *Journal of Traumatic Stress, 9,* 375–379.

Sparr, L.F. & Pankratz, L.D. (1983). Factitious posttraumatic stress disorder. *British Journal of Psychiatry, 140,* 1016–1019.

Spaulding, D. (2005). Intuitive decision making. *Police,* March, pp. 62–64.

Sperry, L. (1995). *Handbook of diagnosis and treatment of the DSM-IV personality disorders.* New York: Brunner/Mazel.

Squire, L.R. (1994). Declarative and nondeclarative memory: Multiple brain systems supporting learning and memory. In D.L. Schachter & E. Tulving (Eds.), *Memory systems* (pp. 203–232). Cambridge, MA: MIT Press.

Staller, M.S., Christiansen, P., Zaiser, B., Korner, S. & Cole, J.C. (2018). Do they aggress earlier? Investigating the effects of ego depletion on police officers' use of force behavior. *Journal of Police and Criminal Psychology, 33,* 332–344.

Steblay, N.M. (1992). A meta-analytic review of the weapon focus effect. *Law and Human Behavior, 16,* 413–424.

Steele, C.M. (1997). A threat in the air: How stereotypes shape intellectual identity and performance. *American Psychologist, 52,* 613–629.

Steidl, S., Razik, F. & Anderson, A.K. (2011). Emotion enhanced retention of cognitive skill learning. *Emotion, 11,* 12–19.

Sternberg, E.J. (2010). *My brain made me do it: The rise of neuroscience and the threat to moral responsibility.* Amherst, NY: Prometheus Books.

Stiles, J. (2000). Neural plasticity and cognitive development. *Develpmental Neuropsychology, 18,* 237–272.

Stroshine, M., Alpert, G. & Dunham, R. (2008). The influence of "working rules" on police suspicion and discretionary decision making. *Police Quarterly, 11,* 315–337.

Stucke, T.S. & Baumeister, R.F. (2006). Ego depletion and aggressive behavior: Is the inhibition of aggression a limited resource? *European Journal of Social Psychology, 36,* 1–13.

Stuhlmiller, C. & Dunning, C. (2000). Challenging the mainstream: From pathogenic to salutogenic models of posttrauma intervention. In J. Violanti, D. Paton & C. Dunning (Eds.), *Posttraumatic stress intervention: Challenges, issues, and perspectives* (pp. 10–42). Springfield: Charles C Thomas.

Sun, I.Y. & Payne, B. (2004). Racial differences in resolving conflicts: A comparison between Black and White police officers. *Crime and Delinquency, 50,* 516–541.

Suss, J. & Raushel, A. (2019). Wallet or gun? Evaluating factors that affect anticipation ability in a use-of-force scenario. *Journal of Police and Criminal Psychology, 34,* 292–302.

Suss, J. & Ward, P. (2012). Use of an option generation paradigm to investigate situation assessment and response selection in law enforcement. *Proceedings of the Human Factors and Ergonomics Society Annual Meeting, 56,* 297–301.

Swanson, J.W., Borum, R., Swartz, M. & Monahan, J. (1996). Psychotic symptoms and disorders and the risk of violent behavior in the community. *Criminal Behaviour and Mental Health, 6,* 317–338.

Swanson, J.W., Estroff, S., Swartz, M., Borum, R., Lachicotte, W., Zimmer, C. & Wagner, H.R. (1997). Violence and severe mental disorder in clinical and community populations: The effects of psychotic symptoms, comorbidity and lack of treatment. *Psychiatry: Interpersonal and Biological Processes, 60,* 1–22.

Swartz, M.S., Swanson, J.W., Hiday, V.A., Borum, R., Wagner, H.R. & Burns, B.J. (1998a). Taking the wrong drugs: The role of substance abuse and medication noncompliance in violence among mentally ill individuals. *Social Psychiatry and Psychiatric Epidemiology, 33,* 75–80.

Swartz, M.S., Swanson, J.W., Hiday, V.A., Borum, R., Wagner, H.R. & Burns, B.J. (1998b). Violence and severe mental illness: The effects of substance abuse and nonadherence to medication. *American Journal of Psychiatry, 155,* 226–231.

Sykes, G.W. (1986). Street justice: A moral defense of order maintenance policing. *Justice Quarterly, 3,* 497–512.

Takagi, P. (1974). A garrison state in a "democratic" society. *Crime and Scholarly Justice, 1,* 27–33.

Taylor, A.J.W. (2001). Traumatic stress and differential diagnosis of malingering. *Traumatology, 9,* 197–215.

Taylor, R.W., Fritsch, E.J. & Caeti, T.J. (1998). Core challenges facing community policing: The emperor still has no clothes. *ACJS Today, 17,* 3–5.

TenBrink, W. & Lester, D. (1984). Reporting fellow police officers for brutality. *Psychological Reports, 54,* 36.

Tennessee v. Garner. (1985). 471 U.S. 1.

Terrill, W. (2001). *Police coercion: Application of the force continuum.* New York: LFB Scholarly Publishing.

Terrill, W. (2003). Police use of force and suspect resistance: The micro process of the police-citizen encounter. *Police Quarterly, 6,* 51–83.

Terrill, W. (2005). Police use of force: A transactional approach. *Justice Quarterly, 22,* 107–138.

Terrill, W., Leinfelt, F. & Kwak, D. (2008). Examining police use of force: A smaller agency perspective. *Policing: An International Journal of Police Strategies and Management, 31,* 57–76.

Terrill, W. & Mastrofski, S. (2002). Situational and officer-based determinants of police coercion. *Justice Quarterly, 19,* 215–248.

Terrill, W. & McCluskey, J. (2002). Citizen complaints and problem officers: Examining officer behavior. *Journal of Criminal Justice, 30,* 143–155.

Terrill, W. & Paoline, E. (2007). Nonarrest decision making in police-citizen encounters. *Police Quarterly, 10,* 308–331.

Terrill, W., Paoline, E. & Manning, P. (2003). Police culture and coercion. *Criminology, 41,* 1003–1034.

Terrill, W. & Reisig, M. (2003). Neighborhood context and police use of force. *Journal of Research in Crime and Delinquency, 40,* 291–321.

Thibault, E.A., Lynch, L.M. & McBride, R.B. (2004). *Proactive police management* (6th ed.). Upper Saddle River, NJ: Pearson.

Thompson, M. & Sekaquaptewa, D. (2002). When being different is detrimental: Solo status and the performance of women and racial minorities. *Analyses of Social Issues and Public Policy, 2,* 183–203.

Toch, H. (1996). The violence-prone police officer. In W.A. Geller & H. Toch (Eds.), *Police violence: Understanding and controlling police abuse of force* (pp. 94–112). New Haven: Yale University Press.

Tonry, M. (2011). *Punishing race: A continuing American dilemma.* New York: Oxford University Press.

Traverniers, J., Van Ruysseveldt, J., Smeets, T. & von Grumbkow, J. (2010). High-intensity stress elicits robust cortisol increases, and impairs working memory and visuospatial declarative memory in special forces candidates: A field experiment. *Stress: The International Journal on the Biology of Stress, 13,* 323–333.

Trawalter, S., Richeson, J.A. & Shelton, J.N. (2009). Predicting behavior during interracial interactions: A stress and coping approach. *Personality and Social Psychology, Review, 13,* 243–268.

Trimble, M.R. (2004). *Somatoform disorders: A medicolegal guide.* New York: Cambridge University Press.

Twersky-Glasner, A. (2005). Police personality: What is it and why are they like that? *Journal of Police and Criminal Psychology, 20,* 56–67.

Tyre, P. (2001). Betrayed by a badge. *Newsweek,* June 18, pp. 38–41.

Uelman, G.F. (1973). Varieties of public policy: A study of policy regarding the use of deadly force in Los Angeles County. *University of Loyola at Los Angeles Law Review, 6,* 1–65.

United States Department of Justice (1992). *Killed in the line of duty: A study of selected felonious killings of law enforcement officers.* Washington, DC: Federal Bureau of Investigation.

Unkelbach, C., Forgas, J.P., & Densm, T.F. (2008). The turban effect: The influence of Muslim headgear and induced affect on aggressive responses in the shooter bias paradigm. *Journal of Experimental Social Psychology, 44,* 1409–1413.

Unsworth, N. & Engle, R.W. (2007). The nature of individual difference in working memory capacity: Active maintenance in primary memory and controlled search from secondary memory. *Psychological Review, 114,* 104.

Unsworth, N., Fukuda, K., Awh, E. & Vogel, E.K. (2014). Working memory and fluid intelligence: Capacity, attention control, and secondary memory. *Cognitive Psychology, 71,* 1–26.

Van Maanen, J. (1978). The "asshole." In P.K. Manning & J. Van Maanen (Eds.), *Policing: A view from the street* (pp. 221–238). Santa Monica: Goodyear Publishing.

Van Zandt, C.R. (1993). Suicide by cop. *The Police Chief,* 60, 24–30.

Vaughn, M.S., Cooper, T.W. & del Carmen, R.V. (2001) Assessing legal liabilities in law enforcement: Police chiefs' views. *Crime & Delinquency, 47,* 3–27.

Verhage, A., Noppe, J., Feys, Y. & Ledegen, E. (2018). Force, stress, and decision-making within the Belgian police: The impact of stressful situations on police decision making. *Journal of Police and Criminal Psychology, 33,* 345–357.

Vickers, J.N. (2007). *Perception, cognition and decision making: The quiet eye in action.* Champaign, IL: Human Kinetics Publishers.

Vickers, J.N. & Lewinski, W.L. (2012). Performing under pressure: Gaze control, decision making, and shooting performance of elite and rookie police officers. *Human Movement Science, 31,* 101–117.

Vinson, D.E. & Davis, D.S. (1993). *Jury persuasion: Psychological strategies and trial techniques.* Little Falls, NJ: Glasser Legalworks.

Violanti, J.M. (1996). *Police suicide: Epidemic in blue.* Springfield: Thomas.

Violanti, J.M. & Drylie, J.J. (2008). *Copicide: Concepts, cases, and controversies of suicide by cop.* Springfield, IL: Charles C Thomas.

Violanti, J.M., O'Hara, A.F. & Tate, T.T. (2011). *On the edge: Recent perspectives on police suicide.* Springfield, IL: Charles C Thomas.

Vohs, K.D. & Heatherton, T.F. (2000). Self-regulatory failure: A resource depletion approach. *Psychological Science, 11,* 249–254.

Vohs, K.D., Baumeister, R.F. & Ciarocco, N. (2005). Self-regulation and self-presentation: Regulatory resource depletion impairs impression management and effortful self-presentation depletes regulatory resources. *Journal of Personality and Social Psychology, 88,* 632–657.

Wadman, R.C. & Ziman, S.M. (1993). Courtesy and police authority. *FBI Law Enforcement Bulletin,* February, pp. 23–26.

Waegel, W. (1984). How police justify the use of deadly force. *Social Problems, 32,* 144–155.

Walker, S. & Fridell, L. (1993). Forces of change in police policy: The impact of Tennessee v. Garner on deadly force policy. *American Journal of Police, 11,* 97–112.

Ward, P., Harris, K.R., Ericsson, K.A., Eccles, D.W., Tashman, L. & Lang, L.H. (2007). Cognitive basis for expert and superior performance in law enforcement. *Proceedings of the Annual Meeting of the Cognitive Science Society USA, 29,* 1884.

Ward, P., Suss, J., Eccles, D.W., Williams, A.M. & Harris, K.R. (2011). Skill-based differences in option generation in a complex task: A verbal protocol analysis. *Cognitive Processes, 12,* 289–300.

Ward, T. (2004). *Attention: A neuropsychological approach.* New York: Psychology Press.

Waters, A.C. & Tucker, D.M. (2013). Self-regulation and neural development. In B.W. Sokol, F.M.E. Grouzet & U. Muller (Eds.), *Self-regulation and autonomy: Social and developmental dimensions of human conduct* (pp. 279–296).

Watson, A.C., Morabito, M.S., Draine, J. & Ottati, V. (2008). Improving police response to persons with mental illness: A multi-level conceptualization of CIT. *International Journal of Law and Psychiatry, 31,* 359–368.

Webb, H. (2011). *Managing the use of force incident: For criminal justice officers, supervisors, and administrators.* Springfield: Charles C Thomas.

Weitzer, R. (1999). Citizens' perception of police misconduct: Race and neighborhood context. *Justice Quarterly, 16,* 819–846.

Werner, N.S., Jung, K., Duschek, S. & Schandry, R. (2009). Enhanced cardiac perception is associated with benefits in decision-making. *Psychophysiology, 46,* 1123–1129.

Wester, S.R. & Lyubelsky, J. (2005). Supporting the thin blue line: Gender-sensitive therapy with male police officers. *Professional Psychology: Research and Practice, 36,* 51–58.

Weyandt, L.L. (2019). *Clinical neuroscience: Foundations of psychological and neurodegenerative disorders* (2nd ed.). New York: Taylor & Francis.

Whalen, P.J., Shin, L.M., McInerney, S.C., Fischer, H., Wright, C.I. & Rausch, S.L. (2001). A functional MRI study of human amygdala responses to facial expressions of fear versus anger. *Emotion, 1,* 70–83.

White, M.D. (2000). Assessing the impact of administrative policy on use of deadly force by on- and off-duty police. *Evaluation Review, 24,* 295–318.

White, M.D. (2002). Identifying situational predictors of police shootings using multivariate analyses. *Policing: An International Journal of Police Strategies and Management, 25,* 726–751.

White, M.D. (2006). Hitting the target (or not): Comparing characteristics of fatal, injurious, and noninjurious police shootings. *Police Quarterly, 9,* 303–330.

White, M.D. & Klinger, D. (2012). Contagious fire? An empirical assessment of the problem of multi-shooter, multi-shot deadly force incidents in police work. *Crime and Delinquency, 58,* 196–221.

Williams, J.M. (1998). The malingering of memory disorder. In Reynolds, C.R. (Ed.), *Detection of malingering during head injury litigation* (pp. 105–132). New York: Plenum.

Williams. M.B. (1999). Impact of duty-related death on officers' children: Concepts of death, trauma reactions, and treatment. In J.M. Violanti & D. Paton (Eds.), *Police trauma: Psychological aftermath of civilian combat* (pp. 159–174). Springfield: Charles C Thomas.

Williams, T. (1991). Counseling disabled law enforcement officers. In J.T. Reese, J.M. Horn & C. Dunning (Eds.), *Critical incidents in policing* (pp. 377–386). Washington DC: Federal Bureau of Investigation.

Wilson, E.F., Davis, J.H., Bloom, J.D., Batten, P.J. & Kamara, S.G. (1998). Homicide or suicide: The killing of suicidal persons by law enforcement officers. *Journal of Forensic Science, 43,* 46–52.

Wittrup, R.G. (1986). Police shooting–An opportunity for growth or loss of self. In J.T. Reese & H. Goldstein (Eds.), *Psychological services for law enforcement* (pp. 405–408). Washington DC: US Government Printing Office.

Wolf, O.T., Schommer, N.C., Hellhammer, D.H., McEwen, B.S. & Kirschbaum, C. (2001). The relationship between stress induced cortisol levels and memory differs between men and women. *Psychoneuroendocrinology, 26,* 711–720.

Wolfe, S.E. (2011). The effect of low self-control on perceived police legitimacy. *Journal of Criminal Justice, 39,* 67–74.

Wolfe, S.E. & Nix, J. (2016). The alleged "Ferguson effect" and police willingness to engage in community partnership. *Law and Human Behavior, 40,* 1–10.

Wolfgang, M.E. (1959). Suicide by means of victim-precipitated homicide. *Journal of Clinical and Experimental Psychopathology, 20,* 335–349.

Worden, R.E. (1989). Situational and attitudinal explanations of police behavior: A theoretical reappraisal and empirical assessment. *Law and Society Review, 23,* 667–711.

Worden, R.E. (1996). The causes of police brutality: Theory and evidence on police use of force. In W.A. Geller & H. Toch (Eds.), *Police violence: Understanding and controlling police abuse of force* (pp. 23–51). New Haven: Yale University Press.

Worden, R.E. & Caitlin, S.E. (2002). The use and abuse of force by police. In K.M. Lersch (Ed.), *Policing and misconduct* (pp. 85–120). Upper Saddle River, NJ: Prentice-Hall.

Worrall, J.L., Bishopp, S.A., Zinser, S.C., Wheeler, A.P. & Phillps, S.W. (2018). Exploring bias in police shooting decisions with real shoot/don't shoot cases. *Crime and Delinquency, 64,* 1171–1192.

Wrightsman, L.S. (2001). *Forensic psychology.* Stamford, CT: Wadsworth.

Yehuda, R. (1998). Psychoneuroendocrinology of post-traumatic stress disorder. *Psychiatric Clinics of North America, 21,* 359–379.

Yehuda, R. (2002). Clinical relevance of biological findings in PTSD. *Psychiatric Quarterly, 73,* 123–133.

Yerkes, R.M. & Dodson, J.D. (1908). The relation of strength of stimulus to rapidity of habit-formation. *Journal of Comparative Neurology and Psychology, 18,* 459–482.

Yu, S. (2017). Nonlethal weapons and technology. In M.J. Palmiotto (Ed.), *Police use of force: Important issues facing the police and the communities they serve* (pp. 51–64). Boca Raton, FL: CRC Press.

Zaiser, B. & Staller,M.S. (2015). The word is sometimes mightier than the sword: Rethinking communication skills to enhance officer safety. *Journal of Law Enforcement, 4,* 1–17.

Zeling, M. (1986). Research needs in the study of post-shooting trauma. In J.T. Reese & H.A. Goldstein (Eds.), *Psychological services for law enforcement* (pp. 409–410). Washington DC: USGPO.

Zillmer, E.A., Spiers, M.V. & Culbertson, W.C. (2008). *Principles of neuropsychology* (2nd ed.). Belmont, CA: Wadsworth.

Zola, S. (1997). Amnesia: Neuroanatomic and clinical aspects. In T.E. Feinberg & M.J. Farah (Eds.), *Behavioral neurology and neuropsychology* (pp. 447–462). New York: McGraw Hill.

INDEX